King Solomon and the Golden Fish

Raphael Patai Series in Jewish Folklore and Anthropology

A complete listing of the books in this series can be found at http://wsupress.wayne.edu.

General Editor
Dan Ben-Amos
University of Pennsylvania

Advisory Editors
Jane S. Gerber
City University of New York

Barbara Kirshenblatt-Gimblett
New York University

Aliza Shenhar
University of Haifa

Amnon Shiloah
Hebrew University

Harvey E. Goldberg
Hebrew University

Samuel G. Armistead
University of California, Davis

Guy H. Haskell

King Solomon and the Golden Fish

Tales from the Sephardic Tradition

Texts Collected and Edited by **Matilda Koén-Sarano**
Translated and Annotated by **Reginetta Haboucha**
Preamble by **Yoel Shalom Perez**

Wayne State University Press   Detroit

Copyright © 2004 by Wayne State University Press,
Detroit, Michigan 48201. All rights are reserved.
No part of this book may be reproduced without formal
permission.
Manufactured in the United States of America.
08 07 06 05 04   5 4 3 2 1

∞ The paper used in this publication meets the minimum
requirements of the American National Standard for
Information Sciences—Permanence of Paper for Printed
Library Materials, ANSI Z39.48-1984.

Twelve of these tales have previously appeared in a
different translation in *Folktales of Joha, Jewish Trickster* by
Matilda Koén-Sarano, published by the Jewish Publication
Society, February 2003.

This book has been published with the assistance of a
fund established by Thelma Gray James of Wayne State
University for the publication of folklore and English
studies.

Library of Congress Cataloging-in-Publication Data

King Solomon and the golden fish : tales from the
Sephardic tradition / texts collected and edited by Matilda
Koén-Sarano ; translated and annotated by Reginetta
Haboucha ; preamble by Yoel Shalom Perez.
  p. cm. — (Raphael Patai series in Jewish folklore and
anthropology)
Includes bibliographical references and index.
ISBN 0-8143-3166-1 (cloth : alk. paper)
1. Jews—Folklore. 2. Sephardim—Folklore. 3. Legends,
Jewish. 4. Folk literature, Ladino. I. Koén-Sarano,
Matilda, 1939– II. Series.
GR98 .K56 2004
398.2'089'924—dc22
                                                    2004013730

A mis inyetos
Para ke konoskan sus raízes
MATILDA KOÉN-SARANO

To the Proud Bearers of the Tradition
REGINETTA HABOUCHA

Contents

Foreword xi
Preamble xv
Preface xix
Introduction xxiii
Abbreviations xxxi

PART ONE   Tales of the Supernatural

1 King Shelomó and the Golden Fish   5
2 The Rights of Widows and Orphans   15
3 *A la Fín* Everything Comes to Light   22
4 The Fisherman and the Gold Fish   29
5 The Wonderful *Tendjereniko*   35
6 The King's Lost Son Transformed to a Dog   41
7 When There Were No Mirrors in the World   47
8 The Father's Will   53

PART TWO   Tales of Fate

9 The King's Daughter and the Gardener's Son   71
10 The Three Sayings   76
11 The Man without *Mazál*   89
12 What Is Written in the Sky One Cannot *Enfasar*   94

PART THREE   Tales of Elijah the Prophet

13 Eliau Anaví and the *Gevír*   107
14 Eliau Anaví and the *Vistozo*   112
15 The Holy Letters   117
16 Eliau Anaví and the Mother-in-Law   122

PART FOUR   Romantic Tales

17 The Power of Love   133
18 The Rose and the Lion   142
19 The King's Daughter and the Three *Fostanes*   149

20 Shlomó *Ameleh* and the Birds' Eggs   156
21 The Arranged Marriage   169

PART FIVE   Tales of Cleverness and Wisdom

22 The King and the *Sandelár*   185
23 The Princess Who Laughed   188
24 To Experience So As to Understand   190
25 The King and the Golden Wheat   195
26 The Donkey Knows How to Read   201
27 Mushón and the *Papás*   208
28 The Tale of the Questions   213
29 When the Mouth Is Used   227

PART SIX   Jokes and Anecdotes

Djohá   235
30 Djohá's *Salata*   238
31 Djohá in the King's House   240
32 Djohá Eats at the King's Table   243
33 It's All in the Asking   247
34 Djohá and the Oil   249
35 Better a Wise Man Should Strike You Than a Fool Help You   251
36 What a Sweet Death!   254
37 Djohá's Questions   255
38 Djohá's Retorts   259
39 Djohá's Invitation to *Pranso*   261
40 Djohá's *Mirákolo*   264
41 Djohá and the *Karpúz*   267
42 The Eggs and the Grain   271
43 Djohá's *Merás*   276
44 Djohá and the Forty Thieves   280

Numskulls: Tales from Makeda   283
45 The Tales of Makeda   285
46 The Seven Repudiated Wives of Makeda   287
47 The Woman from Makeda and the *Papias*   294
48 *Djenitores* in Makeda   296
49 The Mice of Makeda   298
50 The *Makedanos* and the Cat   301
51 The Eve of Yom Kippúr in Makeda   303

52 Yom Kippúr in Makeda   306
53 The *Makedanos* at the Bathhouse   310
54 Snow in Makeda   313

El rey Shelomó i el pishkado de oro   315
Informants   319
A Note on Judeo-Spanish   329
Glossary   333
Type Index   353
Motif Index   357
Bibliography   385

Foreword

More than five hundred years have passed since the expulsion from Spain of our forefathers, and we still carry within us that magnificent culture created during the sojourn of the Jews in Spain over the course of more than a thousand years. Places and names, habits and customs, foods and songs, tales and proverbs have accompanied us to this day in the beloved tongue of our ancestors. Ladino, as it is popularly but inappropriately known, is the language we spoke in the homes of our parents. It is in that tongue in which the traditional Judeo-Spanish tales were narrated, tales known today only by those who transmit them orally, holding within them a treasure worthy of preservation and transmittal to future generations.

In the past, popular tales were told as part of daily life. They were passed from father to son and told among friends and neighbors, on the street, and at the marketplace. Any occasion was appropriate to tell a new tale or an already familiar one. This is how these tales, these *konsejas,* were passed on from one person to the next, from one locale to another, from one generation to the following. Some tales have a magical or supernatural setting; others may be legends with King Solomon or the Prophet Elijah as the protagonist; some are moral tales that illustrate examples from real life; and others are funny tales about Djohá or Moshiko. Still others are familiar tales that immortalize comical or exemplary situations. All are engraved as family memories.

With the telling of these tales our mothers put us to bed at night, introducing us to a world of magic and letting us dream about it. It is with the telling of such tales that our fathers reared us, integrating the tales' universal values within the education and culture of the various countries in which we lived. It is with the telling of tales that our fathers and mothers taught us how to laugh—indispensable to maintaining an inner balance. With the telling of tales they drew the strength needed to overcome the move from country to country, the hostility and persecution they encountered along the way during the long centuries of the Diaspora, and the difficulties of daily life. It is with the telling of tales that they overcame their nostalgia for the beloved Spain they had left behind forever, even as they went through two or even three countries after the Spanish Diaspora, and as they prepared to return to their eternal homeland of Jerusalem.

The principal aim of the traditional Judeo-Spanish tale is thus to educate through example. Another objective, though, no less important, is to produce laughter so as to make personal and social tensions disappear. There were other goals that in general are not acknowledged: escaping the world of reality and taking refuge in a world of kings and queens, or creating a semblance of victory in a world of enmity and repression. No less present were the off-color jokes, those that exceeded the limits of good breeding, told only in the presence of adults. Through these tales kings and tailors, priests and rabbis, fathers and sons, Jews, Christians, and Muslims, at times in friendship and at other times in conflict, were paraded before us. The tendency was to resolve the issue through a liberating joke.

The Judeo-Spanish tale is characterized primarily by the language used to transmit it, the same today as yesterday. This language that our parents spoke and preserved lovingly and faithfully throughout the centuries still has the old sounds of the fifteenth-century vernacular. Over the generations it was enriched by Turkish, Greek, French, Italian, and Slavic borrowings acquired under the Ottoman Empire, by Arabic words from Spanish Morocco and Jerusalem, and by the Hebrew of Israel, before and after the establishment of the state of Israel—even though Hebrew words were already incorporated into the language spoken in Spain. Thus it is that in the various countries where the Sephardim lived, numerous dialects emerged that can be found in the large corpus of tales.

It is through these tales that values, historical and imaginary figures and events, a way of thinking, habits and customs, clothing and food were transmitted from one generation to the next. Thus it is also that a realistic or idealistic setting is expressed in a rich world of tales and traditions—Jewish and non-Jewish, filled with *hohmat hayim,* the wisdom of life, and the values that continue to be relevant in a world still seeking identity and lasting values. It is also through such popular tales that one detects the path encountered by the Sephardim throughout their history—traces of the *Thousand and One Nights.* Spain gave its language and some of its cities as theaters for the tales: Zaragoza, Granada, Maqueda. From Turkey come the figure of the sultan and the tales of Nasr-a-din Hodja, which among the Sephardim became the tales of Djohá. The European tale contributed supernatural elements to another branch of Judeo-Spanish tales.

Today, as a result of radical changes in modern society that eliminated the conditions permitting the thriving of oral tradition—a family and social life based on communal living, without television, where a teller, truly gifted with the art of storytelling, found his or her natural place—the link has been broken. Lately there are those who have noticed the loss of this important means of communication and education. The traditional tale has been recognized as a vehicle for transmitting values, as a source of anthropological information, and as a repository of sentimental values. So it is that, in order to rediscover these tales and bring to light the world hidden within them we seek tellers among the elderly. We use a fluency in Judeo-Spanish, with all its complexities and dialectal differences, to coax informants into speaking freely and to liberate them from the ingrained prejudices that make them feel that such tales have no place or importance in a modern society.

To preserve and transmit oral tales the way they were told is no longer possible. After overcoming this first obstacle and accepting that the milieu created is not a natural contextual one for the telling of stories, it becomes clear that storytelling is still alive and well. The teller becomes an informant, and the tale is recorded. The best results, of course, derive from the recreation of a natural setting, that is, with a circle of habitual tellers, preferably of the same sex, so that they can feel free to say what they wish without censoring the tales that come to mind.

Although the sources of the tales are anonymous, each version derives from the actual telling. Each teller adapts, eliminates, and changes the elements of the tale around a central core that remains more or less stable. This is done with the help of gestures and facial expressions and according to the teller's memory and mood of the moment, the gender of the audience, and the circumstances of the narration. That is why, when trying to record a popular tale in writing, we find ourselves facing the problem of trying to write in an "oral" form, an obvious paradox. But it is the only way to retain the spontaneity of the tale, its orality being one of its main characteristics.

The language of the tale is of utmost importance in this period of decline in the survival of Judeo-Spanish because capturing a tale in its moment of narration is fixing the condition and idiosyncrasies of the language at a particular point in time, directly from the mouth of the narrator. Today, with the language no longer transmitted from mother to child, those of us still able to speak it and who remember the tales we were told have the important duty to record, preserve, and transmit them, in written or oral form, in the original language or in translation into the main languages of today's societies.

Finally, the importance of the tales themselves must be made clear. They serve to link young and old and to create, through their peculiar and universal values, a continuum between generations. This is based on the fundamental concept that the tales represent a way of thinking and living worth preserving because it is filled with wisdom and humor.

In closing, I want first to thank my informants. They have all contributed to the making of this book in telling their tales with love and enthusiasm. I want to recall with affection the memory of all those who are no longer alive, especially my father and mother, Alfredo and Diana Sarano of blessed memory, to whom I owe everything: from my love for tales to my narrative ability, from my knowledge of the Judeo-Spanish language and traditions to some of the tales.

Thanks are due my husband, Aharon Cohen, who helps me in my work with all his heart and energy and without fail. My gratitude goes as well to Professor Raphael Patai, of blessed memory, who encouraged the publication of this harvest of tales; to Professor Dan Ben-Amos, who facilitated its publication; to the researcher and writer Yoel Perez, who worked faithfully to see that this book came to light; and to the scholar Gladys Pimienta, who allowed me to publish a tale from her large repository from Spanish Morocco. Finally, special thanks to Professor Reginetta Haboucha, who conducted the difficult labor of translating the tales into English, trying to preserve their character and flavor, and enriched them with her scholarly annotations of major importance for those who may want to delve deeper into the subject matter.

MATILDA KOÉN-SARANO
Jerusalem, December 6, 1999
Translated from the Judeo-Spanish by Reginetta Haboucha

Preamble

Some years ago the late folklorist Professor Raphael Patai asked me whether I could locate Judeo-Spanish folktales harvested directly from oral tradition, that is, directly from informants, in order to publish them in an annotated anthology.

Naturally I immediately thought of Matilda Koén-Sarano, who for many years has been involved in the task of collecting and publishing Judeo-Spanish folktales, which she records from narrators in Israel and elsewhere. She gladly agreed to help me and opened up her archives to me, which included hundreds of narratives: stories she had recorded from informants in their original language and which, for the most part, had never been published. We sat together for long hours to sort out the material, the main challenge being to select the right mix of stories from this extensive collection. At last, we agreed to the following three goals in tale selection:

1. To take the broader view and have as many narrative genres represented in the book as possible.
2. To bring to readers tales reflecting the Judeo-Spanish culture in its characteristic colors.
3. To identify tales displaying artistic qualities so that even a reader disinterested in the research apparatus that accompanies them would find the tales interesting and derive enjoyment from them.

Dr. Reginetta Haboucha, who for many years has dedicated herself to the research and analysis of the Judeo-Spanish oral narrative, took on the task of translating the texts into English and providing relevant scholarly annotations and commentaries.

Many Judeo-Spanish collections of folktales have been published, some in Ladino and others in various foreign languages. This is the first time, however, that an entire collection of such tales, unadulterated by literary adaptation or significant editing—except, of course, in the process of translation—has been published in English in an annotated scholarly edition. The tales preserve, almost intact, the original text used by the traditional storytellers who narrated them. The anthology thus fills a void that has existed for far too long in this area. This is one of its major values.

In recent decades we have been witnesses to a great awakening of interest in the Judeo-Spanish tradition, both in the United States and abroad. From the materials gathered by researchers, it is clear that the Judeo-Spanish culture and language have retained their vitality far beyond the expectation that most researchers may have held at the onset of their inquiries.

Writing down and documenting folktales is considered by many a last effort to rescue and preserve a vanishing cultural treasure for the coming generations. As far as Judeo-Spanish culture is concerned, however, it seems to me that this nostalgic archival approach is unfounded. Those who already mourn the loss of this particular tradition are grossly mistaken. As this anthology demonstrates, the Judeo-Spanish language and its culture are alive and well.

The publication of texts that preserve the original storytelling form favored by traditional storytellers is significant also for a different kind of reader: the modern, nontraditional performer. In the 1980s a renaissance of the professional art of oral performance began in the United States. From there it spread to Canada and to other countries. Today storytelling is a growing phenomenon that has spread all over the Western Hemisphere and is being followed and studied by folklorists around the world.

As a student of this interesting phenomenon, I am acquainted firsthand with a modern community of storytellers, and it is my impression that one cannot look at those new narrators as followers of a specific ethnic and cultural tradition. Rather, according to my research, the new storytellers use various ethnic and cultural traditions. The large majority of new Israeli storytellers, for example, seem to draw their repertoire from a wide variety of sources from all over the world, including written sources, often heavily. What is true of Jewish-Israeli storytellers today may well apply to modern storytellers in the United States and elsewhere.

There is nevertheless a wave of new storytellers for whom the Jewish storytelling tradition is very dear, and they strive to preserve it in all its glory and with all its flavorful characteristics. In their performances, they frequently use traditional materials drawn from any of the various "tribes" of Israel. Many of them are or have been involved either in artistic or social welfare/education activities. Their intended audience is the entire society that surrounds them, and the percentage of old-fashioned folktales in their repertoire appears to be rather limited.

It is important to stress that the tales included in this volume did not undergo any kind of literary adaptation. They preserve intact the original performance of the traditional storytellers who narrated them, and this is what makes them so very attractive to the new narrators. It is our hope, therefore, that this volume will serve as an inspiration to the community of emerging storytellers, professional as well as amateur, and that it will contribute to the continuity of the oral transmission of such narratives, both within the confines of Jewish-Spanish culture and that of the general Jewish culture in its interaction with other cultures.

    YOEL SHALOM PEREZ
    Haifa, 2002

PREFACE

In an anthology of narratives it is important to conceive of each oral rendition as the narrator's property, which he or she lends to or shares with the collector. Collectors, however, also have an impact on the character of a collection since they are responsible for the overall selection of tales grouped for publication.

In the case of this particular collection of Judeo-Spanish texts, it was harvested in Israel and elsewhere by Matilda Koén-Sarano, an inveterate teller, collector, and editor of Judeo-Spanish tales who has published several volumes of stories in the original language side by side with a Hebrew translation. She recorded, transcribed, and edited these tales and collaborated with her friend and fellow *konseja* enthusiast, Yoel Shalom Perez from Ben Gurion University in Beer-Sheva, to select from among many others the fifty-four representative narratives, three times *Chi*—eighteen, the symbol of life—for publication in this volume. Himself a storyteller, Perez is also a student of the Sephardic performance event today. He has contributed a revealing essay to this anthology about storytelling as living art within the social group that perpetuates the tradition in modern Israeli society. The tales he selected represent many of the major themes and narrative techniques of the Sephardi oral tradition and introduce the reader to the creative imagination and intercultural backgrounds of the gifted bearers of this tradition.

Most of these tales are traditional and in local circulation. They were taken down from thirty narrators, twenty-two of them women and eight men. A brief interview history of each narrator's life is appended, including the year and circumstances of each recording session. Little contextual information, such as the performance art of each narrator, is available from the collector, however, as storytelling has lost much of its traditional role and purpose in the modern setting of Israeli society.

This work was designed for readers familiar with Jewish culture and its folk beliefs as well as for those who come to it with little prior knowledge of the lore. One of my goals for this anthology has been to study not only the strong Jewish elements present in the texts but also the meaning and interpretation of an amalgam of national cultural heritages assimilated into

Sephardic folklore from long-time Muslim and Christian neighbors. The intercultural contacts are often evident; yet the judaized traits and the adaptation of universal traditions reflect the slant and hopes of the Jewish/Sephardic transformation.

For the benefit of the non-initiated reader, analytical commentaries have been appended to each narrative as needed. Included in them is textual study that examines the aesthetic characteristics of the tales, the peculiarities of particular versions, and symbols of the acculturation process. Also included is clarifying information on the cultural references, culture-specific associations, and worldviews that underlie each text or are alluded to in it. It must be understood, though, that any attempt at interpretation is colored by my subjective vision of what each text represents.

While oral texts are by nature tangential to a culture, they are also multidimensional and rely on reflection, pacing, emotions, body language, and sociolinguistic features. The intimacy that eye contact and gestures bring to the performance cannot be rendered on a printed page, and it is important not to overlook that reality. It is also important to remember that translation of a text from oral to written form is an art, or even a re-creation, not a science, and that it sometimes calls for skilled approximations of words and meaning and reflects an attempt at reasonable punctuation. This process is necessarily an imperfect one.

Working with Judeo-Spanish tales is a particularly complex enterprise. Over time, and as a result of geographic diversity, a multiplicity of surrounding languages has had a significant influence on the development of what is today the surviving language of the Sephardim. Thus, the language of our texts is often contaminated—some may say enriched—in varied ways by this influence. The result is a speech heavily peppered with adulterated foreign words and filled with idiosyncratic and colorful characteristics that risk being lost in the traditional process of translation, a possible detriment to the integrity of the oral rendition. Thus, the challenge of translating Judeo-Spanish oral tales lies not only in trying to retain the flavor of the oral retelling while conveying the narrative in writing, but also in attempting to do so through a different linguistic instrument. The static text produced is in contrast to an evolving performance, a transformation that occurs necessarily in the act of transcribing any oral tale.

In presenting Judeo-Spanish folktales in this English translation to scholarly as well as lay readers, it is just as important to reproduce the original style as closely as possible as it is to be faithful to the content of each story. In this work, giving the written form to a narrative has included a serious effort at providing a text in English as faithful to the original telling as syntactically possible, all the while trying to convey the flavor and intercultural complexities as well as the intended nuances and to retain the matter-of-fact approach of the original narration that tells what the protagonists see, say, and do, rather than what they feel. Precisely in this lies the strength of the folktale. By hearing/reading what the protagonists say and do, the listener/reader can sense, understand, and interpret how they feel. I include as many of the "borrowed" terms and phrases as possible in the translation so as to give the readers a sense of the colorful essence of Judeo-Spanish, keeping in mind the need to reduce significant interference to facilitate the ease of the reading process.[1] A glossary is provided at the end of the volume and key linguistic and cultural features are included in notes and commentaries as well in an effort to enhance the reader's understanding and enjoyment.

For illustrative purposes and to give interested readers a sense of the folk flavor of the language and rhythm of a single, discrete performance, one of the translated texts, *El rey Shelomó i el pishkado de oro,* is offered also in its original Judeo-Spanish version at the end of the volume. This tale's title also provides the title for this anthology: *King Solomon and the Golden Fish*. It may be helpful for readers to keep in mind that Judeo-Spanish is an oral language with no single established phonetic system of transcription into Latin characters.

A prototypical tale is the original tale pattern from which copies are made. It has recognizable universal traits and provides the archetype. Each tale's archetype has characteristics unique to its own cultural context; it also has universal traits in common with those of its global counterparts. To render this anthology useful for scholarly consumption as well as for public enjoyment, it includes universal classificatory types (AT or IFA; see type index) and motifs as a base of reference and comparison to existing Jewish and non-Jewish parallels. Indices of tale types and motifs are appended as well for cross-referencing Jewish and universal sources.

For organizational purposes, I have arranged the tales into six conventional generic categories, according to their general thematic content. The choice of appropriate headings is based on the most important features of each group of texts.

Many have contributed to the development of this work—in spirit and scholarship. Of invaluable assistance was my much-admired mentor, Samuel G. Armistead, whose sensitivity to the nuances of Judeo-Spanish always inspires and enlightens. Paola di Robilant offered a careful and critical read of the first version of the text translation for idiomatic fluency and ease of reading. Isaac Jack Levy, Haïm Vidal Sephiha, and Marie-Christine Varol provided meaningful interpretations of obscure colloquial terminology. I am grateful to the late Raphael Patai for his early guidance and to Dan Ben-Amos for his support and continued interest. To Yoel Perez I extend special thanks for his faith and diplomacy. Finally, Matilda Koén-Sarano deserves accolades for her indefatigable contribution to the preservation of the Judeo-Spanish oral tradition and for her patience with this particular project.

Reginetta Haboucha
New York, November 2000

Note to the Preface

1. An aspect of the oral style found in these tales is the frequent lack of agreement in the tenses used. For example, the past tense may alternate with the present. I have retained the same tense sequence in the translation as appears in the original rendition.

Introduction

REGINETTA HABOUCHA

When the Catholic king and queen, Ferdinand of Aragon and Isabel of Castile, imposed the Expulsion Edict of 1492 on those steadfast Jewish subjects who refused to give in to the threat of sword or fire, they unsuspectingly set in motion a remarkable linguistic and cultural odyssey. Among the descendants of those expelled, the nostalgic ties to faraway Sefarad[1] remain strong to this day and are reflected both in their speech and in their oral traditions which, in turn, may have served to preserve Sephardic Jews as a distinct cultural and historic unit.

Medieval Spain had nurtured the emergence of a unique and thriving Jewish-Spanish culture. It is well documented, for example, that throughout the Middle Ages Spanish Jews were noted for their linguistic skills. As translators and storytellers, they were some of the main transmitters of Eastern/Islamic culture to the Christian world. Belonging to an ancient people whose own history goes back thousands of years and whose long tradition teaches to remember stories and live by their teachings, this came quite naturally to the Sephardim.

After all, storytelling holds a cherished place in Jewish culture. According to Jewish tradition, the written Torah—the first five books of the Bible—and the oral Torah—the *Torah she be'al peh*—were both communicated to Moses orally when he ascended to Mount Sinai. Together, among Jews, the Pentateuch and the Oral Law form a whole, encompassing both text and interpretation. Thus, an ongoing interaction between the spoken and the written word has existed from the beginning, and retelling has become central to the annual cycle of synagogue rituals and religious practices, with generation after generation of Jews telling and retelling the stories of their forefathers.

Judeo-Spanish storytelling derives from this distinguished heritage. The power of orality has been central to the transmission of Sephardic customs, wisdom, and values for centuries. Over the course of a five-hundred-year historical journey, the narrative transmission process has remained dynamic, constantly evolving from and being strengthened by contact with the surrounding societies of the past and, more recently, with modern Israel. As Sephardic Jews came into contact with the ideas and institutions of the various people among whom they resided, their speech and thought patterns were naturally affected. What they plucked from surrounding societies led to the creation of traditions and customs that enriched the cultural tapestry of Spanish Jewry.

While other oral genres (now tenuously alive in the Sephardic Diaspora) have displayed a deep and singular faithfulness to their original peninsular roots, the Judeo-Spanish oral narrative—to the wonderment and delight of modern scholars—exhibits a more universal character and reflects an international heritage of folk wisdom. It is true that Sephardic versions of international tale types may contain archaic elements going back to the end of fifteenth-century Spain. They are not, however, some ancient, multisecular relic of the medieval, pre-diasporic past, or even of the purely and more ancient Jewish tradition. They have not survived simply as a marvelously intact and unmodified venerable and monolithic corpus but have acquired a multitude of foreign elements along the way—mostly from the Balkans, the rest from the Near East or North Africa—which have not only influenced but also enhanced them. Dynamic and modified by new imports, they generally conform to time-honored guidelines and standards. Some tales in the Sephardic repertoire are not necessarily indigenous to the Jewish people but may originate with the folk tradition current among their neighbors. These, too, were modified and changed during the process of moving from one place to another and from one people to another.

While they reflect a melting pot of sources and show obvious similarities to the storytelling of other cultures with whom they have had prolonged contact, such tales impart clearly the collective wisdom and morality of a special, identifiable culture. Many are popular all over the world and thus belong to all of us, with no single culture having sole ownership over them, but there is no question that they have specific Jewish features, Jewish folklore and Jewish religion having influenced each other throughout the ages.

As they came to absorb some of the customs and folk beliefs of others into their own culture, Sephardic storytellers did not do so mechanically but imbued their tales with distinctive Jewish and Sephardic characteristics and, oftentimes, with the Jewish religious and ethical spirit. In addition to purely Sephardic/Jewish popular beliefs, intercultural affinities, influences, changes, and visible examples of the acculturation process are discernible. Those elements that could be adapted without conflict with essential Jewish beliefs are colored with a Jewish interpretation or a Jewish slant. We call this adaptation of universal traditions "judaization," a process of transformation to the religion, philosophy, and way of life of the Jews. Many general practices, for example, are judaized merely by the use of a Hebrew term. Such a process of assimilation of elements stemming from other religions and cultures is a syncretic phenomenon, rarely conscious or intentional and often the result of intercultural affinities.[2]

Folklore expression varies, and folk narratives belong to an oral literary genre that encompasses folktales, legends, jokes, and anecdotes, transmitted mainly through word of mouth. Not all of these genres are represented in this anthology. *Konsejas,* or Judeo-Spanish narrative tales, have been a feature of Sephardic life for a very long time, part of its spiritual and cultural heritage. They represent the traditional artistic manifestation of a community, the spirit and essence of its culture, reflecting both continuity and consistency through time and place. Proverbs and folk sayings, part of gnomic or wisdom literature perpetuated in daily speech, instill wisdom and a moral truth. Modern-day Sephardic tales display this wisdom either in Judeo-Spanish or in Hebrew, a sign of the linguistic impact of the traditional Jewish environment on the tellers' daily life and deep-rooted beliefs. Riddles, on the other hand, which are usually woven into the fabric of prose narratives, appear less frequently in the Sephardic repertoire. One narrative example is included in this collection.

While this anthology does not showcase a predominance of religious plots or sacred legends, the narratives represented reflect a society in which Jewish tradition is very much a part of everyday life. They are quintessentially Jewish. Their details are rooted in what is real and familiar to the tellers and the audience. They depict instances from the rituals of the Jewish life cycle, such as birth, the *brit milá* (circumcision), ritualistic wedding celebrations, and customs connected with death, displaying their rhythm as part of the true life of the community that nurtures them. From the general Jewish year cycle, some of the holy days are mentioned, such as the Sabbath or Yom Kippúr[3] and the Kol Nidré, when traditional Jews commonly dress in white. Common occurrences in the tales are observance of the commandments, including the giving of charity, holiday observance, circumcision, ritual bathing, synagogue attendance, and the study of the Torah. The tales give snapshots of these traditional events: prenuptial *mikvah,* or ritual bath, wedding and *brit*/circumcision customs. This is not to say that religious legends do not exist in Sephardic society, but each collection is the result of the social circles from which the collector gathers her tales, and this anthology reflects not only that but also the personal slant of the selector of the tales, himself a performer.

The tales also convey timeless wisdom and a colorful depiction of the way of life of the Sephardic communities that existed until the first half of the twentieth century. The impact that the surrounding cultures have left on the Jews can be detected in many aspects of the narration, such as local tastes and fashions. In overall terms, the tales portray the traditional life of the common people, Jews and Muslims alike, as they lived side by side and observed it, before a major segment of the Sephardic community of the Diaspora found its way to Israel. They describe visits to a coffeehouse, drinking Turkish coffee, playing *tavle,* or backgammon; they show criers at the marketplace, jewelers and silversmiths, the *bakál* or grocer where characters buy everyday staples. They describe shops where women buy their wares and where the incognito king or his spies are sure to encounter the individual they seek; the old hag who seems to know everyone and is able to gain access into every home through her cunning;[4] the poor Jews of the community who live in popular basement dwellings because they are more affordable; the housekeeping and cleanliness of modest but proud homes; the women who do not leave their houses, obeying their husbands' instructions not to appear alone in public; the madman of the village, known to everyone; the prevalent poverty; the journey on foot from one city to another; the village water well where young girls fill their water jars before the Sabbath; and fishing, shoe repair, and barbering as the main means of survival of the poor. Yet the modern world does intrude: finding lodging at a hotel in an unfamiliar city; mailing one's earnings back to one's wife through the post; or identifying the rich with the philanthropic Rothschild.[5]

Sephardic lore as shown here is vitally concerned with everyday situations and the immediate environment. The didactic story rather than the magic tale is dominant, and the landscape of the narrative is one of its key elements. Most of the tales are novelle, with a realistic setting and familiar themes (sexual awakening and courtship; the purposeful quest for a mate; family life; society; values; the universe) and characters drawn from real life (parents and children; bride and groom; husband and wife). The vicissitudes of life can be traced in the stories. They deal with the life of ordinary people and their daily troubles: matchmaking; marital relations; adultery; the heartbreak of barrenness; murder and its punishment; the hardship of earning a living; the unpredictability of luck; poverty; cleverness; the wisdom of the elders; tasks and tests; and other such familiar themes. The tales characteristically use familiar folktale motifs, only on occasion including incidents of the marvelous or supernatural. The typical narratives are similar to those that appear in the *Decameron* and *Arabian Nights.*

The chief characters can be real-life men or women, heroes or heroines who command the audience's attention and sympathies. Usually portrayed as human beings in conditions similar to those of the tales' listeners, they are, more often than not, not bound to actual time or space, although the tales occasionally may be set in Jewish time (within the Jewish calendar cycle). Often there are also biblical characters, such as in tales illustrating the human and amorous side of King Solomon, as opposed to his legendary wisdom, or featuring Elijah the Prophet as the imaginative helper of the desperately needy who meet his challenges. Narrative stereotypes are also popular, prominent among them being Djohá, the innocent simpleton central to many a Sephardic joke. Gentile characters remain anonymous and are referred to only by title: king, vizier, *papás* (priest), etc. Some other players are identified by affectionate or recognizable first names or simply as Jews.

Tasks and tests are common motifs in folktales as the means by which to secure a prize. Sephardic tale renditions do not break that mold. In such narratives, the hero must overcome something difficult or impossible to win the pined-for bride or to save his own life. Usually accompanied in universal parallels by motifs of supernatural helpers who enable the hero to perform the assigned tasks, these tests tend to come in threes and are often imposed at the suggestion of wicked counselors or jealous rivals. In most cases, when protagonists encounter the supernatural or when the hero receives supernatural aid and triumphs unexpectedly, it is seen as part of the everyday course of events. Such outcomes may serve to help the audience disassociate from the familiar and overcome the difficulty of reaching a desired position of secure, socially accepted success, if only for a moment.

Tales are often heuristic, and their moral structure frequently ensures that the good are rewarded and the evil punished. The point of many a tale often stresses specifically Jewish elements of survival or reinforces the teaching of lasting Jewish values. Through their ability to outwit and deceive, our heroes often triumph over an unfamiliar and/or hostile environment, symbolized by heartless rivals or the harsh realities of their condition. In some tales, however, a pattern of inversion of reality may emerge, as in universal folktales: the poor girl may marry a prince, while a princess may disguise herself as a scullery maid; or the hideous beast, frog, or lizard is finally revealed as a handsome prince. Whether the characters are virtuous, clever, lazy, or foolish does not always matter. In the end, they usually achieve the reward, and all ends well against all odds.

Singular among Sephardic narratives is the romantic tale stressing the theme of fate in matters of marriage and luck. Very popular also—and now the most widespread—are jokes and anecdotes depicting the comic aspects of life as seen through Jewish eyes, stories of people whose actions are silly to the point of absurdity. While the use of universal humorous motifs is present, many stories have undertones of sadness and frustration. Through a happy ending, though, the tales carry a note of hope and consolation as well: the wish for all Jews to find their way out of precarious situations.

In these tales of life trials, of cleverness and wisdom, society is divided distinctly into the Good and the Bad, the Rich and the Poor, the Powerful and the Weak. Class differences are black and white. The main characters are tested with hard luck and formidable obstacles, and they are challenged to accomplish extraordinarily difficult tasks. They confront rivalries and betrayal and see things as a whole and penetrate the depth of a situation, demonstrating the knowledge of the world and human nature they have acquired through experience. By and large the message, in the end, is a positive one: humankind—and Jews—will prevail and thrive.

These folktales are imaginative narratives told to entertain, but they have a mysterious authority of their own. Not only have they moved from place to place in various cultural guises and survived, but they also teach us and show us more about ourselves than we thought we knew. Although the stories in themselves have power, the way they are told may give them even more potency. Storytellers have considerable freedom to select their motifs from hundreds of choices, and they usually use those they know well and love that express concerns and feelings that seem to be part of the psyche of their typical community. They preserve and choose from a standard repertoire of culturally appropriate and acceptable motifs, adapting a universal tale to fit comfortably into the conventional tapestry of their own cultural tradition and tailoring the textural features to the needs and interests of their audiences. This makes each retelling fresh and exciting, without sacrificing the basic plot that makes each tale recognizable as a prototype. Such flexibility of interpretation also allows for adaptation of the tales to relevant time and place.

Because folktales of all kinds are archetypal, there is remarkable uniformity in structure across cultures, although content and style may vary. Sephardic tellers often use these fictional tales, intertwined with tradition and ritual, to highlight morals and reiterate messages we sometimes forget. Handed down through generations of telling and retelling, their tales are integrated and remolded to mirror Sephardic norms and traditions and to become an inspiration and an ethical guide. The cogitative folklore that appears in them includes popular beliefs that find their expression in customs and practices. The tales are thus an acceptable vehicle to transmit the normative values of the Sephardic society as well as behavioral principles and traditions. By sharing Jewish and universal ideals, tellers expect their audience to obtain some spiritual nourishment from them, and thus it may be that they seek to instruct through examples.

In order to tell a tale, though, to reformulate and revitalize it, tellers need a reactive audience, and this stresses the important role of listeners in the shaping and perpetuation of any oral tradition. The intimate, reciprocal relationship among the teller, the text, and the listeners/readers creates meaning and an interpretation that can never be a repetition; each retelling makes the tale speak anew. As tales illustrate the human condition, they talk to each one of us at a different level. The experience and struggle of the protagonists are part of our consciousness; each tale speaks to us directly and elicits a response.

What makes these tales Sephardic? Most important, the fact that they have been adopted and adapted and that they have survived in the Sephardic community. As a powerful link between Spanish Jews and their Hispano-Jewish legacy, these delightful narratives must be passed along to keep the legacy alive. The cultivation of this rich tradition has been facilitated in great part by a cherished audio-oral vehicle of transmission. The messages transmitted in the narratives—tensions, anxieties, humor, hope, values, and wishes—come to us not only through plot and choice of motifs but also through a peculiar and colorful language.

The reward of folklore has always been in sharing. The tales in this collection of Sephardic verbal tradition reveal an art that has borrowed from other cultures and transformed. They draw their breadth from diverse outside influences, yet they reveal the will to affirm their own full and deep cultural identity. The value of this anthology is in its color, power, and contribution to the enrichment, preservation, and illumination of Sephardic culture. Each transmitted story is a key to the door of a private treasure. Rather than as a pure reflection of reality, each tale in this collection ought to be read as a window, always only partially opened and not always crystal clear, to the world of the unconscious, both individual and social. In the end, storytelling is a powerful way to teach.

Notes to the Introduction

1. For the name-place Sefarad, see Obad. 20.
2. To some extent, this development parallels the linguistic syncretism inherent in such examples as the "Spanglish" spoken by Latinos in the United States, or the "Franglish" used in Quebec. It is also reminiscent of the modern-day infiltration of Yiddish into the everyday language of many American Jews of Ashkenazic or Eastern European descent.

3. Yom Kippúr is the oldest Jewish holiday mentioned in the Torah, the observance of which is commanded by God.

4. This character is reminiscent of the central protagonist in the Spanish picaresque *La Celestina*. See commentary for tale 20.

5. See commentary in tale 10 for reference to this nineteenth-century magnate.

ABBREVIATIONS

In citing works in the notes, short titles have been used. Works frequently cited have been identified by the following abbreviations:

Alexander-Noy Tamar Alexander and Dov Noy, eds. *Ozaroh shel Abba: Me'ah Sipurim ve-Sipur mi-Pei Yehudei Sefarad (The Treasure of Our Fathers. Judeo-Spanish Tales)*. Jerusalem, 1989.
Alexander-Romero Tamar Alexander and Elena Romero, eds. *Érase una vez... Maimónides. Cuentos tradicionales hebreos.* Córdoba, 1988.
Andrejev Andrejev, Nikolai Petrovich. *Ukazatel' Skazocnich Síuzhetov po-Sisteme Aarne.* Leningrad, 1929. Berkeley, 1993.
AT Antti Aarne and Stith Thompson. *The Types of the Folktale.* 2d rev. Folklore Fellows Co. (FFC) 184. Helsinki, 1973.
AY *Aki Yerushalayim, Revista kulturala djudeo-espanyol.* Jerusalem.
BJ Micha J. Bin Gorion. *Der Born Judas: Legenden, Märchen und Erzählungen.* 6 vols. Leipzig, 1919–24.
BP Johannes Bolte and George Polívka. *Anmerkungen zu den Kinder-und Hausmärchen der Brüder Grimm.* 5 vols. Leipzig, 1913–32. Reprint, Hildesheim, 1963.
Crews Cynthia Crews. *Recherches sur le judéo-espagnol dans les pays balkaniques.* Paris, 1935.
EB Wolfram Eberhard and P. N. Boratav. *Typen türkischer Volksmärchen.* Weisbaden, 1953.
Grunwald, "Motifs" M. Grunwald. "Sipurim spanyoliim ve-ha-motivim she-bahem" ("Spaniolic-Jewish Folktales and Their Motifs"). *Edot* 2 (1947): 225–45.
Grunwald, *Tales* Max Grunwald. *Sipurei 'Am, Romansot, ve-Orakhot Khayim shel Yehudei Sefarad (Tales, Songs and Folkways of Sephardic Jews. Texts and Studies).* Ed. Dov Noy. Jerusalem, 1982.
Haboucha Haboucha, Reginetta. *Types and Motifs of the Judeo-Spanish Folktales.* New York, 1992.
IFA Israel Folktale Archives.

Jason, "Types"   Heda Jason. "Types of Jewish-Oriental Oral Tales." *Fabula* 7 (1965): 115–224.
Jason, *Types*   Heda Jason. *Types of Oral Tales in Israel, Part II*. IES Studies no. 2. Jerusalem, 1975.
JS   *Le Judaïsme Séphardi* (Nouvelle Série)
K   Žamila Kolonomos, ed. *Proverbs, Sayings and Tales of the Sephardic Jews of Macedonia*. Belgrade, 1978.
KS   Matilda Koén-Sarano. *Kuentos del folklor de la famiya djudeo-espanyola*. Yerushalayim, 1986.
L   M. A. Luria. *A Study of the Monastir Dialect of Judeo-Spanish Based on Oral Material Collected in Monastir, Yugo-Slavia*. New York, 1930.
LP   Arcadio de Larrea Palacín. *Cuentos populares de los judíos del Norte de Marruecos*. 2 vols. Tetuán, Morocco, 1952–53.
Marcus, *Mabu'a*   Eliezer Marcus. *Min ha-Mabu'a (From the Fountainhead)*. Haifa, 1966.
MR   Juan Martínez Ruiz. "Textos judeo-españoles de Alcazarquivir (Marruecos), 1948–1951." *Revista de Dialectología y Tradiciones Populares* 19 (1963): 78–115.
[Noy]   Dov Neuman (Noy). Motif index of Talmudic-Midrashic Literature. Ph.D. dissertation. Bloomington, Indiana, 1954.
Noy, *Egypt*   Dov Noy. "Animal Tales in Ancient Egypt." *Makhanayim* 105 (1966): 116–21.
Noy, *Libya*   Dov Noy, ed. *Shiv'im Sipurim ve-Sipur mi-Pi Yehudei Luv (Seventy-one Folktales from Libyan Jews)*. Jerusalem, 1967.
Noy, *Morocco*   Dov Noy, ed. *Moroccan Jewish Folktales*. New York, 1966.
Noy, *Tunisia*   Dov Noy, ed. *Shiv'im Sipurim ve-Sipur mi-Pi Yehudei Tunisia (Seventy-one Folktales from Tunisian Jews)*. Jerusalem, 1966.
Schwili   Dov Noy, ed. *Jefet Schwili Erzält*. Berlin, 1963.
TEM   *A Tale for Each Month*. Israel Folklore Archive.
W   Max L. Wagner. *Beiträge zur Kenntnis des Judenspanischen von Konstantinopel*. Vienna, 1914.
"Ysopete"   John E. Keller and James H. Johnson. "Motif-Index Classification of the Fables and Tales of Ysopete Ystoriado." *Southern Folklore Quarterly* 18, no. 2 (1954): 85–117.

PART ONE

Tales of the Supernatural

Sephardic tales sometimes depict realms of the otherworld, beyond the natural sphere of our everyday life and contrary to the perceived order of things. These are usually reached by means of a magical or supernatural occurrence and are usually accessible to mortals by luck or after a tedious quest.

Colored by the supernatural invasion of the natural order by spiritual or magical forces and the appearance of supernatural beings recognizable to the listeners, such universes are ordinarily depicted in a world in which miraculous deeds are performed mysteriously. Despite the paranormal events, however, there is almost always a realistic understatement. In one way or another, the narratives are set in a semi-Jewish world where such supernatural occurrences are popularly accepted as credible and where didactic messages of societal value are transmitted and understood.

When it appears, the otherworld of popular belief is set in some indefinite place and time, where supernatural episodes are accepted along with the everyday Jewish setting. The supernatural function may be expressed through knowledge of events and happenings hidden in the future or in the past. Fairies are seldom featured, but the Prophet Elijah often appears as a more plausible substitute. Supernatural and human characters interact casually, good is rewarded with a happy ending, and evil is generally punished. Such tales have psychological appeal, as we can see in the section on Elijah the Prophet in this anthology.

Superstition is sometimes woven into the supernatural aspects of some tales. These beliefs or practices usually result from fear of the unknown. Their validity in the narrating society is based on the belief in the power of the supernatural and of such invisible forces as *shedim,* or spirits and demons. They frequently reveal popular beliefs and cherished traditions. Be they fairies, demons, or Elijah, however, the extraordinary understanding of such folk characters and their ability to exercise magic powers enable them to affect the lives of human characters in the tales for good or for evil.

In this section, a speaking fish displays preternatural powers of perception by revealing a secret adulterous relationship in the king's palace. In the end, the fish proves more knowledgeable than King Solomon, who, despite his renown as a wise man, is humbled for his indiscriminate love of women and his inability to see through the deceit of one person or to recognize the worth of another. A second supernatural fish with the power of speech has the ability to fulfill three wishes, but within reason. It serves to punish overweening ambition and to teach listeners to be satisfied with their lot and not become too greedy. The omniscient old man in another tale imparts his wisdom in a crisis and, in the process, changes the behavior of an entire kingdom and effects a valuable social welfare change. A mysterious natural manifestation avenges an unsolved murder in yet another tale and identifies the murderer before the king. The punishment imposed follows a biblical injunction. In another narrative, a magic cooking vessel turns up at opportune moments to progressively improve the lives of a destitute widow and her orphaned daughters. In another tale, child snatching brings to light the belief in the power of demons to steal newborn babies and cast a spell over them. The appearance of beings identified with Lilith, Adam's rebellious first wife, is propelled by the belief in her power to steal newborn babies in Jewish folklore. In yet another tale, the breaking of a vow to a dying father leads a man through a terrifying otherworld experience and, ultimately, to his death. Finally, in the only fairy tale in this collection, a punishing witch transforms a pair of unkind and thoughtless young lovers into hideous and blind beings. Each can only regain the lost good looks through the kindness of the other.

1

King Shelomó and the Golden Fish

Narrated by MOSHÉ IBN EZRA (1987)

At the time of King Shelomó, there lived in the Galíl,[1] next to the Kinneret,[2] an old fisherman who had seven daughters, one more beautiful than the other. *Ma* the youngest, Shulamít, was the most beautiful of them all.

One day the firstborn, the *bohora*,[3] presented herself before her father. She said:

"Today, upon casting your *trata,* your net, say: 'This *trata* is the luck, the *mazál,* of my daughter the *bohora,* the first born.' Let's see what'll come out. Perhaps you'll get lucky because of me."

And that is what the fisherman did, when the time came, there in the Kinneret. He went into his boat and cast his net in the middle of the sea.

"This is the *mazál* of my daughter the *bohora,* the firstborn."

And he waited till the afternoon.

In the afternoon, gathering his *trata,* he found it heavy. Very heavy! With much effort, he dragged the *trata* to the sandy shore. He saw a large stone. Upon returning home, he said to his daughter:

Note: See Koén-Sarano, "El pishkado de oro," in *Lejendas,* 29, for a Judeo-Spanish version of this tale with a Hebrew translation.

1. Hebrew for Galilee, a region in northern Israel.

2. Lake Kinneret, known as the Sea of Galilee in the New Testament (Matt. 4:18, 17:27) and the "Sea of Tiberias" in Talmudic sources (Tosefta Sukka 3:9). Today in modern Israel, the biblical name, Yam Kinneret, has been revived for the lake. See commentary.

3. The firstborn child is often named *bohór*(a), a specially honored name.

"This was your *mazál*! A stone!"

On the second day, the second daughter presented herself. Anyway, we'll make a long story short. All the daughters tried. Once it turned out to be a bundle of old shoes, which they threw back into the water. Another time it was sea weeds. Each single one of them drew a different *mazál*. In the end, Shulamít, the young one, presented herself:

"Father, this time, it's for me!"

"*Ma* you see what's coming out! There is nothing!"

"This time, cast it for me!"

It was Friday. The fisherman wanted to finish early, to return home and welcome the *Shabát*.[4] At dawn, he took himself down to the Kinneret. He cast his net.

"I cast the *trata* in the name of Shulamít, my youngest daughter."

And he waited. Past midday, he gathered his net. He saw that it was a bit heavy. He pulled it in slowly, slowly. And when he drew it in, what does he see? An enormous fish, *senteando,* sparkling with gold and diamonds! He was left struck with wonder! And while he was still struck with wonder, the fish opened its mouth. It said to him:

"Take me out of here immediately, take me to your house, and build a water pool for me, a *djépea,* so that I may live!"

The fisherman went home immediately, with great difficulty. They all came out to meet him.

"Hush!" he said. "Let's all get to work!"

And *kavakaron,* they dug up a *djépea* in the courtyard of their homes, filled it with water, and put the fish in it.

From that day on, the family's delight was this: every morning, they rose and drank their coffee around the *djépea,* and the fish whirled circles around, *solanses,* and told little tales to them, from the thousand and one nights of days bygone. Thus they spent their time.

One day, as they were sitting near the fish, the fisherman was thinking about the fate of his seven daughters, how he would marry them, he who had not even a penny, not an *agorá*. The fish opened its mouth. It said:

---

4. *Shabát* is reserved for relaxing, praying, thinking, and studying Torah. It begins just before sundown on Friday evening and lasts until after sundown on Saturday. It is a day of rest, the queen of days, a time during which religious Jews step out of the hurry of their everyday lives and into the holiness of *Shabát*. The Torah says that on the seventh day God stopped his work of Creation, blessed the seventh day, and declared it holy. The fourth commandment tells us to observe *Shabát* and sanctify it.

"What is there to think about? Stretch out your hand, grab a fistful of diamonds, go to Yerushalayim,[5] and sell them."

"Good idea!"

The fisherman stretched out his hand, grabbed a fistful of diamonds and pearls from the fish's head, took a piece of bread, put it in his pocket, and left for Yerushalayim. After three days, he reached the city and was awed by its splendor and beauty. All the streets led to the center that was the Bet-Amikdásh, the Holy Temple, which was sparkling with gold. Finally, he inquired after the street of the jewelers, the *bijutiés*. They showed it to him. In Yerushalayim there were many streets: the street of the jewelers, the street of the butchers, the street of the *tisheros,* the scissors-makers. Along each street was a different trade.[6]

Finally, he reached the street of the jewelers. The first jeweler before whom he presented himself said to him:

"*Regreto!* I am sorry! It's impossible for me to pay you! What you are showing us is extremely dear. *Avál* there is here a jeweler by the name of Aminadáv. It is he who takes jewels, *bijús,* to the court of Solomon, of Shelomó. He may be able to buy this from you."

The fisherman addressed himself to Aminadáv; *ma,* examining the pearls, the latter saw that he did not have at hand the entire sum needed.

"Listen," he said, "take half the money. Today I'll collect more. Come tomorrow morning!"

Let us leave this and see King Shelomó's court. King Shelomó loved many women, *de todas las sortes,* of all sorts and ranks. And, through them, he became the son-in-law of Pharaoh, Paró, the king of Egypt, and he took his daughter, Tantanhis, who was one of Paró's most beautiful daughters. He brought her to Yerushalayim; he built a palace for her, and Tantanhis came with a following of many servants, and among them a black giant of a servant.

Anyway, it so happens that on that day, Tantanhis went out to the *charshí,* the jewelers' market, she entered Aminadáv's shop, and she saw the pearls.

---

5. Jerusalem, the city of Salem (Gen. 14:18; Ps. 76), is sacred to Jews, Christians, and Moslems, both as an actual historical place and a symbolic idea. After King David had reigned in Hebron for seven years, he moved his capital to Jerusalem (2 Sam. 5:1–13) where he planned to build the Temple. It was his son Salomon, however, who actually built and dedicated the Temple there (1 Kings 7, 8). It remained the holiest of cities during the period of the First and Second Temples. Even after the destruction of both the Temple and Jerusalem, it remained the focus of Jewish prayers. It was under Ottoman rule from 1517 to 1917.

6. Teller's aside, as an explanation.

She went immediately to King Shelomó and demanded insistently that he buy her these pearls. King Shelomó came to examine the merchandise and observed among the pearls the scale of a fish. A suspicion entered his mind:

"There is something here."

He commanded his servants to wait for the seller of pearls: as soon as he comes the next morning to take the rest of the money, let them seize him and bring him before him. And that's how it was. The next morning, when the fisherman came to collect the rest of the money, the soldiers fell upon him and brought him before King Shelomó.

King Shelomó said to him:

"My sword upon your head! You are to tell me how these pearls came into your possession!"

And the fisherman said:

"Nothing can be kept from the king! I will tell you the pure truth!"

And he told him everything.

The king could not stay put. He gathered his ministers immediately and went to see the fish in the Galíl, in the Kinneret. They took their women along as well, and Tantanhis came also, with her court.

Finally, they saw the fish. They all marveled at the sight of its beauty! It was *senteando,* sparkling all over! They sat around the *djépea;* the mistress of the house brought them coffee, and the fish started to whirl *solanses.*

When it arrived before Queen Tantanhis, the fish spitted out a *fishék,* a spurt of contempt that soaked her entirely. This upset King Shelomó very much, and he immediately demanded of the fisherman to kill the fish for its audacity in doing what it did.

The fish opened its mouth and spoke to him:

"Is it you they call King Shelomó, the wisest man in the entire world? *Ma* you don't know what goes on inside your own house! Queen Tantanhis is in love with the black man she has in her house. He is hidden behind the statue of Amún Rá!"

And let them go and find him.

And so it was. They went to Yerushalayim immediately and found this black man who made his home behind the statue of Amún Rá. They took both of them at once and executed them, according to the law of Moshé, the law of Moses.

As time went by, the king was quite sad because he had loved Queen Tantanhis very much. And what had happened to her had scalded his heart. To *afalagar,* to relieve his sorrow a bit, he decided to go to the Galíl and be in the company of the beautiful fish. He took a few servants along, went to the Galíl, and every morning, as was the custom with the members of the fisherman's family, he would sit around the *djépea,* and the fish would begin to tell stories.

Seeing King Shelomó so sad, the fish said to him:

"Why are you thinking so much? Is there a lack of beautiful girls in Israel for you to be so sad? Turn your head and look at the beauty you have by your side!"

Shelomó turned his head and saw the fisherman's youngest daughter, Shulamít. And from then on, his eyes were opened, and he decided to take her as his wife and set her above all the other women in his palace, his *armón.*

After some time passed, they made a beautiful *tálamo*[7] beside the Kinneret, and that is where the marriage of King Shelomó with Shulamít took place. Then it was that King Shelomó wrote in his poem, the *Shir Ashirím,* the Song of Songs: "There are seventy queens, and countless maidens and concubines, *ma* Shulamít is but one."[8]

King Shelomó occupied himself with marrying the six remaining daughters with state ministers, and since then they all lived happily, *orozos.*

May all be well with them and with us too.

---

7. In its use here, the Spanish word *tálamo* probably refers to a *ḵhuppá* or bridal canopy under which bride and groom stand during the marriage ceremony and where the marital union takes place. Symbolically, it represents the groom's home into which the bride is escorted. The usual form of a *ḵhuppá* is a canopy stretched over four posts, with four post holders, one at each corner.

8. The Song of Songs (6:8–9) is translated as:

There are threescore queens,
And fourscore concubines,
And virgins without number.
My dove, my undefiled, is but one.

This dialogue, in which a man and a woman share the delights and anguish of their mutual love, seems on the surface to be a secular amorous poem. While sexual desire is expressed frankly, the rabbis allegorically interpret the lover as God and the beloved as the people of Israel. Also, the bridegroom may be Solomon, personifying spiritual righteousness, and Shulamít, the bride, representing wisdom and fertility. The book appears in the third section of the Bible and is the first of the five Megillót or Scrolls. In the liturgy, the Song of Songs is recited during the morning service, on the intermediate *Shabát* of Passover, and often on the eve of *Shabát.* According to rabbinic tradition, King Solomon is the author of the book, but the Talmudic Baba Batra 15a states that it was actually written down by King Hezakiah and his associates (based on Prov. 25:1). Modern scholarship has generally rejected Solomonic authorship and attributes a much later date for the book.

Commentary

The type of this narrative is IFA *895, *The Miraculous Child,* a novella of infidelity versus innocence, reminiscent also of AT 875D, *The Clever Girl at the End of the Journey,* part 3, in which the vizier's son marries the heroine after she answers the original question (H561.1.1.1). (The fish laughed because there is a man dressed in women's clothes in the harem.)

In another, more complex, published Judeo-Spanish version from Turkey, a Jewish fisherman offers the king three live fish at a time when fish is scarce. The fish are given to the queen as a gift, but they spit on her twice and she demands an explanation from the fisherman under pain of death. When the fisherman's daughter inadvertently swallows the ashes of a burnt skull her father had accidentally found, she bears a son who speaks at birth and reveals the queen's unfaithfulness. The queen's lover is exposed, and she is put to death.[9]

The central motifs of our tale deal with a magic speaking fish (B175, B211.11 [Noy], B211) that has supernatural knowledge (D1810) and spits at the queen to expose her guilt (Q471, D1318.2). It is revealed that she is committing adultery with a repulsive and lowborn slave (T481, T481.2.1, T232.2), and she is punished (Q241).

This most interesting and complex version combines the biblical with the supernatural, weaving a Jewish folktale type with a display of biblical information and Solomonic folklore. It is also reminiscent of the Flood Story of Manu and the Fish, in the Hindu Shatapathat Brahmana. The teller sets the tale in a recognizable historical time (Solomon's reign) and geographical space

---

9. See W, no. 10, "La reina i el nasido/Die Königin und der Neugeborene," 51. That version is from Istanbul and is also classified in Haboucha, 371–74, under *895. For additional Jewish parallels, see Alexander-Romero, no. 7 and p. 244; Jason, "Types," 176–77; Jason, *Types,* 44; Gaster, *Exempla,* no. 354; Grunwald, "Motifs," no. 33; Grunwald, *Tales,* no. 34; Marcus, *Mabu'a,* no. 10 (AT 178A); Nahmad, *Portion in Paradise,* 89; Noy, *Animal Tales,* 217–19, no. 34 (Morocco, AT 178A); Noy, *Ha-na'ara,* no. 11 (Iraq, AT 178A); Noy, *Morocco,* nos. 42, 48; Schram, *Jewish Stories,* 195; Schwarzbaum, *Studies,* 395. For non-Jewish sources, see Al-Shahi and Moore, *Wisdom from the Nile,* no. 25; Ashliman, *Guide to Folktales,* 176 (875D); Basset, *Mille et un contes,* 2:157, no. 71, 2:310, no. 44; BP, 2:349; Chauvin, *Ouvrages arabes,* cf. 2:100, no. 59 (AT 178A), 2:122, no. 115 (AT 178), 5:289, no. 173; Dawkins, *Forty-five Stories,* nos. 20, 21; Grimm and Grimm, *Tales,* (1977) no. 94; EB, no. 100; Laoust, *Contes berbères,* no. 74; Straparola, *Facetious Nights,* 4:1; Thompson and Roberts, *Indic Oral Tales,* 105; Villa, *100 Armenian Tales,* no. 67; "Ysopete" (B330).

(Galilee, Lake Kinneret, and Jerusalem). His narrative reveals knowledge of the Scriptures and of the cycle of homilies and legends that surround Solomon in the Haggadá. It includes historical events (the marriage of Solomon to Pharaoh's daughter), buildings (the Bet Amikdásh), and biblical names or titles—sometimes adulterated but always in Hebrew (Shelomó, Shulamít, Yerushalayim, Paró, Aminadáv, Tantanhis, Amon-Re [Amun-Ra], Moshé), biblical chapters (Shir Ashirím), and rules *(La ley de Moshé)*.

The tale is set in Galilee in northeast Israel and uses the traditional number seven for the number of daughters the destitute fisherman has fathered and needs to feed. The number seven is believed to have mystical power (Z71.5 [Noy]). In the Bible, it is connected with every aspect of religious life in every period. Here, the lot of the youngest of seven daughters is the last net to be drawn and the only successful one. Not only does it bring to light a supernatural catch on the eve of the Jewish Sabbath, but it offers miraculous help (B470), causing the family's luck to change for the better (B292 [Noy], B292). The marvelous fish is found in the Kinneret, a freshwater lake in northeastern Israel fed by the River Jordan in its northern shore. Although fishing on *Shabát,* even from a river or a pond (C631.2+ [Noy]), is forbidden, it is customary to eat fish on that festive day, as it had become a favorite dish from Talmudic times.[10] Fishes were thought to bring good luck because they are the zodiac sign of Adár, the month of Purim in the Hebrew calendar. Because fish are considered ownerless property, anyone catching fish is entitled to keep them, making them highly prized and eagerly sought by those in need.[11] Our tale connects fish with the observance of the Sabbath, easily showing the Judaism of the characters.

The choice of name for the youngest daughter as Shulamít (Shulammite) ties the tale neatly to Solomon. Shulammite may be the feminine form for the Hebrew Shelomó (Solomon), meaning "she who belongs to Solomon." It is often identified with Abishag, "the maiden from Shunem," who was brought to King David in his old age.[12] The name or title of a dancer that appears in

---

10. Shab. 118b. For eating fish on the Sabbath, see also the story of Yosef-Mokír-Shabát (Shab. 119).

11. Fish are proverbial symbols of fruitfulness, and fishing is a livelihood that Jews have engaged in historically. There are many references to fish and fishing in Talmudic literature and an abundance of *halakhót* (laws) and *aggadót* (tales and legends that elaborate on the laws) about fish and fishermen in both the Babylonian and Jerusalem Talmuds and in various *midrashim* (interpretation of Hebrew Scriptures). Jews are said to be clever because they eat plenty of fish.

12. 1 Kings 1:1–4, 15. See also 2 Kings 4:25.

the Song of Songs, the term "Shunammite woman" is synonymous with a beautiful woman.[13] Also known as the Song of Solomon or Canticles, this series of lyric love songs is unique in the Bible.[14]

The poverty of the fisherman in the tale is central, as it is mentioned more than once, first at the beginning of the narrative and then again in relation to a dowry for his unmarried daughters. The listeners understand his condition. The suggestion by the supernatural fish that the father sell the gems taken from its own back leads to the fisherman's travel to Jerusalem and to the mention of Solomon and the Bet Hamikdásh, his Temple, a reference fundamental to Judaism. The beautiful city was the headquarters of royal merchants (P431 [Noy]). The ancient rabbis had said: "Ten measures of beauty came down [from Heaven]; nine measures were taken by Jerusalem and one, by the rest of the world."[15] Solomon was the king of Israel appointed by God to build the Temple, and one of his most important acts was the construction of the Bet Hamikdásh, reputedly a magnificent sanctuary, in Jerusalem. The Temple was famous for its costly materials and technical perfection. Along with a reference to the splendor and layout of Jerusalem, the tale also refers to the Temple's dazzling beauty.[16]

It is rare for names to be given to characters in folktales, especially to minor characters such as a tradesman. And yet the court jeweler is identified anachronistically as Aminadáv (Amminadav), the name of a biblical prince (father of Nahshon) of the tribe of Judah.[17] The identification of the jeweler as the royal jeweler leads to the mention of Solomon's fame as a man who

---

13. Cf. 1 Kings 1:4; Song of Songs 6:13, 7:1–8.

14. See note 8 above.

15. The construction of the First Temple and the adjoining royal palace gave Jerusalem a unique character, a combination of a holy city within a royal city. Under Solomon, the economic advantages of Jerusalem as the center of the Israelite Empire and trade routes became evident.

16. Solomon's beautiful Temple was built as a permanent home for the Ark of the Torah. It was the central Temple for all of ancient Israel and the center of the Jewish religion. It was also the symbol of God's covenant with the Jewish people and stood for four hundred years. When the land was invaded and conquered by armies from Babylon, the Temple was burned to the ground. The Bible provides a detailed description of how the First Temple was built. Angels as well as demons are said to have assisted Solomon in the task (1 Kings 6, 7).

17. Exod. 6:23; Num. 2:3. Nahshon was a chieftain who assisted Moses in taking a census of the Hebrews (Num. 1:7). Refer also to 1 Chron. 15:10–11.

loved women and of his Egyptian wife.[18] The Bible does indeed tell us about the marriage of Solomon to the daughter of Pharaoh.[19] The name of Pharaoh's daughter is not known. In the tale it appears as Tantanhis, which is most likely a corruption of Tahpenes, probably an Egyptian title rather than a proper name. Tahpenes, "she who protects the king or the palaces," is explained by the Hebrew title "Great lady," which refers to the queen mother, wife of Pharaoh, and sister-in-law of Hadad, the Edomite prince.[20] Solomon is said to have brought his bride to the city of David[21] and built a house for her,[22] to which she brought a full retinue.[23] In return, he received Gezer from Pharaoh as a dowry for her.

It was not unusual for non-Hebrew wives in the Bible to bring along their gods and religion, and Solomon himself allows his wives to build shrines and practice their own rituals. The tale's reference to Amon as an Egyptian deity is mentioned in the Bible.[24] In this tale, adultery may be used as a metaphor for idolatry, as it is closely tied to the worship of Amon-Re. Prophets gave such metaphors full and explicit expression: the exclusive loyalty that Israel must give God is analogous to the exclusive fidelity a wife owes her husband.[25]

Understood as voluntary sexual intercourse between a married woman and a man other than her husband, adultery is called abomination in Judaism.[26] The teller reaffirms Commandment 347, which instructs Hebrews

---

18. I have been unable to verify, however, whether there is any historical evidence of her unfaithfulness to him.

19. In 1 Kings 9:16. This is probably Siamon or Psusennes II, of the twenty-first Egyptian dynasty. Reference to Solomon's marriage to Pharaoh's daughter appears also in Sanh. 21b.

20. 1 Kings 11:19–20.

21. 1 Kings 3:1.

22. 1 Kings 7:8, 9:24; 2 Chron. 8:11. The unusual distinction accorded to Pharaoh's daughter by Solomon attests to the special relations between Egypt and Israel at that time.

23. 1 Kings 9:16.

24. Jer. 46:25. He is usually portrayed as a ram or as a human being with a ram's head, with a headdress of feathers in the shape of a sun wheel or a crown with the head of a cobra. After his fusion with Re, Amon became the supreme deity in the Egyptian pantheon (Amon-Re).

25. Hos. 1–2; Jer. 2:23, 3:1ff.; Ezek. 16:15ff., 23:1ff.

26. In contrast, the extramarital intercourse of a married man is not a crime in biblical or later Jewish law. The distinction stems from the economic aspect of Israelite marriage: the wife was the husband's possession of a special sort, and adul-

not to commit adultery.[27] Prohibited in the Decalogue,[28] adultery is punishable by death for both partners,[29] and this is what occurs in this narrative. Although no particular mode of execution is prescribed in the Bible, stoning is mentioned[30] and thus represents an older tradition than Talmudic law,[31] which prescribed strangulation as the most humane mode of capital punishment.[32] Reference to the stoning of adulteresses is found in prophetic allegories[33] and is described in the New Testament as commanded by the law of Moses.[34] Lovers of adulterous women in folktales are usually described as black or loathsome and of a lower status. Here, the queen's lover is a black giant of a slave, connected to her Egyptian origin by way of his hiding place: the statue of an Egyptian god of recognizable gigantic proportions.

As Commandment 288 forbids the pronouncement of judgment on the basis of the testimony of only one witness,[35] there must be sufficient evidence of guilt for the queen and her lover to be punished. The nature of the offense being what it is, however, it is not unusual for an adulterous act to take place in secret, thus precluding sufficient evidence. With insufficient evidence, it was not uncommon for a suspected adulterer to be subjected to the ordeal of the waters of bitterness.[36] Although this motif does not appear in this tale, it is obvious that our male teller is fully familiar with his Scriptures.

Finally, reference is made to Solomon's legendary wisdom (J192+ [Noy]), but the tale also points to his legendary weakness for women.

---

tery constituted a violation of the husband's exclusive right to her. This was consistent with the patriarchal system.

27. Lev. 18:20.
28. Exod. 20:14; Deut. 5:18.
29. Lev. 20:10.
30. In Deut. 22:21–24.
31. Sifra 9:11.
32. Sanhedrin 52b. et al. This book is a Tannaitic midrash to Lev., originating in the first or second century, the R. Akiva School.
33. Ezek. 16:38–40.
34. John 8:5.
35. Deut. 19:15.
36. Num. 5:12–31.

2

The Rights of Widows and Orphans

Narrated by SARA YOHAY (1993)

In the Land of Gluttons, there was a daughter of very wealthy parents who had married the king's son. And she had five children, all skinny and white-faced, sickly, *hazinientos,* and nervous. Of all the good things that the doctors who looked after them and the servants who served them brought before them, they wanted to eat nothing. And so they went on.

Their mother thought that with a change of food the children would grow better, and she sought a fine cook. They introduced a widow to her who also had five children, and who broke her back day and night, doing laundry and cooking for people, so that they would not die of hunger. This woman happily accepted work at the palace, and when she asked how much they would pay her, they said to her:

"Not even a *grosh*! Not a penny! You are obligated to cook for the king's children! It's an honor!"

And so, they gave her nothing. The widow cried bitter tears. How would she sustain her children? At the palace, she kneaded fresh bread every day, and it filled the entire kitchen with its smell, *amá,* to her, they gave not even a small piece. The widow had an idea. Every time she had hands sticky with dough, she would run home and wash them in a *tendjeré,* a pot of water, and she would boil that water, and it would turn into a white soup. This is what her children ate, and they were growing up healthy and strong, with red cheeks, and they weren't catching any sickness, any *hazinura*.

One day, they asked her:

"Why is it that when you go home, you go with your hands sticky with bread dough? Why don't you wash your hands here?"

The *povereta,* the poor one, answered:

"With that I feed my children. Otherwise they would die."

The thing became known, from the servants to the courtiers and from the courtiers to the wife of the king's son.

This one said, much amazed:

"How can children live and grow with only this kind of nourishment? *Sha,* I'll go see with my own eyes...."

She dressed up as an old woman and *suivió,* she followed the widow with hands sticky with dough. And she watched as she washed them in the *tendjeré* and boiled the water, and with what appetite the children ate. And they were tall, strong, and handsome.

Bitter at the thought of her own children, the king's daughter-in-law returned to the palace and told the story to her husband. And the husband summoned his advisor and soothsayer. The two of them agreed that the widow was robbing the king's grandchildren of their health with the dough stuck to her hands that she brought to her children.

The next day, the widow was not permitted to go home with doughy hands. The poor one, the *povereta,* cried out that this was the only thing she brought home to eat, *ma* no one heeded her pleas. With a heavy step and a darkened heart, and weeping ceaselessly, she went back home. The children sat down at the table, and there was nothing to eat. The children asked her what had happened, and she told them.

The next day there was a hullabaloo, a *shematá,* at the palace: tears, loud cries, *dubaras!* What had happened? The king's grandchildren had shut their mouth and would not open it. What didn't they try?! What didn't they do?! They brought magicians! They opened up books of wisdom! Nothing!

They started asking here and there who could come up with an idea on how to save the king's grandchildren. *Amá,* no one wanted the *belá,* the calamity of getting involved with the king!

In the palace kitchen there worked a young boy who, one way or the other, couldn't have been older than ten. He went before the king and said:

"My grandpa, my *nonno,* will give you the solution to this problem. My *nonno* knows everything."

As one can imagine, they ran and fetched the boy's *nonno:* an old man holding in his hand the Book of Truths.

"Help us!" said the king.

"I can't! It just isn't working for me," answered the old man. "Here, in this matter, some injustice exists, which, if you don't redress it immediately, you don't *adovar, pishín,* will make matters not only not get better, *ma* they'll get worse."

"Speak up," said the king. "I give you my word that I'll set everything right."

"*Agora* we can speak," the old man said. "Your Majesty, your kingdom is a kingdom of gluttons. Your life is spent eating and ingesting to excess *(bufar)* until you're ready to burst, to *patladeár.* The poor are dying for a crust of bread and you, you surfeit your dogs! What has happened here is a blow, a *haftoná,* from heaven. You, as king, you should have set a good example; *amá,* instead, you surpass, *depasates,* all limits. Your family, people just like yourself, have pulled away the plate of food from a poor widow who sweats every day for nothing. *Agora,* her children do not eat. Your grandchildren will not eat either. Not until there is food on the widow's table! *Agora* the entire country will make *taní,* a fast, for three days and three nights. You'll give bread to the poor and you'll protect the widows. And you'll bring your grandchildren to the cook's house."

When all of this was done, the widowed cook went back with doughy hands. She made the soup; her children ate, the king's grandchildren ate, and they were cured.

A royal edict was issued that no household should go without food, that the wealthy should help the poor, and that everyone should read and learn from the Book of Truths. And so they all lived happily, and we, even more so.

COMMENTARY

This is an adaptation of AT 750F*, *The Old Man's Blessing,* a religious tale in which God repays and punishes.[1] Only the initial segment of the type appears in our narrative. In the full type, a poor woman gives children water in which she washes her hands after making bread for a rich lady. The children are healthy. An old man blesses the woman for her kindness and her house becomes finer and filled with money. When she borrows scales from the rich lady to weigh money, a coin sticks to the scales, and the rich woman asks how she acquired the money. When the envious rich woman tries to imitate her, she throws out the old man instead of being kind to him and is reduced to poverty in punishment.

Our version is concerned more with moral discrimination and the societal aspect of the condition of the needy family than with a contrast between the kind and unkind, although the contrast does appear in the narrative, albeit

---

1. Universal versions of this type are found in T. Hansen, *Types* (Argentina and Puerto Rico) as well as in Megas, *Folktales of Greece,* no. 39.

in a less prominent or central fashion. The focus here is on the helplessness of orphans and widows—the tragedy of their plight, their social treatment, and their emotional vulnerability. Narrated by a woman, our tale revolves around the central motifs of wealth and poverty (U60), the many children of the poor (P161), the care and sustenance of children (T600), and divine justice (A102.16). It reflects pressing family concerns as well as societal issues: the difficulty of raising a family alone; and the indifference and obliviousness of the rich to the needs of the less fortunate. Also present are the principles that moral law was received by man from God (A182.11.3 [Noy]), that wisdom is acquired from books (J166), and that the Bible (V136) and the study of the Torah (V97) are meaningful guides for conduct. The tale also contrasts the oppressor and the oppressed and highlights a providential punishment that remains unexplained and unresolved, despite consultation with the soothsayer (D1712 [Noy]), until the all-knowing grandfather (J151) refers to the Book of Truths to find an explanation as well as a solution.

The book referred to here is probably the Book of the Covenant, the Bible, where the warning not to oppress widows and orphans is stated with full rigor. God's role as their protector is stated: "A father of the fatherless and a judge of the widows is God in His holy habitation."[2] The commandment to render justice to them and the prohibition against oppressing them are reiterated frequently.[3] The Prophet Isaiah, for example, urges: "Uphold the rights of the fatherless; defend the cause of the widow."[4] There are numerous similar injunctions to avoid taking advantage of their not having a husband or a father to protect them.[5]

With no financial support and therefore defenseless and in need of protection, the orphans and their mother in our tale merit solicitude from the community but receive none. The Talmud holds the community responsible for their support; those who raise an orphan are considered by the Torah to be as righteous as those who are giving constant charity.[6] Widows and orphans are often cited as the object of charity and the subject of social legis-

---

2. Ps. 68:5; cf. 10:14.

3. The Bible mentions no less than twenty-six times the obligation to protect and care for the widow, the orphan, and the stranger. This is the welfare system transmitted from generation to generation, which depends in great part on people's good will and good deeds. It helps create a caring community.

4. Isa. 1:17.

5. Commandment 256, for example, recommends specifically: "Do not afflict the widow or the orphan."

6. Talmud Babli (Babylonian Talmud), Sanhedrin 19b.

lation.[7] Thus charity, especially to them, was considered by rabbis of all ages to be one of the cardinal *mitzvót* of Judaism, being an attribute of God himself: "He doth execute justice for the fatherless and widow and loveth the stranger, in giving him food and raiment."[8]

In Judaism, charity and benevolence are valued most highly. The word *tzedaká* in the Bible denotes "righteousness," which in post-biblical Judaism is used to designate charity. It calls for love and fellowship toward the poor and needy,[9] who have a just claim on the wealthy. It is said that the rich acquire merit through giving (V440+ [Noy]), suggesting that there should be no condescension in almsgiving. The broader picture in our narrative stresses the importance of these helpful relations between members of the community and focuses on the way people should behave toward one another. It shows how justice and compassion are part of the covenant with God and points to the responsibility of each individual to make the world a better place for all. Finally, it stresses that moral law is the counterpart of natural law since evil-doing inevitably brings disaster in its wake.

The setting of the stage appears in the very first sentence of our tale, which takes place in "The Land of Gluttons." The description by the old man, later in the tale, that the king and his court worry more about feeding their pets than helping the poor is a strong rebuke. That description tells us that there is wealth in the spatial realm of the tale, that there is plenty of food, and that overeating takes place routinely. The contrast between this scene of prosperity and abundance, a land of plenty where everyone should have their fill, and the difficult life of the widow and her hungry brood is intended to be striking. The contrast is enhanced further when the widow is brought to the palace as a skillful cook but is forced to use her wit to provide for her family when no compensation is forthcoming from the royal purse. Her doughy hands become the sole source of nutrition and health for her children.

Both mothers in the tale, the princess and the pauper, worry equally about their children's well-being. The parallel between them is clear: they each have five children and care a great deal about their health. Both strive to keep them healthy. The mystery of the sickly disposition of the highborn children is only made clear in the end as the deserved punishment by God for the royal parents' blindness to the dire need of their subjects. Thus diet, as the primary source of life, is associated closely with social justice and divine intervention. While there is much delicious food to be had at the palace, the royal children

---

7. Deut. 16:11 and 14, 24:19–21, 26:12–13; also Maimonides, Yad, De'ot 6:10.
8. Deut. 10:17, 18.
9. Exod. 22:20–26.

do not benefit from it: they are sickly and pale. The orphans, on the other hand, thrive on the meager nourishment provided by a liquid diet from their mother's doughy hands. The contrast is salient and the supernatural intercession unambiguous. The narrating society assuredly believes in the reality of the story line.

When the king takes away the only sustenance available to the widow's children, he fails the test that was sent his way and has to be made to suffer retribution. This illustrates the biblical verse: "You shall not afflict any widow or orphan. If you afflict them in any way, I will heed their cry as soon as they cry out to Me, and My wrath shall blaze forth and I will put you to the sword, and your own wives shall become widows, your children orphans."[10] The widow's silent plea is heard in heaven, and matters worsen for the royal grandchildren: they refuse any nourishment. The old helper, the only man able and willing to speak frankly to the king and open his eyes, explains the miraculous punishment. The aid provided by the old man when all goes wrong in the palace is illustrated by AT 981, *Wisdom of Hidden Old Man Saves Kingdom*.[11] He intervenes to solve the enigma of the young princes' refusal to eat, however, only after the king assures him that he will take action and follow his advice. The generational scheme (king, son, grandchildren vs. young kitchen hand and grandfather) extends the parallels between the poor and the rich. Unlike the king, who is depicted as an insensitive and ignorant glutton, though, the old grandfather demonstrates his knowledge of Judaism and its commandments: "Let everyone read and learn from the Book of Truths," he

---

10. Exod. 22:21–23.

11. Other Judeo-Spanish tales about the wisdom of old age are found in KS, "El rey i el padre viejo," 43; KS, "La kadena de arena," 247; Salinas, "Konsejo de un padre a su ijo"; and L, no. 2, p. 24. See Haboucha, 495ff. Jewish parallels appear in Baharav, *Mi Dor le-Dor*, no. 52 (Iraq); Jason, "Types," 195; Jason, *Types*, 65; Mizrahi, *Beyeshishim khokhma*, no. 27 (Iran); [Noy], (J151); Noy, *Ha-na'ara*, no. 60 (Iraq); Schwarzbaum, *Studies,* 179, 200, 418, 471, 474. IFA versions were collected from Afghanistan, Eastern Europe, Iran, Iraq, Iraqi Kurdistan, Israel (Bedouin and Sephardic), Lebanon, and Turkey. Other traditions also show examples of this type: Ashliman, *Guide to Folktales,* 202; Chauvin, *Ouvrages arabes,* 8:199, no. 244; Dorson, *Folktales Told around the World,* 243 (Japan); EB, no. 197; *Gesta Romanorum,* no. 124; Keller, *Spanish Exempla* (J151.1); Sánchez de Vercial, *Libro de los exenplos,* no. 401 (347); Robe, *Mexican Folktales,* 153; Rotunda, *Motif-Index of the Italian Novella* (J151.1); Thompson, *Folktale,* 266–67; Thompson and Roberts, *Indic Oral Tales,* 123; Tubach, *Index Exemplorum,* 1997.

admonishes. This is advice to make interpersonal and societal choices informed by Jewish values (J151 [Noy]).

The old man prescribes a fast, to be observed across the kingdom for three days and three nights. Fasting is the principle of refraining from eating and drinking, the most widely evident function of which is to avert or seek an end to a calamity. It is also traditionally a way of winning God's forgiveness and eliciting His compassion.[12] This implies that fasting is basically an act of penance and a ritual expression of remorse, submission, and supplication. While this is exactly its function here, it is strengthened by a call for behavioral change: the rich must change their ways and open their heart and purse to those in need. The tale shows how justice and compassion are part of the covenant relation with God. The responsibility not only of leaders but also of each individual is to make the world a better place for all. When the royal children are taken to the widow's house and fed the same spartan diet of doughy soup as her own children, it is a lesson to put their trust in God.

This tale deals with religious values and social tensions between various elements of the community. It stresses commandments that govern relations between people and is essentially didactic, transmitting and reinforcing Jewish norms of behavior. While the tale carries a timeless social message, the end formula is an adaptation of a traditional Judeo-Spanish tale ending.

---

12. Ps. 35:13, 69:10; Ezra 10:6.

3

A *la Fín* Everything Comes to Light

Narrated by SARA YOHAY (1992)

One day, so and so had a fight with his neighbor. The two of them came to blows and, suddenly, so and so killed his neighbor.

"Oh, *bre,* what do I do now?" so and so thought. "If it becomes known, the dead man's family will kill me! And if they don't kill me, they'll take me before the king for a trial, for a *mishpát!* And the king will order that they cut off my head! Let's say that the king takes pity on my wife and my five children: he'll throw me into prison and I'll rot, without food, paralyzed with cold, and no one will ever see my face again! In the end, my wife will marry another; my children will live a life of shame!"

And, always thinking along these lines, he decided to hide the body of his dead neighbor in the cellar, the *kelár,* of the house. He lived in a country house, *de kampanya,* where there were all kinds of old things downstairs, in the *kelár.* The ceiling of the *kelár* was made of wooden planks, of *tavlás,* detached one from the other. There he had sacks of oats for the horses. But upstairs were the *udás,* the rooms where they lived.

The man put the dead body there, and no one suspected a thing. They searched for the neighbor. They wrote about him in the *jurnál,* in the newspaper. Nothing was discovered about him. In time, it was thought that the man had abandoned his wife and run away, or that some wild animal had devoured him.

In short, the widow took her children and she went to another city, where she married and had more children. And of the dead man no one spoke anymore.

But about a year after what happened, from where the dead man was buried grew a vine, a *gefen,* tall and sturdy, full of green leaves that reached up to the rooftop. Everyone marveled at seeing this *gefen,* and they looked at it with curiosity because no one had ever heard that, in a *kelár,* a *gefen* could grow without sun or water!

After a few years, the *gefen* produced grapes. To this day, no one has ever seen such large and beautiful grapes! Of two colors, growing from the same plant. The bunches of grapes, the *chambís,* weighed twenty okes each! What did so and so do? He clipped the best *chambís,* he put them in a basket, and he went before the king. He said to him:

"Good and just king! Take this present, this *peskésh,* from your servant!"

The king tasted and said:

"I have never eaten anything like it in my life!"

Rengrasió, he thanked so and so, and he mandated that he alone will eat from these grapes. The next day, when they served the grapes to the king, he didn't have a chance to taste them because he saw that blood was dripping from the white grapes. The king turned yellow. He said:

"This can't be! I must be dreaming!"

He called the queen, and he showed her the grapes. And the queen also saw the blood. The king sought the advice of the queen and she, like all women, put in her two cents:

"My lord king, my husband, order that they bring you more grapes from so and so, to investigate the matter further and be more certain."

And so it was done. But the second *peskésh* turned out to be just like the first. The same day it was normal; the next day, blood came out of the grapes!

The king said to his soldiers, to his *hayales:*

"Go and see what's the matter with this *gefen,* and come back and tell me about it!"

The *hayales* went. They saw. They came back and told the king about the beautiful *gefen* that was growing in the *kelár.*

"This is not enough for me!" the king replied. "Pull out the *gefen,* and bring it back to me in my palace!"

The *hayales* ran back. And they kept digging and digging to pull out the *gefen* until, when the roots were exposed to the light of day, what did they see? The bones of a dead man, intertwined with the roots! Shouts! *Guayas!* Laments! Cries! Shock! The *hayales* seized so and so; they brought him before the king. They tied him up tightly this way, they pushed him that way, until he confessed to the crime.

The king said to his wise men and to all his attendants:

"Observe and learn that each and every evil deed always comes to the light of day."

They tried so and so, and they hanged him by his legs, by his *pachás*. The *gefen* continued to grow. In the royal palace, however, a decree came out that no one was to eat from the grapes. And when they would see its beauty, they would all shudder at the thought of the revenge of the dead man.

COMMENTARY

A similar but unsubstantiated legend exists about the death of Solomon Ibn Gabirol, the great eleventh-century Spanish Jewish poet. According to the legend, a Moor, jealous of Ibn Gabirol's talent, killed and buried him secretly next to a fig tree. The tree is said to have given such excellent fruit afterward that it caught the attention of the king, thus leading to the discovery of the murder.[1]

Narrated by a woman, this tale belongs to a popular universal type, AT 960, *The Sun Brings All to Light*, a novella about a murder avenged.[2] Just like the universal folktales that belong to the widespread, orally transmitted tale type AT 303, *The Twins or Blood Brothers*, our tale is structurally dependent

---

1. Lomba, *Ibn Gabirol*, 45.
2. There are several Judeo-Spanish versions of this type that I am aware of: one from Tetuán, LP, no. 147, "El limonero por testigo," vol. 2, p. 230; the second from Israel, KS, "El shaet emprevisto," 205, and the third from the *Me'am Lo'ez* in Pascual Recuero, *Cuentos sefardíes*, no. 40. Also Koén-Sarano, "Indjustisia," in *Saragosa*, 154, and "Las buchichikas," in *Lejendas*, 265. The first two are classified under AT 960 in Haboucha, 486–88. For Jewish versions, see Gaster, *Exempla*, nos. 89, 431; Gaster, *Ma'aseh Book*, vol. 2, no. 218; Jason, "Types," 193; Noy, *Morocco*, no. 14; Pascual Recuero, *Cuentos sefardíes*, no. 40; Schwarzbaum, *Studies*, 65, 185, 294, 456; Schwili, no. 110; Sider, *Boryslaw*, no. 5 (Poland); Noy, *TEM 1971*, 107 (AT 960—Syria IFA 9234). For universal versions, see Ashliman, *Guide to Folktales*, 159 (type 780C), 200 (type 960); Basset, *Mille et un contes*, 2:381, no. 109; Baughman, *England and North America*, 23; Boggs, *Spanish Folktales*, 115; BP, 2:531; Briggs, *Dictionary of British Folk-Tales*, pt. B, vol. 2, 497; Chauvin, *Ouvrages arabes*, 2:123, no. 118, 7:146, no. 423; Chevalier, *Siglo de Oro*, no. 74; EB, no. 141; El-Shamy, *Folktales of Egypt*, no. 37; A. Espinosa, *Castilla*, no. 32; Grimm and Grimm, *Tales*, no. 115; Laoust, *Contes berbères*, no. 104; Sánchez de Vercial, *Libro de los exenplos*, no. 96; Rael, *Colorado y Nuevo Méjico*, no. 104; Robe, *Mexican Folktales*, 153; Thompson and Roberts, *Indic Oral Tales*, 122; Villa, *100 Armenian Tales*, no. 52.

on the pattern and motifs of the Cain and Abel story, as expanded in the Aggadá.[3]

The biblical narrative of Cain and Abel, the sons of Adam and Eve, is a paradigm of human conflict and offers the first biblical example of murder. Both brothers gave an offering to God: Cain, a tiller of the earth, gave of the fruit of the soil, while Abel, a shepherd, gave the prize of his flock. After God accepted Abel's gift but rejected his brother's, the firstborn, Cain, killed his younger sibling and became a fugitive.[4] Ultimately, Abel's blood was his witness, just as it is in our tale.

Working the land is considered man's natural occupation, so why did God reject Cain's gift?[5] While there is no reason given for the brothers' quarrel in the Bible, there are many versions in the Aggadá of the dispute that arose between them. It is usually assumed that Cain slew his brother out of jealousy. Our Sephardic teller does not give a reason for the killing that occurs in her tale; all she tells us is that the killing happens without much rhyme or reason, apparently as a result of a struggle. Does the murderer lose his temper or is he drunk? Anger betokens a loss of self-control. At the same time, the motif of the extraordinary *gefen* elicits the thought of wine and the possibility that the murder may have resulted from a drunken act, although drinking almost never appears in Sephardic tales.[6] Although the teller does not tell us what the fight was about, she shows us how the inner man is revealed when restraints are removed.

Our narrative highlights the harmful consequences of quarreling and shows that killings are avenged and murderers punished, sooner or later (Q211), through miraculous intervention and God's justice (A102.16). Thus, it has a religious connotation that leads the audience to focus less on the actual murder and more on the mysterious ways by which God repays and punishes. Crimes inevitably come to light (N270), the teller—in the voice of the king—assures us. In folktales, there is more than one way this can happen, as shown in AT 960: the murderer repeats the last words of his victim as the sun rises; the crime is revealed through the unusual names of young boys; or, as in AT 780ff., *The Singing Bone* gives away the secret of the murderer's identity. Here, it happens through reincarnation into a vine growing from the grave

---

3. The Aggadá is the literary, aesthetic element in the Oral Law and in the Talmud and Midrash. It elaborates scriptural meaning through legends, tales, parables, and allegories.

4. Gen. 4:1–12.

5. Gen. 2:15.

6. See tale 32 for the only reference to the effect of drinking in this anthology.

(E631, F811, F815.4 [Noy]). The vine springs up from the bones of the slain man and his blood appears in the grapes (E631.0.3, F979.12, F991), calling for attention and revenge. The murder is eventually revealed upon digging the miraculous vine out of the ground (N271.7) and discovering the skeleton of the slain man. Incredibly, the vine had grown without light or water.

Commandment 289 admonishes us not to commit murder.[7] Because human life is sacred, killing is a breach of norms and a societal taboo. It is the biblical view that the crime of murder is a social offense and not just a personal wrong. Why the murder occurs in our tale remains unstated. What is unusual in folk renditions, however, is the interior monologue that this teller inserts into her tale. By taking us into the murderer's mind, she makes us witnesses to his fear and to the psychological thought process that leads him to bury his victim in his cellar rather than report the death to the authorities as an accident.

Just as Cain did, the tale's protagonist murders a man, and just like Abel, he gives a quality offering of the soil, the choice first fruit, the best of the grapes, as a gift. The offering here, however, occurs after the crime, not before, as in the Bible, and it brings about the murderer's downfall for, like Abel's blood, the victim's blood eventually cries out (A1344.1). The biblical concept of blood guilt derives from the belief that deeds generate consequences and that sin is a danger to the sinner. The most vivid example of this appears in connection with unlawful homicide, where innocent blood[8] cries out for vengeance.[9] Bones also are symbolic as a powerful relic of the physical soul in folk stories, the most enduring construct of the person. Here, bones and blood mix together to bring to light the protagonist's crime.

In our tale, just like in other universal versions, God is the final guarantor that the homicide is ultimately punished. Although there is divine intervention here, it is the king who becomes the avenger, but he appears to require a confession since there are no witnesses. In Jewish law, however, even the criminal's own confession is not acceptable as evidence, and circumstantial evidence, however convincing, is not admitted. Commandment 290, in fact, prohibits conviction on circumstantial evidence alone.[10] Furthermore, Commandment 288 forbids pronouncing judgment on the basis of the testimony

---

7. Exod. 20:13.
8. *Dam naki,* such as in Jonah 1:14.
9. Gen. 4:10.
10. Exod. 23:7.

of only one witness.[11] The general rule is that in criminal cases and in cases involving claims on property, the testimony of at least two people who have actually witnessed the act is required to establish the facts of the case and convict the accused.[12]

In addition to its didactic divine/supernatural function, our version has a societal emphasis as well. Our example is presumably based on the Hebrew idiom, *heshív damím 'al rosh,* which indicates that God will turn back to the head of the slayer the blood of the slain, the punishment for which he thought he had averted. The way to redress the social order is to avenge the shedding of blood by punishing the culprit. In Moorish Spain, the Jewish courts did rely on the Talmudic statement that as an emergency measure, they had the power to impose an execution or physical penalties. In practice, however, it became illegal for a Jewish court to impose the death penalty. We see that even in the face of the verse "And no expiation can be made for the land for the blood that is shed therein, but by the blood of him that shed it,"[13] God himself cared enough about Cain's life to give him a relatively mild punishment (wandering the earth endlessly).[14] Commandment 225 actually exhorts that one who commits an accidental homicide be exiled.[15] Here, perhaps because the murder appears accidental rather than intentional, the guilty party is neither put to death nor exiled but hung upside down in the gallows.

In this Sephardic narrative, the detection of blood in the grapes has a double significance. In addition to its role in raising the king's suspicion, blood in food brings to mind Jewish dietary laws. Bloody grapes cannot be eaten because the Bible prohibits the consumption of blood, for blood is life.[16] From these and other commandments derive the dietary laws of *kashrút,* which Jews are expected to observe. The king's reaction upon seeing the bloody grapes is one of disbelief and dread. He immediately recognizes that this is an extraordinary sign but seeks the counsel of his trusted queen before he acts. The female narrator seems to agree humorously with the general perception that women always have to put their two cents in, but the queen's sensible advice is what leads to the discovery of the human remains.

---

11. Deut. 19:15.
12. Num. 35:30; Deut. 17:6, 19:15.
13. Num. 35:33.
14. Gen. 4:12.
15. Num. 35:25.
16. Lev. 7:26, 17:10–14; Deut. 12:23–25.

The remarriage of the slain man's wife is an aspect of the tale that diverges from traditional Jewish law. The *halakhá* prescribes that a marriage can only be dissolved by divorce or by the death of a spouse.[17] In cases such as the one described in our tale, when the mere disappearance of the husband was not sufficient proof of his death, the wife would have remained bound to him as to one who would not divorce her. The Bet Din or Jewish court would not have dissolved her marriage nor released her to remarry.

---

17. The *halakhá* is the legal portion of the Talmud and post-Talmudic literature concerned with personal, communal, and international activities as well as with religious observance. It usually refers to the Oral Law, codified in the Mishná, in particular those statements of law that appear without immediate regard to scriptural derivation.

4

The Fisherman and the Gold Fish

Narrated by ESTER KAMAR (1990)

There was a couple, a *zug,* a man and his wife, quite old, who lived in an old shack, a *tsrif,* old and broken down, on the banks of the river. He was a fisherman, and they were very poor.

One day, as was his wont, he went to catch fish from that river. In his net, in his *reshet,* he caught a gold fish. This fish opened its mouth and started to speak to him. It said:

"Do me a favor: put me back in the river! Please!"

The fisherman said:

"What? A gold fish such as this, how can I put it back in the river?"

The fish said to him:

"Look, throw me back into the water, and I'll grant you three wishes. Call me and ask for whatever you want. My name is Sinái Smángalov."

The fisherman said:

"Well, I'll go ask my wife!"

He went to where his wife was, he told her the story, and she said to him:

"Of course! Go, throw it into the river and let it make your three wishes come true!"

The fisherman went back. He said to it:

"I'll throw you into the river. Grant me the three wishes."

"Fine," said the fish. "What is the first wish?"

He said:

"First of all, my wife wants a large and beautiful house!"

The fish said:

"*Beseder!* Alright. Go, and it'll be as she wished!"

The fisherman went home and didn't recognize the place. That *tsrif* he owned had disappeared! He saw a large and beautiful house. He went into the house. He said to his wife:

"Are you happy? *Na,* look at what a beauty of a house you have now."

"Yes," she said. "It's very beautiful!"

A bit of time passed; his wife said to him:

"Look, go and summon the gold fish. I have another wish."

He said to her:

"Isn't it a sin? There should be no asking for anything! We are fine!"

"Go," she said.

She was strong, mean! The poor man, the *miskén,* went; he started to call out:

"*Sinái, Sinái Smángalov,
Dag ben dag alé vehalóf.
Ishtí matrá ahvát beití,
I ahafetsá ve lo aní!*"[1]

The fish came up and said:

"What does your wife want?"

The fisherman said:

"She wants a king's palace, an *armón*. She wants servants, and clothes, and a crown on her head. She wants to feel like a queen!"

The fish said:

"*Beseder!* Go home and you'll find what she wishes for!"

The fisherman left. He found an *armón* more beautiful than that of kings. He said to his wife:

"Are you happy now?"

"Yes," she said. "I am happy for now."

A good bit of time went by, a good *karár* of time. His wife said to him:

"Go back once more and tell the fish:

---

1. This formula is uttered in Hebrew. The word *matrá* is probably an adulteration of *matridá*.

Sinái, Sinái, Smángalov,
Fish, son of a fish, rise and go.
My wife disturbs the peace of my home.
She is the one who wishes, not I!

"Sinái, Sinái Smángalov,
Dag ben dag alé vehalóf.
Ishtí matrá ahvát beití,
I ahafetsá ve lo aní!"

He started:
"No! I don't want to go! I'm embarrassed!"
"Go!" she said to him:
He went and said:

"Sinái, Sinái Smángalov.
Dag ben dag alé vehalóf.
Ishtí matrá ahvát beití,
I ahafetsá ve lo aní, ve lo aní!"[2]

The fish came up once again and said to him:
"And now, what is it she wants?"
"She wants to be the King Messiah, the *Meleh Mashíah!*"
"Ah!" said the fish, and it dove into the sea without giving him an answer.

When the fisherman came home, he found his wife in that shack, that *tsrif,* in which she used to live at the beginning, sitting down and making socks, *churapes*.[3]

Commentary

This moral story about greed and its punishment represents a wonderful version of the tale of magic, AT 555, *The Fisher and His Wife,* in which a supernatural animal helper, a speaking fish, offers to fulfill three wishes for a poor fisherman (D1720.1, D1761.0.2, B470) in exchange for being thrown back into the water (B375.1).[4] The wife's wishes become more and more excessive (to

---

2. For emphasis, this repetition of the formula ends with the reiteration of the final verse: "ve lo aní, ve lo aní" (not I, not I!). This is meant to distance the man and stress that he plays no part in the actual request.

3. She is probably knitting a pair of socks.

4. Another Judeo-Spanish version, also told by a woman, can be found in Koén-Sarano, *Konsejas,* 103. Universal parallels appear in Boggs, *Spanish Folktales,* 71; BP, 1:138 (Grimm, no. 19); Briggs, *Dictionary of British Folk-Tales,* pt. A, vol. 1, 436; Cole, *Best-Loved Folktales,* no. 14; Delarue, *Conte populaire français,* 2:376, 721; D'Aronco, *Fiabe Toscane,* 82; Grimm and Grimm, *Tales,* no. 19; Robe, *Mexican Folktales,* 100; Thompson, *One Hundred Favorite Folktales,* no. 51 (Russia).

be duke, king, pope, God) until she finally loses everything. Likewise, in our version, the fortunate catch by the husband leads to a positive change of luck for the needy couple and a radical change in living conditions (D1761). The henpecked fisherman, however, cannot stand up to his wife's greed. Notwithstanding her husband's reluctance, she makes progressively more extravagant requests, parallel to those found in the type: to dwell in a palace, to live as a queen, and, eventually, to become the Messiah. As she exceeds moderation and her desires become more extravagant, she squanders her opportunity to live well and is punished by losing all she had gained (C773.1).

In Jewish tradition, fish is believed to be a centerpiece of the Meal of the Righteous that will usher in the messianic age. Thought to bring good luck, fertility, and abundance,[5] it is food available to the poor at little expense. This explains the destitute fisherman's hesitation to relinquish his lucky catch. With the words, "Fish, son of a fish," the teller makes clear that this is neither a monster nor an enchanted person in animal form. One of the most interesting elements in this didactic tale is the use of a charm formula (Zo) with a distortion of the names of three angels: Sinay, Sinsinay, and Samengelof. These are the three angels sent by God to overpower Lilith, the more aggressive and less docile first wife of Adam, and bring her back to Adam after she deserted him following a quarrel during which she refused to give up her equality and argued with him about the manner of their intercourse (G303.12+ [Noy]).[6] The parallel between Lilith and the fisher's wife is not difficult to envision, considering the unreasonable and obdurate character of the

---

5. In Gen. 1:22, God blesses the fish and instructs them to be fruitful and multiply.

6. This legend appears in the Alphabet of Ben Sirá, a midrash of the geonic period. Following a Talmudic legend, the Zohar stresses that Lilith was created during the six days of Creation. In legends found in the later *midrashim*, she is associated with Adam, as either his demonic wife or his original wife, created, unlike Eve, from the dust of the ground and at the same time as Adam. She is often considered to be the "first Eve." Legend has it that after a falling out with Adam, she pronounced the Ineffable Name and flew off into the air. On Adam's request, God dispatched after her the three angels Sinay, Sinsinay, and Samengelof. Finding her in the Red Sea, the angels threatened that if she refused to return, one hundred of her sons would die every day. She refused, but was forced to swear, however, that whenever she saw the image of those angels in an amulet, she would lose her power over an infant. Lilith is believed never to enter a house in which the names of these angels are written. The legend of Adam's wife who preceded the creation of Eve (Gen. 2) often merges with the earlier legend of Lilith, a demon who kills infants and endangers women at childbirth.

wife. The fisher complains that his wife upsets the peace of his home and that she is the one making repeated bigheaded demands, not he.

The magic formula or charm used three times to summon the helpful fish (D1273, Z71.1 [Noy]) utilizes the name of only two of the three angels, the third one being mangled. When the magic fish (B175, B211.11 [Noy]) gives its name to the fisher as a means to conjure him, the narrator forgets the middle angel, Sinsinay. Later, when she repeats the charm every time the man summons the marvelous fish, she seems to remember that there are three angels but just does not recollect the name of the missing one. Since the name of the second angel, Sinsinay, is in fact very close to that of the first, Sinay, the teller's repetition of formula as "Sinay, Sinay, Smangalov" instead of "Sinay, Sinsinay, Samengelof" works equally well as a substitute.

As is not uncommon in Sephardic tales, the man defers his decision as to whether to hold or release the fish until he is able to consult with his wife. Traditionally among Jews, wise women were respected and consulted in important matters.[7] As can be seen in this anthology, for example in tale 14, the Elijah version of the clever wife who advises her husband on how to use one wish wisely (AT 750A), women often represent wisdom and good. In contrast, in other tales such as this one, they are featured as the voice of greed and unrighteousness. While this may be a reflection of the dichotomy about women so prevalent in a patriarchal society, it is of particular interest to note the negative image of women as perpetuated by female storytellers.[8] The position of the fisherman's wife is clearly one of influence and importance. Unsure how to act, the husband hopes by conferring with her to acquire the wisdom needed to make the best decision for them as a couple, a decision he seems unable or unwilling to reach alone. Later, his reluctance to accede to his wife's wishes to make successively more covetous requests indicates that he realizes that the granting of wishes should be seen as God's gift to them, undeserving though they (she) may be. He senses that such a gift should not be abused or misused, and he grows more and more uncomfortable with transmitting his wife's immoderate fantasies. At the same time, he is unable to resist relaying her demands to the marvelous golden fish (N810). The tension between husband and wife helps accentuate the strong will and immoderate aspirations of the woman.

Additional elements that shape our tale include appropriate moralizing advice. In Jewish tradition, humility is among the highest of the virtues, yet

---

7. 2 Sam. 14:2ff., 20:16–22.
8. See Haboucha, "Misogyny or Philogyny."

the permanent dualism of the choice between good and evil—evil inclination, *yetzér ha-rá'*—is believed to be in us at birth and to tempt us throughout life. In the end, the moral of this tale is that one should act wisely and try not to be too greedy (J514) because immoderate requests will be denied (Q338) and overweening ambition punished (L420). The unspoken but unambiguous warning is to be prudent in one's demands (J530) and to leave well enough alone (J513).

5

The Wonderful *Tendjereniko*

Narrated by KOHAVA PIVIS (1992)

There was once an unmarried midwife who went from house to house to help women give birth. This midwife came home once, and she wanted to cook for herself something to eat. And she made herself a chicken in a little pot, a *tendjereniko,* she had. When the chicken was finally ready, and she was about to eat, suddenly, *ensupitó,* two knocks were heard at the door:

"Midwife, midwife, come quickly!"

"What is it?"

"It's my mother who is giving birth!"

The midwife left everything—she didn't eat—and went far away from there.

In that same alley lived a widowed woman [no reference to you!][1] with three daughters. When the midwife left, the *tendjereniko* leaped off the stove, the *primus,* and, clunk, clunk, clunk, it went to the widow's house. It knocks on the door.

The widow's eldest daughter, who was tall, came; she opened the door. She saw no one; she closed the door. Her mother says:

"Who is it?"

The daughter says to her:

"There is no one!"

The *tendjereniko* knocks on the door once more. The second daughter opens it. She saw no one and shut the door. The mother says:

---

1. Teller's aside. See commentary.

"Who is it, dear?"

"No one," the daughter says.

Once again the *tendjereniko* knocks on the door. The youngest child came; she opened the door. Her mother says to her:

"Who is it, apple of my eyes?" [One says "apple of my eyes" to the youngest one.][2]

The child said to her:

"*Addió*! My God! Look, mother, what there is here!"

The mother opened the door; the *tendjereniko* came in. She takes the cover off; she sees a nice sautéed chicken, *sofrita*! They all ate and went to sleep. And the empty *tendjeré* went back to the midwife's *primus*.

The midwife returned two hours later; she wants to eat a good meal. She takes the cover off and looks. The *tendjereniko* is empty!

"*Addió*!" she says. "How can that be? There was a chicken in here! Where is it?"

What is she going to do? She took a glass of milk with a sesame bagel, a *semít,* and went to sleep.

The next day, the same thing: the midwife is working all day long, going from here to there. In the afternoon she comes home. She bought herself a little piece of meat from the butcher, the *kasáp*. She said:

"I'll prepare myself something to sustain my soul."

She came; she cooked it for herself. As she is about to eat: knock, knock, knock . . . at the door.

"*Presto, presto*! Quickly, quickly, midwife! My sister is giving birth! She has pains!"

The midwife left the *tendjeré* and went. When the midwife was gone, the *tendjereniko* leaped down from the *primus*. Clunk, clunk, clunk! It went once again, *yené,* to the widow's. At the widow's house, they uncovered the *tendjeré*:

"*Addió*!!!"

Good *sofrito* meat, with peppers, with onions! It had been years since the poor ones had eaten anything like it! They were very poor. They had no livelihood, no *parnasá*! Well, that day they ate, and on the third day it was the same.

After three days of eating meat, and chicken, and vegetables, *zerzavát,* the girls' faces had put on some color. The poor widow came, and she is looking:

---

2. Teller explains the expression used by the mother when talking to her youngest child.

"My daughters, how beautiful they are! *Amá*, they have no clothes! Everything is torn! Everything is old! It's all faded already! Oh, if only they had a few dresses, a few *fostanikos*, they would look like kings' daughters!"

On the fourth day, in the morning, when the midwife had gone to work, the *tendjereniko* hopped down from the *primus* and went . . . clunk, clunk, clunk . . . to the river's edge. At the river's edge, in those days, the countess and her three daughters came to bathe. They would remove their beautiful garments and they would place them on the grass. Now they looked: there is a *tendjeré* there.

"Oh," said the countess, "we'll put them here, rather than put them on the grass."

They took all the clothes, they put them on top of the *tendjereniko*, and they went into the river. The *tendjereniko* . . . clunk, clunk, clunk . . . went straight to the house of the widow and her three daughters.

It went in. They looked:

"*Addió*! Look at these beautiful clothes!"

"Oh, this is for me!"

"No, it's for me!"

"I'll take the red one!"

"I'll take the green one!"

Each one grabbed a beautiful *fostán*, made of lace, of *dantelas*, of velvet, of *katifé*, and with buttons, with *bundjukes*. They got dressed and turned into ladies, into *hanumes*. Now, what did the widow see? That she has three daughters, beautiful and well dressed. She looks up to the sky and says:

"Look what a great God, a great *Dió* there is! *Agora*, what do my daughters lack? They lack three handsome bridegrooms!"

And, because she had said it aloud, her voice was heard above.

On Thursdays, everyone goes to the public bathhouse, to the *hamám*. On that day, the three sons of an important and very wealthy merchant in town went there. And the little marvelous *tendjereniko* also went to the *hamám* . . . clunk, clunk, clunk! It went inside and stood to the side.

After the merchant's sons bathed for an hour or two in hot water, in cold water, and splashed themselves with *kolonia*, they want to rest a bit. They look around for a spot and find none; everything is full. *Ensupitó*, they saw the *tendjereniko* over there, to the side.

"Ah," they said, "we'll sit down for a while over here, to rest."

Ensupitó, the *tendjeré* . . . clunk, clunk, clunk . . . started to hop and skip, and it went out into the alley. People said:

"What's that? Three youths jumping atop a *tendjeré*? Where are they going?"

The youths are screaming:

"*Addió!* Help!"

They only had towels on them. At last they took hold of a big sheet on the way, and threw it over themselves. Eventually they arrived. The *tendjeré* knocked on the door. The three youths saw the three beautiful girls. The three girls saw the three handsome youths. And they fell in love.

A short while later, they made three big weddings in the neighborhood, in the *kartié,* and they were all very happy (and so were we).

Commentary

This delightful tale is an adaptation of AT 591, *The Thieving Pot,* in which a peasant exchanges his cow for a magic pot that brings him bread, beer, money, etc., from his rich neighbors. Most of our narrative's motifs are magic-related. While no exchange transaction occurs here—nor is there any attempt to hold on to the magic cauldron—the *tendjereniko* is, indeed, a magic thieving pot (D1171.1, D1605.1) that ushers in all kinds of wonderful surprises. The teller never makes clear how the magic pot is acquired and whether its rightful owner is even aware of its magic power. Just as in the type, however, once strangers have put objects into it, the pot brings these objects back to the widow's house (D1602). The pot also turns out to be a magic wishing vessel (D1470.1.19), seemingly responding to the wishes of only one master, the widowed mother (D1651.3). Finally, it is a self-returning magic object as well (D1602), hopping back and forth from one house to the other. The door through which it comes and goes is a symbol of transition and change.

Initially the pot serves as provider (D1470, D1470.2, D1472.1), bringing in the basic necessities of life (D1472.1.9) in the form of much-needed cooked meals prepared by the owner of the pot for herself. Physical life predominates in the tale. Local customs appear colorfully in the form of the food described: *sofrito* meat, sautéed with onions and peppers, *sofrito* chicken, and *semít,* a delicious soft bagel-like bread covered with sesame seeds, popular all over the Middle East. As a midwife, the owner of the magic vessel is a tangential character whose traditional occupation is well accepted in the Sephardic community. Her work is often not remunerated, or she may receive only a nominal or in-kind fee for her role in the birthing process. Midwives were very busy women because there were often no doctors in the villages. Tired as they were, they always responded to the call of duty and were ready to spring into action whenever they were needed, even in the middle of the night, leaving the warmth and safety of their own home. There are Sephardic tales of midwives being called out at night to help *shedót* (female demons) in childbirth; in such cases, they are usually warned not to partake of *shed* food if they want to see home again. They are sometimes given garlic as a reward by the demons, but when they return home they find that the garlic has been transformed into gold.[3] While the tale gives only a brief glimpse of our midwife's life and work, the audience easily recognizes her role in society.

The weekly visit to the *hamám,* the bathhouse, on Thursdays is a custom of the surrounding Muslim society, so it is familiar to the tellers, Friday being the weekly holy day of the region. Sephardic Jews clearly relate also to the care of the body, which is prescribed in Jewish teachings. The bathhouse described provides the vapor bath, which causes perspiration and languor, as depicted. The young men are said to take a hot bath first, followed by immersion in cold water. This helps them derive the most benefit from the bath.

The *tendjereniko* in this tale may represent a household spirit which, while inhabiting another home, acts as guardian spirit and benevolent protector of a needy family. It is commonly related in folktales that a domestic spirit that inhabits the characters' home and behaves as a family guardian may sometimes also be a nuisance while looking after the welfare of a particular household, playing pranks and snatching food and objects, just as it does in this version. A mischievous helper who performs household tasks, it can also be easily provoked to malicious troublemaking. The pranks described in this tale occur at the expense of the passive secondary characters: the midwife, who twice loses her dinner; the countess and her daughters, whose garments are stolen as they bathe in the river; and the three sons of a wealthy merchant, who are kidnapped and placed in an embarrassing position as they are transported across town with no clothes on.

Once we probe beyond the magic and humorous aspects of the tale, it is obvious that the main concern is with the helplessness of the orphaned girls and their widowed mother, who have no means of support and need protection. As we have seen elsewhere, to provide for a widow and her family is a *mitzvá,* an obligation the community usually takes upon itself. Here the magic pot appears on the scene to take over the task of helping the fatherless family and to fulfill the mother's wishes: that her daughters be dressed like ladies—the thieving pot furnishes stolen clothes of velvet and lace (D1473)—and that they marry handsome and well-established bridegrooms—the helpful pot brings into the house wealthy suitors (N201), sons of merchants (P431 [Noy]),

---

3. See Molho, p. 128, no. 3, classified in Haboucha as 476*-A*, *A Midwife to Demons*. See also Koén-Sarano, "El moel eskaso," in *Lejendas,* 245.

after affording them miraculous transportation (D1520, D1532). Once the wish for the exalted husbands is realized, the tale ends.

The narrative skill of the teller reveals itself in the artful use of onomatopoeia ("clunk, clunk, clunk"; "knock, knock, knock") and repetition throughout the narrative structure of the tale and its plot development. The formulaic number three is used repeatedly, as in the *tendjereniko*'s appearances at the door of the widow's house. On the pot's third try, the youngest daughter sees it. Because of her small size, she is the only one able to notice the little pot. The pot returns on three occasions, to provide three days of nourishing feasts of meat, chicken, and vegetables. Finally, there are the three daughters of the widow, paralleled first by the three daughters of the countess and then by the three handsome youths and the three weddings. The folk motif of three sisters only the youngest of whom is successful is a popular one in folktales. The teller describes her as the apple of her mother's eyes. This is one of two asides that the narrator allows herself. Another is used kindly and is intended as a protective device for the listener when reference to death is made indirectly at the first mention of the widow. The teller's society attaches magic power to the spoken word and its ability to cause harm or to repair the damage caused by other words. This resonates throughout the Torah and with the audience so that when a word or an expression is used that could be seen as inviting tragedy or disaster, a protective expression is added to safeguard the listeners.

The tale's denouement suggests a supernatural explanation for mysterious events and the belief in a reversal of fortune caused by a concrete object. The widow thanks God for his help, and we are told that her wishes, expressed aloud, are heard directly in heaven. Providence's (God's) role as the protector of the family is illustrated in Psalm 68:6: "A father of the fatherless and a judge of the widows is God in His holy habitation."[4] This is undoubtedly part of the worldview of both the narrator and her audience.

---

4. Cf. 10:14.

6

The King's Lost Son Transformed to a Dog

Narrated by MATY SHALEM (1992)

There were a king and queen who had no children. After much effort, the queen finally conceived, and a son was born to them. They looked after that son like the apple of their eyes *ma,* as it happens in folktales, one day, when the queen was in the garden and was rocking the baby's cradle, a violent wind rose which seized, *aferró,* the cradle, and the child vanished!

Everyone in the kingdom went into mourning, and they went searching for that infant who had been born to the king and queen in answer to so many rogations, and who had vanished! The king and queen did not resign themselves to their hard luck, to their *negro mazál, ma* the queen resolved, *dechizó,* to go out in search of her lost son. And so as not to be recognized, she dressed herself in the simple clothes of a woman of a low station in life. And she began to go from place to place, speaking to people.

In the end, she built a *hamám,* a public bathhouse, and she settled there. And she asked of all those who were to come to this *hamám* to tell her a short tale. She refused to accept money, *parás,* as was the custom in those days, *ma* she requested payment only with the tale. And so, people from various lands came to her, and she heard many, many tales, *ma* she did not achieve what she wanted.

One day, while the queen was at the door of the *hamám,* a beautiful girl came in and said to her:

"I'll tell you a tale, *ma* I don't know if it's true or if I dreamed it."

"Tell me," the queen said to her.

The girl told her that she comes from a very, very poor family. In her home there is no water and that's why, every Friday, she has to go to the well to draw water. On one Friday afternoon, before *shabát,* the girl went to the well. The line was very, very long, and the girl was at the end of the line, waiting to be able to draw water and return home. Time was passing; it had already turned dark, and she was left alone. It was her turn to draw water. Suddenly, she heard loud noises and voices. A racket, a *baraná,* began in the entire area. Brooms, tables covered with white tablecloths, flowers, and foods fall from the sky! And she is near the well, seeing it all. There are people sitting at the tables, and among them all a handsome youth is sitting, dressed in royal garments. And everyone is merry. They are singing:

"*Shabát* has arrived! *Shabát* has arrived!"

The girl stood there entranced, and she fell asleep. In the morning, when she woke up, she looked around her, *ma* everything had disappeared. Only a dog remained, black and dirty, *djirando,* circling here and there.

This was the tale of the girl to the queen, at the *hamám.* The queen said to the girl:

"Listen, young girl, I want you to come with me."

The queen had gone once to a magician who had given her a little vial, a *bokaliko,* of rose water, telling her:

"Look, your son is nearby. If you *riushir,* if you succeed in catching sight of him once, sprinkle a few drops of this water on him *pishín,* immediately, and he'll be yours again."

The girl's tale gave the queen a premonition; she said to her:

"I beg of you! Next week, on Friday afternoon, we'll go together and wait on line to draw water from the well at the same spot where you stood."

The girl was frightened. She said to her:

"What is it you want from me? I am but a poor girl!"

Ma, after the queen insisted a great deal, she agreed, *achetó,* to go back at the same time and to wait at the end of the line, this time intentionally.

The two of them waited there, and nightfall came again. Suddenly: voices, thunders, loud noises! Brushes falling from the sky, tables with embroidered tablecloths! And the queen's son is sitting at the head of the table, dressed very well. In the meantime, he had grown up to become a youth.

The queen began to tremble because she realized that this was her son. She approached him with the rose water and sprinkled a few drops on him. Everything disappeared! Only the youth remained! The mother was wild with joy!

The youth and the girl married, and if they haven't died yet, they are still alive today.

COMMENTARY

A tale of magic, dealing with supernatural adversaries, enchanted relatives, abductions, disappearance, and recovery, this is a version of part 2 of AT 425D, *Vanished Husband Learned of by Keeping Inn (Bath-house),* in which the queen sets up a bathhouse where all must tell a story (H11.1.1). She thus hears of her husband and finds him. In our tale a beloved infant son rather than a spouse has disappeared.[1]

As illustrated in this tale, childlessness is a source of frustration and despair. Because the central purpose of marriage in Jewish tradition is procreation, children are considered a great blessing[2] and barrenness is seen as a curse and punishment.[3] God, however, is believed to hold the key to fecundity,[4] and prayer is one of the ways to appeal for divine benevolence.[5] The barren queen in our narrative eventually conceives (T548), but her joy is short-lived. The prince is a miracle baby whose birth is brought about after much effort and prayer, but this treasure is soon stolen away from his mother, supernaturally (R10.3), as if abducted by a whirlwind (R17). The narrator puts the tale in perspective by saying that what happens at the time of the infant's disappearance is typical in folktales. The mother knows instinctively that her son was abducted by demons (R11.2.2) and consults a sorcerer to help her find him.

The belief in the power of demons over humans and their helplessness in the face of it is generally present but peripheral in Jewish life. It is still prevalent, however, at the level of folk beliefs and is primarily based on medieval superstitious folklore. In patriarchal societies, newborns were believed to be especially vulnerable to evil influences, particularly Lilith, who is identified with the child-stealing demon, a character she retains in later

---

1. For Jewish parallels, see *BJ,* 1:189, 374. Another Judeo-Spanish tale, Crews, no. 10, p. 104, displays the motif of the abducted child and is classified under *324, *The Recovered Child,* in Haboucha. For universal versions, see Megas, *Folktales of Greece,* no. 28; Dawkins, *Forty-five Stories,* no. 8; Thompson and Roberts, *Indic Oral Tales,* 63.
2. Gen. 22:17, 32:13.
3. Gen. 30:1; 1 Sam. 1:10; Lev. 20:20–21; Jer. 22:30.
4. Ta'anit 2a.
5. Sarah, Rebecca, Rachel, Samson's mother, Hannah, and the Shunammite woman were all barren at first, but God granted their and their husband's prayers (cf. Ps. 113:9).

folklore. Infants and their mothers were routinely protected by means of amulets, charms, and other precautions.[6] For example, a mother might be kept awake for the first three days after birth to prevent Lilith from harming her. Protective charms would be placed on the baby or on the cradle (G302.16+ [Noy]). A popular custom was to gather at the home of the newborn to recite the Shemá, the Jewish creed, to protect the child and mother from the evil spirits, particularly the *broshá,* the female demon who is believed to steal newborn children. The belief in female demons that strangle children at childbirth is tied to the personification of Lilith as a strangler of babies (G302.9+ [Noy]).[7]

The long-awaited infant in our tale disappears due to a supernatural event and needs to be found to restore order. Often the motif of the lost child symbolizes the loss of soul in folktales, and the center of the quest for the child is to achieve a greater level of awareness and wisdom. Here, his disappearance causes the mother to search for him for many years, and the story centers on how he is found and freed, with the focus of the tale being the quest for the vanished prince and his disenchantment and recovery.

The motifs of recognition by various means are prevalent in folktales, and often recognition occurs through tokens or the telling of shared experiences. The motif of the telling of stories at the bathhouse is a well-known one as well. What occurs here is a supernatural manifestation, a Sabbath gathering of Jewish demons, which is witnessed by chance by the unpromising heroine. As luck or fate would have it, the poor girl finds her way to the bathhouse to share her story with the queen (N831), thus becoming instrumental in the

---

6. Lilith has two primary roles in cabalistic demonology: as one who harms children and as a seducer of men. Because she was viewed as having designs on Eve's children (she claimed to have been expressly created to harm newborn infants), amulets were routinely written for women in childbirth to protect them from her. The uncircumcised child was considered particularly vulnerable, thus the room where the baby was kept was often protected by written or printed amulets, which included Psalm 126 and Psalm 121, as well as the names of the three angels, Sinay, Sinsinay, and Samengelof (found in the Sefer Raziel, early thirteenth century; see also Simon Bar Yohai, Sefer Hazohar, 1:14b, 2:96b, 111b, 3:19a, 76b). Lilith is said never to enter a house in which these angels' names are invoked for the protection of new mothers and their babies (see Patai, *Hebrew Goddess,* 223, 227, 238, fig. 2). Refer to tale 4 in this section, where these angels are mentioned and for more on Lilith. See also Ben Ami, "Customs of Pregnancy and Childbirth." The offspring of this Lilith are believed to fill the world.

7. 2 Alphabet of Ben Sira, 23a.f.

recovery of the now grown-up prince and earning her unstated reward: marriage to the prince.

The supernatural vision of the young helper occurs at dusk at the onset of *Shabát*. *Shabát* is welcomed traditionally with the lighting of Sabbath candles and is celebrated with prayers and a festive meal. As no work of any kind is permitted on *Shabát*, it is important for the young girl to draw her water before the setting of the sun.[8] When she fails to do so in time, she becomes witness to an extraordinary sight in a realm that extends beyond the natural one and can be reached only by means of such a magical occurrence. The spectacular phenomenon of lightning or discharge of atmospheric electricity is intended to sketch a surreal and frightening otherworld. At the same time, however, a semblance to the Jewish space and time of the tale is established. The *shedím* are Jewish demons that submit to the Torah and celebrate *Shabát* with cheerful merrymaking and delicious food and drink. Thus, the manifestation is depicted in a Jewish world inhabited by spirits or supernatural beings and in which magical deeds are performed.

In folktales, the world of demons is accessible to the living only by chance or after dangerous quests. That is why the narrator feels compelled to stress that the successful second visit to the well and the vision that results are unusual in that they do not occur by chance, as the first ones had. Despite the artificial nature of the event, however, it leads to the witnessing of the Sabbath gathering of demons and the release of the abducted prince. The superstitious belief that the activities of devils that hover in the air take place mainly at night, before midnight, was widespread. Such demons were said to be invisible and responsible for various inconveniences. They were thought to shun light and to linger in isolated, cold, dark, damp places. In particular, it was believed that they lived at the bottom of wells. One was advised, therefore, to refrain from drinking water on *Shabát* evening from pools, rivers, wells, or even from an uncovered glass. The Talmud also commands that a person should not walk unaccompanied in the dark for the same reason.[9]

It was not uncommon for Talmudic rabbis to believe in the existence of demons, the power of witches to do harm by spells, the effect of incantations to ward off evil, and the power of the evil eye. Some cabalists made use of all

---

8. Rebecca also went to draw water from the well outside of Aram Naharaim. There she met a stranger with ten camels who was Eliezer, Abraham's servant. She was kind to him, and he sought her as a bride for Isaac (Gen. 24:10–67).

9. In Nahmanides's opinion, for example, the *shedím* have subtle bodies that allow them to fly through the air, and their sustenance is derived from water and fire. Cf. Lev. R. 24:3 and Ber. 43b.

the motifs in the Talmud and Midrash with regard to demons and mingled them with folk beliefs, thus giving Jewish demonology a markedly syncretic character. Maimonides and other rationalists opposed these views, believing that magic has no power to do harm and no effect other than a psychological one, but traditions of the past as well as the cultural environment and intellectual outlook of each individual cabalist contributed to the diversification of such beliefs.

We are not told how the queen recognizes her son when she finally sees him, except for her "premonition" upon hearing the girl's story at the bathhouse. This could be an example of mystical recognition, in which identification occurs either by "force of nature," when an unknown member of the family is immediately and magically recognized (H175), or through a supernatural manifestation (H192).[10] Both of these elements surface in our narrative, as the mother succeeds in disenchanting and rescuing her son (R153.4) from the otherworld.

In folktales, the interest often shifts from the act of abduction and transformation itself to the breaking of the enchantment. The abduction and transformation of the human child in our tale results in a change of shape (here he is turned into a dog) imposed as a result of enchantment (D141).[11] The dog/prince functions in human form as a spirit, and his restoration to human form in the real world occurs through the performance of a recommended procedure, as is often the case in folktales.

Clearly, there is magic in this tale to influence and change the situation for good, as magic professes. Interpretation and prediction were thought to require special skills, and a specific group was credited with this ability: astrologers, fortune-tellers, and sorcerers. Such diviners used various methods to predict and affect the future. Many of these customs stem from the notion that a wise and learned man can deceive the demons, considered stronger but more stupid than mankind. Here, a magician offers simple rose water as a magic potion with which to disenchant the prince, once he is identified. This is a harmless local reference, as rose water is put to a wide variety of culinary uses in the region. Sprinkled on the enchanted prince, it succeeds in its intent: disenchantment results (D700, D562.1, D766), and all ends well.

---

10. See [Noy] for the last two motifs.
11. Cats and dogs are often viewed as possible reincarnations.

7

When There Were No Mirrors in the World

Narrated by SARA YOHAY (1993)

One day the town criers, the *delales,* went out into the world to make known that Princess Florina had decided to marry and that her tutors [the princess was an orphan][1] were seeking a husband for her, *amá,* on one condition: those who wanted her must bring a gift. He who brought the best gift would become the princess's husband and king of the Land of the Flowering Mountains.

As can easily be imagined, the best, the most valiant, and the most highly educated princes of the region, all of whom had heard praised the unique beauty of Princess Florina, rose up to the occasion. And each one of them was breaking his head over what present to bring.

Among the princes was the son of the King of the Land of the Green Eyes. He was all that a princess could wish for! And he had succeeded in having a portrait of Florina brought to his chamber, to his *udá.* Each time he looked at it, his heart would burn with love.

He, too, arose to seek her hand, and he came up with an idea as a present: the *blús* birds!

Agora, he knew where they were! The Queen of the Woods, of the *bosko,* of his country had possession of them so they would sing to her the Song of Infinite Love.

The prince prepared for the trip, and he went into the *bosko.* The animals went to advise the queen that the prince of the Land of the Green Eyes had

---

1. Teller's aside.

come to see her. The queen and all her retinue came near the Waters of Truth that fell powerfully and gave life to the thousands of trees that filled the *bosko*. The prince bowed a *temená* before her and explained his case in a soft voice.

The queen was very touched to hear his love arguments. She acceded to his request and gave orders that the two *blús* birds present themselves along with the best present in the world: a mirror cut from the crystal waters that fell into the *bosko,* so that Princess Florina could see her own beauty.

The prince expressed his thanks with gratitude and ordered that they make him a large cage to take away the birds. Just at that very moment, an old hag, ugly and loathsome, entered the woods. Her hair was tousled and her fingernails black. The old hag was leaning on a staff, and while she walked, she slipped and fell. Screaming, she demanded that the prince give her a hand to get her up. *Amá,* seeing her so dirty, he did not want to soil the beautiful garments he was wearing, and he refused, *refusó,* asking one of his servants to assist her.

Dark smoke rose up from the earth! And thunder and lightning crossed the sky and shook up the trees! The old hag, who was no other than the Witch Malice testing his character with her fall, threw wrathful words of malediction at him, which said that the punishment for his pride was to become *kambúr,* hunchbacked and hideous, and that the whole world would laugh at him! The prince sought her forgiveness; *amá* the witch laughed like a madwoman:

"Ha! Ha! Ha!"

And she flew away from the *bosko*.

In a second the prince was transformed into a deformed mass, a disgusting sight to behold. Insane with grief, the prince started to cry and cry.

The queen of the *bosko* and all her retinue and all the animals felt themselves turn to stone before such a disgrace. Now, *agora,* the prince could no longer return to his palace, nor could he continue to think about Florina. He locked himself into his grief and began wandering through the world.

The day came when a horseman, a *kavalier,* rode past him, and he was no other than the Prince of Darkness, who was on his way to ask for the hand of Florina. When he saw the *kambúr,* he said:

"Ah, this is Florina's present! There doesn't exist in the world anything more ugly than this!"

He seized the *kambúr,* threw him into a cage, covered it with a cloth, a *mantél,* and proceeded to the palace. When he arrived, the welcoming ceremonies had already begun. One after the other, the princes brought their gifts. More beautiful than ever, Florina laughed and rejected the presents as well as those who brought them.

At last came the Prince of Darkness. He lifted the *mantél,* and everyone present took a step back in horror and shrieked. Florina stood up to look, and with a face that showed disgust, she said:

"This is the most original thing I've seen."

And as she was about to grant her hand to the Prince of Darkness, the *blús* birds came in with the mirror. They said to Florina:

"The Prince of the Land of the Green Eyes is on his way. Wait before you decide!"

Florina saw her own beauty in the mirror, and she was enchanted. She began dancing from joy and showing her present to the paladins. She decided to wait before making a decision because this was the best present she had received. While she waited, she had an idea. She grabbed the mirror and she held it up to to the face, the *facha* of the *kambúr,* so he could see how ugly, how *bruto* he looked. When he saw his *facha,* the wretched *kambúr* went insane with grief. And all the paladins began to kick him. And Florina laughed and laughed at his misfortune.

Supitó, suddenly, thunder and smoke! The earth shook! The witch appeared and she shouted:

"Cruel and heartless princess! So you laugh at the misfortune of the *kambúr*? *Agora* I'll punish you so that you become blind and as ugly as he is!"

In vain were the tears of Florina! There was nothing to be done: *supitó,* she was blinded. Everyone present ran away, leaving Florina all alone in darkness and despair.

The *kambúr,* twice as unhappy to see his beloved in such a state, in such *hales,* drew close to her and embraced her, to console her. And filled with gratitude, she kissed him back. And thus the miracle of love occurred! The two of them became as handsome as they had once been, and the curse was overcome.

The *blús* birds began to chirp, and the world saw the biggest wedding in history. They invited the witch, and they thanked her for the lesson she had taught them. They ruled with justice, and produced many children. And the *blus* birds kept on singing the Song of Infinite Love.

Commentary

A version of AT 425C, *Beauty and the Beast,* this tale begins with a suitor contest and tests connected with marriage (H300), as well as with the bride princess offering herself as prize for the accomplishment of a task (H335, H331, T68).[2]

First recorded in a sixteenth-century Italian collection and popularized by Charles Perrault in the late seventeenth century[3] and by de Villeneuve and Leprince de Beaumont in the eighteenth century,[4] *Beauty and the Beast* is the story of a marriage between a beast—actually a prince who has been transformed by magic—and a beautiful young woman. Because of his unkindness toward an evil fairy, the Beast is cursed and turned into a repellent being described as uncouth in nature. In the end, the princess sees past his unsightliness to the gentle and loving creature trapped inside, and the Beast is returned to his true appearance by the woman's love.[5]

Our tale may be an oral rendition of a literary version of the type, in which the unkind are punished so as to be taught a lesson. It is filled with folk motifs and goes beyond the well-known *Beauty and the Beast* prototype, combining elements of yet another European version of the type, a reversal or mirror tale of *Beauty and the Beast*. In that version, often called *The Loathly Lady* (D732), a handsome knight breaks the enchantment of an ugly hag. Having retained the resonance of the prototype, our version is a variation on both these types. Like many other narratives passed down via oral tradition, it was adjusted along cultural norms in that Beauty herself is temporarily transformed into a blind and ugly being so as to taste the same bitter despair as the Beast.

Our narrative also includes elements of AT 900, *King Trushbeard*. Like the heroine in that type, the princess disdains all the suitors who respond to the invitation to woo her. The hero sees her picture and falls in love with her. After his transformation into a hideous being by the witch, she treats him

---

2. Universal versions of Beauty and the Beast include Baughman, *England and North America*, 11; Briggs, *Dictionary of British Folk-Tales*, pt. A, vol. 1, 487, 495, 511; D'Aronco, *Fiabe di Magia*, no. 12; Dawkins, *Forty-five Stories,* 222; Dawkins, *Modern Greek Folktales*, no. 13; Delarue, *Conte populaire français*, 2:715; Rael, *Colorado y Nuevo Méjico*, no. 163; Robe, *Mexican Folktales*, 76; Thompson and Roberts, *Indic Oral Tales*, 63.

3. In the tale titled "Riquet à la houppe." Refer also to Catherine Bernard's similarly titled tale of the same year.

4. Credit is due to one of the anonymous reviewers of this anthology for pointing out the importance of de Villeneuve and de Beaumont as the true popularizers of the tale type in the eighteenth century.

5. *Cupid and Psyche*, the tale of the philosopher and satirist Apuleius, is often viewed as the earliest example of the *Beauty and the Beast* tale type.

shamefully and cruelly and is punished for it. After her pride is broken and she reforms she is disenchanted and marries her original suitor.

The main characters in our tale are the romanticized princess, the handsome prince, and the evil witch. The tale centers on images of the human body. The princess is a remarkably beautiful woman (F575.1). Her beauty is idealized, of course, but a real princess must have also special qualities, and here she must learn to develop them. Likewise, the prince represents the idealization of a man in his handsome looks, love, youth, heroism, and charm. He is so enthralled by his love for the beautiful princess, however, that he pays no heed to the needs of others. For that weakness of character, the witch, whose purpose in the tale is to test him, puts him under a spell and transforms him into a monster (D1872). Symbolically, this is needed to tame a less civilized side of the hero and prepare him for more socially acceptable behavior. The character of the princess is also later put to the test by the same witch (G200). When the princess fails, she is instantly punished.

Witches seldom appear in Judeo-Spanish tales, so ours is a rare example, with the witch applying her supernatural power for apparently harmful ends but in reality for a good cause: to teach the main characters a lesson by changing their physical appearance when they fail to show kindness. She punishes their heartlessness and mockery (Q288) by cursing them (M411.12, G269.4) and magically transforming them (G263, D683, D5) into hideous beings (D1870, F576, D1871). Her casting a spell is a magical act of transformation that turns the hero from a handsome lover to a loathsome and deformed outcast, taking away his most cherished dream, the prospect of winning the hand of his beloved. In time, the witch also causes the princess to go blind (Q559.2 [Noy]) and become repulsive to make her pay for delighting in the plight of her deformed suitor. Once she uses her new mirror to cause pain to the distraught prince, she can no longer enjoy the reflection of her own beauty in it.

The purpose of these changes of shape imposed by another is to teach the prince and princess a lesson in kindness and humility (H1550). As Kafka's *Metamorphosis* suggests, the form into which one is transformed is related to some aspect of that individual's personality or behavior. In similar tales, a bewitched human can only be released when the love of another becomes stronger than the spell that binds him/her. Usually the hero, imprisoned in animal form, can be freed by the love of the woman. Both remain transformed, however, until a change of heart causes them to earn their disenchantment. In most folktales, as in this one, the interest often shifts from the act of transformation to the final breaking of the enchantment. It is clear that the witch has the power both to curse and cause harm and to bless and repair the damage caused by her earlier curse.

Although he does not know it, the bewitched prince's only hope of recovering his original form is the heroic love of the princess, whose main role is to free him through kindness. Though never actually stated, the message is easily understood by the audience: when each character overlooks the other's deformity and offers love and support, the couple is finally united and disenchanted (D700, D735, M420).

8

The Father's Will

Narrated by LEVANA SASSON (1992)

There was once a very, very wealthy merchant. This merchant had but one son, and he gave him everything. The son never lacked for anything.

The son grew up, he married, and a grandson was born to the merchant. And they were leading a good life. At the end of some years, the father saw that he was getting older. He called his son and he said to him:

"*Agora,* now that I am about to die, I want to tell you a secret. All the *parás,* all the money, that I have has come to me from far away, from across the sea. *Amá,* I am leaving you this testament, this *tsavaá:* you'll take all the *yerushá,* all the inheritance, if you promise me that you'll never go on a boat, on a *fluka,* that you'll never cross the sea."

The son said:

"Very well, father, I'll do as you say."

The father said:

"All the *parás,* all the money, all the gold that I have, it's all for you."

The father died. The son said:

"My father told me that I have *parás* for a lifetime."

And his son was learning the Torá. He was a *talmíd hahám,* a scholar of the law. And he grew up.

A year passed. A *fluka* arrived at the city. Those on the *fluka* asked the people:

This tale appeared in Judeo-Spanish and in Hebrew in Koén-Sarano, "El testamento del padre," in *Lejendas,* p. 237.

"Where does this merchant live?"
They said to them:
"The merchant died, *amá* he has a son. To this son he left all his *parás.*"
They came to the son, and they said to him:
"Look, we were good friends of your father's. We came on a *fluka* filled with gold and *parás.* All of this belongs to your father. *Agora,* we have heard that your father has died. We are honest people: we want to give it to you."
He said to them:
"From where did all of this come to my father?"
They said to him:
"Your father went across the sea and he worked there; and he made money. *Agora,* take all of this and come with us, because there are still many treasures left over there, and you must take possession of them."
He said to them:
"No! My father made me vow not to leave my home and never to cross the sea."
They said to him:
"That cannot be, because your father worked over there! And if he told you this, he must no longer have been in his right mind!"
He said:
"No! I promised him! I'm not going!"
They kept talking and talking to him. In the end, they convinced him. He went to sea along with them. A great storm started. The *fluka* sank; everything sank. The clothes, the *parás*! Everything sank into the sea. He alone was left: naked and *desbragado,* with no clothes on. He swam and swam. He came to a desolate place. He is walking and walking. . . . Suddenly he saw a tree. He said:
"There is no one here. I'll sleep here, under the tree, and I'll see what tomorrow morning will bring."
And he lay down there. Suddenly a lion passed near him. He began to plead with God to save him. He says:
"I now know why all these evils are befalling me! I promised my father not to cross the sea. The entire *fluka* sank, and *agora* He has sent me this lion to devour me!"
Pishín, quickly he climbed up the tree. The lion circled around and around, then left. He said to God:
"*Bemét*! Truly! I want to thank you! Forgive me! I realize that I have done a really bad thing."
He climbed up on the tree, and suddenly he sees that there is a really large bird, an eagle. He was terrified that it would bite him. *Aferró,* he took hold of

its beak, of its *biko,* climbed on its back, and remained there for the entire night. In the morning, the eagle began to fly. It flew and flew and flew. It arrived at a place where people were speaking Hebrew. Immediately, *pishín,* he jumped down from the tree. He said:

"It looks like there are many Jews here who are going to save me."

He saw young children. He said to them:

"Excuse me, are you Jewish?"

They gave him no answer. They went inside. They called the rabbi, the *rav.* The *rav* came out. He said:

"Who are you?"

He said to him:

"Come, I'll tell you all that has befallen me on the way!"

"Whatever you went through is nothing," the *rav* said to him. "What you'll go through here is much worse!"

"Why? Aren't you Jewish?"

The other one said:

"No! This is a place of demons, of *shedím*! Know that we kill whoever comes from the outside!"

"No!" he said. "I know that I have made a mistake, *amá* I want you to forgive me."

The other one said to him:

"Tonight, stay with me. Tomorrow we'll see what we'll do."

The next day, he said to him:

"Come to the synagogue, to the *kal.* We'll ask all the *shedím* what their decision is."

The next day, he took him to the *kal,* and he covered him up with his own coat, his own *palto,* so that people would not see him first and kill him. The *shedím* are saying to each other:

"I smell the scent of a human, of a *benadám*!"

The *rav* saw that they had already noticed that there is someone with him. He stopped the prayer, *afsikó* the *tefilá,* in the middle, and he said to him:

"*Agora,* I can no longer keep you with me. I must ask them what we are to do with you."

He said to them:

"This and that happened to this young man. He is a good man, a learned man, a *talmíd hahám.* He learned the Torá!"

They said:

"No! God, the *Dió,* brought him here so that we should kill him, not because He wanted to be kind to him!"

And they came over to kill him. The *rav* said:

"I'll take him to my house, and we'll ask Ashmedáy, the king of the *shedím*. Let's see what he has to say. Whatever he says, we'll do."

The next day they went before Ashmedáy, and they said to him:

"Look, the story is this and this! This man didn't do what his father had told him. *Amá,* he didn't do it on purpose, *mahsús.* They forced him to."

Ashmedáy said:

"Look, I have a son. I want this man to teach him a bit of Torá. I'll see how he behaves here."

And the man taught Ashmedáy's son for three years. And Ashmedáy would say to him:

"It's now *beseder* here. Remain here with us."

After some time, Ashmedáy went out to war with an army, a *tsavá,* and everything! Before he left, he said to this man:

"Look, I have seen that you are *neemán,* good and trustworthy. I'll give you the keys to all the houses that I have here. You can enter wherever you want. There is only one palace that has no keys; it's open. *Amá,* there, you must not enter."

"Very well," he said to him.

He was walking and walking. The evil inclination, the *yetzer ará,* gave him no rest. He said:

"Why did he tell me not to enter there? Who knows what there is over there?"

He went in, and he saw a seated woman dressed entirely in gold, like a queen, and many maidens dancing around her. He drew closer and closer. She saw him.

"What are you doing here?" she said to him.

He said to her:

"Who are you?"

"I am Ashmedáy's daughter. My father told you not to come near this palace. Why did you, once again, not do what you were told? *Agora* they'll kill you!"

"I don't know," he said. "I walked and walked. Suddenly I saw you, and I came in."

She said to him:

"Do you know what? If you want my father not to kill you, tell him that you have come here because you're in love with me and that you wish to marry me. Come, let's marry and you'll stay alive."

Az, he said:

"Very well! You're very beautiful, and I want to marry you."

At that moment, while he was there, Ashmedáy came in, as he had returned from war. He saw immediately that he is in his daughter's palace. He said to him:

"Didn't I tell you not to come here?"

He unsheathed his sword and prepared to kill him, but he said to him:

"Forgive me. I wish to speak to you before you kill me. I came here because I want to marry your daughter. I fell in love with her. She is very beautiful!"

Ashmedáy said to him:

"If you want to marry her, that's okay, that's *beseder. Amá,* if not, I will not spare your life."

The daughter said to him:

"Look, I am a demon, a *shedá. Amá* I have a woman's ways: I can have children, I can do everything."

He said:

"If that's so, I am ready. We'll get married."

They made a big wedding. They got married. Two years later, a son was born to them, and he named him Shelomó, Solomon. Every time he looked at his son, he would start sighing:

"Oh! Oh!"

His wife said to him:

"Look what a handsome son we have! Why is it that every time you hug your son you sigh?"

He said to her:

"Shall I tell you the truth? I left a wife and son in that other city. And every time I look at this child, I remember my son, and my heart aches."

She said to him:

"Do me a favor. When you're with me, when you are with your son, don't sigh."

Once again, upon holding his son, he sighs:

"Oh! Oh! Oh!"

His wife said to him:

"Look, I can't live this way any longer! Do you know what? I'll let you go for a year to where your wife is. Go, see her, and then come back to me."

He said to her:

"Very well."

Ashmedáy came. He summoned all the *shedím,* and he asked who could take him.

One of them came and said to him:

"I'll take him in twenty years."

Another one came and said:

"Ten years."

Another one said:

"One year."

One came, a hunchback, with one eye. He said:

"I can take him in a day."

Ashmeday's daughter said to her husband:

"Look, keep in mind that this hunchback is very prickly. Don't ask him anything."

"Very well," he said.

The hunchback took him, and within a day they came to his city. It was nighttime. He waited until daybreak. In the morning he met some people on the street. They said to him:

"Aren't you the merchant's son, the one who went away on the *fluka*?"

He said to them:

"Yes, I am. *Amá,* don't ask what has happened to me! The *fluka* sank, and I have lived in other places. *Agora* I have returned to my wife and son."

They said to him:

"Don't ask!?! Your wife is just like a widow, an *almaná,* with her son in the house! She doesn't know what to do!"

He came home. He said to his wife:

"*Na,* there! I have now come back to you."

And he told her everything that had happened to him. *Amá* he did not tell her that he had to go back. And he stayed with her. One day, he said to the hunchback:

"Tell me why you are hunchbacked and why you have only one eye."

The hunchback was annoyed. He said to him:

"I'll tell you, *amá* I'll no longer remain with you. I'll go back to Ashmeday." He said to him: "I've only one eye because I struggled against someone, and he took out one of my eyes. And I'm a hunchback because that's the way I was born! *Amá agora,* now it's all over! I'll leave you and go back to Ashmeday. Tell me what you want me to tell your wife."

He said to him:

"Tell my wife that I'll no longer return to her side!"

The demon, the *shed,* said to him:

"What? You promised her that you'd come here for a year and then go back to her!"

"No!" he said. "Tell her that I'll never come back!"

The other one went back to her. She asked him:

"What did my husband say to you?"

The *shed* said to her:

"Your husband said that he'll never come back!"

She didn't know what to do. She went to her father. She said to him:

"What shall we do? He gave me his promise."

Ashmedáy said to her:

"Let's wait out the year. I told him that he could stay there for a year. Let the year take its course. We'll see."

The year went by. He sent him the hunchback with others, so they can bring him back. He said:

"No! I'm not going back!"

They said to him:

"*Amá* you gave her an oath and a marriage contract, a *ketubá*. *Agora* you can't just leave her like that!"

He said to them:

"I gave them an oath because I was frightened that they would kill me. *Amá* I have a wife. I don't want to be married to *shedím*. I want my wife to bear me more children."

They went back, and they told Ashmedáy's daughter everything. And she went to her father and asked him what to do. Ashmedáy said to her:

"You sent him the hunchback. Send him someone more respectable, more *mehubád*. Maybe that one can speak to him nicely and convince him."

One, more *mehubád,* came. He spoke to him nicely:

"Look, they gave you nothing but kindness over there. They saved your life! They gave you whatever you wanted! Ashmedáy arranged a marriage for you! He put his faith in you, his *emuná*! He placed his keys in your hands! He gave you his daughter! What more do you want? You had a really good deal! *Agora,* is this a way to pay him back? It isn't nice!"

He said to him:

"No! *Agora* I have returned to my wife and son! *Beshúm ofen,* on no account do I want to go back there!"

That one returned and reported everything to Ashmedáy, and he said:

"I'll go myself and I'll kill him, he and all the dwellers of his city!"

His daughter said:

"No! I'll take a few people with me and I'll go to him myself, with my son."

She took the boy and they went there. They remained at the door. She said to the boy:

"Do you know what? It's time to get up. You go. Enter. Tell your father that we have come."

The son knocked on the door. He woke up his father. He said to him:

"Get up! What's the matter? I'm your son. Didn't you recognize me?"
He said to him:
"I was asleep. Why did you come?"
His son said to him:
"I came with my mother to take you back."
He said:
"No! Go back to your mother! Tell her that I will not go back!"
The son told him:
"You're my father! You promised my mother that you'd come here for a year and that you'd go back! The year is over! *Agora* you must return!"
He said to him:
"No! Go away, you and your mother! I am never going back! *Skapó*! It's over! Your mother is a demon, a *shedá*! I have a wife who is human, a *benadám,* and I don't want to go back!"

The *shedá*-wife came. She went inside. She said to him:
"I want all the people of the city to come out. I want to speak to them. I want to tell them everything."

And so it was. She made them all come out. She told them everything that had happened with him:

"We rescued him! We gave him everything! We made him... and, *agora,* he refuses to come back to me! And I also have a *ketubá* that he signed for me! What do you have to say?"

Az, he said:
"I am ready to give her back the *ketubá*. I am rich. My father left me much at the end of his life. I'll give you the money, the *parás,* and go away!"

She said to him:
"I don't want *parás*! *Agora* that the entire community, the entire *edá,* found out all about it, *agora* that you have humiliated me enough, I no longer want to take you back with me! *Agora* I'm going to leave," she said, "*amá,* before I go, I'll give you a kiss."

She went into the house and came to kiss him. While kissing him, she took him and choked him. She choked him and left him there. She went out and told the people who were there:

"I'm done with him because he shamed me so much. And I'll not take my son back because, if I take him back with me, I'll always keep the memory, the *zikarón,* of my husband! And I want to remember nothing of him! I want you to watch over my son, to find him a bride, and to provide well for him."

She went back to her land. And they took the son, they provided well for him, and they found him a bride. And he was happy.

May they be well and so may we.

COMMENTARY

As in AT 911*, *The Dying Father's Council,* the heart of this narrative is the last request of a merchant father to his son (P431 [Noy], P233) and the solemn promise the son gives at his father's deathbed (M250), a promise he later breaks (M256). Eventually, the counsel of the father is proven wise by experience (J154), and the disobedient son pays a heavy price for this breach of trust. The teller presents the son's action as the cause of his downfall and, eventually, of his death. Her narrative is filled with belief in demonology and the power of retribution. It also intertwines several types of family and social relationships: father/son (P233), husband/wife (P210), father/daughter (P234), the breaking of bargains and promises (M205), and marriage (T100).

Jewish tradition emphasizes respect for the dying and the dead. The Talmud stresses that the oral testament of a dying man has the same legal force as his written and witnessed instructions (M258).[1] There are many examples of adherence to such last wishes in the Bible. Consider how the final requests of Jacob[2] and Joseph,[3] and the advice of David,[4] were all faithfully heeded and observed. Thus, deference is traditionally given to the last wishes of a dying person.

In our tale, the immediate punishment suffered by the protagonist for disobedience is reminiscent of Jonah's biblical ordeal. Like Jonah, he becomes the victim of a violent storm miraculously caused in reprisal for breaking the rules. This is as far as the similarities go, however. In our tale, when the ship sinks the hero is the sole survivor. Yet he does not repent. It is only after a lion threatens his life that he begins to link his streak of misfortunes to his own behavior. This realization is reinforced once he is subjected to yet another danger when, after traveling on the back of an eagle (B552), he reaches the otherworld realm of demons (G302.2+ [Noy]) where he is exposed to the threat of paying the ultimate price for his failure to honor his vow to his dying father.

The teller shows us how the spirits of good and evil struggle within the human soul. Judaism proclaims that individuals have the power to choose between good and evil and need but the will to make the right choice. Our hero faces this dualism of choice when confronted with a unique prohibition. Unique proscriptions are well-known folk motifs, which heroes and heroines

---

1. Gittin 13a.
2. Gen. 49:29.
3. Gen. 50:25.
4. 1 Kings 2:1–9.

often fail to honor. This weakness of character takes place twice in our tale: the first time when the hero disobeys his father's instructions not to leave home and travel on a ship and later when he disobeys the king of demons' single interdiction not to set foot in one of his residences. In both instances, the protagonist is forbidden to do one particular thing; everything else he is free to do (C600, C610, C611). In both instances evil inclination, *yetzer ha-rá'*, tempts the hero, and his curiosity or greed gets the better of him (W137, W151). Through a series of difficult experiences, he is brought to confront a marital dilemma and a third breach of promise when he fails to honor his marriage vows to his demon wife. His broken promise to return to her side after a year's absence leads to his final demise.

It is typical of folktales to put protagonists through dangerous quests and situations in order for them to gain entrance to the otherworld. This otherworld of popular belief is depicted here as a world of demons, a realm beyond the natural one, reached only after a dangerous voyage. Inhabited by spirits or demons, it is represented as a universe in which magical deeds, such as rapid journeys and the detection of the human scent, are normal occurrences. Interestingly, as soon as the hero recognizes that his hosts speak Hebrew, he assumes that he has found safety among Jews. The expectation is that Jews anywhere in the world would help a fellow Jew in distress.

Belief in the power of demons over humans and their vulnerability in face of it is still common at the level of folklore and superstition. The belief is implied in the Talmud in several places, especially in the Babylonian Talmud,[5] and demonology is more prominent in the Palestinian *midrashim* than in the Jerusalem Talmud. Some medieval thinkers, Talmudic commentators, and codifiers accepted such beliefs while others, such as Maimonides,[6] rejected them as contrary to the doctrine of divine providence.

Demons enter quite naturally into folktales as if it were commonplace to experience the presence of supernatural beings. As enemies of humankind, they tend to represent darkness and temptation. Their role is often conceived as that of tempting men to do evil. Human confrontation with demons, therefore, is the age-old struggle for enlightenment and knowledge instead of ignorance and confusion. The term *shedím*, rendered as "demons" or "devils" in most translations,[7] is often used to describe evil spirits born from the union

---

5. This may be because Babylonian Jews lived in a world believed to be filled with demons and spirits, malevolent and sometimes benevolent, which inhabited the air, trees, water, etc.

6. The foremost medieval Jewish philosopher (1135–1204).

7. See Deut. 32:17; Ps. 106:37.

of Lilith and Adam. The female demon in this tale reflects the image of Lilith, who is generally considered a hostile power.[8] She and her offspring, the *lilím* or she-devils, embody the image of the femme fatale: the seductive, sensual, vengeful woman who tempts men to their downfall.[9]

The consequence of a union of human and fairy/demon in folklore is often tragic. This is the case in our tale, where the demon-wife turns out to be harmful to the hero when he finally opposes her. She is an attractive temptress. Her beauty is an external manifestation, though, not the reflection of the inner self. At the beginning, the hero does not recognize her as a dangerous and possessive lover, as the heroine in *Blue Beard* does in Perrault's tale. She appears benign and loving and gives the hero helpful advice to rescue him from the wrath of her father and from certain death (G530.2). She woos him with sex and life (G302.12+ [Noy], T463 [Noy]), and he appears to abandon his worldly wife and child. The result is the marriage of a mortal with a supernatural being (T111, T111.3 [Noy]), another common folk motif.

The sexual element in the relationship of man and demons holds a prominent place in the demonology of the Zohar. Midrashic literature expands the legend that Adam, having parted from his first wife after it was ordained that they should die, produced demons with spirits that had attached themselves to him. The offspring of this union are said to fill the world. Such mating of female devils with human males was believed to have continued throughout history, and their devil progeny was believed to resemble humans and to be mortals.[10]

Belief in evil spirits is reflected in our tale. Though set in some indefinite land and time, the world of demons depicted here is described as a Jewish one in which demons speak Hebrew, have a rabbi, attend prayer services at the synagogue, learn Torah, and give brides a marriage contract.

Some of the demons were considered "Jewish demons," or *shedím yehuda'ím,* and were said to accept the Torah. This was supposed to be true, particularly of demons ruled by Ashmedáy or Asmodeus, the king of demons (F402.2.1 [Noy], G302.2+ [Noy]). Note in the tale that Ashmedáy invites the

---

8. Legend tells us that the less docile first wife of Adam, a jealous and angry Lilith, returns to the Garden of Eden after the creation of Eve and tempts her in the form of the snake, thus bringing about the fall of humanity. She is often depicted as queen of the demons and a consort of Samael, the demon king.

9. Mentioned in the Talmud and in midrashic and cabalistic literature, Lilith was originally a succubus believed to cohabit with mortals. See Isa. 34:14.

10. In the later cabala, demons born to man out of such unions are considered his illegitimate sons. They are called *baním shovavím* (mischievous sons).

human visitor to teach his son the Torah; at the beginning of the tale the hero himself had been described as a student of the Torah (G302.9+ [Noy]).[11]

Ashmedáy was considered by some to be the son of King David and Agrath, the queen of the demons. Often characterized as a cherub, he is described as "king of the demons" in the Talmudic Aggadá and as a great philosopher.[12] Being an opponent of Solomon and "ruler of the south," however, with sixty-six legions of spirits as followers, Ashmedáy was usually regarded as an evil spirit himself, although not harmful. The Talmud itself does not identify him as an evildoer and often assigns him the function of preserving the ethical order of the world. In rabbinic lore, he is a messenger of God, hence an angel.[13] He appears in this tale as a benevolent king and judge who goes out to war with his army to fight an unnamed enemy.[14] Unlike the hero, who once again breaks his word, Ashmedáy keeps to the letter of his agreement to allow him a full year's visit to his human family.

Many superstitious Jewish customs dealing with *shedím* stem from the notion that a wise and learned man can deceive the demons, which are stronger but less clever than men. In Jewish folklore, although still the king of demons, Ashmedáy sometimes appears as a dupe of the men with whom he enters into partnership. Here he is depicted as a beneficent demon and a friend of his human son-in-law who, in the end, succeeds in deceiving him and rendering him powerless.[15] Ashmedáy keeps his promises and goes out of his way to help the hero by giving him three opportunities to change his mind and return to the world of demons. It is as if he does not really want to punish him. When all fails, however, the stage is set and death occurs.

As in many folktales, there is a realistic understatement in our narrative, despite the extraordinary events, and supernatural occurrences are easily

---

11. In rabbinic Judaism, study of the Torah is given the highest value, for men at least, and great emphasis is placed on teaching children religious observance and the Torah.

12. Pesakhim 110a. One popular view, however, is that "Ashmedáy" is merely the title of the office of the king of the demons, just as Pharaoh is the title of the office of the king of Egypt.

13. In the writing of Isaac ha-Kohen, as in the writings of many cabalists, Lilith the younger is the wife of Asmodeus (Tarbiz. 4).

14. As an evil spirit or demon, Ashmedáy appears first in the apocryphal book of Tobit and in the Testament of Solomon (first century CE). In Tobit, he is a demon that has slain the first seven husbands of Sarah, who becomes the wife of Tobias, son of Tobit.

15. The author of Ra'ayá Meheimná, in the Zohar (3:253a), distinguishes a type of demons resembling humans who are also good-natured and prepared to help men.

accepted along with the everyday events. Two spatial worlds at parallel levels are depicted here—the human world and the otherworld of demons—and the demons travel freely from one to the other. The magic journey back to earth that the protagonist undertakes, carried by a moody hunchbacked demon (D2121.5, N810, N813, G302.22 [Noy]), is a marvelous air voyage with extraordinary speed (D2135, F411.0.1). As expected, travel takes place at night, as does the journey that the demon wife and her son undertake to reach the world of humans. The method of travel is magical not only as an actual passage through space but also as an expression of the urgent desire for change, a symbol of the hero's restlessness (D2122).

In other folktales of marriage to a supernatural being in which the hero breaks the taboo that ensures the continuance of his relationship to his supernatural wife, the offended woman returns to her own world and the benefits she bestowed on her husband cease. In tales in which a character's return from the otherworld occurs, many years have gone by and protagonists sometimes crumble into dust from old age. Often those who return after having tasted otherworld food are doomed to pine and die, losing all interest in the everyday world. Typically in Judeo-Spanish tales where characters experience the otherworld, they make sure not to taste any food there.[16] These motifs are missing here, but an uncommon episode takes place. Because the human husband had married his demon wife under duress and not out of love, he pines for his old life and his first son and expresses the desire to see his human home again. When he is allowed to do so, many years of real time have passed, and his first wife has mourned her disappeared husband as dead.

Yet, as the *halakhá*[17] prescribes that a Jewish marriage can only be dissolved by divorce or by the death of either spouse, his wife could only be released from marriage with proof of her husband's death or by receiving from him the *get* (bill of divorce). The mere disappearance of the husband with no proof of his death is not sufficient for the declaration by the court (Bet Din) that a wife is a widow and that her marriage is dissolved. Thus, while the hero's deserted wife lived like an *almaná,* a widow, with no means of financial support, she had in fact become an *aguná*. An *aguná* is bound to a missing husband as she is to one who refuses to divorce her.[18] If she cannot

---

16. See tale 5, note 3.

17. The *halakhá* is the legal portion of the Talmud and post-Talmudic literature. It deals mostly with personal and communal issues as well as religious observance.

18. Ruth 1:13. For another folk narrative example of a woman whose husband disappears, see tale 3 in this section.

obtain a divorce from her husband, or if it is unknown whether he is still alive, she cannot remarry.[19]

A motif of the traditional Jewish marriage ritual enters into the tale when the hero offers to pay his demon wife the settlement of her *ketubá* to get rid of her (T135.8 [Noy]). Through the *ketubá*, or marriage contract, a bridegroom essentially obligates himself to provide a settlement for his wife should he divorce her. In principle this obligation is imposed upon him by law for the purpose of protecting the woman. It is important to remember that before Talmudic law, the wife's consent was not required for a divorce to be valid. The main purpose of the *ketubá* was thus to prevent the husband from divorcing his wife against her will, and "so that he [should] not regard it as easy to divorce her."[20] The *ketubá*, therefore, served as a check against hasty divorce because the husband was obliged to assume the full responsibility of compensation for the stated amount.[21] As the bride's dowry was recorded in the *ketubá*, she could claim this sum from her husband's estate once he died or divorced her.[22] The hero here is ready to compensate his demon-wife with the sum prescribed in her *ketubá*.

When he refuses to return to her, she bestows upon him the kiss of death, which chokes him (K951.0.1 [Noy]).[23] Before taking her leave, however, she ensures the future and well-being of her orphaned son by making him the responsibility of the Jewish community.[24] Such responsibility is in line with Jewish societal tradition. Many Jewish communities throughout the ages provided for the care of orphans.

---

19. A husband, on the other hand, is not affected by *aginút,* the state of being abandoned by a spouse, without divorce. He can remarry.

20. Ketubot 11a; Yev. 89a; Maimonides, Yad Ishut 10:7.

21. The sum was two hundred *zuzim* if the bride was a virgin and one hundred *zuzim* if a widow or divorcee. In addition to this basic settlement, the husband vowed to protect his wife, work for her, and provide her with her rights and sustenance.

22. In Jewish law a widow does not inherit from her husband, but she is entitled to the sum stipulated in her marriage contract, her *Ketubá,* and the rights due to her by virtue of its provisions that relate to her maintenance. This should be the same as that which she was entitled to receive during the husband's lifetime.

23. See Levi, "Recueil de contes juifs," 50–54, in which the writer refers to a Hebrew manuscript (no. 1466 of the Neubauer Catalogue) which displays a collection of tales, legends, and anecdotes of an edifying nature. One of these tales is very similar to our tale in its plot and many of its details.

24. See Ben Ami, "Customs of Pregnancy and Childbirth" for more details about these customs among Sephardic and Oriental Jewish Communities.

PART TWO

Tales of Fate

Singular among Judeo-Spanish narratives is the romantic tale that stresses the problem of fate and pre-ordination in everyday life.[1] The lesson such tales highlight is that because there are unknown reasons for events to evolve the way they do, there is no use trying to evade one's destiny. Everything is foreseen,[2] and the inevitability of one's luck in life and one's predestined lot is absolute. The tales stress the relationship between God's omnipotence and human weakness.

This stress on the finality of the heavenly decree is especially illustrated in matters of love and matrimony. Universal stories about heroes finding their way to each other, often after overcoming difficult obstacles and dangers, are at the heart of Jewish matrimonial lore. This is no less so among the Sephardim in whose narratives someone's *mazál*[3] is unavoidably met, despite the use of various means to try to circumvent or influence fate. According to the Zohar,[4] the souls of the truly matched couple derive from a common soul-essence. For this reason, even before birth, the bride and groom are destined to be joined in matrimony.[5] Then, as marriages are believed to have been decided in heaven, the question often asked is whether the fateful decision can be evaded or if it is irrevocable.

It is human nature to long to know what the future holds. The belief that destiny is determined, or at least affected, by the stars and planets in the ascendancy when a person is born leads the kings in our tales to consult astrologers about their daughters' future. This is done either out of inherent curiosity or in order to anticipate and try to thwart the fate that awaits them. Jewish writings have a somewhat ambivalent attitude toward astrology. There is no explicit prohibition in the Bible against consulting astrologers and there is no denial that astrology actually works. The Shulkhan Arukh[6] rules that one must not inquire of the astrologers and not consult lots. The Prophet Jeremiah inveighs against those resorting to astrologers.[7] Maimonides rejected astrology on theological grounds, declaring it complete nonsense. Such repeated admonitions against it, though, perhaps speak to its popularity.

The concept of the predestined mate is the focus of many Judeo-Spanish tales. Belief in divination and in the stars as influencing one's destiny is highlighted in some of the narratives in this section. In one case, the king tries to alter his daughter's destiny by ordering her mismatched intended, her *mazál,* to be killed. Elijah the Prophet intervenes just in time to change the order of death against the youth, and thus the lowly hero is eventually able to marry his princess, as predicted, leading the king to concede the immutable power of fate. Likewise, in a different tale, the king tries to change the course of his daughter's destiny by sending off her intended to be killed. The youth elicits the pity of his executioners, who spare his life. He then experiences various lucky episodes and ends up winning the princess's hand anyhow. Here as well, the king is forced to acknowledge the power of fate. In yet another story, the king does not consult the stars but tests his daughter's luck by forcing her to marry a destitute man. Through her patience and loyalty, the husband becomes rich, and the daughter teaches her father a lesson in charity and generosity toward the less privileged. He learns that no human can escape fate and should not even attempt to do so. And, as the fourth tale points out, a luckless man remains without luck despite repeated attempts to help him. Here the teller indicates, however, that his dim wit also has something to do with his repeated lack of success.

The tales weave a few magical and supernatural details into the framework of the plot, and these episodes are accepted within the everyday Jewish world of the tellers and listeners. The magical elements are sometimes central to the development of the tale: the miraculous appearance of the all-knowing Elijah and the timely help he provides, unsolicited, to the endangered youth; the magic lake's waters that cause the hero's dark skin to become lighter. More often than not, however, such magical details serve to embellish rather than shape the plot: the preternatural writing in the sky warning the king not to interfere with fate; the help of enchanted animals who reward the hero with wealth when he responds wisely to their query and thus helps disenchant them. Despite these extraordinary happenings, there is almost always a realistic environment in the world of these narratives. At all times the affirmation of God's omniscience is conclusive and final, albeit not always understood by humans who have to face the perils and insecurities of life.

Notes

1. See Haboucha, 436–81, for versions of Judeo-Spanish tales of fate.
2. Abot 3:19.
3. The term *mazál* can be viewed as a planet and its influence, the fate as determined by the stars. It means "luck" but also alludes to a predestined marital match.
4. 3:43b.
5. Bereshit Rabba (Gen. R.) 68:3–4; Wayikra Rabba (Lev. R.) 8:1.
6. Yoreh Deah, 179.1.
7. 10:2.

9

The King's Daughter and the Gardener's Son

Narrated by SHOSHANA LEVY (1988)

In one city there was a king, and in another city there was a gardener. As fate, as *mazál*, would have it, they gave birth: the queen gave birth to a girl and the gardener's wife gave birth to a son.

Time passed. Five years.... Ten years.... The king, who had the daughter, wanted to know what *mazál* his daughter would have. He summoned his advisor and asked him to peer into the stars for he whom his daughter would marry. The advisor went up to the observatory and saw that this king's daughter was to marry a gardener's son. He came. He told the king about it:

"My lord king, your daughter will marry the son of a gardener who lives in such and such a place!"

"Is that so?" said the king. "I'll take care of that!"

Time went by after that. One day, he summoned his advisor and said to him:

"You will go before the king of such and such a place, and you'll give him this letter from me."

"Fine!" said the soothsayer and left.

When the king of that place received this letter, he said:

"Call the gardener's son for me, for I want to speak with him."

The gardener's son arrived. The king said to him:

This tale was published in Judeo-Spanish and Hebrew translation in Koén-Sarano, *Saragosa,* 35, and *Lejendas,* 129, under the heading "La ija del rey i el ijo del guertelano."

"Look here, young man, you'll do me a favor. You'll travel to such and such a city. We'll give you a *letra* for you to deliver to the king."

"Fine," said the youth, and he was on his way.

Traveling across one field and then the other, the youth felt very tired. He sat down under a tree and fell asleep. He had the little letter, the *letrezika,* outside his *jaketiko,* his little jacket.

Eliau Anaví passed by. He looked at the *letra.* When he looked at it, it was written there:

"My lord king, as soon as you see this youth, *pishín,* without delay, have him beheaded!"

The youth woke up in the morning. He is going to the king. He knows nothing. He arrived at the king's *saráy.* They received him. He took the *letra* out; he gave it to the king. The king read the *letra.* As he reads the *letra,* he sees:

"My lord king, *pishín* you see this youth, wed him to your daughter. Do not put it off!"

Pishín the wedding was done. Among the guests, the *musafires,* came also the king of the other city. He saw the youth. He said to the king:

"What have you done? This is the gardener's son! I wrote as you asked me to: '*Pishín* you see this youth, you'll have him beheaded!' And you have married him to your daughter!"

The king read the *letra* once more. He called his advisor and said to him: "What does this mean?"

The advisor said to him:

"My lord king, what God does in Heaven, the earth never *enfasa,* never wipes out. This was the *mazál* of your daughter!"

Commentary

Chance and fate play an important role in this tale from the onset. The simultaneous birth of the hero and the princess (T22 [Noy]) suggests immediately that events surrounding the characters are predestined. The ruling of fate comes true in the end, as decreed by the heavens whose decision cannot be evaded, the teller tells us. This version is a good variant of AT 930, *The Prophecy,* with part 1 (*The Prophecy*) and part 3 (*Uriah Letter*) included but part 2 (*Abandonment*) and part 4 (*The Sequel*) missing.[1]

---

1. The type has literary analogues. The theme, probably Eastern in origin, first appears in Europe during the Crusades (twelfth century). The *Gesta Romanorum* and

The king, a symbolic patriarchal figure of rule and authority, assumes the role of the father who longs to know what the future holds for his daughter, perhaps to foresee and protect her from the dangers that may lie ahead for her. To that end, he uses divination to discover the heavenly will. Divination was the practice of forecasting the future, especially by magical means.[2] Diviners used signs to make their predictions, so they had to learn the means by which to interpret them. Interpretation was thought to require special skills, and astrologers, soothsayers, and fortune-tellers (P420+ [Noy], D1712 [Noy]), credited with this ability, often served as advisors at the royal court.

---

the *Book of Sindibad* use it. Other Judeo-Spanish tales of predestination are found in Attias, *Nozat ha-zahav,* 153; LP, vol. 2, no. 111, p. 82; LP, vol. 1, no. 14, p. 55; LP, vol. 1, no. 30, p. 103; LP, vol. 1, no. 86, p. 256; Rozenzweig, "El ijo del rey i la ija del karreador de agua," 39, an identical version of which appears in Koén-Sarano, *Saragosa,* 143. See also Koén-Sarano, "Del mazal no se fuye," in *Lejendas,* p. 73. IFA versions of AT 930 exist from Afghanistan, Eastern Europe, Egypt, Iran, Iraq, Iraqi Kurdistan, Israel (Ashkenazic, Sephardic), Morocco, Tunisia, and Yemen. For additional Jewish sources, consult Attias, *Nozat ha-zahav,* no. 9 (Greece); Bar Itzhak and Shenhar, *Jewish Moroccan,* 189; *BJ,* 1:219, 221, 375; M. Cohen, *'Edot Israel,* vol. 1, no. פס, צו, קפ. Frankel, *Classic Tales,* no. 180; Jason, "Types," 187; Jason, *Types,* 56; Kagan, *TEM 1963,* no. 4 (Iran); Marcus, *Mabu'a,* no. 12 (Iran); Noy, "First Thousand Folktales," p. 107; Noy, *Folktales,* no. 49 (Iraq); Noy, *Ha-na'ara,* nos. 5, 80 (Iraq); Noy, *Tunisia,* nos. 54, 66; Noy, *TEM 1970,* no. 2 (Iraqi Kurdistan); Sabar, *Kurdistani Jews,* 172; Schwarzbaum, *Studies,* 6, 273ff., 442; *Schwili,* nos. 97, 99. For non-Jewish versions, see Andrejev, (type *934); Ashliman, *Guide to Folktales,* 192–93; Baughman, *England and North America,* 21; Boggs, *Spanish Folktales,* 112; Boulvin, *Contes populaires persans,* 1:5, 2:55; BP, 1:267, 276, 4:137; Briggs, *Dictionary of British Folk-Tales,* pt. A, vol. 1, 225, 236, 497, pt. A, vol. 2, 380; Bushnaq, *Arab Folktales,* 147, 172 (Iraq); Calvino, *Italian Folktales,* nos. 75, 112, 152; Chauvin, *Ouvrages arabes,* 8:145–47, no. 145C; Clouston, *Popular Tales,* 2:458–66; D'Aronco, *Fiabe Toscane,* 106; Dawkins, *Modern Greek Folktales,* nos. 50, 51; EB, nos. 124, 125, 126, 128, 214; *Gesta Romanorum,* no. 20; Grimm and Grimm, *Tales,* no. 29 (and AT 461); Grimm and Grimm, *Other Tales,* 27; T. Hansen, *Types* (Puerto Rico) (930*B Cuba); Laoust, *Contes berbères,* no. 83; Megas, *Folktales of Greece,* no. 46; Thompson, *Folktale,* 139–41; Thompson and Roberts, *Indic Oral Tales,* 117; Tubach, *Index Exemplorum,* no. 647; Villa, *100 Armenian Tales,* nos. 27, 47.

2. Diviners served the needs of the country and the king, as was the case in the biblical world. Although divination was forbidden by the Bible (Deut. 18:9–11; Lev. 19:26, 31), Talmudic rabbis tried to distinguish between actual divination and the use of a sign. The acceptable techniques of divining mentioned in the Bible include astrology, a more advanced method of predicting the future from the behavior of heavenly bodies. Dreams were also considered a proper method.

Foreknowledge is a puzzle that has exercised the minds of philosophers as well as simple people: how to reconcile God's foreknowledge with human free will. From the beginning of time, diviners served certain needs of their country and king. This is the case in the biblical world.[3] Divination, however, was also considered an abomination that the Israelites were forbidden to learn and practice.[4] The only exception was the consultation with the Prophets and the *Urím ve Tummím,* a type of lot oracle placed on the breastplate of the High Priest.[5] Although forbidden by the Bible, Talmudic rabbis adopted an ambivalent attitude toward divination, particularly the Babylonian *amoraím* who laid the foundation for the gigantic work, the Babylonian Talmud, and lived in an environment in which divination was extensively practiced.

The seer in this tale envisions the future after peering at the stars (D1311+ [Noy], M302.4 [Noy]) and is not believed to err. Thus, when the future husband of the princess is foretold (M369.2+ [Noy], M369.2.1), the king, while not pleased, accepts the prediction as true and tries to influence or change it through preventive means, albeit not through magic. In his attempts to escape the fulfillment of the unfavorable prophecy (M340, M369.2, M370) and get rid of the unpromising hero (H931), he assigns him a task: he arranges for him to be a messenger with a written order for his own execution. This is known as the Uriah letter, a letter of death (K978). This order for the recipient to kill the bearer is a commonly used device of many folktales of Asia and Europe. Unbeknownst to the hero, it puts him in a position of extreme danger, as David did to Uriah the Hitite.[6] The motif of the Uriah letter changed by a helper is the companion to this, as is the case in our tale. On the way to deliver the letter, the hero receives supernatural help from the Prophet Elijah (N847, N810), the most miraculous figure among Jewish "saints" (V295 [Noy]) and a popular feature in folktales in which a character is in desperate need of assistance.[7] While the youth sleeps Elijah emerges as his helper in the tale instead of the robbers featured in the AT type. He changes the message of the letter,

---

3. There are references in the Bible to apparently approved methods of divination. Astrologers or stargazers are mentioned in the prophecy concerning Babylon in Isa. 47:13: *"hoveréi shamayim."*

4. Deut. 18:9–11; Lev. 19:26, 31.

5. See [Noy], 606.

6. See 2 Sam. 11.

7. See the Elijah section in this volume for other examples of the role of the prophet in Judeo-Spanish folk stories. Because of the appearance of Elijah here, this tale could have been included in the Elijah section of this anthology, but its focus was deemed to be more on fate than on the miraculous help of the prophet.

falsifying the order of execution so that the bearer is honored rather than killed (K511). In many universal tales, the helper is often the princess herself, who acts to save her beloved. In effect, the altered letter gives the princess in marriage to the lowly hero she was fated to wed (T121.3.1, L161, K1355), thus bringing about the fulfillment of the prophecy (M391).

The fleeting but effectual presence of Elijah the Prophet introduces another kind of supernatural element in the tale. As we see in a separate section of this anthology, Elijah is gifted with extraordinary knowledge and qualities that enable him to perform miraculous changes and acts. Here as elsewhere, he appears on the scene quietly and unexpectedly as a messenger from heaven, altering the wording of the message in the death letter and thwarting the ill intention of the sender. This is a kind of miracle of a healing nature, to redress the injustice of the intended killing of the innocent bridegroom. By saving the bearer's life, he brings about his fated marriage to the princess (T107 [Noy]), thus fulfilling the divine matchmaking plan (N120.0.1 [Noy], N121+ [Noy]). And then, as is his wont, as soon as his task is accomplished, Elijah vanishes, only the teller and her audience aware of the role he has played.

10

The Three Sayings

Narrated by REBEKA COHEN-ARIEL (1989)

There was a king who had an only daughter, *regalada*.[1] This king would say:

"This daughter of mine, I shall not give her in marriage except to a *prove aní*.[2] And *kare ke* he be so poor that, *afilu*, he wouldn't have anyone to *arremendar*, to mend his clothes."

The daughter would say:

"What's my father saying? Has he gone crazy?"

One day, he put his daughter in the coach and took her for a ride. He said:

"The one about whom she says: '*Maskeniko!* Poor man!' That's the one who will be her fate, her *mazál*!"

She knows nothing of this. They are riding to the city where they sell. They came to an alley, a *kaleja*. There was a beggar there. And it wasn't enough that he was poor, he had no one to sew patches for him. He put up pins to hold his clothes together.

The king's daughter came. She said:

"*Maskeniko!* He doesn't have anyone even, *afilu*, to mend his clothes for him!"

"Get out of the coach!" her father said to her.

---

1. Literally, *regalada* means "given or received as a gift." A child referred to as *regalado* or *regalada* is particularly beloved because he or she is often an only child. *Regalada de su madre* is a common expression meaning "her mother's dearest child."

2. The expression *prove aní* emphasizes the poverty and need of the character. The repetition of the concept of poverty in *prove* (Sp. *pobre*: "poor") and *aní* (H. "poor") creates a particular narrative style.

"Why, father? *Aba?*"

"Get out of the coach, I tell you!"

The *maskenika* got out. Her father said to her:

"Go with him!"

"*Aba,* I'm to go with him? I, the king's daughter?"

"Yes! Go with him! I'm leaving!"

The king pulled away in the carriage and was gone. The daughter said:

"What am I to do?"

She went over to the *aní,* the poor man. She removed a piece of jewelry, and she said to him:

"You are my *mazál.* Go, rent a little room."

He went. He bought himself clothes. He bought beds. And she remained with him for a year on the money, on the *parás* he had. When they were left with almost no *parás,* his wife said to him:

"*Na,* take those *parás* and go, buy me some wool. We'll make a carpet, a *tapét,* to sell."

He went to buy wool. At the city's gate, before entering the *soko,* there is there a *dallál,* a town crier. The *dallál* said to him:

"I have a saying. He who buys it is sorry, and he who doesn't buy it is sorry!"

This one said:

"My wife gave me *parás* to buy wool. Isn't it better if I buy the saying?"

He gave the *parás* to the *dallál* and he bought the saying. The *dallál* said to him:

"Everything has its appeal!"

"*Addió*! Oh, God! Doesn't everyone know that saying?"

"Hey! I already told you: if you buy it you're sorry, and if you don't buy it you're sorry!"

He remained a while at the coffeehouse, the *kavané,* and he returned home in the evening. His wife said to him:

"Where's the wool?"

"I didn't buy it!"

"Why not?"

"I bought a saying!"

"What saying?"

"Everything has its appeal!"

"And you didn't know that?"

"Hey! I didn't know that he would tell me this."

She said to him:

"Fine, it doesn't matter. Tomorrow you'll go back."

The next day, also, she gave him *parás* and said to him:

"You'll buy wool. I want to make a *tapét,* a carpet, to earn some *parás.*"

He went back once more. Once more the *dallál* is there:

"I have a saying. He who buys it is sorry, and he who doesn't buy it is sorry!"

He says:

"Yesterday I bought a saying. I'll buy another one today as well. How bad can it be? Maybe this one will turn out better."

He said to him:

"So, give me the saying!"

The *dallál* said:

"*Kare ke* you concern yourself with the welfare of others more than with your own."

He says:

"Hey, who doesn't know this saying?"

"I already told you: he who buys it is sorry, and he who doesn't buy it is sorry!"

The *maskín* went home. He does not have the courage to speak to his wife. Twice now he hadn't bought the wool.

And on the third day, also, it was the same; he bought the saying:

"To cure an ill, one needs patience. When angry, be patient."

He came home. He told the saying to his wife. His wife said to him:

"*Yalla,* it doesn't matter. Let's forget about this!"

One day, the wife heard that some young men, some merchants, were going on a trip to bring cloth from India. She said:

"I'll send him along. Maybe he'll learn a trade."

She went. She said to the merchants:

"Who is the leader of the merchants who are going to fetch merchandise?"

They said to her:

"*Fulano.* So and so."

She went to find *fulano*. She said to him:

"Look, are you the leader of all of them?"

"Yes."

She said:

"I'll give you a youth. You'll take him along. I'll give him *parás, avál* you must take care of him as you would your own eyes!"

"Sure, why not?"

"Whatever you yourselves buy, let him buy as well."

"Fine."

"*Amá* listen. He'll say: 'The king's daughter is my wife.' Don't answer him."

"Fine."

She gave him *parás*. She gave him a horse, and dry biscuits as food, as they used to give everyone in the old days, to last months and years. And he left with the merchants. Along the way, they all spoke of their wives, and he would say:

"*Addió*! Do you know what? My wife is the king's daughter!"

Amá, they did as she had bid them: they did not answer him.

They journeyed a long way. There was no water left. They are searching for water in the midst of the mountain, and they found a well there. Who will go down to fill up? This one says:

"No."

The other one says:

"Yes."

He says:

"I'll do it."

"You? No! It's impossible. If something should happen to you, who knows what your wife will do to us?"

"I'll go. I'll sign a paper saying that I volunteered to go down into the well to fetch water for you."

He was stubborn, he put up *innát*. And he went down. *Avál,* what?

"You'll give me *parás*!"

From the hundred merchants they were, if he took only a *shilín* from each one, it's one hundred *shilinis*. He took the *parás* and hid them in his saddle-bag, in his *hursh*.

He went down into the well. He filled bucket after bucket for everyone. And he told them to give water to his own horse as well. As he was coming back up, a frog and a lizard appeared. The frog said to him:

"Who is prettier, the dark one or the fair one?"

He recalled the first saying he had bought:

"In this world, everything has its appeal. Some people like them dark and others like them fair."

The frog and the lizard gave him a pomegranate. He took the pomegranate and saw that the grains were small diamonds. He took the *parás* that the merchants had given him and immediately, *pishín,* he put them in the *posta,* in the mail to send to his wife.

They traveled for another two or three months. They want to rest. They came to a city in Iraq, close to Turkey. They dismounted in a field. There they set up the camels, the *hurshes,* and the sacks of food supplies. And they said:

"Who'll go out at night to keep guard? One man is needed for the beginning and another for the end."

"I'll go out!" he said.

"No! Not you! Anybody but you!"

"No," he said. "I'll go out. I am just like everyone else."

Well, the others went for a walk. The partner, the *havér,* who went out with him fell asleep. He kept making the rounds from one end to the other, because he remembered the second saying he had bought.

All of a sudden, a woman came running. She slipped something into the *hursh* of the camel, and she ran away. He ran after her. She ran and he ran! She ran and he ran! He caught up with her, grabbed her by the hair, cut it off with a knife, and she escaped. He made a ball out of the hair, a *top,* and put it away. In the morning, he revealed nothing to the others. He sees *askeres, pulizis,* soldiers, policemen! They are looking around. All of a sudden, they found an infant boy in the *hursh* of the camel, whom that woman had killed and concealed inside.[3]

Maskenikos, the poor merchants! They know nothing. They hadn't even entered the city yet, and *pishín,* they are all in jail! They were there one day. They were there two days. They are weeping:

"We'll give up all the *parás* and go back home! We didn't get to buy anything, but we have had a taste of prison!"

He came. He said:

"Give the *parás* to me!"

"We would give them to you, but what will you do?"

"I'll do whatever I know. But on one condition: you'll give me all the *parás* you have!"

"We'll give you everything!"

After the merchants gave a paper on which it was written that only one of them would speak for all, the king came and he said:

"Very well, take this one."

He said to the king:

"Look, I'll look from house to house for the one whose hair is the color of this hair. The woman whose hair has been sheared, that's the one who killed the child."

Pishín, the *pulizis* went with him from house to house, *amá* they found nothing.

---

3. This episode is reminiscent of the *terafím* (spirit statues) in connection with divination: those that Rachel stole from Laban were small enough to be concealed in a camel saddle (Gen. 31:34).

The king said to him:

"You've walked the entire city already and found nothing!"

He said:

"I want to look in your houses."

"In my houses?"

"Yes, in your houses!"

"Fine! Let them look at all the ladies, all the *hanumes,* in the king's houses!"

And they found that it was the queen herself who had killed the baby boy, borne to the king by his second wife, because she herself had not conceived. And she did not want the boy to become king.

The king came. He said to her:

"You have done this to me? You killed him because he was to become king? Now we'll kill you!'

The young man said to the king:

"Well, I have given you the owner of the hair, now set us all free."

The king released the prisoners, *pishín,* and he said to him:

"Thank you very much! *Todá rabá!*"

The merchants do not know any of this, because he had not told them what had happened. They took the mules, the camels, the horses, to go back.

On their journey, they came once more upon the same well to drink water. He said:

"I'll go down."

"*Bre!* Man, we don't want you to! You've already done so much for us. Someone else will go down."

"No, I'll go down!"

He went down. He gave water to everyone. The camels drank, the horses, everyone. On his way back up, once again the frog and the lizard appeared. They asked him:

"Who is more beautiful? The dark one or the fair one? Tell the truth!"

He said:

"I am telling you that each one has its appeal. The dark one has appeal and the fair one has beauty."

The frog and the lizard clapped their hands and were transformed into a bride and groom. They had been enchanted! They gave him another pomegranate filled with small diamonds, and he came out of the well.

He collected all the *parás,* and he sent them to his wife. The wife became rich, and she opened up a large inn to distribute food to the poor.

The merchants finally came to the city. And he is looking for his house, and he can't find it. The house where he used to live is not there. In the end, he asked someone:

"There was a little room down here. Where is it? And there was a woman: my wife."

They said:

"Oh! Now there is an inn. *Agora* there is a *malón*. Go up these stairs. It belongs to her!"

It was nighttime. She was sleeping. He had left her pregnant, and by the time he returned, his son had grown up and was asleep next to her.

He comes in and he looks. The son said:

"I want water."

To him it looked as if she were lying with another man. He grabbed the knife. He said:

"Ah, I went into the well, I went to jail, and she has a lover?!"

He was about to kill her. All of a sudden he remembered the third saying he had purchased, and he held back. At that moment, the son tells his mother:

"*Ima,* enough sleep already! Wake up!"

He heard "Mother! *Ima!*" He said:

"Can this be my son?"

She said to the boy:

"Ah, you interrupted my dream. I was dreaming that your father had finally returned!"

And he was standing there. He said:

"Oh, I was about to kill you for no reason!"

He threw himself on her. He kissed her. He hugged her. He said:

"We've become very rich!"

His wife and son got up, and they welcomed him. He stared at that big boy. He kissed him and he hugged him. She gave him food. He took a bath and lay down to sleep.

The next day, he looked over the *malón* where many people come and go every day. Any poor person who has no food to eat! Let him come in! Let him eat there! And they will even give him *parás* in his hand!

The king heard that a *malón* had opened up that gives poor people food and *parás*. He said:

"Let's go see who is this Baron of Rothschild who has enough to give out *parás* as well as food to eat!"

He said to his *vizír:*

"Let's go."

They rode on their horses and they came. They saw a large door. They are before a large *malón*. People are going in and out. They eat and they drink. They take *parás* and they say:

"Such a thing there never was in the world!"
The king came. He was dressed in civilian clothes. He said to the *vizír:*
"Let's go in as well!"
They went inside. They ate. They drank. He looks around. It's his own daughter who is telling everyone:
"Have you eaten? Take *parás*! Have you eaten? Take *parás*!"
"I gave her away to one who had not even patches to be mended!" said the king.
The *vizír* came. He said to him:
"Do you see? Whatever God does, man, the *benadám*, does not undo!"
The king said to his daughter:
"Come here! Do you know who I am?"
"Who are you?"
"I'm the king! I'm your father!"
"You used to be my father. Now, I am wealthier than you are. I am wealthy because I give to the poor. You gave me a poor husband, *avál* you didn't know how to give to the poor!"
"*Bemét*," said the king, "whatever God does the *benadám* does not undo!"

COMMENTARY

Interestingly, this narrative, a combined version of AT 923B, *The Princess Who Was Responsible for Her Own Fortune,*[4] and AT 910, *Precepts Bought Or*

---

4. LP, vol. 1, no. 43, p. 142, gives a Judeo-Spanish version of this type that describes a poor woodcutter who struggles daily to support his seven daughters. Commenting on his situation, the queen remarks to the king that a woman is often behind her husband's success or failure. The king misinterprets her statement and banishes her. She moves in with the woodcutter's family and helps the man improve his condition by skillful housekeeping and providing good advice. After he establishes himself as a successful merchant, the woodcutter builds a replica of the king's palace and invites him to a housewarming reception at the suggestion of the exiled queen. The king's curiosity is piqued when he sees the sumptuous house and the special meal prepared by the queen, which includes his own favorite dishes. Recognition and reinstatement of the queen follow. See Haboucha, 418ff. Another Judeo-Spanish parallel appears in Koén-Sarano, *Konsejas,* 141. Parallels from Jewish sources come from Alexander-Noy, no. 11 (Morocco); Babay, *Tovah be-'ad tovah,* no. 8 (Persia); Gaster, *Exempla,* no. 148; Gaster, *Ma'aseh Book,* vol. 1, no. 68; Jason, "Types," 184–85 (*923, *Love Like Salt*); Jason, *Types,* 53; Noy, *Egypt,* no. 48; Noy, *Folktales,* no. 57 (Yemen);

Given Prove Correct,[5] stresses societal values as well as the dual concepts of fate and free will. Once again, it suggests that good luck is not only predestined but also unalterable unless by divine decree. At the same time, the tale points to the obligation of acting generously toward those in need (*gmilút hasadím*).

The narrative illustrates a confrontation between a father and his daughter. It begins when the king abandons his daughter in a marketplace teeming with poverty and destitution. The king as father is a symbolic figure representing patriarchal authority. His intention in casting his daughter out and giving her in marriage to a beggar remains enigmatic. Was he testing her or punishing her? Had she reproached him for letting poverty exist in his reign, as we are led to believe at the conclusion of the tale? Were they at odds about the inevitability of fate and the responsibility for one's kismet? Had she claimed, as in AT 737A*, *Why Have I Nothing?* and in AT 737B*, *The Lucky Wife,* that a lucky woman could help her luckless husband overcome his fate? Or had she disdained a suitable man (P234+ [Noy]) and refused to marry him, as in AT 900, *King Thrushbeard?* This is never clearly elucidated. The archetype, AT 923B, shows the princess claiming to be responsible for her own good fortune. This motif is missing here, albeit made implicit by the teller's obvious support for the heroine against her father.

In folktales, the abandonment of the heroine is often a form of taking her life. When her father casts her out and forces her to marry a beggar (T121.3.1), she is made to live in humble circumstances. The contrast between wealth and poverty (U60) is present. On the surface, our heroine appears passive and helpless. We are not told how she feels when she is thrust out of her royal surroundings, but feelings seldom are verbalized in folktales. Her marriage to the beggar is a test of her patience and fortitude as a wife (W26, H465). As she had not rebelled against her father, likewise she does not rebel against her husband when he behaves foolishly. If her father's intention was to break her

---

Noy, *Libya,* no. 12; Noy, *TEM 1961,* no. 2 (Morocco); Noy, *Tunisia,* n. to no. 32, no. 39; Schwartz, *Elijah's Violin,* 263; *Schwili,* nos. 21, 44; Shenhar and Bar Itzhak, *Bet She'an,* no. 9. Versions from Egypt, Iranian Kurdistan, Iraqi Kurdistan, Morocco, and Tunisia are found in IFA. Also in IFA are versions of *923, *Love Like Salt,* from Afghanistan, Egypt, Iran, Iraq, Israel (Arab, Ashkenazic, Druze, Sephardic), Libya, Morocco, Tunisia, and Yemen. Other traditions are represented in Armistead and Katz, "Soria," nos. 1, 2; Ashliman, *Guide to Folktales,* 190; Chauvin, *Ouvrages arabes,* 2:174, no. 16, 8:180, no. 212; EB, 487–88; Grimm and Grimm, *Tales,* no. 179; Kent, *Turkey,* 74; Thompson and Roberts, *Indic Oral Tales,* 115; Villa, *100 Armenian Tales,* nos. 3, 6; Walker and Uysal, *Tales in Turkey,* 172.

5. See M. Cohen, *'Edot Yisrael,* vol. 3, no. ריל.

pride, she endures poverty and menial work with fortitude as she settles into this unequal arrangement (T121, L113.1.0.1), but she turns out to be the perfect wife, giving up her past life and bearing all her husband's apparent foolishness without complaint. All the while, she explores ways to help him change his luck (N831) and make him earn a living. When she succeeds, her patience is rewarded by his success (Q64). The couple prospers in part because of the heroine's good luck and ingenuity (N145).

At the same time, we see the character of the hero develop. The archetypal figure of the chief protagonist of folktales is one who overcomes a series of trials to arrive at an ideal state. He is distinguished for bold enterprise, courage, and fortitude, and commands the listener's wonder and sympathy. Portrayed as a person in similar conditions of those hearing the tale, he helps the audience disassociate from the familiar and overcome its own difficulties, if only for a moment, to reach a position of success.

At first, the husband is made to look not only destitute but also simple-minded (L111, L123). In what appears to be an absurd move, he wastes precious money buying a penny's worth of wit in the form of three self-evident yet enigmatic sayings rather than spending it on a much-needed practical purchase (J163, J163.1, J163.4), as in AT 910G, *Man Buys a Pennyworth of Wit*. That the precepts turn out to be wise and helpful to him in the end becomes apparent only much later in the tale. Following his wife's initiative, the man embarks on a journey, which is at once a quest and a test. The change of place/change of luck motif is a commonly held belief in Judaism.

The purpose of the hero's journey is for him to achieve greater awareness and wisdom, which causes his inner transformation. He undergoes a form of internal quest that is more than a mere adventure, and he returns to his wife a different man (L123.1, L160). What emerges is an inversion of reality. Not only is he now wealthy, but he has also become wise.

The husband's luck begins to change during his travels when he uses the three counsels purchased in the marketplace (J21, N134, N131.5). Buying wisdom helps the hero acquire the knowledge he lacks, which is not available to him otherwise. Here, the three penny-counsels teach him that tastes vary and differences must be respected, that one must be unselfish and watch over others, and that it is unwise to act when angry and better to deliberate before taking action (J570, J21.2.6).[6] Once he has come to know the "higher truth," he does not forget it and uses it to his advantage, thus achieving self-realization.

---

6. A Judeo-Spanish version of the application of this counsel appears in Koén-Sarano, "La ravia de la nochi déshala para la manyana," in *Saragosa,* p. 81.

In storytelling, heroes often must prove themselves by passing tests. When the husband volunteers to be lowered into a dangerous well, he descends into the underworld and faces death. The external reason for his adventure is the need to test himself. When the hero encounters the supernatural in the well in the form of enchanted animals, it is part of the everyday course of events. In most tales, the ability of animals to converse with humans is taken for granted. Here, they are helpful actors who assist in defeating the bad luck of the hero. He wins their gratitude by remembering one of the purchased counsels and providing an evenhanded response to their question. Frogs and toads are a symbol of the power of water and are a favorite form of transformation in folktales. Witches often transform into toads those who offend them. The pomegranate given to the hero by the grateful animals as a reward is the many-seeded fruit cultivated since ancient times in the Mediterranean region. It is regarded as a symbol of fertility, fecundity, and hope.

When the hero's descent is successful, he is able to achieve what he and his wife set out to attain. Symbolically, his ascent back to daylight signifies renewal and rebirth. When he returns home to the earlier space, this symbolizes his success in overcoming difficulties. His transformation is reinforced even further when he sees a stranger in bed with his wife, thinks it is a lover, and prepares to kill them both (J21.2) but restrains himself (J171+ [Noy]).[7] He thus avoids a rushed judgment and a hasty punishment (J571, J571.4).[8]

---

7. Eccl. 7:9.

8. This motif appears in AT 910B, *The Servant's Good Counsels*. For Judeo-Spanish parallels of this type, see Koén-Sarano, "La pasensia es madre de la sensia"; also "Los tres konsejos," in *Lejendas,* p. 43. This tale gives a version of AT 910B reminiscent of the life story of Rabbi Akiva. In the tale, the king wishes for his only daughter to marry, but she rejects all her suitors. When she reveals her love for a poor student, her parents demand that she give him up or leave the palace. She chooses to marry her beloved and they live happily until he travels to a faraway place in search of more knowledge, leaving her behind for eighteen years. He learns the wisdom of restraint. When he returns, he finds his wife in bed with a young stranger. As he is about to kill them both, he remembers the advice and waits till morning, when he finds out that the youth is his son. Rabbi Akiva himself was a poor, ignorant shepherd betrothed to the daughter of a very wealthy Jerusalemite whose parents drive her out for agreeing to marry him. She had done so, however, on the condition that he would study Jewish law. Eventually he returns to her as a scholar. IFA versions come from Afghanistan, Eastern Europe, Egypt, Iranian Kurdistan, Iraq, Iraqi Kurdistan, Israel (Ashkenazic, Bedouin, Sephardic), Libya, Morocco, Turkey, and

The narrative art of the teller shows itself initially through triple repetition (Z71.1 [Noy]) when the *dallál* recites his enigmatic formula in the marketplace on three consecutive days: "I have a saying: he who buys it is sorry and he who doesn't buy it is sorry" (J171.1). The three precepts bought prove wise during three separate episodes in the tale. For good measure, the teller adds a fourth episode—the second descent of the hero into the well and his second encounter with the enchanted frog and lizard (B178. [Noy], B211.12 [Noy]), which leads to their disenchantment (D700).

In the epilogue, the king approaches his daughter's philanthropic institution without knowing who owns it but equating it sarcastically with a Rothschild enterprise. The Rothschilds were a prominent family of European financiers and philanthropists throughout the nineteenth century. Their name has come to represent the embodiment of privilege and philanthropy,

---

Yemen. Other Jewish parallels can be found in Baharav, *Mi Dor le-Dor*, no. 34 (Iraq), *BJ*, 3:100; bin Gorion, *Mimekor Yisrael*, vol. 3, no. 76; Cheichel, *TEM 1968–1969*, no. 9 (Tunisia); Gaster, *Exempla*, no. 367; Gaster, *Ma'aseh Book*, vol. 2, no. 198; Grunwald, "Motifs," no. 17; Grunwald, *Tales*, no. 15 (AT 507C and AT 910); Jason, "Types," 180; Jason, *Types*, 45; Marcus, *Mabu'a*, no. 9 (Iraqi Kurdistan); Noy, *Hana'ara*, nos. 22, 23, 53, 64 (Iraq); Noy, *Folktales*, nos. 14 (Afghanistan), 46 (Poland); Noy, *Libya*, no. 33; Noy, *Morocco*, no. 69; Noy, *Tunisia*, no. 30; Prov. 4:7, 20:15; Schram, *Jewish Stories*, 81; Schwarzbaum, "Alphonsi," 36, no. 18; *Schwili*, nos. 85, 87; Yehoshua, *Afghanistan*, no. 11. Many parallels appear in non-Jewish sources: Ashliman, *Guide to Folktales*, 185; Basset, *Mille et un contes*, vol. 1, pp. 226–27; Baughman, *England and North America*, 20; Boggs, *Spanish Folktales*, 109; BP, 4:149–50, 343; Briggs, *Dictionary of British Folk-Tales*, pt. A, vol. 2, 504; Bushnaq, *Arab Folktales*, 94 (Iraq); Calvino, *Italian Folktales*, no. 192; Chauvin, *Ouvrages arabes*, 2:126, no. 130, cf. 8:138, no. 136; Chevalier, *Siglo de Oro*, no. 61; Clarkson and Cross, *World Folktales*, no. 53; Clouston, *Popular Tales*, 2:317–21, 491–93; Manuel, *Conde Lucanor*, no. 36; D'Aronco, *Fiabe Toscane*, 102; Dawkins, *Forty-five Stories*, no. 19 (Greece); Dawkins, *Modern Greek Folktales*, no. 75A; Dawkins, *More Greek Folktales*, no. 16; Disaplina Clericalis, 73, no. 18; EB, nos. 204, 256, 307, 308; A. Espinosa, *Cuentos populares*, vol. 1, nos. 63, 64, 65, 66, 67, vol. 2:271–86; A. Espinosa, *Castilla*, no. 28; M. Espinosa, *Folklore of Spain*, 185; *Gesta Romanorum*, nos. 18, 56, 103, 133; T. Hansen, *Types* (Chile, Cuba, Dominican Republic, Puerto Rico); Keller, *Spanish Exempla*, (J21.2, J571); Kent, *Turkey*, 119; Sánchez de Vercial, *Libro de los exenplos*, nos. 219 (148), 414 (362, 363); Paredes, *Mexico*, no. 43; Rael, *Colorado y Nuevo Méjico*, nos. 88, 89, 90, 317, 318, 319, 320, 492; Robe, *Mexican Folktales*, 146; Thompson, *One Hundred Favorite Folktales*, no. 81 (Greece); Thompson and Roberts, *Indic Oral Tales*, 111; Tolstoy, *Fables and Fairy Tales*, 82; Tubach, *Index Exemplorum*, nos. 70, 2879, 4111; Villa, *100 Armenian Tales*, nos. 6, 17.

serving as a symbol of Jewish success, prosperity, influence, and giving (for the benefit of Jews and non-Jews alike). Baron Jacob Rothschild opened a general hospital in Paris in 1852; thus the reference in our tale.

Finally, the female narrator never condemns the king for his role in the tale, but it is clear that she identifies with the heroine. She weaves her narrative to prove that the father is so mistaken that in the end he must be brought down. Showing him as blind to the true worth of his daughter, from the beginning of the tale to the end, she does not develop his character fully. The only change that occurs in him is that he is brought to acknowledge that fate is predestined and that no human action has the power to change it. The father-daughter conflict is never resolved (P234). When they finally meet again, the daughter rejects her haughty and unbending father, both as a ruler and as a parent, reproaching him, not for having abandoned her but for his lack of humanitarian concern for the poor and for his lack of generosity toward his subjects. These traits mark him as one who disregards the societal value of helping the poor. This is the clear social message of the tale.

11

The Man without *Mazál*

Narrated by ESTER VENTURA (1992)

There was a man who was very, very poor. He had to work day and night to sustain himself alone. He wasn't even married! And what was his work? He carded cotton.

One night, he was working and saying:

"I'm poor and I have no *mazál*! I'm poor and I have no *mazál*!"

Just on that day, the king decided, *se dechizó,* to go out for a walk. *Amá* he was dressed in civilian clothes, and he went out with his *vizír*. They passed nearby and saw that this man is muttering and working, muttering and working.

"What can be the matter with this man?" the king said to the *vizír*. "Come, we'll go in and see."

The two of them went inside. The man greeted them and said to them:

"May your coming be in good tidings!"

They sat down. The king said to him:

"What are you doing? What are you saying?"

The man said:

"What shall I tell you? I am saying that I have no *mazál*. I am a man who works day and night. *Mazál* to earn a little more, I don't have. It's just enough to eat!"

The king said to him:

"Do you have anything to drink?"

This tale appears in Judeo-Spanish in Koén-Sarano, *Saragosa,* 127.

"Nothing. I have nothing in the house!"

The king sat down for a while. He saw that, in truth, *bemét,* he is poor. He got up and left. The next day, he went to his kitchen. He told them:

"You are going to make a *tifsín* of *baklabá,* a tray of *baklabá*.[1] In the middle, you'll put gold pounds, gold liras," he said. "And you'll send it to this man. Let him eat, let him find the liras, and let him be merry!"

In the morning, they made it for him. Around noon, they knocked on his door. They said to him:

"The king sent you this."

Agora, that night, the king had not revealed that he was the king.

"The king?" said the man. "What?! How come?"

They said to him:

"The king wanted to send you this."

When he saw the *tifsín* of *baklabá,* he, by himself there, he says:

"*Addió!* What am I going to do with this *tifsín* of *baklabá?* I am not going to be able to eat it all! *Amá,* if I cut it, *kare ke* I eat it."

He went to one who was a *baklabadjí,* a seller of *baklabá*. He sold it to him and he returned home.

At night, the king again went out with the *vizír.* He knocked on the man's door. He went in again. He said to him:

"How are you?"

"As always."

The king said to him:

"Don't you have anything sweet?"

"I have nothing," the man said. "I will tell you only," he said, "that the king sent me a *tifsín* of *baklabá. Agora,* what am I to do with this *tifsín* of *baklabá?* I went, I sold it," he said, "and bought myself something to eat."

The king struck his forehead with his hands and said:

"*Bemét* this man has no *mazál.*"

He got up. He left. The next day he told his kitchen staff:

"*Agora* you'll make a *tifsín* of *kadayíf*.[2] And, *yené,*" he said, "inside the *kadayifes,* you'll put gold liras."

---

1. *Baklavá* is a Turkish sweet, a delicacy prepared with flaky fillo dough. It is usually filled with chopped walnuts or pistachio nuts and soaked in honeyed syrup, and then cut in lozenges.

2. *Kadayíf* is a different kind of Middle Eastern sweet, also honey-drenched but made of shredded wheat filled with custard or pistachio nuts. Both *baklavá* and *kadayíf* are usually displayed in large circular trays in the marketplace and sold by the piece.

That one, when he saw this again, what is he going to do? Again, he took it and went and sold it.

At night, the king again went back to his house. He said to him:

"Don't you have anything to offer us?"

The man said:

"*Na,* today the king sent me a *tifsín* of *kadayíf.* What am I to do with it?" he said. "I went, I sold it."

The king said:

"It is that he has no *mazál,* and that he is a little stupid, a little *tipésh*!"

The next morning, the king said:

"*Agora* you'll go, you'll bring this man back here. And here," he said, "take him to my treasure vault; put a shovel in his hand and a sack. Let him fill the sack with any *karár,* any amount, of liras he wants. Only in this manner," he said, "will his *mazál* change."

They went. They got him. They said to him:

"The king wants you."

He almost died of fright, of *sar.* They said to him:

"Don't be frightened. The king will not do anything to you. Just come along."

They brought him there. They put a shovel in his hand. Let him fill up as much as he wishes. That unlucky one, the *dezmazalado,* rather than hold the shovel this way, he held it backward. He can't even scoop up a single lira!

An hour went by, two, three. The king said:

"So, what has he done?"

They said to him:

"He hasn't scooped up a single lira yet!"

"Why not?"

"He is holding the shovel backward."

"*Agora,*" said the king. "Take a sack, stuff him inside, and throw him into the sea!"

Commentary

This narrative is another typical example of Jewish lore that stresses the problems of inevitable fate. In essence, it underscores that we do not know how the rich become rich or why the poor remain poor. The main concept here is that events surrounding the central character are predestined and that fate and the divine plan play an important role in his life.

Tales of unchangeable luck are universally popular. AT 947A, *Bad Luck Cannot Be Arrested*, describes a rich man leaving money for a poor man, but the latter closes his eyes and fails to see it.³ Other related types are AT 745A, AT 841, and AT 842. In all three, the role of destiny is central. In AT 745A, *The Predestined Treasure,* the treasure always finds its way to the man for whom it was destined, whether it is hidden inside a hollow tree or baked within a loaf.⁴ In AT 841, *One Beggar Trusts God, the Other the King,* the king gives each man a loaf of bread, but the loaf of the second beggar is filled with gold. Not knowing the nature of the loaves, the beggars exchange them.⁵ Finally, in AT 842, *The Man Who Kicked Aside Riches,* a man who practices austerity for many years asks the gods for wealth in reward. The gods grant the request in the form of a pot of gold that is placed in the man's way. On the way home, the man decides

---

3. A Judeo-Spanish variant of this type appears in Moscona, *Sipurei Sefarad*, 77, in which, to test his poor brother's luck, a rich man places a purse full of money on the path the other is sure to follow on his way home. On that day, however, the brother decides to walk with his eyes closed, trying to determine whether he is able to find his way without looking. When the rich man observes with his own eyes how his brother misses seeing the purse, he concludes that he must be luckless and provides him with a secure income. Another Judeo-Spanish version of this tale of fate, in which poverty cannot be averted despite repeated efforts, appears in Koén-Sarano, *Konsejas,* 203. IFA versions originate from Bukhara, Iran, Iraq, Tunisia, and Yemen. IFA versions of a similar type, AT 947A*, *Bad Luck Refuses to Desert a Man,* were collected from Eastern Europe, Iraq, Israel (Druze, Sephardic), Turkey, and Yemen. Other Jewish parallels can be found in Alexander-Noy, no. 46 (Salonica); Alexander-Romero, *Maimónides,* nos. 74 (Iraq), 85 (Bukhara), also 259–60, 262; Baharav, *Ashkelon,* no. 46 (Turkish Kurdistan, AT 947A*); Frankel, *Classic Tales,* no. 195; Jason, "Types," 192; Jason, *Types,* 61 (AT 947A*); Noy, *Folktales,* nos. 10 (Iraq), 34 (Afghanistan, AT 841), 67 (Turkey, AT 841); Noy, *Tunisia,* nos. 64, 67; Sabar, *Kurdistani Jews,* 148; Schwarzbaum, *Studies,* 77, 259–61, 264, 266–67. For sources from other traditions, see Boggs, *Spanish Folktales* (*948); Bushnaq, *Arab Folktales,* 286 (Iraq); Chevalier, *Siglo de Oro,* no. 72; Dawkins, *Modern Greek Folktales,* no. 79A; EB, no. 131; Megas, *Folktales of Greece,* no. 48; Thompson and Roberts, *Indic Oral Tales,* 102.

4. Versions of this type appear in Gaster, *Exempla,* no. 414; Shram, *Jewish Stories,* no. 135; Shenhar and Bar Itzhak, *Bet She'an,* no. 6; Tubach, *Index Exemplorum,* no. 3613; *Gesta Romanorum,* no. 109; Briggs, *Dictionary of British Folk-Tales,* pt. B, vol. 2, 268; Boccaccio, *Decameron,* 10:1.

5. For Jewish parallels, see Frankel, *Classic Tales,* no. 174; Hanauer, *Holy Land,* 120; Noy, *Folktales,* nos. 34, 67; Pascual Recuero, *Cuentos sefardíes,* no. 64 (Mitrani). For non-Jewish variants, see Basset, *Mille et un contes,* vol. 3, no. 323; Dawkins, *Forty-five Stories,* no. 26; Dawkins, *Modern Greek Folktales,* no. 81; Laoust, *Contes berbères,* vol. 2, no. 64; Lorimer and Lorimer, *Persian,* no. 55; Robe, *Mexican Folktales,* 133; Thompson and Roberts, *Indic Oral Tales,* 102; Tubach, *Index Exemplorum,* no. 703.

to close his eyes to feel how a blind man feels when he walks. When he encounters the pot of gold, he kicks it aside, thinking that it is a stone.[6]

It is not uncommon among the Sephardic poor to believe that only God decides one's fate before birth (N121). If God earmarks for one no more than the bare minimum, even if one moves heaven and earth to increase one's earnings the effort will not be successful. The destitute man in our tale works day and night and barely earns enough money to meet his basic needs. His workaday plod seems hopeless. As a result, it is inevitable for him to conclude that he is purely and simply *dezmazalado,* an unfortunate man born without *mazál.* The teller, who points out that the man is not lucky enough even to be married, stresses the unlucky stars of her main character even further.

The king, on the other hand, refuses to accept the premise of predestination. When he goes out at night in disguise to observe his subjects (P14.19) and discovers the plight of the cotton-carder, he sets himself up as helper in competition with God, thinking that he is powerful enough to arrange for a change of luck, albeit anonymously (N836). Rather than help the man directly, he goes to various lengths to lead him to participate in the changing of his own luck (N131). The king's remedies are reminiscent of Marie Antoinette's memorable line: "Let them eat cake," except that here the cakes are delicious Turkish sweets, and they are filled with gold. When the unlucky man unwittingly gives the money away (N351), not once but twice, it is proof that he has no luck indeed.

In the end, when the king's schemes repeatedly fail and the man's bad luck persists (N250), the monarch is forced to realize that no amount of effort will lead to a change in the man's living conditions. He continues to deny the inexorableness of fate (N101), however. Rather than acknowledge that the man is simply powerless to escape God's decree and should not attempt to do so, he comes up with another explanation, with the teller's complicity. If all his plans have failed, it must be because the man is too stupid to recognize the opportunities afforded him. This indirectly alludes to the well-known dispute over which is more powerful, luck or intelligence (N141).

With the use of AT 1572F*, *Turning the Shovel Backwards,* our tale of fate ends in a humorous fashion, perhaps to provide relief and diffuse the tension and frustration caused by the dire lack of *mazál* or perhaps because the teller herself does not believe in the immutability of fate. What is described in the end is the caricature of the dumb, dim-witted man who never catches on because he is not really meant to do so. He becomes Everyman.

---

6. See M. Cohen, *'Edot Israel,* vol. 2, no. קב; Thompson and Roberts, *Indic Oral Tales,* 102.

12

What Is Written in the Sky One Cannot *Enfasar*

Narrated by KOHAVA PIVIS (1992)

There was once a very rich sultan. One day, when he went out hunting, while looking in the distance, he suddenly saw something like a flame on the mountain. And from this flame, letters began to be written in the sky. The sultan looks on, very curious. What could that be?

It was written so:

"What is written under the sky one can *enfasar,* one can wipe out. What is written in heaven one cannot *enfasar.*"

The sultan said:

"This is foolishness!"

And he went home with his guards.

This sultan had an only daughter, very beautiful. When this daughter turned eighteen, the sultan summoned his soothsayers. Let them consult the stars. And he said to them:

"Find out for me who will be my daughter's fate, her *mazál.*"

The soothsayers left and returned three days later. *Ma* they didn't want to speak.

"Speak up!" the sultan said to them. "Who will be my daughter's bridegroom?"

"You speak!" said one of them.

"No, you do it!" said the other.

"Speak up, *bre?!*" said the sultan.

"We don't want to speak," they said.

"Why not?" said the sultan.

In the end, the oldest one came. He said:

"Look, sultan of ours, we don't know what to tell you. We saw in the heavens that your daughter's bridegroom is the black youth, the *negrito,* who works as a *gizandón,* a cook, in your kitchen, in your *mutbáh.*"

"What?!" said the sultan. "There must be some mistake here! I asked who my daughter shall marry!!"

"No, lord king. We have looked it up again and again! And this is what we saw. What can we do about it?"

Very upset, the sultan dismissed them from the chamber, and he summoned the *vizír.* He said to him:

"Look, this is what the soothsayers have told me. *Agora* what shall I do? What's the solution? The *charé?*"

"Look," the *vizír* said to him, "there is one and only *charé:* let them take this *negrito.* Let them take him to the countryside. Let them kill him and let's be done with it. There will be neither wedding nor anything else!"

The king's guards went. They picked up the *negrito* from the kitchen, and they took him to the countryside to kill him. The *negrito* says:

"What do you want from me? What have I done? I haven't done anything! I'm no thief!"

"This is the sultan's order," they said to him. "We have no choice."

They took him to the countryside. The *negrito* said to them:

"Look, leave me here, far away from the city. I'll run away, and you tell the sultan that you have killed me."

"Fine!"

The guards felt sorry for the poor youth. They said to him:

"Run far, far away! Don't come back to the city! Let us not see you! Otherwise, we'll be the ones they'll kill!"

The *gizandón* ran away. And the guards slaughtered a goat, took a shirt, soaked it in its blood, and took it to the sultan, saying:

"Here, we have killed him!"

The sultan was feeling calmer *agora.*

Time passed. The *negrito* is walking. The sun is beating on his head. He is in a field, from here to there, like the *midbár,* the Sahara Desert! His mouth is dry, and he is about to faint. He sees a flock of black storks, of black *laylekes,* flying. They come down on the other side of a mountain, and five minutes later, they rise up again, white.

"What's that?!" the *negrito* said. "It looks like I am dizzy from the sun."

He took another look, and he saw another flock of black *laylekes* that turned white. He went in that direction, and suddenly he sees a lake, a *havúz*. This is where the *laylekes* had gone in and turned white. He said:

"I'll go in myself, and maybe I'll turn white!"

He removed his clothes *presto,* he went into the water and felt refreshed. When he came out, he looked at his hand. It had turned white!

"*Addió*!" he said. "How marvelous!"

Amá he had forgotten to take off the sash, the *kushák*, he had, rolled many times there, around his waist, around his *bel*. He said:

"*Agora,* I'm afraid that, if I go back into the water, this marvel which happened to me will disappear. *Ayde,* nobody will notice it under the clothes!"

He put his clothes back on and he left. He came upon a palm tree in the middle of the place. He lay down under it. He was tired, and, what with the fright he had experienced earlier, he fell asleep. Suddenly, he hears.... Two men are talking. One says to the other:

"Here, we'll put it here!"

"No! No!" said the other, "here, we'll hide it here!"

"No, here! Here is a good place!" said the first.

After a while, the youth heard: Dippity clop! Dippity clop! Dippity clop! Two horses drawing away! He got up. He went behind the trees. He looks down. There is a hole in the ground that they have just dug up. He removed the earth and is looking there. There is a small box filled with jewels! These were thieves who had stolen an extraordinary treasure. They had put it there, and they had run away!

He said:

"*Agora* I have a treasure, and I am already white. I'll go back to the city and, there, I'll see my fortune, my *mazál*. Where else shall I go? I know no one. There, it is closer."

And he went back to the city of the sultan. What did he do? He opened up a *butika* of jewels, a jewelry store. And, there, he put up some jewels, some *bijús*—some brooches, some *agrafes;* some earrings, some *orojales;* some pearls—the like of which no eyes had ever beheld.

Agora, the sultan's daughter had friends. While strolling in the market, the *shuk,* those friends saw a new shop, a new *butika*. They went in and they are seeing some beautiful things! They shopped. *Presto,* they came to the sultan's daughter and told her all about it. They said to her:

"Look, there is a new *butika*. There are there some necklaces, some *koliés,* some *orojales* such as you've never seen! Even you, who are the sultan's daughter! You have countless jewels, *amá* there, really, there are some extraordinary things!"

Well, the sultan's daughter also went there. And she is looking. And she began going there one day.... She went back a second day.... And the young man is handsome. He is no longer *negrito,* he is white! And he has things worth millions!

In the end, she fell in love. She went to the sultan. She said to him:

"I want to get married."

"You want to get married?" her father said to her. "Fine. To whom?"

"To a jewelry merchant."

"What?! We want to arrange your marriage to the son of the king of Kush, to the son of the king of India, of Japan! You want to marry a merchant?!"

"No, father, you'll see him! He is wealthy! He is very handsome!"

The father won't hear of it. She began a fast, a *taanít,* and she refuses to eat. She started to take ill. The sultan saw that he might lose his daughter. And he has only one! What can he do? He said:

"Well, we'll see him."

When the youth heard that, he came with more jewels. The sultan had no choice, and he married them. There was a large and beautiful wedding, and the sultan gave them a palace so they can live near him.

After the wedding, a week went by, two, and the two of them are very much in love. One evening, while the husband is washing himself, he said to his wife:

"Come, scrub my back."

She came. She is scrubbing his back. Suddenly, she sees that he has a black mark around his *bel.* She said to him:

"What is this mark you have here?"

"Oh," he said to her, "this is a birthmark."

"A birthmark?" she said to him. "It can't be! A birthmark can be a small *nishán, ma* the entire *bel,* black? This is not a birthmark!"

The first night, he refused to tell her.... The second night, he refused to tell her.... The sultan's daughter said to him:

"You don't love me very much! *Kare* that you tell me what it is!"

And she refused to make love to him. The youth cannot stand it. How can he not be with his wife? After three nights, he broke, and he told her the truth: he told her that he had been the *gizandón* in the sultan's kitchen!

She went and told her father, and the sultan remembered those *flamas,* those flaming letters he had seen in the sky, while he was hunting, where it was written that what is written under the sky one can *enfasar, ma* what is written in heaven one cannot *enfasar.*

Commentary

A variant of AT 930, *The Prophecy,* this tale of fate illustrates and reinforces the belief that marriage is decreed in heaven (T107 [Noy]) and that the divine decree cannot be revoked.[1] It serves to show not only that man cannot escape God's will but also that it is in vain that he should try to do so. The term *mazál* used in this tale means "luck" or "destiny." Here, the "luck" referred to is the "intended" or fated husband. Popular belief among many Sephardic Jews is that whatever happens in life is preordained by divine foreknowledge and eventually comes about through a long chain of cause and effect.[2] Clearly, the teller and her society put faith in the belief that marriages decreed in heaven cannot be evaded (M369.2+ [Noy], N120.0.1 [Noy]). This is not altogether different from the assertion prevalent in popular universal tales of prophecy.

Our narrative follows the basic outline of the predestination types: prophecy, attempt to evade its fulfillment, exposure of undesirable intended, compassionate executioner, return home, marriage to destined mate, and recognition by parents of the inevitability of fate. Motif T53.4 is a predominant Jewish motif depicting the Almighty occupied with matchmaking (N121+ [Noy]). While "a match made in heaven" is a popularly used pronouncement among Sephardic Jews, it is also a common folk motif in non-Jewish tales as well as a widely accepted universal axiom. Other salient popular motifs in this narrative include lovesickness (T24.1) and the fulfillment of the prophecy (M391).

Astrology, or divination from the behavior of heavenly bodies, is one of the earliest of all sciences (D1311+ [Noy]). Stars have long been regarded as omens, and here the king draws upon his royal seers' stargazing skills to find out what the future holds for his daughter (M302.4 [Noy], P420+ [Noy], D1712 [Noy]). When they discover the unpleasant truth of her ill-fated match, they fear revealing it to the king and try to withhold it, dreading his anger (J815). He does not kill the bearers of bad news, however, despite their affirmation of the infallibility of signs and their interpretation. Instead, he does what other royal fathers do in folktales when faced with such forewarning. When he learns that the princess is fated to marry a lowly black youth, he attempts to get rid of him. Predictably, the compassionate executioners charged with killing the innocent youth do not do the king's bidding. They

---

1. See tale 9 in this section for parallels of AT 930.
2. God making things occur is depicted as early as in the Talmudic-Midrashic tale of the matron and Rabbi Yossi ben Halafta.

spare his life, let him escape, and smear the blood of an animal on a shirt as proof of his execution (K512.1). This is another widely used motif.

Unlike the teller and her audience, who seem to accept the inevitability of fate, the king does not believe that everything is preordained. He goes to great lengths to foil the unfavorable prediction (M340). His attempts to escape its fulfillment are in vain (M370), however, as his efforts are inevitably frustrated by the divine plan. When he is finally confronted with the fulfilled prediction, he recalls the supernatural warning in the sky he had previously dismissed and acknowledges the inexorability of destiny. This is the teller's way of reinforcing the intended message of the narrative. In the manner of tales of fate, the decree of fortune comes true as the story reaches its close. The father is in no way singled out for reproach as an unbeliever, yet the teller is satisfied that by conceding that his schemes were thwarted, he finally realizes that it was because they went against the divine plan.

Confrontation in the tale appears at several levels: between the king and fate, and the king loses; between the king and his predestined son-in-law, and the king loses again; and finally between the king and his daughter, and, once again, the king loses. The tale is set against a backdrop of different economic backgrounds and of race. In the eyes of the king, not only is the fated bridegroom an unsuitable choice for the princess because he is nothing but a lowly cook but also because he is a black man. Dark people traditionally play the role of villains and traitors in universal folklore (A1614.1 [Noy], A1614.1+ [Noy]), as Ham did in Noah's ark, for which he was cursed to become a black man.[3] The lower status of the black youth is reinforced in his self-image. When he finds out that the color of his skin has lightened by dipping his body into a magic lake (D921, F1082), he is overjoyed. "How marvelous!" he exclaims. This element of societal prejudice is diffused, however, when the king resists his daughter's desire to marry a rich white merchant (P431 [Noy]) and reveals that he was seeking to arrange her marriage to one of several kings, including the king of Cush. Cush is the ancient kingdom in northeast Africa, named Cush by the Egyptians of the Pharos and Nubia by the Greeks. Its inhabitants are dark-skinned.

Magic appears in the tale to counter the king's plot and improve the hero's situation. The magical elements of the tale are pivotal. The king's supernatural vision of the letters in the sky at the beginning of the tale is a heavenly sign that augurs the future. His failure to grasp the significance of the message that what is written in heaven is irreversible sets the stage for the development of

---

3. Midrashim; Sanhedrin 108b.

the plot. Later, the divine plan leads the hero to the magic water that will transform him into a white man (D30, D562.1) and to the accidental discovery of the treasure (N630, N455) that will facilitate his meeting with the princess and help win her heart. Chance here is obviously the result of Providence, which facilitates the realization of the prophecy. The transforming lake (F713) is in a realm beyond the natural one, a place where a mysterious occurrence—transformation to another race—takes place. It is reached by means of a long and painful voyage the hero is forced to undertake and becomes accessible by luck and as a way out of a dangerous situation. The outcome—a jewelry store—features a traditional and well-seasoned profession among Sephardic Jews.

In the end, while the lowly hero indeed marries his predestined princess (T121.3.1), the blood relationship of father and daughter (P234) is depicted as a stronger bond than the newly created one of husband and wife (P210), despite the sexual bond between them. The bride tests her new husband's love by withholding herself from him for three consecutive nights. When his lust overpowers his determination and he finally reveals the truth to her about his racial and social origins, she immediately betrays his confidence and discloses his secret to her father. This illustrates—perhaps unintentionally—a well-seasoned counsel: "Do not tell a secret to a woman" (J21.22). However, the focus here is not on the wife's inability to keep the secret but on the reaffirmation of God's omniscience and the immutability of fate, for the benefit of king and listeners alike. The teller and her tale are reconciled to the workings of destiny.

PART THREE

Tales of Elijah the Prophet

Probably the most beloved figure in Jewish folklore, the Prophet Elijah—or as he is popularly known, Eliau Anaví—performs miracles in folktales in mysterious, unexplained, extraordinary ways. He is seen as having the authority of God behind him.

Who is Elijah, and what is the source of the authority that underlies his words and deeds and makes them so powerful? We learn Elijah's story from the Old Testament. Known as the Tishbite, he is a biblical prophet of the kingdom of Israel believed to have lived under Kings Ahab and Ahaziah in the ninth century BCE. While we know little about his ancestry and early history, we are told that he incurred the anger of King Ahab and his Queen Jezebel when he threatened Israel with years of drought as punishment for its sins. When his prediction came true and a famine occurred, the prophet sought refuge on the banks of a brook, where ravens miraculously fed him with bread and flesh.[1]

One of the miracles attributed to Elijah is the restoration of life to the child of his hostess.[2] Also, in a contest with the priests of Baal who repeatedly and in vain summoned their god on Mt. Carmel, God answered the prophet by sending fire from heaven.[3] Another Elijah wonder is his miraculous translation from earth (he was conveyed to heaven without having died). Upon being forewarned of the forthcoming end of his life, he anointed Elisha as a prophet in his place by casting his mantle on him.[4] He then crossed the Jordan and ascended to heaven, without dying, in a chariot of fire carried away by a whirlwind.[5]

These astonishing events foster the notion that the prophet is a frequent and willing messenger between heaven and earth and that he travels easily back and forth. The character of Elijah in Jewish folklore emerges from such notions. His traditional depiction is that of a supernatural being who possesses extraordinary knowledge and qualities and who provides hope for social justice. As a legendary figure, he mediates between God and humanity and attends to important social issues. He is popularly endowed with moral prominence and believed to come to earth to help threatened Jewish communities in hostile surroundings, to rescue individuals in distress, and to bridge the gap of social inequality. These abilities enable him to perform miraculous acts and to rule over nature. Worshiped as the Angel of the Covenant, he is believed also to be present at each act of circumcision.

This favorite hero occupies a prominent place in Judeo-Spanish folk narratives. He is portrayed principally as an idealist upholding the values of community, social responsibility, justice, and humanity. In many tales, he suddenly appears incognito as a heavenly emissary bearing the appearance of a regular person. He displays extraordinary knowledge and qualities, accomplishing supernatural changes and transformations, fighting against social injustice, and responding to the cry of the dejected, the poor, and the unjustly treated. He attempts to right wrongs by rewarding the poor, particularly those who are hospitable and kind. He acts as provider for those in need, rewards positive social interaction, and does not hesitate to punish the proud, the unfair, and those who violate norms. As a wondrous messenger from God, he performs supernatural deeds and is accessible only to deserving mortals through good fortune. As soon as his work is completed, he disappears, as if by a miracle.

As can be seen in the tales included here, Elijah displays godly attributes, including divine omniscience. As God knows the future,[6] so is Elijah inextricably connected with foreknowledge. He also tests and heals. Although the tales ignore notions of natural law and are set in neither time nor place, the realistic setting is ever present in them. In one tale, Elijah is gifted with the ability to ward off the Angel of Death and saves a rich man from an untimely demise by warning him that only good deeds and charity can annul the severe decree of his imminent death. He also teaches him to put his faith in God as provider, showing him how the poor place their hopes for the morrow in the Almighty.

He sees into the heart of a poor, simple-minded Jew and acts as the guardian angel of an unlearned but worthy man, providing him with instant religious knowledge and the courage to become successful. He protects a newborn Jewish child and meets expectations by playing a role at the circumcision ceremony. At the same time, he does not shy away from teaching the infant's grandmother the power of kindness through fear and humiliation. Finally, he is depicted as a healing agent who performs miracles such as curing the blind or blessing the barren with fertility. When a pious and worthy individual needs consolation, Elijah reveals himself[7] and provides the blind, destitute, and childless man with the fulfillment of a single wish to cure all his ills at once. In tale 9, he appears unexpectedly to change the letter of execution carried by the hero and thus quietly saves him from certain death.[8]

Elijah thus often takes the place of the supernatural helpers and fairies that typically turn up in universal narratives. The marvelous elements occur after an unexpected alteration of reality takes place—a miracle, a privilege—which favors a particular individual while extending the limits of reality. To believe in these extraordinary occurrences and allow the supernatural to flow freely out of reality requires faith in the prophet's intervention. This is what takes place because Elijah has gained a hold on Jewish imagination, being idealized and invested with a charm that stirs the heart and mind. It seems perfectly natural that miraculous events are accepted as valid.

In many respects, Elijah tales are religious stories with anonymous rewards and punishments. They deal with conflicts and their resolution, vital problems of the individual and society that are solved by the prophet's sacred powers to the benefit and stability of the existing social order. They are culture-specific and display a Judaism that emphasizes ethical behavior and faith in divine providence. Elijah's appearance and role are clearly established in Jewish consciousness. He is real, plausible, and easily acknowledged within the semi-Jewish universe of the tales where he performs his meaningful supernatural deeds. His actions are at once extraordinary and natural because they are linked to the characters' own actions: cause and effect. More often than not, tellers and audience hold them as true. They never register the awareness that these miraculous actions are marvelous, unexplainable, and strange. They do not doubt that they are possible as a result of interference by Elijah. The pre-existing faith is confirmed by the tales. These tales are not told to create this faith, but to confirm and strengthen it.

Notes

1. 1 Kings 17:1–6.
2. 1 Kings 17:17–24.
3. 1 Kings 18:19–39.
4. 1 Kings 19:19.
5. 2 Kings 2:7–12.
6. Sanhedrin 90b.
7. *Gilui Eliyahu* is Elijah's revelation. Viewed as a gift, it occurs rarely and only to highly deserving individuals.
8. Tale 9 is not included among the Elijah tales because it is predominantly a tale of predestination. Elijah's role, albeit important to the development of the story, takes second place to the crucial emphasis on fate.

13

Eliau Anaví and the *Gevír*

Narrated by YAAKOV ELAZAR (1991)

There was once a rich man in Yerushalayim who, at the onset of winter, went and bought many food provisions for a rainy day. One night, sleep eluded him, and he was unable to sleep because he saw that he was missing a few flasks of oil.

The next day, Eliau Anaví appeared to him in human form, and he said to him:

"Come with me."

And he took him to the neighborhood, the *kartié*, of the poor. He knocked on a door; a woman came out. Eliau Anaví said to her:

"Sultana, do you have anything to eat today?"

She said to him:

"Blessed be God! Blessed be the *Dió!* We have a little bit of bread and a little bit of lentils!"

"And what do you have for tomorrow?"

"For tomorrow I have nothing; *avál* let's hope that, with God's help, *bezrát Ashém,* tomorrow my husband will bring home something."

Eliau Anaví left Sultana. He went to another house. He knocked on the door and called out:

"Malkuna, what did you have for dinner tonight?"

"A little bit of zucchini."

"And what do you have for tomorrow?"

"Tomorrow, the *Dió* is great!"

Eliau Anaví took the rich man to several houses, and the answers were always the same. He said to the rich man:

"Mister *Gevír,* do you see how people live? They have nothing to eat for the next day, and you, you prepared yourself for the entire winter! You were upset. You felt *sehorá* because you are missing a few flasks of oil! You should know that you have been marked from above as someone about to die. *Agora,* if you want to save yourself, all the food provisions you have at home, go and distribute them to the poor. It's possible that, by doing this, the decree, the *gezerá,* of your death, will be annulled."

Hearing this, the rich man went. He distributed everything to the poor. The man who had been with him disappeared; and he knew that it was Eliau Anaví who had saved him from death.

Commentary

Contrasting wealth and poverty (U60), this religious narrative appears to have no exact equivalent in universal folktale classifications but falls under the Jewish oicotype IFA 934*F, *Charity Saves from Death.* It is one of countless Jewish stories that contrast the rich and the poor for a didactic purpose. The contrast here is between the poor, who are shown to have faith in God because they have no other hope, and the rich, who suffer from unnecessary worries coupled with a certain lack of charity, which their wealth seems to invite.[1]

---

1. This tale was published in Koén-Sarano, "El gevir," in *Lejendas,* 159, in Judeo-Spanish and Hebrew translation. For another Judeo-Spanish version that highlights the need to put one's faith in God, refer to Shahar, "La konfiensa en el Dio," 41. In that tale, a rich but unhappy man seeks a destitute person on whom to bestow charity. When he finds someone he thinks has no hope left in the world, the beggar rejects his charity, proclaiming his faith that God will help him. Later, the rich man himself becomes a beggar, and the governor who saves him reveals himself as the former destitute. The ultimate lesson is that one must place one's faith in God. Other Judeo-Spanish analogues of the type illustrating how charity saves one from death may be found in LP, vol. 2, no. 29, p. 101, "La limosna" (Tetuán) and KS, "La sedaká abalda la gezerá," ("Mas saven los muertos ke los bivos"), 227; see Haboucha, 457–59. Jewish versions of our tale appear in Ausubel, *Jewish Folklore,* 125; BJ, 2:260–62, 356–57, 368; bin Gorion, *Mimekor Yisrael,* vol. 3, no. 36; Frankel, *Classic Tales,* no. 173; Gaster, *Exempla,* nos. 314, 318, 384, 414; Gaster, *Ma'aseh Book,* vol. 2, no. 189; Ginzberg, *Legends,* 4:169–71; Kagan, *TEM 1964,* no. 10 (Morocco); Marcus, *Mabu'a,* no. 35; Mizrahi, *Be-yeshishim khokhma,* no. 7 (Iran); Noy, *Egypt,* no. 5; Noy, *Folktales,* no. 6 (Iran); Noy, *Morocco,* nos. 16, 39; Schwili, no. 76; Noy, *TEM 1965,* no. 3; Noy, *TEM 1976–77,* no. 4. Non-Jewish parallels are found in Boccaccio, *Decameron,* 10:1; Manuel, *Conde Lucanor,* no. 51, *Gesta Romanorum,* no. 109; Tubach, *Index Exemplorum,* no. 3015.

Indirectly, the tale also reproves the rich man for not living up to his moral responsibility toward the poor in his community. The supernatural function of the tale is personified by Elijah, around whom the tale evolves.

As the most miraculous figure among Jewish "saints" in Jewish folklore (V295 [Noy]), Elijah appears here incognito as a guide and a teacher (K1811.3+ [Noy]). While he performs no miracles, he is shown to be God's messenger and to possess extraordinary knowledge of a hidden event: the forthcoming demise of the rich man (D1810, D1812, V223). This highlights the only supernatural aspect of the tale. Elijah's forewarning (V246+ [Noy]) is offered just in time to give the man the opportunity to perform a specific act of charity to redeem himself, thus nullifying the divine decree set against him (V315+ [Noy]). This metaphor illustrates rabbinic writings that advise us to repent one day before death (J171+ [Noy]).[2] This is interpreted to mean immediately, since the exact date of one's death is unknown. By warning the *gevír* and advising him to distribute his belongings among the needy, Elijah acts as a prescient advisor and fulfills one of his traditional roles in Jewish folklore: the ability to ward off the Angel of Death. The teller and his audience have no difficulty accepting as plausible the appearance of Elijah as a being who comes in and out of the tale as a supernatural advisor (N847). They view his appearance as a gift of life.

Foreknowledge is a problem that has exercised the minds of medieval Jewish philosophers: how do we reconcile God's foreknowledge with human free will? Maimonides believed that every person is granted free will and can choose to be righteous or unrighteous. Thus, the power of doing good or evil rests in one's own hands. In our tale, free will is exercised at the conclusion of the tale when the rich man is moved by Elijah's advice to become righteous, thus earning merit that helps reverse his death decree, as illustrated by Solomon who said that righteousness delivers from death and purges away all sins.[3] The assumption here is that the man's generosity was not simply an act of self-protection but a sincere transformation that saves not only his life but also his soul.

The teller structures the tale in two separate yet interrelated, edifying components. The first teaches faith in God, which the rich man is shown to lack. This is done through examples, with the heavenly guide leading his charge from door to door to show him the humbling reality faced by the rest of humanity. Having nothing to hoard, the poor are not concerned with more than one meal at a time. Sultana and Malkuna and all their neighbors trust in

---

2. Shab. 153a; Abot 2:15.
3. Prov. 10:2.

God and firmly believe that He will provide according to His will, whenever and wherever He wishes. They are depicted as free of worry and more at peace with their lot than the *gevír* is with his. Thus they are shown as rich in faith and their implicit trust in God's benevolence to provide for their daily sustenance[4] is set as an example to emulate. This is presented in stark contrast to the rich man, whose behavior is illustrated by the saying, "Whoever has a morsel of bread in his basket and says 'What shall I eat tomorrow?' [J320+ (Noy)] belongs to those who are small of faith."[5] Faith here then appears to be acceptance of one's fate and trust in God's protection.

The second component teaches the importance of the social institution of charity, which becomes a cardinal demand. Giving generously and sharing one's blessings with others, *Gmilút hasadím* (V404 [Noy], V400 [Noy]), is considered the third pillar on which the world stands (V405 [Noy]),[6] with the other two being prayer and repentance. Jewish folktales often use a traditional motif that shows how charity helps reverse the sentence of death ordained from above. Charity is thus used as a means of expiation and has saving power (V410+ [Noy]). The rich man's hoarding rather than his not helping the poor makes him worthy of untimely death: "There is a sore evil that I have seen under the sun; riches hoarded by their owner to his misfortune."[7] The lesson to be learned here is that it is far more advisable to store up treasures for the world to come in the form of good deeds and charitable actions.

Protagonists in Judeo-Spanish folktales are rarely named, yet two minor characters in this narrative are given a first name, perhaps in an attempt to cloak them with an exalted moral status. They are identified as Sultana and Malkuna, common first names for women among Sephardim. In a way, this shows one more aspect of the syncretic nature of the culture. Both names derive from the word "queen": Sultana, popular among those who lived within the Ottoman Empire, is understood to be the wife of a ruler, the sultan; Malkuna comes from the Hebrew *malká,* or queen.

Almost all the elements of the tale are based on the Scriptures, which the male narrator clearly is intimately familiar with yet never actually cites. "Who is rich?" his tale asks, and the answer given is: "He who is happy with his lot."[8] The tale contrasts the strong faith and contentment of the poor (J347.4) with the rich man's lack of trust about the future, as evidenced by his troubled

---

4. Hab. 2:4.
5. Sota 48b; Tanhuma 3.
6. Abot 1:2; Sukka 49b.
7. Eccles. 5:12.
8. Abot 4:1.

sleep. Had not Solomon himself said: "A worker's sleep is sweet, whether he has much or little to eat; but the rich man's abundance does not let him sleep"?[9] God has granted the man riches, property, and honor, yet He does not permit him to eat from it and enjoy it.[10] The message is that wealth takes away peace of mind, and the more possessions a person acquires, the more worry he accumulates, causing him restlessness.[11] There is a Judeo-Spanish proverb that addresses just such a condition. It warns that much wealth causes many worries: "Fortuna muncha, dertes munchos." A benefit of trusting in God is that those who rely on Him are able to detach themselves from worldly concerns, which the rich man in our narrative cannot do. By stockpiling a large amount of oil for a rainy day, the tale also stresses, our *gevír* acts as if he were never to leave this world, overlooking the teaching of the sages: "Do not fret about tomorrow's trouble, for you never know what the day may bring."[12] His poor neighbors do not share the anxiety that plagues him, and the teller wants us to believe that they are better off.

What does the tale teach us? In its societal context, it praises the poor who trust in God's help and censures the uncharitable rich. It ends on a hopeful note, nonetheless, since the wealthy man experiences a change of heart and shares his possessions with the less fortunate. We are led to assume that the sentence of his imminent death has been lifted (Q151). Perhaps the message intended here is that one ought to live one's life righteously as if every day were the last.

---

9. Eccles. 5:11.
10. Eccles. 6:2.
11. Abot 2:7.
12. Sanhedrin 100b.

14

Eliau Anaví and the *Vístozo*

Narrated by ESTER LEVY (1992)

There was an old man who was very, very poor, and blind, *vistozo*. And the poor one, the *miskeniko,* he always said:

"What kind of luck, what kind of *mazál* do I have?! I have no children, no property, no eyes! What am I to do?! There will be no one to name my name."[1]

And he was a good man. He went to the synagogue, to the *kal,* regularly. He prayed, he spoke with people, and he always said that God is great and that He will not forsake him and that, some day, He will make things right.

One day, while at the *kal* praying, very sad, after the others had gone to their homes already, he began to weep. Suddenly, a man appeared beside him; he tapped him on the shoulder and said to him:

"Why are you weeping? What's the matter?"

"Ah," he said to him. "I have a wife whom I love dearly, *amá* she has not conceived! I have no children. And also, I have no sight and I don't make enough of a living, of a *parnasá.*"

"Well," the man said to him, "in what way do you want me to help you? I am ready to help you."

---

1. This is a reference to the reading of *kaddísh,* a brief doxology, a prayer for the dead in Aramaic recited by children for their deceased parents, whose memory they recall by naming their name. Sons in particular are thought to perpetuate the name of their father with the recitation of *kaddísh,* thus the intense longing for a son. The formula is also recited at the close of each section of a public prayer service.

"Ah," he said to him, "in what way? In what way can you begin to help me? I am a man who is very unlucky, very *dezmazalado!*"

"Look," the man said to him, "I am Eliau Anaví, and I came to help you out. *Amá* I can realize only one wish for you, not all of them. Tell me what you want."

He said to him:

"Wait a moment. I'll go ask my wife."

The man went to his wife, and he told her what had happened to him. His wife was very moved, and she said to him:

"What? Eliau Anaví came to you?"

"Yes!" he said to her. "And he said to me that I can make one wish only, and that he is ready to make it come true."

His wife said to him:

"Wait! I'll tell you what you'll ask for! Ask him for this and for that...."

After a few days, while the man was alone at the *kal*, Eliau Anaví came back again. He tapped him on the shoulder, and he said to him:

"Have you made up your mind yet? How do you want me to help you?"

"Yes," the man said to him. "I want to see my children eat out of gold plates, of gold *chinís!*"

"Ah," Eliau Anaví said to him, "since you knew how to make such an intelligent wish, I'll make it come true for you."

And so it was.

Commentary

This religious narrative is at once an interesting version of AT 750A, *The Wishes,* and a typical Elijah miracle tale.[2] The pious character of the tale is

---

2. This tale was published in Judeo-Spanish and Hebrew in Koén-Sarano, "El vistozo," in *Lejendas,* 153. An almost identical version was published by Shahar, "El prove i Eliau Hanavi." Another Sephardic variant appears in Alexander-Noy, no. 69. IFA holds parallels from Egypt, Iranian Kurdistan, Israel (Sephardic), Morocco, and Turkey. See also Jason, "Types," 162; Schwarzbaum, *Studies,* 242, 405, 483. For international versions, see Andrejev; Ashliman, *Guide to Folktales,* 150; Baughman, *England and North America,* 17; BP, 2:210; Boggs, *Spanish Folktales,* 84–85; Calvino, *Italian Folktales,* no. 41.3; Clarkson and Cross, *World Folktales,* no. 51; Cole, *Best-Loved Folktales,* no. 54; Delarue, *Conte populaire français,* 4:122; T. Hansen, *Types* (Chile, Dominican Republic, Puerto Rico); Grimm and Grimm, *Tales,* no. 87; J. Jacobs, *Aesop,* no. 54; Mathers, *Thousand Nights,* 3:27; Perrault, "The Foolish

reflected in the behavior and religious disposition of the blind man who continues to pray (V50) and demonstrate his faith in God despite his multiple misfortunes. The appearance of Elijah takes place at the synagogue (V112.3).

Here is an unlucky mortal unexpectedly visited by a supernatural being in disguise (V235, K1811, K1811.3+ [Noy]), who acts as a helper (N847). The wretched hero is clearly deprived of any luck, truly *dezmazalado*. Except for his beloved wife, nothing good has ever befallen him. Yet he is depicted as a good man who does not seem to deserve his ill fate. He prays to the Almighty at the synagogue (V112.6+ [Noy]) and, most of the time, treats his condition with equanimity. In Judaism, righteous people are often said to suffer their burden with patience and continue their service to God, demonstrating piety in spite of their troubles. The man places his faith in God's ultimate compassion and is thus worthy of Elijah's sympathy and direct interaction. *Gilui Eliyahu,* Elijah's revelation, is a gift long wished for by the sages but rarely bestowed. Note that Elijah does not immediately reveal his identity to the blind man but at first tries to retain his usual anonymity. Note also the wonder and awe expressed by the wife when she learns of Elijah's extraordinary appearance before her husband.

As a legendary figure, Elijah is popularly believed to come to the help of individuals in distress. Here, the prophet bursts onto the scene as a supernatural messenger of heaven who can overcome and rule over nature (V295 [Noy], D1713+ [Noy]). He is depicted as a healing agent who, as is his wont, causes miraculous happenings. Two of the miracles he helps perform here with his supernatural power (V221) are of a healing nature: he cures the man of his blindness (V221.12) and makes conception possible for the barren wife. In addition, he acts as a provider for the couple by bringing about a change of luck for the *dezmazalado* (N130). When his work is finished, he disappears into thin air, as he usually does.

When Elijah offers to help, he also tests the man's ingenuity and character (H1550), giving him the power to make a single wish, to come up with a single remedy for his many ills (D1720.1, D1761.0.2, D1761.0.2.2). Without a doubt, of the three misfortunes that afflict the man, it would be hard to pick the worst one: to be *vistozo* (a euphemism for blindness)[3], without issue (in a

---

Wishes"; Thompson, *One Hundred Favorite Folktales,* no. 73 (Germany); Thompson and Roberts, *Indic Oral Tales,* 99.

3. The society attaches magic power to the spoken word, so euphemisms, such as *vistozo* (the blind one), are often used superstitiously, contrary to their actual meaning, when referring to ills that might make the teller or the listeners nervous.

society that cherishes progeny), or destitute. How can the hero be asked to choose? Worse yet, what should he choose? The hardest ill for him to bear appears to be the barrenness in his marriage. Having children is an integral part of the human life cycle, and infertility is sometimes seen as part of a hidden plan revealed only to those who can penetrate the secret. Enter Elijah, who intervenes and participates in changing the course of events.

As one of the central purposes of marriage in Jewish tradition, procreation was considered a great blessing and a biblical commandment.[4] Children were seen as "a heritage of the Lord,"[5] who assured the continuance of the family name.[6] In contrast, barrenness is a curse and a punishment,[7] a source of frustration and despair. The greatest misfortune that could befall a couple was childlessness,[8] for a childless man was regarded as dead.[9] An offspring (especially a male offspring) was particularly prized in Judaism because it meant that *kaddísh* would be recited in one's memory, thus the character's reference in his lament to the naming of names.[10] While there is no notion in the Jewish tradition that the fate of the dead depends on whether or not their names are remembered, among the unfortunate beings in the next world, Akkadian texts name "the man who has no one to recall his name."[11]

An interesting sideline here is the relation between husband and wife (P210) and the wisdom of the wife, who shows astuteness in articulating the single wish that will fulfill all of the couple's needs (J1100, J1112). She saves the day with an ingeniously worded request that asks for a combination of riches, children, and the restoration of eyesight. The tale here changes character from a religious tale to a test of cleverness and ingenuity, a challenge the wife meets successfully. A parallel universal motif exists (K2371.3) in which the wish is stated in the following way: "Oh God! I want to see from above the seventh story of my mansion my great-grandsons playing in the streets and eating their cakes from golden vessels."

---

4. Gen. 1:28, 9:7; Rashi.

5. Gen. 22:17, 32:13; Ps. 127:3–5.

6. Num. 27:4, 8; 36:8b.

7. Lev. 20:20–21; Jer. 22:30.

8. Gen. 30:23; 1 Sam. 1:10.

9. Gen. R. 45:2. Joshua b. Levi, an early scholarly rabbi (an *amoraí*), commented that to be without children was like death (Nedarin 64b).

10. Intended for the peace of the dead person's soul, the recitation of the *kaddísh* requires a *minyán,* traditionally a gathering of ten men above the age of thirteen.

11. Cf. 2 Sam. 18:18.

The position of the wife was one of influence and importance among the rabbis, and wise women were held in respect and consulted in important matters.[12] In folktales, women often prove more judicious than their husbands. The teller, herself a woman, employs a dramatic device that heightens our interest in the tale. She does not tell her audience what the wife whispers in her husband's ear as the answer he is to give to Elijah. This makes the audience curious as to what the final outcome will be. It should be noted also that tales in which women or wives shine are almost always told by women narrators. In the end, the couple is rewarded for the ability to put together a clever wish (Q91) when it is realized with miraculous results (N201 [Noy], D1761).

---

12. 2 Sam. 14:2ff., 20:16–22.

15

The Holy Letters

Narrated by ESTER VENTURA (1990)

There was a man who worked with carpets, with *tapetes, avál* he did not do it at home: he went from hamlet to hamlet, from *kazál* to *kazál*. He would leave in the morning. He would take along whatever God had provided to eat. He would take a jug of water and his loom for making *tapetes,* and he would go.

One day, when he was in the middle of a mountain, all of a sudden, *ensupitó,* he remembered that he had not taken the water. He is saying:

"Ah, gracious God! Gracious *Dió*! I didn't take any water! I forgot! And there is no one here!"

This man knew neither how to read nor how to write, or anything. What he knew were only the letters, from *alef* to *taf,*[1] and that was his prayer, his *tefilá. Az* he started. He said:

"Alef, bet, gimel, dalet . . ."[2]

Three or four times he said the letters, till *taf.* While he is saying that, *ensupitó* a man appeared before him. The man said to him:

"What are you doing here, man? Where are you going?"

He said to him:

"What shall I tell you? I make *tapetes,*" he said. "I'm going to the *kazales.* And *agora* I have remembered that I haven't taken any water!"

See Koén-Sarano, "Letras sakras," in *Lejendas,* 141, for a Judeo-Spanish rendition and Hebrew translation of this tale.

1. This is the equivalent of A to Z in the Hebrew alphabet.

2. A, B, C, D. . . .

The other one said to him:

"Don't worry. I have here a little jug of water. I'll give you water."

He gave him water. The man drank. The other one said to him:

"If you want, take the jug as well. *Avál,*" he said to him, "*agora* you shall not go on. You'll go back home."

"Why so?" he said to him.

The other one said to him:

"Do as I am telling you. You'll go home," he said. "You'll take your wife and your children and you'll go to such and such a city. In that city," he said, "there is a great rabbi, a *rav*. In another three days that *rav* is going to die. You are to go in his place."

"How can that be?" the man said to him. "Why are you putting such ideas into my head? I can't read! I only know the alphabet, the *alef-bet*. This is what I have learnt and no more!"

The other one said to him:

"You just go there, and everything will turn out alright, *beseder.*"

And he got up; he left.

He said:

"He gave me water. He must be some holy man."

Turning around, he went back home. He said to his wife:

"Get yourself ready and get the children ready as well. We're leaving."

"Where to?"

"We're going away from here."

When they arrived in that city, he was well received, and they took him to the congregation, to the *killá*. They thought that he was truly, *bemét,* some great cantor, some great *hazán,* and they are taking him up to the *tevá,* to the pulpit.

He said to them:

"Look, I am still tired from the trip. *Agora* I can't. Tomorrow."

He is not saying that he doesn't know.

"Fine."

The next day, they took him up to the *tevá*. He took the book in his hand and they all are going crazy. He is reading the book as if it were water![3] *Afilu* the *rav* they had didn't do it this way, this *karár*!

And he himself, in his soul, cannot believe it. He said:

"I'll teach my children as well."[4]

---

3. That is, easily, fluently, fluidly.
4. Teaching children Torah helps impart moral values to them.

Three days went by. The *rav* died. They came to him. They said to him: "Welcome! You'll take the *rav*'s place!"

Who was the man who had offered him water in his mouth? It was Elijah the Prophet, Eliau Anaví, who had taught him the entire law.

Commentary

It is often an anonymous, innocent simpleton, such as the hero of this narrative, around whom religious tales originally centered. The story brings to mind the *Lamed-vav zaddikím,* the thirty-six anonymous and mysterious pious men to whose humility, just deeds, and virtues the world is said to owe its continued existence.[5] Through a seamless combination of realism and the supernatural, the woman teller weaves in the miraculous intervention by Elijah the Prophet, which occurs at the religious level of the tale to turn the life of the traveler around. The relocation of the protagonist to another space may be understood as an attempt to escape his fate, according to the following belief: change of place, change of fate (N131.5). The move away from the home space brings about a vision of Elijah, which causes a change of fortune.

The hero of this unclassified Jewish tale is not an educated man but an *'am ha-aretz,* a common euphemism depicting a man of little religious learning (P193 [Noy]). Carpet weaving is his craft, and he earns his living as a traveling tradesman. The tale reveals the dangers of traveling on foot from village to village through isolated and mountainous terrain. The fear of dying of thirst leads the man to pray for help the only way he knows how (V50). His ignorance is stressed at the beginning of the tale so as to set it up in contrast with the dramatic change the character undergoes in the course of the narrative. At first he displays only the most rudimentary learning, and we are shown how he makes use of that learning: the recitation and repetition of all the letters of the Hebrew alphabet as a heartfelt prayer when he finds himself in dangerous circumstances. True prayer is thus shown to be more than mere utterance from the lips. It must come from the heart for a prayer to be heard by God. Not only must it be sincere but the person who offers it must be worthy of having his petition answered.[6] It soon becomes apparent that our

---

5. See *Yeda-'Am: Journal of the Israel Folklore Society* 18, no. 43–44 (1976): 20–44, for four articles dealing with the legend of the thirty-six hidden righteous persons, "Lamed Vav" in Jewish folklore.

6. Shemot Rabba (Exod. R.) 21, 3; Bereshit 6b.

character's piety, humility, and fervor turn his scant knowledge into a wholesome and sincere prayer, earning him the guidance of divine providence and setting the stage for a miracle. A related non-Jewish motif exists about a man who is so holy that he walks on water even though he does not know how to pray (V51.1).[7]

The man's prayer is the *alef-bet,* the Hebrew ABC. Figuratively, *alef-bet* means the most elementary knowledge, and learning the *alef-bet* is the first step in learning how to read. The Hebrew alphabet has twenty-two letters, all consonants, to which vowels have to be added (usually placed below the letters) to form words. Each letter also has a numerical value (*Gematria*) and meaning,[8] and acts as a symbol (Z140 [Noy]). The Talmudic rabbis attributed special sanctity to the letters of the alphabet, ascribing each one a symbolic meaning.[9] Some believe that the writing of a Hebrew letter constitutes the material stage, its utterance the spiritual stage, and its evolution from oral pronunciation to thought the third, highest stage. When a person utters the letters of the alphabet, he is thought to stir up their spiritual essence, thus giving them the freedom of forming themselves into words. Hence the special purity of prayer performed with feeling and *kavaná,* or purpose, for it transforms the letters of the prayer into a spiritual essence that is believed to rise toward heaven.[10] This is well illustrated in our tale.

The tale reveals itself to be a religious narrative only after the messenger comes from above in response to the man's fervent prayer, recited with purity of soul and *kavaná,* and gives him unexpected assistance and counsel. It is Elijah who appears incognito as the guardian angel of this simple-minded Jew (V235, V238, V238+ [Noy], K1811, V295 [Noy], K1811.3+ [Noy], N848) to protect him from harm. The teller does not feel that it is necessary to identify the supernatural helper as Elijah until the end of the tale. He remains nameless until then, even for the hero himself who appears to be unaware of his rescuer's identity and suspects only that he must be some holy man (N848 [Noy]).

---

7. AT 827, *A Shepherd Knows Nothing of God.* He goes afoot across the water to the priest to ask about God, but on returning, sinks to his knees in the water.

8. This is used in Talmudic interpretation when a Hebrew word is artificially equated with another due to their identical numerical value. The cabalists resorted to this method as a basis of homiletic interpretation of the Torah.

9. *Alef-bet,* for example, means "to learn wisdom" (*alef biná*), while *gimmel dalet* means "to show kindness to the poor" (*Gemal dallím*) (Shab. 104a). The expression "from *alef* to *tav*" (Shab. 55a and Av. Zar 4a), corresponding to that of "Alpha and Omega" (Rev. 1:8 and 22:13), denotes complete integration.

10. Cordovero, *Shi'ur Komah,* 19.

In the end, the narrator stresses that Elijah himself had taught the man all the prayers, as only Elijah can (V246+ [Noy])—not only the reading of them but also the cantillation[11]—at miraculous speed and without the hero's knowledge of his newly acquired proficiency (V51, D1713+ [Noy], D1722+ [Noy]). With extraordinary power that enables him to have foreknowledge of people's fate and to perform magic changes and miraculous acts (V223), Elijah teaches the man *hazanût* (cantorial chant) in an extraordinarily short time (F695.3, V223.4) through the drinking of water (N810, N847). This is well in character, for Elijah is believed to be in the habit of revealing divine secrets to pious mortals (V246, V246+ [Noy]).[12] It is probably also an allusion to Hillel, the Jewish scholar said to have taught the entire Torah to a man standing on one foot (J914 [Noy], X370+ [Noy]).[13]

The belief in Elijah's supernatural appearance does not seem to conflict with the realism of the tale. It fits within the realm of possibilities for the teller and her audience. Although he has sufficient faith in the instructions given to him to follow them, the carpet-maker initially questions Elijah's instructions when told to move to a different setting (V246). This relocation is to be understood as an attempt to elude fate. Throughout her narration, the teller shows us that the main character never loses his sense of who he really is and what he really knows. This can be seen when he is invited to go up to the pulpit, the *tevá,* in the new community (V112.3). Still unaware of his miraculously acquired knowledge, he postpones the moment of truth, but when, to his own surprise and delight, he performs to everyone's satisfaction and wins over the congregation, his first thought is to take advantage of his newly acquired knowledge to instruct his own children in the Torah. The tale thus highlights the value of Torah study as an important form of worship leading directly to prayer and righteous living and, hence, as an activity that makes life meaningful.

---

11. This is the musical notation developed in post-Talmudic times and used for the chanting of the Torah at the synagogue. The reader or *hazán* usually has to learn these by heart, as the Torah scroll carries no notes.

12. Baba Metsía 59b.

13. Hillel, the great spiritual and ethical leader of his generation, was born in Babylon around 30 BCE. He is credited with laying the foundation of a systematic legal interpretation of the Hebrew Scriptures. His most famous maxim is "Do not unto others that which is hateful unto thee." Shab. 31a indicates how Hillel deals with a Gentile who wants to make him angry: he teaches him the whole Torah "on one leg" by quoting one sentence: "Love thy neighbor like yourself." See n.1, p. 256.

16

Eliau Anaví and the Mother-in-Law

Narrated by MALKA LEVY (1988)

There was a great rabbi, a *rav,* who was a great cabalist, a great *mekubál,* and they came to him from everywhere to make queries, to ask him *sheelót*. This *rav* was very poor, and they wanted to pay him, *amá* he would say:

"No! I do not sell the Torá for money, for *parás*! Come whenever you want, and I'll give you the answers."

The *rav* had a daughter, and some young men who wanted to pay him back said:

"Let's do something for him! Let's do him a *tová*. We'll arrange for the marriage of his daughter to the son of such and such a *rav,* who is very rich."

They went before this *rav* and they said to him:

"Look, so and so, who is *mekubál,* has a very good daughter. Very nice, very *nehmadá*. She is suitable for your son."

"Fine," said the *rav.*

His wife came. She said:

"No! I don't want poor people! Yes, I want! Fine! But let it be on one condition, one *tnáy*. Let her mother and father not come to the wedding!"

"Fine," the young men said to her.

They came to the *rav;* they told him everything, and they said to him:

"There is only one thing. You won't be able to go to the wedding because they don't want you to go. You're poor!"

A Judeo-Spanish version of this tale, together with a Hebrew translation, was published in Koén-Sarano, "La s.huegra," in *Lejendas,* 157.

The mother said:

"It doesn't matter. Let my daughter have good luck, a good *mazál*!"

Only that, when her daughter was about to leave, she said to her:

"*Na*! Take this little box, and whenever you find yourself unhappy, spit into it."

The daughter left. *Amá* she always dispatched the beadle, the *shamásh*, to her mother. One day, he said to her:

"She's now with child!"

And the mother is counting the days.

When the day finally came on which the daughter was to give birth, there was very, very heavy rain. And the mother was like a madwoman. At that moment, a little old man came. He knocked on her door, and he said to her:

"Could I lie down in your house for the night? It's raining!"

"Why not?" said the mother. "My bed is empty! I can't sleep because my daughter is about to give birth!"

As soon as the little old man came in, she said:

"*Na*, I'll go, I'll make you a little tea, a *chayiziko*."

As she went to make him the *chayiziko*, what did she see? A kitchen with everything just right! And when she came in to where the old man was? The house? Chandeliers! *Almenaras*![1]

The little old man said to her:

"I'm Elijah the Prophet, Eliau Anaví." [May he appear to us with good tidings!][2] "Your daughter has already given birth to a baby boy tonight, and tomorrow you'll go to her, you and your husband. I'll bring you a coach, with everything right. *Amá* you, until you see my face again, you are to keep fighting with your daughter's mother-in-law."

Well, the mother and father left. As soon as the daughter's mother-in-law saw all the good things they are bringing, she said:

"May your coming be propitious!"[3]

"What's this 'May your coming be propitious'?!" the mother said. "Now? *Agora*? I was not at the wedding! I'll be the one to take the boy to the synagogue, to the *kal*!"

---

1. This expression indicates that the house was filled with lights (chandeliers). The old man had transformed it into a richly furnished home with plenty of bright lights shining.

2. Teller's aside. In this case, it is a traditional blessing usually recited when Elijah's name is uttered.

3. This is a welcome greeting.

Amá the mother-in-law said:

"No! This is the son of my son. I must be the one to take him to the *kal*!"

"No!" said the mother.

And they are killing each other the entire week about who will take the boy to the *kal*! Just on the day of the circumcision, of the *brit*,[4] Eliau Anaví came, and he asked the daughter:

"Where is the little box that your mother gave you?"

As soon as he opened the little box, a large snake came out of it. Eliau Anaví said to the snake:

"Wrap yourself around the mother-in-law."

And to the mother he said:

"And you, take the baby boy and let's go to the *kal*! We'll do the *brit*!"

The daughter's mother-in-law was left shaking all over, with the snake on top of her.

When he returned from the *kal,* Eliau Anaví said to her:

"How did you feel, *kómo arguishates,* when you were left with the snake on top of you? That's how the mother felt when you did not let her come to the wedding of her daughter!"

The daughter's mother-in-law, *pishín,* asked for forgiveness and said that never again will she behave in such a manner.

Commentary

A Judeo-Spanish variant of this tale falls under the Jewish oicotype IFA 899*H, *Tree of Sorrow.* In it, a dying mother advises her daughter to consider a tree as her best friend and thus to trust it with her sorrows. Years later, the daughter notices the tree wilting and dying. Only then does she realize the wisdom of her mother's counsel. Had she not poured out her heart to the tree, it is she who would have wilted and died.[5] The oicotype illustrates a similar concept. We see that when a man locks up his wives while he is away, they all die of boredom and loneliness. Advised by an old woman, the new wife con-

---

4. *Brit* means both covenant and the covenant of circumcision between God and the Jews.

5. This variant was published in 1986. See KS, "La sava," 83. IFA versions come from Afghanistan, Eastern Europe, Iraq, and Rumania. Other Jewish parallels are found in Avitsuk, *Ha-ilan,* no. 5 (Rumania); Frankel, *Classic Tales,* no. 178; Noy, *Folktales,* no. 47 (Iraq); Patai, *Gates to the Old City,* 663. EB, no. 305 provides a non-Jewish version.

fides in a wax doll and survives. The returning husband jealously thinks the doll to be a man and stabs it. The wife's grief oozes out in the form of pus.[6]

Such tales are often told by women about women. The wisdom of older women highlights the psychological need to unburden oneself of personal problems and concerns from time to time; keeping them private and not sharing them is harmful. An inanimate object (a tree, a doll, a box) is used as a confidante when no one else is available. When followed, this counsel saves the person from loneliness and depression. Our teller adopts this motif as one of the components of her tale. In her version, we witness the young bride's loneliness and bitterness emerging as a dangerous snake out of the box. This is reminiscent of Pandora's box, which looses illness and vice upon the world when, overwhelmed by curiosity, Pandora opens it against orders from the gods. While the aspect of female curiosity does not appear in our tale, the concept of accumulated bitterness turning into a snake is a striking one. As far back as the period of Genesis, snakes symbolized an ancient and wise power generally associated with evil.[7] Yet the snake sheds its skin and emerges anew, a symbol of resurrection and renewal, and Moses himself lifted up a brass snake with the power to heal all those who looked at it during a plague in the desert.

The main character takes this tale beyond the concept of the inanimate friend in its didactic intent. Its goal is to teach humility and kindness by showing that the reverse is deserving of punishment. In Jewish tradition, humility is among the highest of virtues while pride is among the most serious of vices. The rabbi/scholar in this narrative represents the prototype of modesty and humility, and the pious nature of the tale is reflected in his behavior and stature (W45 [Noy], J171+ [Noy], J900, J910). As a cabalist, he takes no pride in his accomplishments and accepts no payment for his work. Jewish moralists stress that avoidance of pride is not to be confused with self-deception or self-deprecation. If a person has a good mind and worthy qualities, he is not expected to ignore them, but he is advised not to take credit for them.[8] Whatever talents a person possesses should be seen as God's gifts, undeserving though he/she may be of them. This is just how the teller praises her male protagonist: he is exalted but humble, and reluctant to earn a living from his intimate knowledge of the Torah (W45+ [Noy]).

Because his peers look upon him as a reliable authority in religious matters, they consult him on aspects of Jewish law and ask him to answer *she'elót,* or questions. In the nineteenth century, autonomous Jewish jurisdiction existed in

---

6. Jason, "Types," 177.
7. Num. 21:5–9.
8. Abot 2:9.

Turkey and the Balkans, and a respected rabbi was usually qualified to act as a respondent on *halakhic* matters (statements of religious law), civil law, financial matters, and business dealings for the Jewish community. The questions raised probably concerned problems that arose out of new conditions for which no direct answers could be found in the Talmud, the final authority for Jewish law. *Responsa* are the answers given by authorities in Jewish law to such queries. In Hebrew this exchange is referred to as *she'elót u-teshuvót,* "questions and answers."[9] Such a function is illustrated in our tale in the figure of the rabbi/scholar, a cabalist filled with knowledge and righteousness, able and willing to answer the *she'elót* that arise within the community.

Interestingly, once the worth of the bride's father is established, and as soon as the marriage proposal surfaces, the renowned rabbi disappears from the scene only to reappear in a passive role when he and his wife travel to their daughter's new home upon the birth of her son. The rest of the tale revolves around women, except for Elijah and the infant boy, focusing on conflict between in-laws and the clash of social classes. Rather than both parents making the decision regarding a marriage partner for their children, the mothers of the bride and groom take on the main role. Through the stereotype of the cruel mother-in-law, the teller introduces the motif of false pride. As we see in other tales in this anthology, while it is common for a man to take a bride from a lower class, it is also typical to send generous gifts to her home before the wedding. This does not take place here, another negative reflection of the mother-in-law's insensitive personality.

The bride's mother accepts the humiliating condition imposed by her daughter's future mother-in-law (S50), her main concern being that her daughter's *mazál* be a good one, that is, that she marry well. Later, after the synagogue beadle (P426.4 [Noy]) brings her the joyful news of her daughter's pregnancy, we watch as she anxiously paces the room on the night of expected delivery. The dramatic setting for Elijah's appearance as a beggar seeking shelter (K1817.1) is not an uncommon one in similar tales. The rain is falling in torrents when he materializes as a pitiful figure seeking shelter. This is his test of the anxious mother's character before extending his supernatural assis-

---

9. Collections exist of rabbinic *Responsa* activity, which date back to the period of the *geonim* (heads of Babylonian academies), when scholars developed the practice of addressing questions to the leading authorities of the period, the leaders of the great Babylonian communities. From the third to the tenth centuries, Sura and Pumbedita were the two foremost seats of learning in Babylonia. In addition to their importance to Jewish law, these collections of geonic *Responsa* serve as a rich source for the study of Jewish society.

tance to her. When she proves to be not only hospitable but also generous and kind, he rewards her (Q45, Q45.1) in the same way as the grateful old man in AT 750F*, *The Old Man's Blessing,* rewards his hostess: he blesses the charitable woman for her kindness by making her house become finer.

In this particular narrative, Elijah plays the role of the angel concerned with social justice who comes in to right wrongs and to bridge the gap of social inequality (V235, V295 [Noy], K1811, N847, K1811.3+ [Noy]). The teller reveals her belief in Elijah when she exclaims: "Ke mos apareska para bueno!" (May he appear to us with good tidings!) She accepts that he recognizes the anguish of the mother, wronged by the proud and oppressive mother-in-law, and that he visits her to ease her grief and help end her separation from her daughter. She believes that he is justified in punishing the unjust woman despite, or maybe because of, her social status. Finally, she depicts Elijah playing his traditional role as Angel of the Covenant, believed to be present at every circumcision ceremony to ensure the continuation of that agreed upon ritual between God and the Israelites.[10] This is one of the favorite roles for Elijah in folk culture, where he is considered the guardian angel of the newborn Jewish child during the critical period of thirty days from the date of birth.[11]

Although circumcision dates back to prehistoric times, according to the biblical account (V82) Jewish circumcision originated with Abraham. At God's request, Abraham circumcised himself at the age of ninety-nine[12] and performed Isaac's *brit* (abbreviation for *brit milá*) eight days after the boy's birth. In Genesis as well as in Leviticus,[13] the age of circumcision is given as

---

10. According to Jewish tradition dating as far back as the eighth century, Elijah is present at every circumcision ceremony and a seat of honor is specially prepared for him on these occasions. The first mention of this is in Pirkei de-Rabbi Eliezer 29, which explains the connection between Elijah and the *brit*. (See 1 Kings 19:10, 14 in which Elijah complains that the children of Israel "have forsaken thy Covenant" and God replies that because he has brought such charges, he "shall have to be present at every circumcision ceremony.") Thus, Elijah is identified as the Angel of Covenant (Mal. 3:23, 1).

11. Yalkut Me'am Lo'ez, *Sefer Debarim,* Alef: 33–34. The Me-am Lo'ez is an eighteenth century biblical commentary in Ladino, the outstanding work in Judeo-Spanish. It was begun by Jacob Culi around the weekly portion or the Pentateuch to popularize Jewish lore from the Mishná, Talmud, Midrash, and Zohar. First published in 1730 in Constantinople. Culi died before completing the undertaking and others sought to cover the rest of the Bible.

12. Gen. 17:1–11.

13. Lev. 12:1–3; Gen. 17:9–13.

eight days old. The operation removes the foreskin as evidence of the "sign of the flesh" of the covenant made with Abraham. Circumcision is thus part of the Jewish life cycle and a happy occasion, because a new Jewish child comes into the fold of the Jewish people. The entrance of the child into the covenant of Abraham is a symbol of the strengthening of the Jewish community and the family. It is Commandment 215, which the Jewish people promised to keep as a special covenant with God. The tale thus depicts a community that faithfully observes that commandment.

Although there are no special rules about the location in which circumcision is to be carried out, preference and tradition are that it be done in the synagogue during the morning service (V112.3, V112.6+ [Noy]).[14] As we see accurately sketched in the tale, the ritual of the ceremony usually is that the infant is taken from his mother's arms by the "godmother." Although there is no specific name for her in the ceremony, the grandmother is usually given the joy and honor of being godmother. In our tale, she carries the baby to the synagogue. Traditionally she hands him over to the *sandák* (godfather), who holds the newborn on his knees during the rite. The *brit* is then performed by the *mohél*, or circumciser, with a special chair usually set aside for Elijah, near the seat of the *sandák*. The baby boy is named at the circumcision ceremony.[15] Before the cutting of the foreskin, the child is often welcomed by the congregation with *Barúkh ha-bá* (Blessed be he that comes), and the Sephardim sing a *piyyút* (liturgical song) in which they bless those who keep the covenant. Grandparents participate in the ceremony not only by bringing the child to the *mohél* on the way to the circumcision but also by taking him out of the room after the ceremony has been completed.

All in all, our tale describes a pious Jewish environment and polarizes the tensions that may exist between social and economic classes within the Jewish community (U60). It examines social interactions and highlights the role of punishment in maintaining cooperative behavior in human societies.

---

14. In medieval Jewish life, the synagogue served not only as a house of worship and study but also as a political, communal, social, and administration center. The community council met there, and social and religious ceremonies were held there as early as the thirteenth century. In Spain, circumcisions were known to have been held at the synagogue.

15. Because a baby girl is "Jewish" from birth, there is no need for a special ceremony. Still, it is customary to give her a Jewish name in the synagogue soon after her birth, when her father is called up to the reading of the Torah. Since biblical times much significance has been attached to the names given by parents to their children.

PART FOUR
Romantic Tales

Many Judeo-Spanish narratives are considered novelle, or romantic tales, elaborate narratives that try to remain as close to reality as possible.[1] Typical stories are similar to those that appear in the *Decameron* and *Arabian Nights*.

In mythology, a hero is usually the son of a deity and a mortal, a demigod. In modern usage, however, s/he is understood to be distinguished for bold undertakings, courage, and fortitude. More often than not, the archetypal hero and heroine overcome a series of trials to arrive at an ideal state. The chief protagonists of folktales, they command the listener's wonder and sympathies. Usually portrayed as human beings in conditions similar to those telling and hearing the tale, they provide listeners with a way to disassociate from the difficulties in their lives. Everyday human conditions are overcome, and the heroes' good fortune ultimately asserts itself.

They triumph over an unfamiliar or hostile environment and are not bound to actual time or space. Often they must prove themselves by passing three tests to secure the coveted prize (a bride), and grateful animals speak and express emotions and sometimes provide crucial help in fulfilling these tasks. Oftentimes a pattern emerges in which an inversion of reality takes place. The unpromising heroine becomes a princess by marrying someone above her station, or the princess hides behind the disguise of a kitchen maid to escape a predicament. Protagonists may be virtuous, clever, lazy, or foolish, but in the end they always succeed.

In the five narratives included in this section, love and marriage and their convoluted intrigues take central stage. Women are depicted as virtuous or unfaithful, clever or capricious. In one tale, the new bride must use all her wiles to win the attention of her groom, who is convinced that he has been tricked into marrying a girl he did not wish to marry. In another, the heroine in ugly disguise must attract the prince's attention so as to make him notice her and fall in love with her. She had escaped her home to thwart her father's incestuous intent. He, in turn, was simply trying to fulfill his dead wife's last wishes by using a marriage token (a ring), which could fit only his own daughter's finger. In yet another tale, the wife must confront her husband's suspicion that she has not remained virtuous, despite proof to the contrary. In three of the tales, the bride puts her suitor to the test, and he willingly undergoes the trials of love to win her hand or pines for her when circumstances seem to interfere. Naturally, all ends well.

Note

1. See Haboucha, 295–518.

17

The Power of Love

Narrated by SARA YOHAY (1993)

A young man from a good family, but poor, fell in love with the king's daughter. And he was very sad, very *sehoriento,* because he knew that he would not be able to marry her due to the class difference.

This young man stopped going out with his friends. He stopped working. He barely ate. And he was breaking the heart of his widowed mother!

One day, while sitting in the *bahché,* in the garden, of his house, he saw a small wounded bird with little wings, with broken little wings, which was about to turn into a snack, a *mezé,* for the house cat. He took it in his hands, shooed away the cat, and ran the tiny bird to his room, to his *udá.* A few weeks later, the wings of the bird mended, and it began to fly and sing joyfully.

The young man told the small bird about the king's daughter and about his impossible love. The small bird tried to console him, and it said that it was time for it to fly away, to seek its own love. And so it was that they parted.

The king's daughter was very clever, and she wanted a husband more clever than she. And so, when it was time to marry, she imposed three tests on those asking for her hand. First, that they walk for an entire day with chickpeas in their boots, in their *chizmés*. Second, that they climb up to the black mountain, the *preta* mountain, where there is a monster with an eye that can see the entire world all at once, and that they fetch that precious eye. *Amá* the monster kept it hidden inside his mouth, and who could kill the monster?[1] Third, the king's daughter wore a chain around her neck, with a

---

1. Here the teller stresses the enormity and dangers of the task.

medayón, a medallion, hanging from it. That *medayón* had shut one day, and the key was inside, and it could no longer be opened. In it, the princess kept a picture of her mother who had died when she was but a small child. If they would force the *medayón* open, it would destroy the mother's photograph. This last task was the most difficult of all because no one could touch the *medayón* since the king's daughter slept with it, and she always had it around her neck.

When these three tasks became known, the young men lost their courage, their *koraje.* Let's say that they would *reushir,* that they would succeed in the first task, which in itself was very difficult. What fool would want to climb the *preta* mountain? And even more! Who could succeed in killing the monster? And, even in the event that one succeeded in doing so, the monster kept the eye in its mouth! He could easily swallow it up! And it was well-known that in the monster's belly there were a thousand snakes! And that the eye could see everything! And the serpents would thus know all that was going on! And, to simplify matters, let's say that the thousand snakes would be killed, and that the eye was given to the king's daughter, how could one open a *medayón* worn around the neck the key to which was inside of it?! And let's imagine, further, that one could devise a way to do such a thing, who would dare touch the king's daughter without getting his head cut off?

So they all raised up their hands and said:

"May the plague, the *landra,* affect her! Who would want such a capricious and crazy wife anyhow?"

The king *se sikleó.* He was very saddened by this situation, this *hal.* His daughter would laugh and say:

"Father, do you see how there is no one with whom I can be married? I am more intelligent than any man!"

One day, the small bird came to the youth's window and pecked at the glass. The young man saw the bird as a ray of sunshine! He rejoiced and asked if it had found its love.

"Here it is!" said the small bird, and it showed him its companion, which was also at the window. "We have come," it said, "to bring you happiness. You'll see! You'll be happy with the king's daughter!"

The young man hung his head and said:

"There is no hope...."

The small birds said in one voice:

"We already know about the tests, and we'll help you. But," they said, "we'll advise you on what to do, one thing at a time. Before you present yourself, put on your best clothes and eat well for a week so that your face, your *facha,* fills out and you take on some color."

And so it was done. After a week, the birds said to him:

"When the princess will place the chickpeas in your *chizmés,* we'll bring our friend, the nightingale, the *uzinyól,* to sing a sad song, and the eyes of the princess and of all those present will fill with tears. At that moment, you'll take out an identical pair of *chizmés,* hidden under your cape. Inside of them, you'll put boiled chickpeas. You'll travel on your way for the day, followed by the emissaries of the king and the princess. Upon your return, you'll remove the *chizmés.* And if the princess says: 'What happened to the chickpeas?' You'll say that the fire of your love cooked them!"

And so the king and his daughter and all their retinue arrived, along with many curious onlookers, to see what would happen. And in truth, *bemét,* when the princess inserted the chickpeas, her heart was saddened because she wanted this young man to succeed, as handsome as he was, and with such intelligent eyes. *Amá* the royal words are words that cannot be taken back. She sighed, and at that very moment a family of *uzinyolos* appeared and sang a sad song about someone who goes away never to return. It broke everyone's heart, and with eyes filled with tears, they all followed the flight of the *uzinyolos* overhead. At that moment, and in less time than it takes to say "amen," our young man switched his *chizmés.*

Well, the tears dried up, the youth was given the blessing, the *berahá,* and they began their journey. Walking steadily on, climbing up and down, *aite* the day went by! *Aite* it was time to take the road back! *Aite* back at the palace! There they removed his *chizmés.* What did they find? Flattened chickpeas!

"This can't be!" they all said. "There is something not right here!"

"No!" said the youth. "My love is so great that the burning heat it gives me cooked the chickpeas."

"This matter is settled," said the king's daughter with haste, with *adjilé.* "Tomorrow you'll attempt the second task."

Thinking that she was sending the youth of her dreams to his certain death, the king's daughter spent the entire night praying for his success. *Amá* royal words cannot be taken back.

As for us, the youth consulted with the tiny birds.

"Don't lose any sleep," they said to him. "Our king, the eagle, will help you because I have told him that you saved my life. It is well-known that eagles alone can reach to the heights of the like of the *preta* mountain. You'll have to show that you are climbing, because that's where they sent you. Only that they are all afraid to go up with you! Once you reach a point where people can no longer see you, you'll conceal yourself behind some boulders until we call you. All the rest is our business. Only, take some torn clothing along, to show that you have struggled against the monster!"

The next day, whatever had been decided upon was done. Everyone greeted the young man, and they gave him the *berahá*. The king's daughter felt faint, *amá* she gathered up her strength and climbed up to the highest spot in the palace, facing the *preta* mountain to await the return of the youth.

The youth took one road after another, and he began to climb up the mountain. He had the two small birds perched on top of his hat, of his *chapeo*. When he arrived at a spot where the eye of man, of a *benadám*, could no longer reach, that's when he hid. And what does he see? That the biggest and most beautiful eagle that one could imagine came like a *lampo,* in a flash! And its sheer size cast a shadow over the sun!

"King of the Birds," said the youth, "I thank you for your willingness to help me!"

"Son of man," replied the eagle, "you rescued one of my subjects. We must all help you. We shall never forget your good heart."

The small birds flew away and came to settle on the wings of their king, the eagle; and here is what happened. With the same speed, the same *zveltés*, with which the eagle had come, that's how it flew away until it was out of sight. It kept on flying. It reached the peak of the *preta* mountain and concealed itself behind large boulders.

The two small birds sprang into action. Flying, they drew close to the monster, sitting on a chair made of animal bones, and asleep, with its mouth shut tight so that the eye would not drop. Breath came out of its nose like smoke, like *bafos,* out of a volcano. At the risk of their life, the small birds went up its nose and began to tickle it. The monster shook itself this way, it shook itself that way, and when it could bear it no longer, it gave out such a powerful sneeze that its mouth fell open and the eye fell out and started to roll on the ground! The earth covered up the eye, and the sightless monster began to roar, to emit fire from its ears, and to stomp the ground so much that it felt as though the mountain would crumble.

The eagle pounced! It grabbed the eye, which was as large as a *karpúz,* a watermelon! And, giving the small birds time to hop on it, it started to fly down rapidly, cutting through the air like a *yatagán*. The bellowing of the monster could be heard halfway down the mountain!

A few seconds later, the young man had the eye of the monster in a bag, in a *torbá* [it was as big as a *karpúz!*],[2] and he was on his way back after having given thanks to the king of the small birds and to his friendly subjects.

---

2. Teller's aside.

The youth arrived at the palace where a multitude of people awaited. Shouts of joy were heard. The king's daughter invited him to supper, and she received the eye of the monster.

The king's daughter wanted to know how he had succeeded in doing what he had done, *amá* the youth said to her:

"If some day I marry you, I shall tell you."

The king granted the youth three days of rest, and he told him to ready himself for the final test. The small birds came to the young man's window, and they said to him:

"You'll ask the king to have your hands and feet tied in the room, the *udá*, of the princess, and let them give you a *milizina,* a sleeping potion to put you to sleep. Everything else is our business."

At the end of the three days, this was done. The king said:

"He is now tied up and asleep. There is no reason why he shouldn't be left alone in the *udá* of the princess."

At night, thrilled to have this courageous young man in her *udá* and tired out by the events of the past days, the princess *se aferró,* she grabbed unto sleep with hands and feet.

The small birds sought out a spider secreting a thread of silk from its abdomen. They stood before it and said to it:

"We'll let you live if you help us."

"Ask!" said the spider. "I'll do whatever you want, only let me live and make a home for my children!"

The small birds gave instructions [and this is what I'll tell you].[3] The spider clambered to the ceiling, the *taván,* and let itself down on one of its silken threads until it was level with the neck of the king's daughter. Twisting itself this way and that, it made itself small enough to enter the *medayón* through the keyhole. There it found the tiny key that had fallen inside. It threaded through it a silk thread and raised it, putting it through the keyhole, always making sure to keep the other end of the thread attached to its abdominal spinnerets. It went through the keyhole and came out. As they watched it come out, the small birds took hold of the thread in their beak and flew around in circles, in *rodanchas,* until a click was heard and the *medayón* opened up.

The spider saluted and left. And the tiny birds created a ruckus, a *dubara,* until the paladins came to see. They summoned the king and roused the daughter. No one could explain how the *medayón* had been opened without

---

3. Teller's aside.

touching the princess and under such tight precautions, while the young man continued to sleep! They gave him a *milizina* and woke him up.

And with happiness, admiration, and a thousand questions, they busied themselves preparing for the wedding. Was there anyone not invited to that wedding? From the wealthiest to the poorest, from among human beings and animals! The birds came along with their king. The spiders spun the bride's veil with threads of silk and gold. The *uzinyolos* sang songs of happiness, and the groom's widowed mother was the happiest mother in the world because, for a mother, there is no greater joy than to see her son happy, *orozo*.

One day, the king's daughter asked her beloved:

"*Agora,* tell me how you managed to succeed in the three tasks."

And he replied to her:

"Is there anything greater and more powerful than love?"

And she agreed. After all, why should it matter to her how it had been done? *Aikár,* the point was that the strongest and most intelligent man in the world was hers.

How has all of this come to be known? The little birds told me.

Commentary

While this narrative would generally be considered an ordinary folktale and be included with tales of magic with animals as helpers, it is also a romantic tale that shows how the princess's hand is won. In the most traditional folktale fashion, it is filled with folk motifs, tasks, tests, and tribulations, as well as a happy ending. When a poor young man falls in love with the king's daughter (T10, T91.6.1), wealth and poverty are at loggerheads, and the disparity between social classes emerges. Hopelessness and lovesickness (T24.1) lead the hero to refuse food and drink (T24.6) and to take to his bed out of sorrow (F1041.9.1). Lovesickness is described as a terribly painful experience to go through and to watch, but the center of the tale may well be to guide the hero to achieve a greater level of self-awareness and wisdom. Before becoming a real man, worthy of the princess's hand, he is forced to develop and prove his own merit, for what use is a soul that has never known suffering? Without trial he remains juvenile, not having been measured against serious obstacles. When the trial of love is overcome, he is transformed from a condition of ignorance and naïveté to a higher level of consciousness of what love and life really are.

A version of AT 554, *The Grateful Animals,* this narrative shows that a youth earns the gratitude of a bird he rescues from death (B360, B450). With its help and that of the eagle as king of the birds (B242.1.1, B455.3), he performs the three tasks imposed to win the hand of the beautiful princess (B582.2).[4] Marriage tests are common motifs in folktales, the means by which to secure the pined-for princess as a prize. In this tale, as in many like it, the unpromising hero must accomplish difficult or seemingly impossible tasks to secure the hand of his longed-for but otherwise unattainable bride. Such severe tests and excessive demands to prevent marriage are known as suitor tests (H300, H301, H310). Often the scheme is set up as a suitor contest, where the winner marries the princess.

The princess is not only beautiful but also rich and powerful. The man who weds her becomes king and master of her possessions. Thus, she puts her suitors to severe tests as rites of passage and offers her hand as the prize (H331, H335, H335.0.2, T68). The assignment of a task, test, or quest to a suitor by a prospective bride is less common in folktales than its imposition by the father of the maiden.[5] The assignments typically come in threes, as in our tale, and can be superhuman (H1130) or impossible (H1010). Here, for example, the hero must prove himself in multiple ways. One of the required tests is one of endurance (H328): to walk all day with hard chickpeas inserted in his boots.[6] Another demands fearlessness (H1400) in stealing a single, huge, all-seeing eye from a terrifying, fire-breathing monster of enormous size living at the top of a dark, mysterious mountain (B11.2.11, B11.2.12, G610.3, B11.3.2). The one-eyed monster stands for a fabulous, negative being that

---

4. A Jewish version of this tale appears in Schram, *Jewish Stories,* 209. Non-Jewish parallels can be found in Boggs, *Spanish Folktales,* 71; Briggs, *Dictionary of British Folk-Tales,* pt. A, vol. 1, 365, 369; Cole, *Best-Loved Folktales,* no. 26; D'Aronco, *Fiabe di Magia,* no. 20; D'Aronco, *Fiabe Toscane,* 81; Delarue, *Conte populaire français,* 2:370; A. Espinosa, *Cuentos populares,* 3:26–33, no. 140; Grimm and Grimm, *Tales,* no. 17 ("Die weisse Schlange—Le serpent blanc"), no. 62 ("Die Bienenkönigin—La reine des abeilles"); Kent, *Turkey,* 35; Megas, *Folktales of Greece,* no. 33; Pino-Saavedra, *Chile,* no. 23; Rael, *Colorado y Nuevo Méjico,* no. 220; Robe, *Mexican Folktales,* 99; Thompson and Roberts, *Indic Oral Tales,* 83.

5. See Thompson, *Folktale,* 106.

6. See Schwarzbaum, *Studies,* 152, for a Jewish example of the stratagem of boiling peas to soften them before inserting them in one's boots. This refers to tale no. 130 of Naftoli Gross's collection of Yiddish tales, *Ma'aselech un Mesholim* (New York, 1955), in which two Yeshiva students are punished by the rabbi for some wrong they have committed. One of them circumvents the punishment by boiling the peas before walking on them. Other Jewish versions are Ausubel, *Jewish Folklore,* 370; Learsi, *Filled with Laughter,* 223; and Richman, *Laughs from Jewish Lore,* 339–40.

must be overcome. He represents the antithesis of the hero. Overcoming the exterior monster can also signify slaying the monster within, to be replaced by a higher self. The last task required is a difficult and delicate one, requiring skill as well as resourcefulness (H326, H506). The hero must repair a jewel worn by the princess without touching her body. The sleeping potion given to the hero, who is to pass the night with the princess, adds to the suspense for the audience (K675).

The tasks selected by the teller from a multitude of possibilities lead her to weave images of likely sexual symbolism into the text: boots; the fire of love that supposedly softens the peas that would otherwise render walking unbearable; and keys and locks. In the Middle and Far East, footwear is often used in reference to female sexuality, but whether such a connection is the case here is not entirely clear. Keys are symbolic of the double role of opening and closing, of a mystery or an enigma, or of a task to be accomplished and the method for doing so. It is also a symbol of getting to the treasure: the princess.

These marriage tests are usually accompanied by motifs of supernatural helpers who enable the hero to perform the tasks (H970). Such helpers can be grateful animals, as they are here. The act of kindness toward a wounded swallow at the beginning of the tale earns the hero assistance from the grateful bird and its king (W27, B350). The birds offer their aid voluntarily and are helpful actors in this odyssey (H982). They hold the center of interest, advising the hero (B560) and performing tasks for him (B292, B292 [Noy], B571), defeating the monster with the all-seeing eye and facilitating the accomplishment of the other tasks through resourceful strategies. Like the eagle in our tale who rules over all the birds, the *ziz,* a giant bird featured in Jewish legends (B242+ [Noy], B242.1.10), is said to have been created on the fifth day of Creation and to be so huge when in flight that it blocks the sun.[7] In most tales, the ability of birds to converse with humans is taken for granted (B211.9 [Noy]). Here, the birds advise the protagonist in an undetermined language (B211.3). Also helpful is the nightingale, a small thrush renowned for its sweet crescendoing song, which can often be one of pain, as it is here, when it sings about the tortures of love (A2426.1.1). Finally, the spider as helper is a common motif in folktales. As a spinner of webs, it produces silk from within itself—drawing out and patterning the thread of destiny. In the end, after the monster is defeated (G500) and the other tasks accomplished, enabling the lowly lover to triumph unexpectedly, the hero marries his beautiful princess (L161, T100).

---

7. Schram, *Jewish Stories,* 32.

The princess is idealized, and we witness her transformation from a demanding young woman to a compliant and adoring wife. In addition to her function as the assigner of tasks, it is also her role to facilitate the hero's success. We are invited to witness how she becomes attracted to the suitor and worries about his welfare because she wants him to succeed so she can have him as a husband. As in many versions of the same type, she voluntarily extends a helping hand to the handsome suitor; in this case she accepts his far-fetched but pleasing explanation about the cooked peas. The resolution of courtship takes place after the story's climax, which allows the possibility of hope. In the end, predictably, success culminates in marriage.

18

The Rose and the Lion

Narrated by ALICIA BENDAYAN (1982)

Once upon a time there was a very rich man who was dying from a grave illness, and he summoned his son and said to him:

"I am dying, and everything I have is for you and for your sister. But I'm always worried about her because she is a good girl, sensible, and she is very pretty. And I charge you with taking care of her as you would your own eyes and to look after her. And don't give her in marriage to anyone who comes to ask for her hand until you know his true worth."

The son promised him this, and the man died. After some time had passed, a great *rav,* a rabbi, came and asked for her hand, and the brother sought to find out that he was a good man and everything, as his father had wanted. He gave her in marriage to him, and it looked like the woman was happy.

A long time passed. They lived very happily. One day, there was in the land a king who went in just like that, unexpectedly, *de improvizo.* He would enter the home of a woman, and she couldn't deny herself to him because he was the king! And he had a purse of money in his hand, and he always left it behind in the house he entered.

Now, this king passed by that house one day, and he came in. She was startled and she said to him:

"Welcome, my lord king. But I'll go bathe myself. I can't present myself dirty, with the smell of cooking all over me, before a king such as you. Give

---

This narrative was taken down by Gladys Pimienta. See acknowledgments in Koén-Sarano's foreword.

me some time: I'll go take a bath. Meanwhile, take this book. Look it over. And I'll come when I've finished bathing."

She didn't go bathe. She left the house. She went into a house across the street, and she kept a lookout through the peephole to see whether the king would leave or wouldn't leave. The king took the book and began reading with such interest in the book that he didn't realize that she was taking long to return, or anything else. He finished reading the book and said:

"Blessed be she among all other women. For sure this woman will not come back."

He picked himself up and left; but he forgot the purse filled with money on the parlor room table as well as his sword.

She came back when she saw that he had left. She locked the door and went up to the kitchen to continue cooking. And she noticed neither the money that he had left nor the sword. Now her husband came. He saw the parlor room open. He went inside and he saw the money and the sword, and he said:

"The lion has entered. And if the lion has entered, he touched the flower!"

What did he do? He said nothing to her. It wasn't her fault. But he went out, he bought a bed, set up separate rooms. He didn't seek to see her again. She was desperate now. She didn't know what had happened to cause her husband to do these things to her, and she became ill. Like . . . she wasted away. She didn't eat. She didn't sleep. Until she became very, very ill.

Her brother came and saw her, and he said:

"What's the matter with you? Why are you like that?"

She said to him:

"Look at what's going on: I don't know what's the matter. Why my husband is this way. It's been so long since. . . . It's as if he were not my husband. He doesn't speak to me! He doesn't take anything from my hand! I don't know what's the matter with him!"

The brother said to the husband:

"Look, I want you to come with me before the king so that he may adjudicate, to find out what's going on with my sister."

Now the two of them entered the palace. The king said:

"What's the matter?"

He said to him:

"I'll tell you what's the matter with me. Before he died, my father had placed a garden in my care. In this garden was a rose, much beloved by my father and by myself. And he recommended strongly that I not hand it over to just anyone. And I promised that to my father, and I gave it to this man to care for. And he promised to watch over it even better than I had. But, for a while now, the flower is wilting, and we don't know why. I want this man to say why."

Then he said:

"Yes, sir. I took the garden and I took the rose. But I entered the garden and found that the lion had entered, and if the lion entered, he touched the flower!"

Then the king understood what it was, and he says:

"I was the thief who entered into the garden, who saw the rose. But may God punish me if I touched the flower!" And he says: "She is blessed among all other women. She gave me this book and, through it, brought me to understand what a grave sin it is to lie with a married woman, and that all women— be they prettier, uglier, older, or younger—are all alike. And she is the one who earned the *mitsvá* that, since that day, every woman, be she married, single, or whatever, is safe in her house. And I will not molest her any more."

COMMENTARY

This is another illustration of a solemn promise connected with death (M250), and once again it involves a father and son (P233). Often a symbolic figure in folktales, the father represents supreme authority over his children. Here, he envisions the true worth of his daughter and, as if in premonition, commands his son to take over his role as her protector. As mentioned elsewhere, deference to the last wishes of a dying person, especially a father, had to be faithfully adhered to.[1]

A tale of fidelity and innocence, this version is representative of AT 891B*, *The King's Glove,* and is reminiscent of the biblical David and Batsheva story[2] as well as of the *Othello* episode in which a handkerchief left in a woman's room causes an implicit accusation (K2112.5.1).[3] In our tale, the king

---

1. Gittin 13a. Other tales in this anthology that include this motif are tales 8, 19, and 20.

2. 2 Sam. 11.

3. Judeo-Spanish versions of this type appear in Crews, *Judaïsme Sephardi* 6, 278 (AT 891B*) as well as in LP, vol. 1, no. 1, and vol. 2, no. 112, the latter two classified under **881B, *The Suspected Maiden Proves Innocent,* in Haboucha. Other Jewish versions are found in Farhi, *Osé Pelé,* 3:70–72; Jason, "Types," 175; Jason, *Types,* 43; BJ, 1:254–64, 356–58, 377, 384; bin Gorion, *Mimekor Yisrael,* vol. 3, nos. 22, 23; [Noy] (Q255+); Noy, *Folktales,* no. 59 (Yemen); Schwarzbaum, *Studies,* 64, 455; *Schwili,* no. 81; Song of Songs 4:12. IFA parallels originate from Iraq and Yemen. Parallels from

forgets to take away his sword and trademark royal purse, which he uses to compensate each married woman he violates. The husband's discovery of these objects leads him to consider them sufficient evidence to suspect the worst. The tale highlights how easy it is for the innocent to appear guilty (K2150).

Since such illicit affairs usually take place in secret, often precluding the sufficient evidence required by Jewish law for punishment, the conclusion the husband reaches is not unrealistic. While he acknowledges to himself that his wife may have had little alternative in the matter of the king's visit, he nonetheless takes immediate measures to distance himself from her, suspecting her of having become an adulteress, no matter how unwillingly. Thinking that she was defiled by the king, he refuses to resume marital relations with her, moves out of the marital bed, and cuts off all physical relations with her without explanation (T315, T315.2, Q255+ [Noy]). In fact, he observes the law of ritual and family purity, which demands sexual separation, separate beds, and sometimes even separate quarters. Note the wife's complaint that he will not even take anything from her hands, as if she were unclean, that is, in a state of menstrual *niddá*. The measures he imposes are drastic enough and so unjustified in the eyes of the innocent woman that she begins to wither.

As the central rite of passage, marriage is an occasion of celebration vitally connected to the interest and continuation of the group. Among the Sephardim, the practice of arranged marriages was widespread. Although romantic unions were not unheard of, parents usually arranged an appropriate match for their children. After her father died, the girl's brother performed all the duties of a father.[4] This responsibility takes on a primary place in our narrative, when the brother finds a suitable match for his sister and ascertains that she is well treated by her husband. True to his deathbed promise to his father, the doting brother upholds his responsibilities vis-à-vis his sister by reappearing to seek justice on her behalf before the king. He thus looks after her welfare, even after she marries, and speaks up for her when the need arises. The tale thus focuses not only on the fragility of marital relations (T100, P210) but also on the supportive sister-and-brother relationship (P253).

---

non-Jewish sources appear in Ashliman, *Guide to Folktales,* 181; Calvino, *Italian Folktales,* no. 160; Chauvin, *Ouvrages arabes,* 7:121, no. 391B, 7:122, nos. 391C, 391D; Elisséeff, *Thèmes et motifs des Mille et une nuits,* no. 126A; *Livro de los engaños,* 11; Mathers, *Thousand Nights,* 4:227; Rotunda, *Motif-Index of the Italian Novella* (K2112.5.1, N348); Shakespeare, *Othello.*

4. See Gen. 24:50, 55.

In marriage, it is understood that husband and wife would remain faithful to one another until death. Commandment 347 admonishes us not to commit adultery.[5] Voluntary sexual intercourse between a married woman and a man other than her husband is prohibited in the Decalogue.[6] In the old days, the wife was the husband's possession of a special sort, and adultery constituted a violation of the husband's exclusive right to her. This was consistent with the patriarchal system. In our tale, the peace of the household, *shalom bayit,* is broken when the king seeks to turn the wife into an adulteress. To protect her reputation, she cannot allow herself to remain alone with the king in her own house; thus, she escapes with a false plea: she dupes him into believing that she needs to bathe (K551.4.7) before complying with his amorous desire. According to the law of ritual and family purity, a woman is forbidden to maintain sexual relations with her husband during and for some time both before and after her menses. Marital relations during that time are a severe offense according to *halakhá*.[7] While the king is not the woman's husband, he apparently understands and respects the need for immersion, the purpose of which, stressed in the Book of Leviticus, is spiritual cleanliness. Immersing oneself ritually cleanses one of all physical as well as spiritual impurities and contamination.

The woman's absence gives the king time to read and reflect on the book of wisdom that she judiciously hands him as she leaves (J166). The book, in all probability the Bible, apparently serves to remind him of the commandment not to covet his neighbor's wife. Eventually, once that lesson is learned, he changes his mind and leaves the woman's house. The model wife thus tactfully resists the king's sexual appetite (J816.4)[8] and by shaming him (T320.4) escapes from his undesired and lustful pursuit (T320).

The tale is told in the form of an allegorical riddle highlighting a beautiful rose in a garden and ending with the unspecified but unmistakable motif of AT 983, *The Dishes of the Same Flavor* (J81).[9] The king, who covets his sub-

---

5. Lev. 18:20.
6. Exod. 20:13; Deut. 5:17.
7. After the destruction of the Temple, the law of *mikvá* has become relevant essentially to a menstruating woman, who is viewed as being "unclean" (in a state of *niddá*) during and for seven days after her period.
8. Keller, *Spanish Exempla.*
9. Two Judeo-Spanish parallels are found in KS, "Siempre perdiz?" 49, and Moscona, *Sipurei Sefarad,* 61, "Los guevos boyalis." In KS, when the cardinal reproves

jects' wives (T481.5), is brought to realize that one woman is like another and thus is dissuaded from his amorous pursuits.[10] While the king's behavior initially belies the societal values regarded as important in that society, flouting the conventions and offending the moral laws, the heroine represents the positive values of the chaste woman.

Several powerful metaphors are used in the tale: the lion for the king; the rose for the wife; and the garden for her virtue, her well-being, and the family reputation. The male characters in the tale—the brother, the husband, and the king—easily use and recognize all three. The lion metaphor is obvious; the lion is considered the king of animals. The king, who should represent the symbolic patriarchal figure of rule, the symbol of law, order, and authority, breaks his pact with that role at the beginning of the tale. The allusion is probably to King Solomon, known for his sexual adventures and lust for beautiful women. To conform to the didactic nature of this tale, however, the king reforms in the end, thus living up to his societal and religious responsibilities. When he acknowledges his part in the affair and mends his wayward ways, he rehabilitates the injured wife in her husband's eyes and publicly vows never to invade the privacy of a woman's home again.

Another figure of speech likens the heroine to a rose, the handsome queen of all flowers. The delicate rose needs care and attention because it wilts easily. While on the surface the heroine appears passive and helpless, waiting to bear whatever happens to come her way under her father's, her brother's, and her husband's protection, eventually, however, she is put through a test of character (H1550) and undergoes an internal form of quest. She rises above

---

Louis XIV for his sexual escapades, the king serves him many elegant courses, all pheasant. When the cardinal complains that all the dishes taste the same, the point is made. Moscona's version uses colored eggs to show that with women as well, only the exterior changes. The type is also found in additional Jewish sources, including *BJ*, 3:109; bin Gorion, *Mimekor Yisrael*, vol. 1, no. 82, 164; Cheichel, *TEM 1967*, 139 (Morocco IFA 7776), Frankel, *Classic Tales*, no. 105; Fus, *Khavilot Zahav*, no. 1 (Lithuania); Jason, "Types," 195; Jason, *Types*, 65; Nahmad, *Portion in Paradise*, 97; Schwarzbaum, *Studies*, 64, 123, 455, 464; *Schwili*, no. 81. IFA variants were collected from tellers from Afghanistan, Eastern Europe, Iran, Iraq, Israel (Sephardic), Morocco, Poland, Syria, and Yemen. Non-Jewish versions appear in Andrejev, (*981); Basset, *Mille et un contes*, 2:25, no. 13; Boccaccio, *Decameron*, 1:2; Chauvin, *Ouvrages arabes*, 7:122, no. 391C; Chevalier, *Siglo de Oro*, no. 80; Rotunda, *Motif-Index of the Italian Novella* (J81, J81.0.1).

10. See Wesselski, *Marchën*, 209; Balys, *Index*, no. *981; Andrejev (type 8981 [II]).

her predicament, using her love for her husband and her sense of the respectability of her role as the source of an inner transformation, which gives her the strength and presence of mind to evade the king's advances and tactfully reprove him while teaching him a lesson. She thus proves herself fully capable of preserving intact her virtue and the purity of the marital garden.[11]

---

11. This tale in praise of women illustrates Solomon's saying in Prov. 31:10–31: "A woman of valor, who can find? Far beyond pearls in her value."

19

The King's Daughter and the Three *Fostanes*

Narrated by MATILDA KOÉN-SARANO (1988)

Once upon a time there was a king who had a wife and a daughter, both of whom were very beautiful. One day the wife became very ill, and she had not many days left to live. She called her husband and said to him:

"My beloved, I'm dying, and you, *kale ke* you promise me one thing: that you'll marry again, one year after my death, but only to the woman on whose finger will fit this diamond ring, which I'm giving you. If not, *kale ke* you never remarry!"

The king took the ring; he promised her whatever she wanted, and his wife died in peace. Time passed, and the king began to think about marrying again. He began trying the ring on the daughters of his noble subjects, *ma* it did not fit any of them. Seeing that, he handed the ring to his emissaries, and they began to roam the entire kingdom, trying it on all unmarried women, of all ages and all stations. *Ma* the ring didn't fit any of them.

The king began to despair and, one day, seeing that his daughter was the only woman left in his kingdom who had *deynda* not tried the ring, he insisted that she try it on. As if by magic, the ring fitted her perfectly! The king said to his daughter:

"You'll be my wife!"

"How can this be?!" his daughter said to him. "I am your daughter! This is forbidden!"

"No," the father said to her. "This is the will, the *savá,* of your mother. If you do not agree, I'll marry you by force!"

"If that is so," she said to him, "before I marry you I want you to have a dress, a *fostán,* made for me of the moon's color!"

She thought that he would never *reushir,* that he would never succeed. *Ma* the king, who had a magician for a friend, brought her a beautiful *fostán* of the moon's color.

"That's fine," the daughter said to him, "*ma* one *fostán* is not enough! I also want another *fostán* the color of stars!"

Before too long, the king, her father, brought her a brilliant *fostán,* of the color of the stars. The daughter said to him:

"Two *fostanes* alone a queen do not make. I want also a *fostán* the color of the sun, and in it I'll be married!"

And the king, with the help of the magician, brought her a magnificent *fostán,* the color of the sun.

"Fine," the daughter said to him. "*Ma* I also want a tiny chest, a *kutiko,* made of diamonds, in which I'll be able to keep these beautiful *fostanes* so that no one would steal them from me."

This time, again, the magician succeeded in producing what the king asked of him, and the king brought the *kutiko* to his daughter.

"Very well," said the daughter. "I'll marry you within a month's time."

Nightfall came, and the daughter dressed herself as an old woman, with a black *fostán,* grubby and ragged. She stored the three *fostanes* and her mother's ring inside the *kutiko* of diamonds. She went down to the kitchen, she dirtied her face with ashes, and she slipped away from the king's palace.

She started to walk. She walked and walked, day and night. She crossed fields and vineyards, and she arrived before a beautiful royal palace. She entered the palace and asked if she could *lavorar* there as a dishwasher. The kitchen staff agreed, *achetaron,* and they took her into the king's service. And she began working there. The only thing that astonished everyone was how such a grimy and tattered old woman could have such a youthful and clear voice! This made her beloved by all, including the king's son.

One day, everyone in the palace had gone to a *balo,* to a ball, and the king's son, who was feeling a bit ill, a bit *hazino,* remained alone in the palace. In the evening, he went down to the kitchen to request that they bring him hot soup. The kitchen was locked, and from the small keyhole shone a brilliant light. The king's son bent down and looked, and what does he see? A very, very beautiful woman wearing a *fostán* the color of the moon.

He almost died! He knocked on the door, demanding to be let in. *Ma,* when the door was opened, he found himself before the little old woman in black. The little old woman asked him:

"What is your wish, my lord?"

The king's son said to her:

"I want hot soup!"

The little old woman made soup for him, and the king's son ate it with pleasure.

The next night, the king's son went down to the kitchen once again and, once again, the door was locked. He looked once more through the small keyhole and saw the same woman, dressed in a *fostán* the color of the stars. Immediately, *pishín,* he banged on the door and, this time also, it was the little old woman in black who came out and asked him, in her young girl's voice:

"What is your wish, my lord?"

"I'd like a *gató,* a cake, baked with your own hands," the king's son said to her.

The little old woman made it for him, *pishín,* and he ate every last crumb of it.

On the third night, also, the king's son went down to the kitchen and found the door locked. He looked through the small keyhole and saw the same woman dressed in a marvelous *fostán,* the color of the sun, with, on her finger, a diamond ring that sent brilliant sparkles, *senteas,* all around it. The king's son banged on the door more vigorously, *ma* this time, as well, he achieved nothing. The door opened and the little old woman in black appeared who, at his request, prepared a good pâté for him, which the king's son ate, licking his fingers!

The king's son went down to the kitchen many other times in the hope of seeing the beautiful woman through the keyhole, *ma* she never appeared before him again. And so it was that, in despair, he became ill, *hazino,* from too much love. He lost his appetite for food and drink, and he took to his bed. And very soon, *presto,* the news spread throughout the palace that the king's son was dying!

They started bringing him the best dishes in the world from every corner of the kingdom to make him regain his appetite. *Ma* he would try a small spoonful. He would say:

"I can't! I can't!"

And he would send them back to the kitchen.

Seeing that, the little old woman came. She prepared a rice pudding, a *sutlách*. She threw in her mother's diamond ring, and she sent it to the king's son. The king's son received the *sutlách* and tasted it without appetite. *Ma,* upon tasting it, the diamond ring came to his mouth, the one he had seen on the finger of that beautiful woman through the small keyhole of the kitchen. He said *pishín:*

"Go! Bring me here whoever made this *sutlách!*"

They went down to the kitchen and found the little old woman dressed in black. And they asked her:

"Were you the one who made the *sutlách* for the king's son?"

"Yes!" said the little old woman.

"Come *presto!*" they said to her. "Because the king's son wants to see you."

And she went upstairs and presented herself before him. The king's son said to her:

"Tell me *pishín* whose ring this is!"

The little old woman extended her hand, and the king's son slipped the diamond ring on her finger, which fitted her perfectly! At that moment, the little old woman in the filthy black *fostán* disappeared, and in her place the king's son found himself before a most beautiful woman, dressed in a marvelous *fostán* the color of the sun. The king's son recognized her *pishín* and asked her:

"Who are you?"

And she told him all that had happened to her because of the king, her father.

All the illness of the king's son *amahó*, it cured itself on the spot. He jumped out of bed and asked the young woman for her hand. She accepted *pishín*. A very big and very beautiful wedding took place to which all the kings of the world were invited and, among them, the bride's father, who came, saw her, and began to weep, asking for her forgiveness for what he had done. The daughter pardoned him with all the goodness of her heart. And from that day on, they all lived happily and contentedly.

Commentary

This narrative combines three interrelated tale types. It begins with a Jewish oicotype, IFA 510*C, *The Maiden in the Chest,* in which the dying wife asks her husband to remarry only if one of her ornaments—here a ring—fits the new bride-to-be. The object fits only one woman (Z320), however, and that is the man's daughter. When he attempts to force her to marry him, she flees from home before the wedding.[1] AT 510B, *The Dress of Gold, of Silver, and of Stars (Cap o'Rushes)*[2] illustrates the segment of the tale in which the father

---

1. See Jason, *Types,* 18. IFA parallels are from Iran, Israel (Arab), Morocco, Tunisia, and Yemen.

2. There are two published Judeo-Spanish versions of this type from Tetuán: LP, vol. 1, no. 79, p. 238, "La muñeca de palo" and LP, vol. 1, no. 87, p. 260, "El anillo suelto." LP 79 tells of a girl who fits her mother's gloves and escapes from her wooing father in a hollow wooden doll. She appears three times at a ball wearing her mag-

who wants to marry his own daughter gives her the presents she demands. She then flees and works as a servant for a prince. This is a version of Perrault's "Peau d'âne." AT 510, *Cinderella and Cap o'Rushes,* part 1, *The Persecuted Heroine* (b), describes the offended heroine fleeing in disguise from her father who wants to marry her.[3] In part 3, *Meeting the Prince* (c), she is seen in the kitchen wearing her beautiful clothes. Part 4, *Proof of Identity,* shows how

---

nificent dresses and wins the prince's heart. Identification follows with the ring baked in a cake. In LP 87, the heroine escapes in a hollow golden throne. She attends a ball three times and secures tokens from the prince. Recognition follows when she bakes the tokens in a cake. In both cases the heroine marries the prince. Another version appears in Koén-Sarano, *Konsejas,* 57. Other Jewish versions of AT 510B appear in Alexander-Noy, nos. 9 (Morocco), 76 (Turkey); Jason, "Types," 151; *Schwili,* nos. 24, 38. An IFA parallel comes from Tunisia. Parallels from other traditions can be found in Al-Shahi, *Wisdom from the Nile,* no. 22; Ashliman, *Guide to Folktales,* 108; Basile, *Pentamerone,* Day 2, Tale 6; Day 3, Tale 2; Baughman, *England and North America,* 12; Boggs, *Spanish Folktales,* 67; Boulvin, *Contes populaires persans,* 1:19, 2:20; BP, 2:45–56, 4:219, 250; Briggs, *Dictionary of British Folk-Tales,* pt. A, vol. 1, 137, 164, 177, 179, 416, 455, 456, 460, 502, pt. A, vol. 2, 387; Bushnaq, *Arab Folktales,* 193 (Egypt); Calvino, *Italian Folktales,* no. 103; Chauvin, *Ouvrages Arabes,* 5: 196–97; Chevalier, *Siglo de Oro,* no. 38; Cole, *Best-Loved Folktales,* no. 22; D'Aronco, *Fiabe di Magia,* no. 16; Dawkins, *Forty-five Stories,* nos. 7, 9, 14 (Greece); Dawkins, *Modern Greek Folktales,* no. 40; Delarue, *Conte populaire français,* 2:256, 718; EB, nos. 188, 189, 244, 245; A. Espinosa, *Cuentos populares,* vol. 1, nos. 108, 109, 110, 111, 112, vol. 2, 406–21; Grimm and Grimm, *Tales,* no. 65; T. Hansen, *Types* (Cuba, Dominican Republic, Puerto Rico); Huerta, "Motif-Index of Juan de Rael" (T411.1); Perrault, "Peau d'âne"; Pino-Saavedra, *Chile,* no. 20; Rael, *Colorado y Nuevo Méjico,* nos. 106, 107, 108, 109, 110, 111, 114, 116, 117, 118, 119, 237; Robe, *Mexican Folktales,* 89; Straparola, *Facetious Nights,* 1:4; Thompson, *One Hundred Favorite Folktales,* no. 41 (Norway); Thompson and Roberts, *Indic Oral Tales,* 73; Villa, *100 Armenian Tales,* no. 24.

3. Additional Judeo-Spanish versions appear in LP, vol. 1, no. 13, p. 50, "La Cenicera" (Tetuán) and LP, vol. 1, no. 47, p. 154, "Lo que cada una se merece" (Tetuán). See also LP, vol. 2, no. 91, p. 17, "Las tres peticiones" (Tetuán) (classified in Haboucha as AT 480), as well as nos. 1, 3 (Skoplje), no. 8 (Salonique) (classified in Haboucha as AT 480), and no. 16 (Bitolj) (classified in Haboucha as **403 D). For other Jewish parallels, consult Grunwald, *Tales,* nos. 2, 51; Hanauer, *Holy Land,* 167; Meyukhas, *Ma'asiyot,* 6–12, no. 2 (Israel Sephardic); Noy, *Egypt,* no. 12 (AT 480); Noy, *Libya,* nos. 2, 67 (AT 403), 170; Noy, *Morocco,* no. 1 (AT 480); Schram, *Jewish Stories,* 414, 427; Schwarzbaum, *Studies,* 90; Shenhar and Bar Itzhak, *Shelomi,* 44. There are IFA versions of this type from Afghanistan, Eastern Europe, Iranian Kurdistan, Iraq, Iraqi Kurdistan, Israel (Sephardic), Morocco, Turkey, and Yemen. For non-Jewish

she is discovered through a ring, which she throws into the prince's pudding. In the end, predictably, the orphaned heroine marries the prince (L111.4.2), as she does in all the types listed above (T100). In part 5, *Marriage with the Prince,* the father is invited to the wedding feast and forgiven.

Because our tale is more romantic than fantastic, it features few magical elements, and they are all connected with the delaying tactics of the reluctant bride: the magician provides the means of securing the marvelous by helping the king meet the challenge set by his daughter. He is required to produce extraordinary clothes for her (F821) and the motif of the gowns of the color of the sun, moon, and stars (F821.1.5) comes into the tale. The impossible tasks are satisfied when the king magically produces dresses so fine that they can all fit into a tiny chest (F821.2). Once the task is accomplished, the tale reverts to a more realistic development, which could also possibly help categorize it as a tale of the clever heroine who succeeds in marrying the prince.

As we can see elsewhere in this anthology, promises connected with death (M250) are binding. This time it concerns a marriage test imposed by a dying wife about the choice of a second wife. The surviving spouse promises his ailing wife that he will not marry unless the new bride meets the specifications the first wife imposes (M255, H363). The bride test is for the deceased wife's ring to fit the bride perfectly (H363.2). Respect is accorded the last wishes of a dying person, which are viewed as having the same binding force as a legal document. The king feels bound by his promise to the extent of defying the biblical injunction against incest, even when the potential infraction is called to his attention. Usually a symbolic figure of great authority, the father in this

---

parallels, see Armistead-Katz, "Soria," nos. 1, 2; Ashliman, *Guide to Folktales,* 107; Boulvin, *Contes populaires persans,* 1:14, 2:7; BP, 1:65; Briggs, *Dictionary of British Folk-Tales,* pt. A, vol. 1, 138; Bushnaq, *Arab Folktales,* 181 (Iraq); Calvino, *Italian Folktales,* nos. 54, 64, 70, 148; Carvalho-Neto, *Ecuador,* nos. 37, 38; Clarkson and Cross, *World Folktales,* no. 4 (Canada); Cole, *Best-Loved Folktales,* nos. 1 (France), 10 (Germany), 179 (Canada), 187 (Haiti); D'Aronco, *Fiabe di Magia,* no. 15; D'Aronco, *Fiabe Toscane,* 77, 78; Dawkins, *Modern Greek Folktales,* no. 21; Delarue, *Conte populaire français,* 2:245; Dorson, *Folktales Told around the World,* 57, 177; EB, nos. 60, 240; A. Espinosa, *Cuentos populares,* vol. 1, no. 105, vol. 2:396–98; M. Espinosa, *Folklore of Spain,* 184; Grimm and Grimm, *Tales,* nos. 21, 186; Grimm and Grimm, *Other Tales,* 44; J. Jacobs, *European Folk and Fairy Tales,* no. 1; Kent, *Turkey,* 15, 148; Legey, *Maroc,* nos. 3, 54, 55; Lorimer, *Persian,* nos. 16, 39; Mathers, *Thousand Nights,* 4:191; Pino-Saavedra, *Chile,* no. 19; Rael, *Colorado y Nuevo Méjico,* nos. 112, 113, 115, 139; Robe, *Mexican Folktales,* 87; Thompson, *One Hundred Favorite Folktales,* no. 40; Villa, *100 Armenian Tales,* no. 30.

case is clearly in the wrong, and he must be humbled and shown the error of his ways.

The father-daughter interaction (P234) occurs only at the beginning (escape from the threat of incest) and the end (remorse and forgiveness) of the tale. In most of the universal versions listed above, the unwelcome lover is put off repeatedly by the use of a deceptive respite (K1227). The daughter assigns her incestuous father tasks, agreeing to marry him once they are accomplished (T151.0.1, T411.1). These excessive demands are made with the expectation that the assignee will be unable to fulfill them and, thus, in the hope of delaying and eventually preventing marriage (H301). In the end, while the daughter exacts the price she seeks, she flees to escape the incestuous marriage (T411.1 [Huerta], R210, R213, T311.1).

The motif of the attractive woman disguised as a menial at the lover's court (K1816, K1821.7, K1816.0.2) and that of the prince whose attention is drawn when he discovers the heroine in her beautiful clothes lead to other common motifs: his falling in love (T10, P30) and then falling prey to lovesickness (T24.1). Recognition follows (H151, H151.6) with the identification of the disguised princess by the ring she bakes in a pudding (H94, H94.1). That recognition token—the dying mother's ring—is a widely used plot device that serves to identify the central character with an object of love.

The narrative skill of this teller stands out. She artfully weaves in the distinct segments of the tale in episodes of threes: the extraordinary dresses; the visits the prince makes to the kitchen; and the special meals the princess prepares for the prince. She uses food as a repeated motif to connect the prince to the heroine. The threefold visits of the prince, for example, take place not at a church, as in AT 510B, but in the royal kitchen. The teller takes apparent pleasure in describing how much the prince enjoys the princess's cooking: the first time he eats the soup with pleasure; the second time he eats every last crumb of the cake; and the third time he licks his fingers after eating the pâté.

20

Shlomó *Ameleh* and the Birds' Eggs

Narrated by SIMHA COHEN (1993)

King Solomon, Shlomó *Ameleh*, married many women. He once saw a girl, he fell in love with her, and he wanted to marry her. This girl said:

"I'm ready to be your wife, *ma* I have one condition."

"Which one?"

"I want you to have a house built for me from the eggs of all the birds that are in the world. I want the ceiling, the *taván,* to be made entirely of eggs."

As there is nothing that the king can't do, he summoned the eagle, the king of the birds, and said to him:

"*Presto*! Quickly! Bring me the eggs of all the birds in the world!"

The eagle went away and brought him back egg after egg. Shlomó had the room built and had the eggs placed in the *taván*. He called the girl and said to her:

"Come see. I have now built you a room just as you want it."

Ma she was smart, *hahamá*. She looked and looked, and she said:

"No! There is an egg missing here!"

The king was very surprised. He summoned the eagle. He said to him:

"There is an egg missing here! Why didn't you bring it?"

"My lord king," said the eagle, "there is a little bird that refuses to give its egg: 'For a woman?' it said. 'No! Women cannot be trusted!'"

This tale appears in Judeo-Spanish and Hebrew in Koén-Sarano, "Los guevos de pasharó," in *Lejendas*, 83. See also p. 51 for an aborted parallel in anecdotal form, "Saver kuando demandar."

The king said to the eagle:

"Go fetch it *presto*! If you don't, your head will roll!"

The eagle went *presto, ma* the little bird entered quickly, *pishín*, into his hole. The hole was small, and the eagle, the king of the birds, who is large, was unable to enter it. He stood outside, waiting and waiting. He was boiling: how can he go back to the king without the egg?

Another little bird passed by. He said to him:

"Why are you so upset?"

"Do you know why?" the eagle said to him. "All the birds in the world gave their eggs to Shlomó *Ameleh*. Only this little bird doesn't want to give it to him. That's why he has fled into his hideout!"

The little bird said to him:

"*Aspera!* Wait! I'll go bring you the egg."

This little bird went into the hideout. He said to the other one:

"Shalóm. Peace be with you! How are you? Tell me why it is that you don't want to give your egg. We have all given ours. The king demanded it. It must be given!"

"Come, sit down," the other one said to him. "I'll tell you what happened."

"What happened?"

"My nest was in a garden, on top of a tree. There was there a husband and wife who loved each other very much. All of a sudden the husband sighed:

'Ah!'

His wife said to him:

'What's the matter, my beloved? Why are you sighing? What are you longing for?'

'Today we're together,' the husband said to her. '*Ma* there is life and death in the world. Tomorrow I'll die, and you'll take another husband.'

'No! God forbid! *Has ve-halila!*' said the wife. 'Don't utter such words from your mouth! I'll never remarry. I'll always remain faithful to you. And if I die before you do, you yourself will go and take another....'

'No! I'll never take another one!'

A few days passed. The husband died. The wife wept. She used up her eyes. She went into a small cave, a *meará,* and she buried him there. She sat there and wept:

'Oh! Oh! Oh!'

She loved him very much.

In that city, the king had ordered a thief seized and placed under guard. He told the guard:

'Hang this thief tomorrow morning. When I see him dangling, I'll let you go.'

'Very well,' said the guard.

While the guard was watching over, *bekleando,* the thief, all of a sudden, *ensupitó,* he heard:

'Oh! Oh! Oh!'

Someone is weeping. Where is this weeping coming from? The guard followed the weeping to its source. He entered the *meará* and saw this woman who was very beautiful. She was the one who was weeping.

The woman saw him; she said to him:

'Come in.'

All at once she forgot about her husband. She said to him:

'Come.'

And he went.

The guard said:

'*Addió*! Oh God! I had to guard, to *bekleár,* this thief!'

Oops! The thief had escaped. *Agora,* what would the king say? They'll hang him instead of the thief! The guard returned to the woman; he said to her:

'See now? You said to me: "Come, come!" and the thief has run away....'

'Silly man,' the woman said to him, '*na*! Here is my husband. We buried him two days ago. We'll put him in place of the thief.' [Look at what kind of woman she is!][1]

He said to her:

'*Ma* this thief was missing an eye!'

She said:

'We'll take a nail; we'll gouge out one of his eyes.'

And that's what they did: they removed the husband from his grave, they gouged out his eye, and they hung him in place of the thief. The king saw from the window that they had hung the thief. He told the guard:

'Go now! You're free! You are *líbero*!'

"That's why," said the little bird, "I will not give my egg. Women cannot be trusted!"

The other small bird came. He said:

"*Agora* I'll tell you what happened to me. My nest, just like yours, was on top of a tree, in a garden.... There lived a man and his son. The father was old; he said to his son:

---

1. Teller's aside.

'My son, there is life and death in this world. In a little while I'll die, and you'll remain alone. *Kale ke* you marry. I'll give you a shoe. You must marry the girl whose foot fits into this shoe.'

These two made rugs, *tapetes*. When the old man died, the youth remained. He kept making and making, but he was not successful in selling them. All his warehouses were filled with *tapetes*. His father had told him:

'Until you have a bride, go from village to village to look for her. When you find her, build a fence, a *gadér*, and don't go outside of here anymore.'

The youth took the shoe, and he went from house to house seeking a wife. *A la fín,* in the end, he came to the hut of a villager who worked the land. He knocked on the door and entered. He was a good-looking youth, well dressed.

'*Barúh abá*! Welcome! What is it you want?'

'I'm seeking a wife. Do you have any daughters?'

'I have three daughters, *ma* you must be jesting with me! A *gentleman* such as yourself, how could you marry a village girl?'

'Yes, I could!'

They brought out the oldest daughter and they tried the shoe on her. It doesn't fit her. They brought out the second one. Neither did it fit her. As for the third one, it fit her perfectly.

The youth said:

'This is the one I'll take as my wife.'

He took the girl. He gave her parents, her *djenitores, parás* and gifts, and he married her. He had a palace built, with a fence, a *gadér,* a swimming pool, a garden with trees and flowers and everything in it, and he said:

'I will not step out of here.'

Ma business is not going well for him. He makes *tapetes;* but he does not sell them. He forgot that his father had told him:

'You must never leave this land again.'

[No matter how much one has, it is never enough.][2] *Agora,* what will he do? He took his *alates,* his tools, and he went to Estanból. He opened up a shop, a *botika,* and he began making *tapetes*. And everyone liked his work, his *lavoro,* very much.

The king of Estanból heard that there is such a man who makes *tapetes*. He called him:

'Come here. Can you make me a large *tapét,* from one wall to the other wall?'

He said to him:

---

2. Teller's aside.

'Certainly!'

And he set down to *lavorár*. *Ma* he had taken along the picture of his wife, and each time he thought about her, he would take out the photograph and look at it, saying:

'Ah!'

And he would work more willingly.

The king said to his *vizír:*

'Go see if this man *lavora* well!'

The *vizír* went; he came back, and he said to him:

'Yes, he *lavora* very well, *ma, ensupitó,* he takes something out, looks at it, then goes back to *lavorár.*'

'What can it be?' said the king. 'I want to see it with my own eyes.'

He concealed himself there and saw that, indeed, the man was doing just that. He said to him:

'Come here! What is this that you're taking out?'

'Nothing!' he said. 'It's the picture of my wife.'

The king looked at it:

'Ah, what a beautiful woman! Ah, you didn't want to show it!'

He took him; he put him in prison. The poor man—they tied up his hands and feet. [Why? Because he had not followed the will, the *savá,* of his father!]³

Agora, the king desires this woman. He convened his entire parliament and he said to them:

'I want one of you to go get this woman for me!'

The *vizír* said:

'I'll go!'

The king gave him *parás,* and he went. He opened up a *butika* in the city where that man used to live. He started to sell very cheaply. Every woman who came in, he would look at and say:

'No, this is not the one!'

A la fín, in the end, an old hag came in, a witch, a *mahshefá.* The *vizír* showed her the picture of the woman. He said to her:

'Do you know this woman?'

'Yes, I know her.'

'Get me a *randevú* with her.'

'Fine.'

---

3. Teller's aside.

The *vizír* gave her *parás*. The old hag went knocking on the woman's door, *ma* the woman did not come out. She never went out because her husband had said to her:

'Don't go out!'

She looked out of the window; she saw the old hag. The old hag said to her:

'I am your aunt. I came to find you.'

The woman opened the door for her; the old hag went upstairs.

'What do you want?'

'One of your nephews wants to come and visit you. Can you receive him?'

'Yes! Sure! Bring him over!'

The old hag went back to the *vizír*. She said to him:

'I have already arranged it with that woman. Go tomorrow at such and such a time.'

The *vizír* placed the *parás* in the old hag's hand; he closed shop and went. He knocked and knocked on the woman's door. She saw from the window that a young man had come. She let him in; he went upstairs. At the entrance to the house there was a long hallway, a *korridór*. In the middle of that *korridór* there was a pit. Over that pit there was a *tapét*. The man, who saw that the woman was so beautiful, wanted to reach her side more *presto,* and take her hand and say to her:

'Shalóm!'

He came to the middle of the *korridór,* and boom! He fell into the pit.

She looked down at him from above; she said to him:

'Ah, *mamzér*! Bastard! What did you want? *Agora, kare ke* you work. If you are going to work, to *lavorár,*' she said to him, 'you'll receive food. If not, you will not eat.[4] You'll die here. What is it that you know how to do?'

The *vizír* said to her:

'When I was a boy I enjoyed making hats, *chapeos*. . . .'

She brought him needles and threads, and he settled down to making *chapeos*. If he made them, she brought him food. If he didn't make, she didn't bring.

Meanwhile, the king saw that six months had gone by and the *vizír* wasn't coming back. He said:

'Sure! He found that woman and he is having a good time with her!'

Again, he convened his most loyal men. He said to them:

---

4. "Who has not worked shall not eat" (Bereshit Rabba [Gen. R.] 14:10).

'Who will go *agora*?'

The *ḳadi*, the judge, came. He said to him:

'I'm loyal to you. I'll go!'

In short, the *ḳadi* took the *parás;* he went to that city; he opened up a *butiḳa*. The women came to shop. He looked. He saw no one until that old hag arrived. He showed her the photograph:

'Do you know this woman?'

'Sure, I know her!'

'Fix me a *randevú* with her!'

'Fine.'

The old hag went; she knocked on the woman's door. This one recognized her, and she let her come up.

'Your uncle's son wishes to see you. Can he come over to find you?'

'Let him come tomorrow.'

The same thing: the *ḳadi* closed the *butiḳa;* he put the keys in the hand of the old hag:

'Take the *butiḳa* for yourself!'

He knocked on the woman's door. She saw another man; she let him come up. He came to the *ḳorridór*. He saw a very, very beautiful woman. He wanted to get quickly, *presto,* to her side. Oops! He fell on the other one's head.

She said to him:

'Stay here *agora*. And you are going to *lavorár*! If you won't *lavorár,* you won't receive any food!'

She looked at the two of them from above, and she said to them:

'*Mamzerím*! Bastards! What did you want from me? *Agora* work!'

And she brought them more threads.

The king is waiting and waiting. . . . Six months went by, and they still have not returned. The king said:

'I'll go myself!'

He said to his son:

'Do you know what? You'll sit in my place and you'll govern the country. I'll go to where that woman is.'

In short, the king went. He too opened up a *butiḳa*. Women kept coming and coming, *ma* he did not see the woman in the photograph, in the *stampa*. Until the old hag came in:

'Do you know this woman?'

'Yes, I do know her!'

'Fix me a *randevú* with her!'

'Fine.'

In short, the old hag went to the woman. She said to her:

'There is a nephew of your mother's who wishes to see you.'
'Very well. Come with him tomorrow.'
The next day, the old hag went to the king. She said to him:
'She said that we should go together.'
The king closed the *butika*. He went with her and knocked on the door. She saw the two of them downstairs. She dressed up more beautifully, much more beautifully. The king came in and he saw a very beautiful woman. He wanted to reach her side more *presto*. How can he do it? He ran toward her! Boom! He fell on top of the other two.

'What is this?' the king said.

'That's what it is,' she said to him. 'If you are going to *lavorár* you'll receive food. If not, nothing!'

'*Ma*, I'm a king! I never do any *lavoro*!'

'If you don't work you don't eat!'

The other two taught him, and he worked. Later, the king wanted to go back home. How is he going to do it? His son is in his place.

What did this woman do? She wrote a *letra* to the king's son:

'You should know, my son, that the son of the king of Germany has to come to you. Receive him well, and let him do whatever he wishes in the state.'

And she said to the king:

'Sign here!'

The king signed so that he would be released from there. She sent that letter to the king's son with his father's seal, so that he would ready himself to receive the son of the king of Germany.

The king's son put out flowers, banners; he fixed up his city. What did she do? She dressed up as the king of Germany—[she had the garments][5]—and she boarded the steamship. She told those of the steamship:

'I want only one person to steer the steamship. How much do you earn? One hundred? I'll give you two hundred. I'll take the ship; I'll leave and come back.'

Az, they gave it to her, and she left. When she arrived in Estanból, she put on the garments of the son of the king of Germany and she entered the king's palace. They all received her very well.

'The son of the king of Germany has arrived!'

The king's son gave her great honors, great *kavód*. She asked him:

'How is your state?'

The king's son said to her:

---

5. Teller's aside.

'I want you to visit my prisons.'[6]

When she visited them, she said:

'I went into the prisons. I saw a sad man, a desperate man [her husband!].[7] What did he do? Is he a thief?'

'This one used to make *tapetes* for my father. He did not want to show him the *stampa* of his wife!'

'Ah, *mamzér*! Bastard! *Rashá*! Wicked man! Bad Jew! Put more shackles on him, *pishín*! Tighten the fetters on his hands and feet!'

A day later, she said to the king's son:

'Do you know what? I'll take this Jew back to Germany and have him killed.'

As the king, his father, had written to him, 'Let him do whatever he wishes in our state,' the king's son let her have him, and she took him with her and left. She removed his shackles and gave him food. *Ma* she wished to test her husband. And she spoke to him as king of Germany. She said to him:

'I have a very beautiful sister. I want you to amuse yourself a bit with her.'

The husband said:

'No! I have only one wife and one *Dió!*'

'What's the matter? I rescued you, I removed your shackles, I fed you!'

'No! I don't do this! *Beshúm ofen*! Not on any account! Throw me into the ocean!'

Seeing that her husband does not want to do this, she took him with her and brought him back to their city. She brought along also the son of the king of Estanból. They set the table next to the pit where the three men were held. The king's son looked down; he saw him; he said:

'Oh, father!'

'Save me!' his father said to him.

'Do you want to come out?' the woman said to him. 'Sign here for me that, if a man who is *lavorando* for you looks at a *stampa,* you have no right to cause him grief, to make *tsarót* for him. Why should it matter to you? He is making you a *tapét*! As for this old hag,' she said, 'hang her and shred her to pieces! The *vizír* and the *kadi,* kill them!'

She removed the king from there. She sent him back home with his son, and from that day on they began to live in peace."

When the little bird heard that such a woman exists, one who did all of

---

6. This is an interesting concept based on the wise saying: "Let me see your courts and your prisons, and I'll tell you the state of your society."

7. Teller's aside.

this for the sake of her husband, he took his egg and brought it to Shlomó *Ameleh*. And so it was that he was able to marry the girl he loved.

In his garden grew an apple tree. There were only three apples on that tree. They gave one to the teller of this tale. The second one they gave to Simha, and the third one they gave to me!

COMMENTARY

The structure of this narrative is that of a frame tale that incorporates two other tale types within it. *The Thousand and One Nights* gives a classic example of the frame tale in which the cohesive plot device concerns the efforts of Sheherazade to keep her husband, Shariar, legendary king of Samarkand, from killing her. She does so by entertaining him with a tale a night for one thousand and one nights.

A marriage test is at the center of our tale plot in which a king (P10) falls in love (T10) with a girl who assigns him a task (H335.0.2) and offers herself as the prize for its accomplishment (H335). The suitor must do something difficult, almost impossible, to win the bride. This frame tale is a version of the Jewish oicotype IFA *981 I Andrejev, *Tales of the Talking Birds*,[8] in which, to fulfill the wishes of his beloved, the king is required to build a palace of bird eggs. To accomplish the task, he seeks the help of all the birds in the world. One bird does not contribute its egg and, through the telling of a tale, illustrates the per-

---

8. See Crews, no. 5, p. 91 (Bitolj) and Haboucha, 497ff. This Judeo-Spanish tale was also published in translation in Crews, *Folk-Lore,* 43:216–25. In addition to the types listed below, the Bitolj version features other episodes not included in the present narrative: AT 888A, *The Wife Who Would Not Be Beaten* pt. 2, *The Prince Enslaved* (b), shows how the husband loses his freedom at a chance game with the trained cat (c) in the land of cheaters and is enslaved. Pt. 3 or AT888A, *The Rescue,* features the wife winning the game by letting mice loose, which the trained cat chases. AT 217, *The Cat and the Candle,* describes the actual game and how it is won. For the study of a parallel of this tale, see Haboucha, "Misogyny or Philogyny." IFA versions exist from Libya, Egypt, and Morocco. For Jewish parallels, see Alexander-Noy, nos. 6 (Morocco), 54 (Turkey); *BJ,* 3:293–94, 315, 325; bin Gorion, *Mimekor Yisrael,* vol. 1, no. 66, 128, vol. 1, no. 82, 164, vol. 3, nos. 24, 25, 26, 1141–42. Frankel, *Classic Tales,* no. 99; Gaster, *Ma'aseh Book,* vol. 1, no. 107; Ginzberg, *Legends,* 4:142; Grunwald, *Tales,* no. 56; Hanauer, *Holy Land,* 186; Kurt, *Zar prakhim,* nos. 22, 42 (Afghanistan); Mintz, *Tales of the Hassidim,* 418; Nahmad, *Portion in Paradise,* 56, 98; Noy, *Libya,* nos. 8, 54; Noy, *Morocco,* no. 44; Noy, *Tunisia,* no. 68; Sabar, *Kurdis-*

fidious character of women. Ultimately the frame tale culminates in marriage: King Solomon wins the beautiful maiden by accomplishing the difficult task she had set. Note the formulaic and unusually playful ending.

Well-known secondary motifs of helpers enabling the wooer to perform the task are used here. As we have seen in other tales in this anthology, tests connected with marriage (H300) and help received in performing these tests (H970), especially from animals (B571), are part of the plot; they help the suitor win the bride (B582.2). In this case, the helpful animals are speaking birds (B211.3, B211.9 [Noy], B450). Birds are at the center of interest here and act as assistants to King Solomon, a biblical figure endowed with the extraordinary ability to understand the language of birds and other animals (D2198+ [Noy]).

Solomon's goal of winning a bride is almost thwarted by one bird, however, and this twist allows for the incorporation of the two fidelity/infidelity tales within the frame tale (H1556). The first narrative inserted, AT 1510, *The Matron of Ephesus (Vidua)*,[9] highlights a disloyal widow. It illustrates motif K2213.1 in which a woman mourns day and night by her husband's grave. A watchman guarding a prisoner about to be hanged is in danger of losing his own life after the prisoner escapes while the widow distracts the guard. To save him, she offers the latter her love and substitutes her husband's corpse on the gallows so that the guard can escape. In our version, when the woman mourns her dead husband (T85), she shows excessive grief (T211.9). Yet, she proves to be a faithless widow (T231), ready to marry a new man soon after her husband's funeral (T231.1). She then subjects his body to indignities. Historically, the Matron of Ephesus is a widow famous for her beauty and marital devotion and equally famous for her faithlessness. She is the object of a motif that has passed through world literature. The episode was a medieval

---

tani Jews, 55–61; Schram, *Jewish Stories*, 253; Schwarzbaum, *Studies*, 47; *Schwili*, nos. 12, 80. For universal parallels, see Andrejev (type 1352*); EB, no. 278; Laoust, *Contes berbères*, no. 33; Legey, *Maroc*, no. 67; Voltaire, *Zadig*, chap. 2.

9. See Koén-Sarano, *Lejendas*, 41, for a Judeo-Spanish parallel of the faithless wife, "No ay konfiensa en la mujer." IFA versions were collected from tellers from Afghanistan, Egypt, Libya, and Morocco. For Jewish parallels, refer to Ausubel, *Jewish Folklore*, 635; *BJ*, 3:239–42; Gaster, *Exempla*, no. 442; Hadas, *Jewish Aesop*, no. 80; Jason, "Types," 205; Jason, *Types*, 74. For international versions, see Andrejev (type 1352*); Ashliman, *Guide to Folktales*, 256; Briggs, *Dictionary of British Folk-Tales*, pt. A, vol. 2, 207; Chauvin, *Ouvrages arabes*, 8:210–13, no. 254; Chevalier, *Siglo de Oro*, no. 157; Clouston, *Popular Tales*, 1:29–35; EB, no. 278; A. Espinosa, *Cuentos populares*, vol. 2, no. 93, vol. 2, 356–67; Handford, *Aesop*, 203; Tubach, *Index Exemplorum*, no. 5262; "Ysopete" (K2213.1).

"merry tale," thought to be of Eastern origin, and well-known to classical antiquity.[10] It is also known among Jews.[11]

In the second tale inserted into the main narrative, another bird sets out to prove that women can also be faithful, and in so doing succeeds in convincing the first bird to contribute its egg so that the king may win his bride. This second tale within a tale features a father and son (P233) and a promise connected with death (M256). The dying father imposes a unique prohibition, forbidding his son to do one particular thing; everything else he is free to do (C600). Following his father's instructions, the son goes in search of a bride (H1381.3.1), whom he puts through a bride test (H360, H300). The slipper test identifies as the fated bride the one whose foot it fits (H36.1) since, as usually happens in folktales, the slipper will fit only one woman (Z320). The motif of the slipper test, of course, appears in AT 510, *Cinderella*. Later, the breaking of the son's promise to his dying father (M250, M256) leads to his captivity and to the opportunity for his wife to prove her love for him (P210) as well as her cleverness (J1112). In the end, the counsel of the dying father not to leave home proves wise by experience (J154).[12]

AT 875C, *The Queen as Gusli-player*, introduces the episode in which the husband disobeys his father's instructions and travels to a foreign land, where he is thrown into prison. After the sultan falls in love with the wife by looking at her picture (T11.2), he imprisons the husband and attempts to seduce the woman. His repeated attempts are punished (Q243.2.1) and she deals with him cleverly (J1675). That type, as well as AT 888, *The Faithful Wife*,[13] describes how the enslaved husband is later rescued by his wife, disguised as a visiting prince.

AT 888A, *The Wife Who Would Not Be Beaten*, part 2(a), *The Prince Enslaved*, shows how the husband sets out to win his fortune. Part 1 of AT 888,

---

10. Her story is told by Petronius (Sat. 111–13). Voltaire incorporated it in his *Zadig*.

11. Tosafot to Kid. 80b (R. Hananel Gaon, 11c); *Jewish Quarterly Review* 6:516; *Zeitschrift der deutschen morgenlandischen Gesellschaft*. Leipzig, 1847ff.

12. The motif of the deathbed promise appears in several other tales and is analyzed elsewhere in this anthology.

13. IFA versions are from Afghanistan, Iraqi Kurdistan, Morocco, and Yemen. Jewish versions include Jason, *Types*, 43; Kagan, *TEM 1964*, no. 9 (Poland). For non-Jewish versions, see Ashliman, *Guide to Folktales*, 180 (AT 888A); BP, 3:517; Briggs, *Dictionary of British Folk-Tales*, pt. A, vol. 2, 252, pt. B, 223; Grimm and Grimm, *Tales*, no. 218; Grimm and Grimm, *Other Tales*, 128; Thompson and Roberts, *Indic Oral Tales*, 107 (AT 888A).

The Enslaved Husband, describes how the husband is taken into slavery, and part 2(b), *The Chaste Wife,* how the messengers of the sultan seek in vain to seduce his wife. Eventually the wife, disguised in man's clothes (K1837), succeeds in rescuing her husband (N831, R152, R110). Dressed as a foreign prince, she travels to the hostile land. In the end, as in AT 875C, once the wife receives permission to take back with her one of the prisoners, she chooses her husband and thus rescues him from prison (R152.1). He does not recognize her.

This second tale within a tale illustrates an unequal marriage (T121), in which the unpromising heroine is the typical successful youngest daughter (L102). An interesting detail here is the groom's giving gifts and money to the parents of the bride to seal the marriage agreement and as a sign of future well-being and prosperity. Traditionally, the dowry is offered by the bride's family.

The old hag in the tale, who serves as a go-between for the king's emissaries and eventually for the king himself, seems to know everyone and is able to gain access into every home through her cunning. The means by which she enters the woman's home are deceptive, and her motive is pecuniary. This episode easily brings to mind the well-known Spanish picaresque novel *La Celestina* and its disreputable protagonist by the same name.

21

The Arranged Marriage

Narrated by IMANUEL BEN EZRA (1992)

In the city of Izmir, there was a young man who was a jeweler, and they called him Avraam the *djevaerdjí,* Abraham the jeweler. This young man had already reached the age of twenty-five. He does not want to marry. He just is not finding a bride for himself.

[And you know that, in the old days, it was not customary for young men to meet with young women in order to take each other in marriage. It was the parents, the *parientes,* who looked for a bride for a young man.[1] And that's the way it was with Avramachi.[2]]

The mother was always weeping. She would say to her son:

"Look, son, what else can I hope for? I want to see a happy occasion. I want to rejoice in this world, and leave it happy. Don't you want to get married? I'll find a good bride for you. All that you wish for I'll find for you."

"No, no, no, no!" he would say to her.

In short.... His mother nagged him so much that one afternoon, while drinking coffee, he said to her:

"*Ima,* do you want me to marry? Find me a bride! The one you'll pick will be good enough for me!"

Tov! The next day his mother took along a few small purses of ducats. [In the old days, the currency, the *parás,* was ducats.][3] She got dressed and fixed herself up, and where did she go? She goes to the Jewish Quarter, to the *Djudría.*

---

1. Teller's aside.
2. This is an affectionate nickname for Abraham.
3. Teller's aside.

She entered the *Djudría*. The houses were below ground level, with small staircases leading down. She saw a girl, a young girl, *spondjando,* mopping the stairs to her house. The old woman, Avraam's mother, stood there watching her.

"*Hanum*! My dear!" she said. "Can you give me a glass of water?"

"Sure! Come in," the young girl said. "This is a Jewish household. Come on in!"

And she led her downstairs. The mother looked around: everything clean, everything fine, *ma* poor. She was surprised. She says:

"For such poor people to have these kinds of manners, of *niúr*...."

The young girl brought her the water. She said to her:

"*Hanum,* what's your name?"

"My name is Merkaducha."[4]

"Don't you have a mother? Where is your mother?"

"Yes," she says, "she serves in houses."

The woman says to her:

"When can I see her? I want to speak with her."

She says:

"Tomorrow."

The woman says:

"Look, *hanum,* you'll tell your mother not to go out tomorrow. If she has to go somewhere, whatever they pay her, I'll give her twice as much. Let her stay at home. I'll come and talk to her about an interesting matter, an interesting *kestión.*"

"Fine."

The young girl went and made her a coffee, and the good woman drank it and left. *Ma* what did the woman do? On her way out she slipped a purse of money into the armchair, the *chelték*. When she left, the young girl started to tidy up, because her mother was about to come back from *lavór*. All of a sudden, *ensupitó,* the little purse fell to the floor.

"*Addió*! What's that? Master of the universe, it seems that this fell out of the woman's pocket, and she didn't notice it! *Guáy de mozotros*! Woe unto us!" she said. "She'll think that we are thieves! What'll she say? What'll she think?"

In short, the mother already arrived. She sat her down. She gave her a *kavé*. She gave her a cigarette.

"What went on today, *hanum?*" the mother says to her.

"Mother," she says, "today was a really beautiful day!"

"What happened?"

---

4. See commentary for background on this name.

The young girl told her that this woman had come and that she had asked her not go to the *lavoro* the next day because she'll come back. She'll speak to her about a *kestión*. And she'll pay her for the day she would be spending at home! *Ma* she said nothing to her about the *parás* she found!

The next day, this woman returned, and they received her with great pleasure. The young girl came. She said to her:

"Look, *madám*, this and that: I found a little purse of ducats that fell out from you here yesterday."

"No, for charity's sake! For *sedaká*'s sake! I have no knowledge, no *habér* of it!" the woman says to her. "It's from the heavens that have taken pity on you. These *parás* are yours."

Avraam's mother sat down. She called the girl's mother over and she started speaking with her. She said to the young girl:

"Merkaducha, would you do me a favor? Go to the grocer, to the *bakál*. Buy me a pack of cigarettes."

The young girl got up and left. In the meantime, she began talking with the young girl's mother, and she told her that she had come and found the girl to be suitable for her son. And she told her not to think about anything, because her son is Avraam the *djevaerdjí,* and whatever is needed he will take care of, himself. He wants nothing from the girl!

The mother started to cry from happiness. She says:

"Very well, I for one accept, *amá* let's see if she herself wants it."

When the young girl came, they asked her if she wanted to. She said:

"Why not! If I found approval in the eyes of this young man, why not?"

In short, they began sending her many things, and they settled on, *fiksaron,* the wedding date within a month's time. Bags of sugar started to arrive, bags of *kavé. Amá* before they sent her these things, they had taken her out of that house and moved her into a better neighborhood, a better *kartié.*

The day of the wedding is getting closer, without the bride and groom having seen each other. [Of course, they wouldn't see each other until they got married.][5] The day before [as is still customary today],[6] they led the bride to the bathhouse with songs and dances. And for the groom the same thing. Her girlfriends came. They picked up the bride. They took her to the bathhouse, they perfumed her, soaped her up. And his friends picked up the groom.

They are now finished and are on their way back already. His friends said to him:

---

5. Teller's aside.
6. Another aside, connecting past and present.

"*Addió,* let's go take a look at your bride!"

"What for?" he said. "Tomorrow!"

"No," they said to him. "Let's go see who your mother has picked for you. You haven't seen her yet. Go! Look!"

And they led the coach to the area where the young girl lived. Just at that moment, her friends gathered. They were dressing up the bride, and are singing to her. Among all these girls was one a bit slow-witted: Esterika[7] the Mad they called her. This young girl, seeing the clothes and what they are singing to her, started:

"Oh! Oh! Oh! I want that too! I want that too!"

Her friends said to the bride.

"Who will ever marry her, the *povereta,* the poor one? She'll remain this way. Let her put on your gown for a second. Let her be happy."

They insisted so much that she took off her wedding gown and put it on Esterika the Mad. At that moment, the coach passed by, with the groom and his friends. They looked inside and saw Esterika the Mad with everyone singing to her. The groom struck his head with both hands and fainted.

Enfín, they did what they did. They took him home, and the wedding took place the next day. *Amá* he did not raise his eyes to look at her anymore! He now has her by his side, and he doesn't know who she is, still thinking that she is Esterika the Mad.

They finished the wedding. He jumped up, went into a room, locked himself in with a key, and stayed there.

Agora, this girl was very intelligent. She thought:

"Something must have gone through this young man's mind. We'll let some time pass."

She didn't say anything to him. The next day she got up. She made coffee for him, everything. He isn't raising an eye to look at her. *Enfín,* some time passed. She is looking:

"*Addió*! What will it be? Why did I get married? I was better off in my mother's house. What benefit do I get from this marriage?"

What did she do? She got dressed. She fixed herself up. She went over to her mother-in-law. She said to her:

"Mother, I have come to ask for your *permisión,* your permission."

The mother-in-law said to her:

"*Permisión* to do what? What is it you want?"

She says to her:

---

7. This is an affectionate nickname for Esther, literally "Little Esther."

"Your son is behaving in such and such a manner," she says. "Why did I get married? All the things you gave me are of no value to me. I was better off, single, in my mother's house. I have come," she says, "to ask your *permisión* to do something to my husband so as to reform him, to restore him to *mutáv*."

"*Hanum,*" the mother-in-law said to her, "you already know that he is the only son I have. Don't go and do anything to him now."

"Mother," she said to her, "it's true that he is your son, *ma* he is also my husband.... Would I want to hurt my husband?"

Enfín, the mother-in-law said to her:

"*Tov*! Do as you wish!"

This young girl had a friend who was the daughter of the *pashá* of the area, a Turkish girl. She went to her house to visit her. She said to her:

"You'll do me a favor? Give me your gown and, if you can, lend me also your coach for an hour. Do me this favor, I beg of you!"

"Sure!" her friend said to her.

She called out:

"Hassán, give her the gown I wear and get the coach ready. Take her to the place she wants to go to."

"Fine."

And that's the way it was. The young girl got dressed. She fixed herself up [*zatén,* of course, she was very beautiful].[8] She climbed into the carriage. Where was she going? To the *kuyumdjulár,* to the jeweler's, to Avraam's.

Poor Avraam! Every evening he would go drink. He would get himself drunk, and he would return home. He was....

"*Addió*!" he says. "What could my mother have been thinking? Couldn't she find...? Couldn't she find...? She picked that crazy one for me! What shall I do?"

Ensupitó, he sees that in front of the *butika* a coach has stopped. He took a look. He sees a most beautiful woman. The woman came down, speaking in Turkish, *aziéndose hadras,*[9] playing the coquette, pulling her veil. She entered the *butika*.

"*Yaudí*! Jew!" she says to him, "I came because I want this, and this, and this."

He started to bring things out. He started to show her earrings, bracelets, *koliés,* everything. After he brought out everything, she says to him:

---

8. Teller's aside, probably realizing that she had never commented on the girl's physical appearance.

9. The expression *hadras i baranás* denotes excessive display or ostentation.

"Wrap it up. I'll take it all," she says. "*Amá, parás* I don't have to give you. I'll send them to you with my servant tomorrow."

"Fine."

"Do me a favor," she says to him, "my throat, my *garón*, is dry. Fetch me a glass of water."

Avraam went running. He took a glass, he washed it with soap, he cleaned it, he dried it, he filled it up with water, and he brought it to her. She started to drink; the glass slipped from her hand. It fell on her foot and broke. She started to curse him:

"*Yaudí*, are you blind? Didn't you see?"

Poor Avraam, he was going crazy with fright. She took everything along as it was. She climbed into the coach. She left. *Pishín,* Avraam went out to see which way she's going. Who is she? Where did she come from?

That night was worse than other nights. He came home. He locked himself into the room, and there he is.

Amá, before, the young girl had already gone and had a key made for her husband's room. She took some string, entered her husband's room, stretched the string over the bed, and hung all the jewels she had taken: the bracelets, the *koliés,* the earrings.

Her husband arrived, half crazed. He threw himself on the bed like a log, like an *udún,* and he fell asleep. She came. She let herself into the room. She slid into bed, and at midnight, when she saw that her husband was sleeping soundly, she started saying:

"Foot, my dear foot, cut by a glass cup and bandaged with the kerchief, the *rizá* of my husband!" she is saying.

Avramachi, who was sleeping, woke up. He is hearing the same voice he had heard earlier in the day, at the *butika*.

"*Addió!*" he says. "I must be dreaming. It can't be!"

He opened one eye and peeked. He sees her, who is in bed. That's when he understood that she is his wife. She explained to him what she had done and, in this way, they lived happily together, *orozos*.

Commentary

This romantic tale focuses on the rite of marriage and many of its ceremonies, from matchmaking to life after the wedding. The importance of marriage (T100) and preparations for the wedding (T132) are at the core of the introduction to the tale, which has no universal type equivalent.

Many believe that the concept of marriage originated at the time of Creation.[10] In Judaism, it is a highly religious obligation to marry and have children. Although one of the main purposes of marriage is widely held to be procreation, marriage is also considered necessary because it provides both partners with companionship. An occasion for celebration vitally connected to the interest and continuation of the group, the union of men and women has been invested with significance and ritual—with emphasis on both the sexual nature of the coupling and often its religious and economic implications.

Among Sephardim, until the turn of the century, the practice of arranged marriages was widespread. While the bride's and groom's wishes were not ignored when a marriage agreement was made,[11] and their consent was usually sought, as it is in this tale, it was not required (at least not the woman's consent). Although romantic pairings were not unheard of, by and large marital matches were agreed upon by parents, and we see that the role of the mother as a matchmaker who arranges for the marriage of her son (T53.0.1) to an unpromising heroine (L100) is given prominence in this narrative.

The tale polarizes class differences. To seek a bride for Avraam, his mother proceeds to the Jewish Quarter, the *Djudría* (*Djudería*), which was considered an area housing people of a somewhat lesser socioeconomic class. In many Jewish communities within the Ottoman Empire, wealthy Jews tended to live outside the Jewish Quarter. Note the teller's stress on the landing below street level and on the cleanliness of the girl's home, despite her poverty. While health and poverty (U60) are contrasted here (the bride is shown to be of a lower status [L162]), this feature is not uncommon in Sephardic reality or in folktales. Finding a poor but worthy bride was not beneath wealthier Sephardic parents.

As we note here as well, once the match was agreed upon, the parents of the bride and groom would come to an understanding on the gifts to the young couple and on the date of the wedding. When needed, community funds provided for a dowry for an orphan or a poor girl (V405+ [Noy]). The groom's mother makes two generous and socially laudable gestures in our tale. First, she secretly leaves a purse behind during her first visit to the bride's house, later denying doing so, so as not to shame the bride's family and because when the poor do not know to whom they are indebted, this is a

---

10. With the possible exception of the Essenes, there has never been anything like a religious order of celibates in Judaism. Thus, the weight of Jewish tradition is against the celibate life, even for the most dedicated students of the Torah.

11. Gen. 24:5, 8.

higher form of charity (V407 [Noy]).[12] Soon afterward, the woman finds it necessary to reassure the bride's mother that she is not expected to incur expenses. On the contrary, she tells her that the groom is wealthy enough to take care of all expenses himself, and he indeed does so generously. Since biblical times, the accepted practice was for the groom to give the bride gifts and she to bring along some property recorded in the *ketubbá* or marriage contract. The custom prevailed until modern times, with various alterations, one of which is that the father of the groom makes a contribution equal to that of the bride's father. The tradition of giving gifts is meant to establish a pattern of prosperity for the new couple, a way to let the bride and her family know that the suitor is generous and well-to-do.

Since the daughter was often excluded from paternal inheritance, the father traditionally gave her a dowry. Usually the bride's parents presented a gift of property or money to her future husband; this emphasized the fundamentally economic nature of marriage, often demonstrating the worth of the family and the bride. The property a wife brought to her husband at marriage (*nedunyá*) was institutionalized during the Talmudic period. Traditionally, 50 *zuzim*, the equivalent of 180 grams of silver, was the minimum amount of the gift,[13] but parents generally gave according to their ability and social standing. In this tale, it is stressed that no dowry is expected.

Set in the city of Izmir, Turkey, the narrative is permeated with a realistic Jewish/Sephardic atmosphere. Some marriage customs are given central stage here. The social or community performance related to the cycle of marriage includes a ceremony during which participants act out certain roles. To begin with, the bridal couple must not see each other before the wedding (T134.1), and the commandment of the *mikvá* before the ceremony is observed (V96). The *mikvá*, or ritual bath (V99+ [Noy]), is stressed in Leviticus 2 and associated with levitical purity.[14] Stressing the importance of Jew-

---

12. This emphasizes the social value of humility. The greatest type of charity is believed to be that which is given anonymously, with neither the taker knowing who gave the gift nor the giver knowing who received it. It is considered best to keep such good deeds hidden from those who need not know about them. By flaunting their good deeds, even the most charitable persons could embarrass those receiving help if they know that others are aware of their poverty. We are told also not to look for honor or glory for an act of charity, for it will diminish the deed; the reward for charity is greater if it is done secretly.

13. Ketubot 6:5.

14. Literally, it means "the gathering of water," and it is rather like a small swimming pool, constructed so that there is a tank of rainwater connected to the waters of

ish family-purity laws, a prenuptial ceremony marks the first immersion in a *mikvá* by the bride, who performs *tebilá,* or ritual immersion, to purify herself in preparation for marriage. The ceremony evokes the joy of song and mirth as the bride-to-be gets ready for the immersion accompanied by an intimate group of women. Female friends and relatives of the bride and groom make the occasion a memorable and joyous one, marked by singing, dancing, and ululation. The bride is showered with candy and often proceeds from her home to the bath accompanied by musicians.

The tale tells us also that in his own quarters, as he prepares to enter marriage in a state of purity, the bridegroom is attended by his friends. It is also customary for a groom to sanctify himself in the *mikvá* before his wedding.[15] Afterward, all his friends celebrate with him by going from house to house, as he is usually not left alone before the wedding. The day of the wedding, he would proceed with his companions to the house of the richly attired bride who awaited him. She was then conducted to his house. The essence of the marriage ceremony seems to have been the transfer of the bride to the house of the groom.

In this tale, the groom lets himself be deceived by appearances (U110). In a case of mistaken identity, once the wedding takes place, he and his new bride (P210) are left to their own devices to work things out. The tale shows that rather than being concerned with meeting his bride's needs and trying to achieve a genuine, mutual relationship that would sweeten with time rather than grow bitter—the foundation of a happy married life—the groom is absorbed with self-pity. He neglects his marital duties (T271) by observing

---

the pool. Ordinary water from the tap may not be used, since the water must not be poured from a container. After the destruction of the Temple, the law of *mikvá* has had relevance chiefly to a menstruant, who is considered to be in a state of *niddá* (menstrual uncleanness) during the menstruating period and for seven days afterward. According to the law of ritual and family purity (*taharát ha-mishpakhá*), a woman is forbidden to maintain sexual relations with her husband during and for some time both before and after her menses. The laws of *niddá* are detailed in the *Mishná* and in the Babylonian Talmud. According to *halakhá,* marital relations during that time are a severe offense. Only after counting seven "clean" (bloodless) days and after the obligatory ritual immersion in the *mikvá* can the couple resume marital relations. The minimum sexual separation is twelve days during which husband and wife keep separate beds and sometimes separate quarters.

15. According to the Talmud, men must immerse themselves also after they have had marital relations or other emission of semen and before being allowed to study the Torah.

continence in marriage (T315, T315.2). Rather than confront her husband directly, the bride cleverly finds a way to attract his attention. When she dresses up in the attire of her wealthy Muslim friend, daughter of a *pashá,* the contrast is meant to be so striking that it would never occur to the husband that she could be his wife. Disguises are commonplace in folktales, and here the wife's disguise succeeds in bringing about the couple's reconciliation (J1112, T298) after she slips into her husband's bed pretending to be the Turkish woman he so much admired (K1843.2). The sexual component of marriage is stressed throughout this second part of the tale. Without it, the bride wonders, why did she have to marry at all? The teller emphasizes through repetition that the bride would have been better off in her mother's home. She thus stresses the societal value of procreation in marriage.

The mother's relationship with her son (P231) and her position as a mother-in-law are underscored here. In her search for a wife for her son, the mother observes and tests. The potential bride she identifies is a good housewife, as evidenced by the clean house she keeps. She is generous and hospitable, as evidenced by the way she welcomes and entertains a total stranger. She is honest and discreet, as evidenced by the way she responds to the purse of ducats left behind. She is obedient and reliable, as evidenced by the way she arranges for her mother to meet the visitor. After the wedding, Merkaducha shows additional qualities: determination, imagination, and wisdom. She also shows due respect for her mother-in-law when she expressly seeks her permission to undertake the unusual charade meant to attract her husband's marital interest. These are all feminine qualities prized within Sephardic society.

Interestingly, in the episode of the disguised wife's visit to the jewelry store, the male teller seems to allude knowingly to the unequal status of the Jew vis-à-vis a higher class of Turks in Izmir. Dressed as the daughter of the local pasha, the wife calls her husband *Yaudí,* or Jew, and treats him as an inferior rather than as the wealthy merchant he actually is. The contrast between his position in the Jewish community as Avraam the *djevaerdjí* and his standing among the Turks is striking. Bedazzled by the woman's beauty, but also intimidated and frightened by her apparent position of wealth and power, he has no choice but to allow her to depart his store with his entire inventory without paying for it. He does not even dare ask her to identify herself. After she leaves, he runs to see the direction her coach travels to try to find out who she is.

Finally, the use of name symbolism should be noted here. From biblical times, much significance has been attached to the names given by parents to their children. Traditionally, the Jewish boy is named at his circumcision ceremony and a girl in the synagogue when her father is called up to the reading of the Torah soon after her birth. Hebrew names were common among

Sephardim, and children were often given nicknames or called by diminutives, such as Avramachi for Avraam (Abraham), Esterika for Esther, and Merkaducha for Merkada. The latter is a symbolic name (Z183), which means "bought back" through a symbolic purchase, to ensure the child's survival against the forces of evil. It is not uncommon when more than one child dies in infancy within the same family that the next child is symbolically "bought back" by a close relative so that s/he would escape the fate of her or his siblings. Thus, the name Merkada may imply that the child had been sick or that earlier siblings had died at a very young age. She may have been "sold" to another person to fool fate and safeguard her from the family's destiny to lose infant children.

PART FIVE

Tales of Cleverness and Wisdom

*T*ime and again, through a continuous process of retelling, reinterpretation, and reintegration of the past into the present, narrators illuminate situations and dramas in ways that reflect their own experience and worldviews. Keeping their tradition vital and perpetuated, they adapt the tales to the spirit of the times, alerting us to the ironies and suffering in their own lives while retaining the essential aspects of traditional storytelling.

Sephardic narrators blend and elaborate on folklore motifs from Jewish and universal oral traditions, reasserting pride in their own practices. The theme of their tales sometimes reflects real-life situations in which support for the underdog emerges. In many instances, the characters they create live within some of the same constraints and circumstances as in the narrating society. The listeners can thus easily identify with the heroes of the tales, and the narratives provide comfort or release.

A theme that typically shows up is the conflict between Jew and Gentile that once threatened the very existence of the narrating society. The atmosphere of rivalry between groups depicted in these Judeo-Spanish tales acquires a serious, almost threatening dimension. For the Jewish characters, failure often means death, while success wins survival rather than riches or a royal marriage. In the competition between court advisors, the rise and fall of the priest, rabbi, or vizier affects the future of the entire group. Though it may appear that the tales deal with confrontation between religions, often they also give a picture of envy and rivalry. Even as, in the beginning, the opponent may resent the Jew whom he sees as a rival—and try to destroy him and his people—the ultimate advantage of the Jewish characters is not necessarily the result of a religious contest that establishes the superiority of their faith. For not only is there an ethnic and religious struggle in the background, but personal careers are also part of the equation.

The conflict is frequently between different social classes as well. If the conflict involves Jews, it is not necessarily because of their religion but because of their comparative success and repeatedly demonstrated resourcefulness. This perception is reaffirmed over and over again in the tales, which sometimes set up an unpromising Jew against the most successful of Gentiles in order to highlight the humorous way through which the weaker Jew is able to pull a fast one on his powerful non-Jewish counterpart. In such tales, the focus sometimes is on instances of deceit with which the Jew diffuses a crisis by playing a clever trick on those who threaten him. The tactic is one that the weak often use in folktales to defend themselves.

The tale structure frequently depicts the ruler receiving misguided counsel that sways his sound judgment. He appears to be caught in a somewhat ambiguous role between the Jew and the envious minister, almost as an unwilling referee. At first, it often looks as if the heartless challenger is gaining the upper hand, when his insistence seems to tip the scale against the Jews. In the end, though, it may be a matter of proving Jewish cleverness and ingenuity. As there is no divine intervention to save the Jews, and the characters usually confront their enemies and triumph over fear and injustice on their own, such tales of persecution and salvation may not be considered sacred legends.

In two of the eight selections in this category, difficult tasks are imposed on Jews: in one tale they are compelled to teach an animal how to read, with the survival of the entire community at stake; in another, the lowest of the low among the Jews is required to double a substantial sum of money within a month, or else. In both instances, they are saved by their wits, and their ingenuity is highlighted from a perspective of superiority—so as to stress the success of their group—with the least capable member of the community easily fooling superior individuals of the competing group.

While other narratives also display the clever actions or responses of unpromising individuals, they do not focus specifically on Jewish survival: a shoemaker gives the king a cleverly worded symbolic answer; an old man helps cure a princess through the most humble and obvious of remedies; an old rabbi shows a rich man the road to empathy and charitable giving by making him experience some of the discomfort of the needy; a rejected son shows his royal father the absurdity of his actions; and, in a courting dance of sorts, a young man and woman compete in a marital contest of cleverness before they settle on each other as mates. Finally, when a Jew's position is threatened or belittled, he cleverly sets up a situation where he is vindicated without appearing to have caused the downfall of his opponent.

In these tales of life trials, of cleverness and wisdom, the main characters are tested with hard luck and formidable obstacles and challenged to save themselves and others from extraordinarily difficult situations. They are asked to find answers and solutions to impossible questions and conditions, or to explain the inexplicable. The least promising of them demonstrate the knowledge of the world and of human nature they have acquired through life experience and a keenly developed power of survival. This is an affirmation of humankind and of Jewish vitality against overwhelming odds. In the end, these successful heroes often share that wisdom with others. Human resilience and imagination assert themselves.

22

The King and the *Sandelár*

Narrated by SARA BENREY (1990)

Finding his mind filled with many thoughts that robbed him of sleep, one night, the king put on casual clothing and went out to the street.

As it was already very late—close to midnight—everyone had gone to bed already, and the streets were in darkness. *Na,* he saw a tiny light far away, and he walked toward it. As he drew near, he saw that it was a shoemaker, a *sandelár,* who is singing while repairing shoes.

The king asked him:

"How can you be so happy, so *orozo,* with your work?"

"Blessed be the *Dió,*" the *sandelár* said to him. "I eat and I drink, I pay my debts, and I get ahead, and I even have two girls, two *mosas.*"

"And if you earn that much," the king said to him, "how much do you pay in taxes, in *taksas?*"

"This is my secret!" the *sandelár* said to him.

"What do you mean, it is your secret?! I can report you to the king and it can cost you dearly!"

"I'm not afraid," the *sandelár* said to him, "because, when the king will hear my secret, he will give me even more *parás!*"

"*Alora,* so, I'm the king! And you, you must tell me this secret!"

And so as to make him believe it, the king showed him his seal. This time the *sandelár* found himself forced to reveal his secret, and he said to him:

"My lord king, I am nothing but a poor shoemaker, a *povereto sandelár,* who sometimes has to work past midnight simply to support himself! I have with me my father and mother. I take care of them, and these are the debts that I repay. I also have three sons that I'm raising. May I never be deprived of them! They are the ones who will look after us in our old age, and these are my savings. As for the two girls, the *mosas,* they are my two unmarried daughters. *Malgrado,* despite all of these obligations and my hard work, here, *yené,* I sing, because I expect much good from the heavens."

Hearing this, the king took out a purse of ducats and gave it to him, and he said to him:

"You're right to keep your faith in the *Dió* and in your king!"

May they be well and so may we.

COMMENTARY

This tale, which can be found in the Midrash Hagadol,[1] belongs with others illustrating clever acts and words. It is a version of AT 921A, *The Four Coins, (Focus),* in which a puzzling conversation takes place between the king and one of his subjects (H585).[2] The king asks the peasant what he does with the four coins he earns and the peasant answers enigmatically: "First I eat; second I put out at interest; third I pay debts; and fourth I throw away." The answer is eventually elucidated: "First I eat (feed myself); second I put out at interest (give to my children); third I pay debts (keep my parents); fourth I throw away (give to my wife)" (H585.1). The king rewards the man for his cleverness (Q91).[3]

---

1. Gen. Lekh Lekha.

2. For Judeo-Spanish parallels of this type, see KS, 261, in which the king is identified as King Solomon and rewards the shoemaker by appointing him vizier, and Koén-Sarano, "El chapinero," in *Lejendas,* 101. Other related versions appear in K, no. 7 (Bitolj) reprinted in *AY* 26–27, p. 43; Salinas, "Un diálogo," 84, all versions of AT 922B, *The King's Face on the Coin.* The first two include AT 921A as part of their tale development. For AT 922B, see Haboucha, 413.

3. Other Jewish parallels can be found in M. Cohen, *'Edot Israel,* vol. 3, no. רמב; Gaster, *Exempla,* no. 211; Jason, "Types," 181; Jason, *Types,* 50; K, 140–41, no. 7 (Bitolj); Marcus, *Mabu'a,* no. 8 (Iranian Kurdistan); Noy, *Ha-na'ara,* no. 2 (Iraq); Noy, *TEM 1966,* no. 4 (Iraqi Kurdistan); Noy, *TEM 1970,* 177 (Poland, IFA 8913); Schwarzbaum, *Studies,* 221, 475. Additional IFA versions have been collected from Afghanistan, Iran, Iraq, Israel (Ashkenazic), and Yemen. Non-Jewish parallels of this type appear in Andrejev (type 921 I*); Ashliman, *Guide to Folktales,* 188; BP, 4:137; Chevalier, *Siglo de Oro,* no. 64; Dorson, *Folktales Told around the World,* 127; *Gesta Romanorum,* no. 57; Laoust, *Contes berbères,* no. 75; Megas, *Folktales of Greece,* no. 54; Thompson and Roberts, *Indic Oral Tales,* 115; Tolstoy, *Fables and Fairy Tales,* 22.

The clever symbolism of the type, simplified here, focuses on a poor, simple, unsophisticated person who toils day and night barely to make a living. While the universal tale type describes the response of a peasant, our tale easily substitutes a shoemaker (P453), one of the traditional Sephardic occupations in the Balkans. The wisdom of the response remains intact, however. It shows how popular lore is vitally concerned with everyday situations and the immediate personal environment of teller and audience. The symbolism is slightly downplayed here, while the traditional faith in God and king as benevolent protectors is highlighted. As a person who trusts in God and in his own ingenuity, the shoemaker is serene and his disposition calm, no matter what trouble befalls him.

Finally, the common motif of the king's nocturnal rounds around town in disguise to observe his subjects and learn their secrets (K1812, P14.19, N467) is a well-honed tale device that serves to help him take the pulse of his people and learn their secrets. In the process, he hears a good amount of sensible judgment and learns much that is helpful to him as he rules over them but that would not otherwise have come to his attention.

23

The Princess Who Laughed

Narrated by SARA YOHAY (1993)

This story they tell in Russia.

A powerful king had a daughter who always laughed. When everyone else cried, she laughed. When she was in pain, she laughed. When she was upset, she laughed.

It got so that the king thought that she had an illness, a *hazinura,* and he called upon all the doctors to find a remedy. No one knew what to do.

One day, a quack arrived from faraway, and he said to the king:

"Leave her for a month with only bread and water."

And so it was done. *Amá* the laughter did not subside.

A little old man came who was, give and take, a hundred years old! And he said to the king:

"Almighty king, I brought you two things that make all women cry, and your daughter will not escape from this!"

"Ah!" the king said to him. "I'll give you much *pará* and gold!"

"Thank you," said the old man. "*Amá,* at my age, wealth is of no importance. What counts is to convey my experience to others."

The old man called for the princess to come before him. And, putting a knife and an onion in her hand, he ordered her:

"Mince it!"

The princess did as the old man said! First came the tears, and then endless weeping! And, of her laughter, there was not even a memory. They say that rivers swelled from all the years that the princess had failed to cry.

Thus she was cured by the simple experience of life. And she thanked the old man. And the king was very happy to finally have a normal daughter!

COMMENTARY

While laughter is primarily associated with fun and amusement, in our tale it turns into an illness that appears impossible to cure. In fact, it is the mirror condition to that of the sad-faced princess who never smiles (F591) but who is finally brought to laughter upon seeing a procession of people sticking fast to a magic object or a golden goose. Such extraordinary motifs appear in both AT 559, *Dungbeetle,* and AT 571, *"All Stick Together,"* in which a sad-faced princess is offered to the man who can make her laugh. In both types, she is finally brought to laughter when shown an absurd parade of people magically sticking fast to objects, grateful animals, or to each other.

In similar types, the task of making the princess laugh is a marriage test which, when successfully completed, brings about the winning of her hand in marriage as a reward. Our tale focuses instead on the experience and wisdom of old age—*hokhmát hayím*—to bring to tears the always laughing princess (J151, J151 [Noy]). Similar wisdom appears in AT 981, *Wisdom of Hidden Old Man Saves Kingdom.*[1] It includes none of the magical elements and animal gratitude present in the types listed above. In the end, the abundant tears of the princess cause rivers to swell (A1012.1ff, F162.2.12, F715.2.5), and the old man hero refuses all reward.

The onion used to cure the laughing princess is the same pungent vegetable highly prized for culinary and medicinal purposes (J2412.1). The strong flavor of the onion and the potency of its sulphuric oil, which brings tears to the eyes and stings the skin, have led to its folk use as a powerful medicine. It is widely credited with the power of drawing sickness and maleficent influences unto itself, and it has been used in widely varied times and places against a multitude of ills, including colds, bites, warts, earaches, and fever.

---

1. For other Judeo-Spanish versions of the wisdom of old age, see Koén-Sarano, "La kadena de arena," in *Lejendas,* 67; KS, "El rey i el padre viejo," 43, and "La kadena de arena," 247; Salinas, "Konsejo de un padre a su ijo"; and L, no. 2, p. 24 (Monastir). See Haboucha, 497, for parallels of wisdom of old age.

24

To Experience So As to Understand

NARRATED BY ESTER VENTURA (1992)

There were a man and a woman who had nine children. After some time, she became pregnant, and she gave birth to the tenth child, the *diezén*. And they are so poor that they don't have enough even to eat. The man looked: the *diezén* has now arrived. He has nothing to eat, nothing to wear. What shall he do? He found no solution. He got up; he went to the neighborhood rabbi, the *rav* of the *shehuná*. He said to him:

"*Amán*! Have pity! My tenth child has just been born, and I don't have either to clothe them or to feed them!"

The *rav* said to him:

"Don't worry. I'll find things for you. Go home and it will be fine, it will be *beseder*."

The *rav* changed his clothes and he went out. And it is so rainy and cold outside that the skies have opened up! Where did he go? To the house of one of the richest men in town!

Who saw him coming but the rich man's servant, who went immediately, *pishín,* to his master, to his *patrón*. He said to him:

"Look, the *rav* of the *shehuná* has come. I don't know what he wants."

By now it's already nighttime.

"I am getting up," his *patrón* said to him. "Don't open up for him. I'll go open up for him myself."

The rich man opened the door to the *rav*. He said to him:

See Koén-Sarano, *Lejendas,* 117, for this tale in Judeo-Spanish and in Hebrew, "Provar para kreyer."

"Come in! Come in!"

"No," the *rav* said to him. "You come outside. There is something I want to talk to you about."

The rich man went outside. The *rav* said to him:

"Look, there is a family with ten children. They don't have enough to feed them or to clothe them. That's why," he said. "I plead with you to give me a check for them. Next week is the circumcision, the *birít*. You'll be the godfather, the *sandák*."

There was no way out. The *rav* himself had come! *Pishín,* immediately, he went inside, wrote out a check, and handed it to him.

The *rav* went and handed it to the father of that family, of that *mishpahá*. And those poor unfortunate ones now bought food. They are now *beseder.*

We'll make a long story short. The day of the *birít* arrived. The *rav* said to the new father:

"Look, let the *sandák* be that wealthy man, because it is he who has sent you the money, the *parás*."

"There is no problem, no *baayót,*" the father said.

They seated the rich man in the chair; the *birít* was performed. After the *birít* was done, the rich man says to the *rav:*

"Look, there is one thing I want to ask you," he said. "I can see that, *bemét*, really, the *mishpahá* is very poor. *Avál,* when you came to ask me for the *parás,* why didn't you come inside but made me step outside?"

"Ah!" the *rav* said to him. "*Agora,* sit down. I'll tell you something. Look," he said, "there was a war between two governments. The leader of one of the governments wanted to win the war at any cost, *avál* he didn't know how he was going to enter the other country. He dressed in civilian clothes and crossed the border, the *gevúl.* He went in. Despite all of that, they already knew him by sight because they had already seen him in the newspapers. A *polís* came. He recognized him. He said:

'This is the one who wants to wage war against us. How is it that he is walking here?'

'No, it's not!'

'Yes, it is!'

They ran after him. He ran and ran. He entered the house of a Jew.

'Hide me,' he said to him, 'they'll kill me. Afterward your reward will be very large!'

Where could this one hide him? Where could he hide him? He lifted the *rima,* the pile of mattresses he had, put him underneath, and put the *rima* back in its place. All the policemen, the *shotrím,* entered in there. They are saying:

'This is where we saw him enter. Where did you hide him?'

'No one has come in here!' said the Jew. '*Na,* go ahead and search! Go ahead and search!'

They started removing the pillows, the quilts. They looked: there was nothing underneath.

Ayde! They gave up. They got up and left. Once they left, the Jew took the man out of there and asked him:

'Tell me, how did you feel when the *shotrím* were pulling the mattresses off?'

The man didn't answer him. He said to him only:

'If I win the war, I am ready to do whatever you wish on behalf of all the Jews.'

And he left. When he finally won the war and came back to the country, the Jew is. . . . Hadn't he saved his life?

The other one said to him:

'Look. Everything is well. For all the Jews I'll do anything you wish. *Avál* you, I'll have you hanged.'

'Is this the reward?!' the Jew said to him. 'I who saved your life?!'

'That's the way it is,' he said.

And he gave orders that the man be hanged.

'*Addió,*' the Jew is saying, 'My God! After I saved him! I'll no longer do favors for anyone anymore!'

They seized him. They took him away, and he is already at the gallows. As they are about to pull the rope, he came in and said:

'No! Don't pull that rope on him!'

When he took him down from the gallows, he came in, he asked him:

'Tell me, how did you feel when they were about to pull that rope? That's the way I felt under the mattresses.'

"And I," the *rav* said to the rich man, "I wanted you to come outside so that you yourself would experience the rain and the cold, and feel compassion so that you would give the check to those unfortunate ones!"

COMMENTARY

Depicting life where individual members of the Jewish community—in this case the local religious leader (N848)—serve as intermediaries between the rich and the poor (U60), this realistic tale has no specific classification. By showing a wealthy man—a wealthier member of the extended Jewish family— responding to his social obligation of helping the poor (N835, V404 [Noy], V400 [Noy]), the narrator appears to stress not only charity but also the importance of helpful relations between members of the community, where the wealthier ones are expected to provide for the needier ones.

In Judaism, compassion toward the needy ranks high among virtues (V405 [Noy]). It was considered by rabbis of all ages to be one of the cardinal *mitzvót* (commandments) of the faith. The obligation to help those in need is stated many times in the Bible, and the rich are believed to become meritorious by giving alms. The opportunity to do a *mitzvá* is granted one as a favor. As we do not really understand why the rich become rich and the poor remain poor, the dependent condition of the poor was not regarded as having been brought on by themselves but by the evils of the social order. The poor are said to have a just claim on the wealth of the rich. In fact, Rabbi Akiva is supposed to have said that God allows the poor to remain poor so that the rich can acquire merit by helping them (V440+ [Noy]).

A higher form of charity is said to be when the donor is not aware of whom he benefits, and the poor do not know to whom they are indebted (V407 [Noy]). If for some reason one cannot hide one's generosity and will receive honor or praise from the recipient, it is understood that one should not come to demand or expect that honor. Thus it is surprising, in our tale, that the help of the benefactor is not kept anonymous. The recipient is made aware of the need to honor his wealthy helper (Q40, Q42, Q113.0.1) by inviting him to act as the *sandák* or godfather at the circumcision of the newborn. The *sandák* holds the baby during the surgical procedure, and it is not unusual for the honor to be given to one who gives charity.

Our tale is filled with the fulfillment of other Jewish obligations. The use of symbolic numbers in folk stories is common. The number ten used here, for example, is associated with completion: the Ten Commandments of the Bible and the ten divine manifestations of cabala that correspond to the ten secret names of God. The teller does not pass judgment on the poor father for not making better use of family planning despite the obvious fact that he is unable to support his growing brood. This is because, according to the rabbis, the first *mitzvá* of the Torah is the command to procreate.[1] Another commandment is to perform the ritual of *brit milá,* the removal of the foreskin on the eighth day of life to make manifest the "sign of the flesh," the covenant made with Abraham.[2] The Elijah seat on which the *sandák* sits and the performance of the *brit* at the synagogue as a religious ritual are elements that help affirm the link to Judaism. It also involves the participation of the family and the community.

---

1. Gen. 1:28, 9:1.
2. Gen. 17:9–13.

Because Elijah is viewed as the Angel of the Covenant, there is a chair provided for him at every circumcision ceremony.

The secondary tale within the frame tale is used to explain to the rich man why he had been asked to step out of the warmth of his home and into inclement weather when the rabbi had initially asked for his assistance. Based on the belief that one best understands the situation of others when one experiences the actual plight and conditions in which they live (Q46), the rabbi exposes the rich man to the raw elements to cause him to feel deep compassion and, consequently, to be more generous in his giving. His illustrative tale within a tale makes clear that concept (R175). It is based on a historical character, Napoleon, whose life is said to have been saved by a Jewish tailor during the 1812 Russian campaign. Napoleon, who had swept through the country with his army, was defeated in Moscow and was in flight. Unaware of his identity, the Jew does not hesitate to hide him. After all, a man in danger must be helped. The foolishness and cruelty of the question he poses to him afterward, however, reveal the lesson to be taught: to experience is to understand.[3] It is clear that the teller remembers the narrative in all its details, but in all probability she does not associate the king in her tale with the historical figure of Napoleon.

---

3. For a Jewish parallel, see Serwer-Bernstein, *Jewish and Arab Folktales,* no. 8, pp. 47–51. Cf. also p. 6, a foreword by Dov Noy.

25

The King and the Golden Wheat

Narrated by JULIDE AVZARADEL (1992)

Once upon a time there was a king whose wife, the queen, was with child. One day, with her morning sickness, her *konchentos,* and her discomfort of pregnancy, the queen could not hold back and [pardon the expression][1] she farted in the king's presence.

The king was very angry that the queen had made such a mistake in front of him, and he cast her out of the palace.

Powerless, the unfortunate queen went to live in a place where the poor lived, and she gave birth to a beautiful and healthy son. She did her best to raise him, to educate him, to satisfy his needs, and to give him all her motherly love.

When the youngster finally went to school, to the *skola,* his friends began asking him who his father is and where he lives. As he could give no answer, they began to make fun of him and to torment him, saying that he was a fatherless boy, a bastard, a *mamzér.*

The mother, seeing him so sad, asked him one day:

"My dear son, why are you so dejected and unhappy these days? It breaks my heart to see you so. Tell me what's troubling you."

And the youngster told her that at school the pupils, the *elevos,* are making fun of him because he has no father, and they say that he is a bastard, a *mamzér.* And he pleaded with his mother to tell him who his father is. The mother said to him that he is the king's son, and she told him what had happened to her when she was pregnant with him:

---

1. Teller's aside.

"Because I made the mistake of farting before the king, he cast me out of the palace in anger," she said to him.

The youngster listened to everything and said nothing. Years went by and the youngster, who was very intelligent, hardworking, and ambitious, grew up and succeeded in becoming one of the richest and most honorable young men in the city.

One day he prepared a cart, a *talega,* filled with wheat of gold and went to the king's palace, saying that he has a present for him. As he was already well-known in the city for his good deeds, his *bienfezensias,* the guards agreed to take him before the king. The youth opened up the *talega* filled with wheat of gold and he said to the king:

"When they'll sow this in the field, wheat of gold will grow."

Very pleased, the king summoned his gardener and ordered him to sow the wheat and to look after it well. From time to time he would ask the gardener if something had grown in the field. Months went by, and in the field neither wheat of gold nor anything else had grown! The king sent for the young man who had given him the gift of wheat of gold, and when he came before him he said to him:

"How could you mock me this way?! The wheat of gold that was supposed to grow in the field has not grown. What happened to your promise?"

"My lord king," the youth said to him, "it looks like someone who farted passed across the field. That's why the wheat didn't grow!"

The king got up from his seat. He said to him:

"Is there a person who doesn't fart?"

And the young man answered him:

"My lord king, if that is so, you cast my mother out of the palace in anger because she farted before you while she was pregnant with me!"

The king understood that this was his son! He came down from his throne. He kissed him, he embraced him, and he ordered that the queen be brought back to the palace. They held sumptuous festivities, with songs and dances, and they lived happily, *orozos,* till the end of their days.

Commentary

A version of AT 1431, *The Contagious Yawns,* this is a reductio ad absurdum tale (J1190, J1191.1).[2] Using a series of appropriate motifs, the narrative illus-

---

2. See Briggs, *Dictionary of British Folk-Tales,* pt. A, vol. 1, 238.

trates cleverness in rebuking the king (J1536, J1675, J1280). As this cannot be done directly without the risk of incurring punishment, the hero uses a roundabout way to make his point and bring the king to recognize his error. The illogical behavior of the "strong" royal figure provides the opportunity for the unpromising "weaker" character to show that he is superior to the king through the use of one absurdity to rebuke another (J1530). After attracting his father's attention, the hero puts him out of countenance by showing him that his decision to banish the innocent queen from the palace had been unwarranted (J1212). After the king acknowledges the foolishness and injustice of his former judgment, he reinstates his outcast wife (S451).

The prototype of the absurd judgment and its clever undoing appears in AT 821B, *Chickens from Boiled Eggs,* and is listed as a religious tale because the devil materializes in it. The plot is as follows: many years after the guest has eaten twelve boiled eggs, a host demands an enormous sum for them, claiming that by this time they would have hatched out chickens who, in turn, would have laid eggs, etc. The devil as advocate comes in and demands that the host cook his peas for planting (J1191.2). "Boiled peas may grow as soon as chickens can be hatched from boiled eggs." The devil carries off the judge.[3] This type is represented by *The Eggs and the Grain* (tale 42) in the Djohá section of this anthology, a tale about a suit over chicken produced from boiled eggs in which Djohá, the quintessential fool, plays the role of the devil's advocate. The irrationality of the host's demand is counteracted by the equally ridiculous argument used by Djohá: to harvest a crop produced from boiled seed.[4]

---

3. For parallels from non-Jewish traditions, see Andrejev; Ashliman, *Guide to Folktales,* 165; BP, 2:368 n. 1; Briggs, *Dictionary of British Folk-Tales,* pt. A, vol. 2, 100, pt. B, vol. 1, 145; Clouston, *Noodles,* 120; Delarue, *Conte populaire français,* 4:262; EB, nos. 294, 295; A. Espinosa, *Castilla,* no. 31; García Figueras, *Yehá,* no. 91; Megas, *Folktales of Greece,* no. 53; Rael, *Colorado y Nuevo Méjico,* no. 34; Robe, *Mexican Folktales,* 131; Walker and Uysal, *Tales in Turkey,* 236.

4. For a Judeo-Spanish version of this type, see Shahar, "La valor del guevo haminado," 51–52, in which young Solomon reproves his father by using the usual argument of cooked beans vs. boiled eggs. Other Jewish versions can be found in the IFA (Libya, Iran, Turkey); *BJ,* 3:58, 61, 64, 83, 259, 301; bin Gorion, *Mimekor Yisrael,* vol. 1, no. 60, 120; Frankel, *Classic Tales,* no. 86; Gaster, *Exempla,* nos. 329, 342, 403, 441; Ginzberg, *Legends,* 6:285; Jason, "Types," 167, 181 (920*E); Jason, *Types,* 35, 49–50 (920*E); Nahmad, *Portion in Paradise,* 44; Noy, *Libya,* no. 23; Noy, *TEM 1970,* 178 (AT 920A, Turkey IFA 8892); Schram, *Jewish Stories,* 69, 112. IFA versions of 920*E, *Children's Judgment,* an equivalent Jewish oicotype, exist from Afghanistan, Greece, Iran, Iraqi Kurdistan, Israel (Sephardic), Morocco, Tunisia, Turkey, and Yemen.

In part 3 of AT 875, *The Clever Peasant Girl,* the same principle of using one absurdity to discredit another appears.[5] A young girl marries the king, and as he decides a dispute over the possession of a colt unjustly, she advises the abused subject how to show the king the absurdity of his decision by putting forward an equally foolish act.[6] Part 2 of AT 920A, *The Daughter of*

---

5. For Judeo-Spanish versions of this type, see Baruch, "El judeo-español de Bosnia," 140; Shahar, "La mujer i el marido ke keria divorsar," 51; KS, 219, 259; LP, vol. 1, no. 39; MR, no. 6. IFA versions were collected from Eastern Europe, Egypt, Greece, Iraq, Israel (Bedouin, Sephardic), Libya, Morocco, Syria, Tunisia, Turkey, and Yemen. Other Jewish sources are Alexander-Noy, no. 98 (Israeli Sephardic); Ausubel, *Jewish Folklore,* 95, 97; Baharav, *Ashkelon,* no. 1 (Lybia), no. 7, p. 57 n. 16; Bar Itzhak and Shenhar, *Jewish Moroccan,* 129; *BJ,* 4:108–14, 280 (AT 875A and 875D); bin Gorion, *Mimekor Yisrael,* vol. 3, no. 15, 1292; Cheichel, *TEM 1968–69,* no. 3 (Bukhara); Frankel, *Classic Tales,* no. 157; Gaster, *Exempla,* no. 196; Grunwald, "Motifs," no. 18; Grunwald, *Tales,* no. 13, and 92 n. 1; Haimovits, *Shomrim,* no. 8 (Yemen); Jason, "Types," 171–72; Jason, *Types,* 40; Lehrman, *World of the Midrash,* 103; Meir, "Nuskhaot ha-yehudiyot"; Mizrahi, *Be-yeshishim khokhma,* no. 5 (Iran); Na'ana, *Ozar,* 408–9 (Syria); Nahmad, *Portion in Paradise,* 90; Nehmad, *Glima,* no. 4 (875D I*[c]); Noy, *Folktales,* no. 61; Noy, *Ha-na'ara,* no. 101 (Iraq); Noy, *TEM 1961,* no. 4 (Yemen) (875D I*); Noy, *TEM 1962,* no. 7 (Egypt); Noy, *TEM 1971,* no. 11 (Yemen); Noy, *Libya,* no. 170; Noy, *Tunisia,* n. to no. 4; Rappaport, *Folklore of the Jews,* 31; Richman, *Jewish Lore,* 319; Schram, *Jewish Stories,* 112, 195; Schwarzbaum, *Studies,* 47, 90, 295, 394–95; *Schwili,* nos. 11, 77, 78, 79, 92, 167.

6. Versions of this type from other traditions include Al-Shahi, *Wisdom from the Nile,* nos. 25, 27; Andrejev; Ashliman, *Guide to Folktales,* 175–76; Basset, *Mille et un contes,* 2:39, no. 17; Baughman, *England and North America,* 19; Boggs, *Spanish Folktales,* 106; Boulvin, *Contes populaires persans,* 1:46, 47, 48, 2:46, 48; BP, 2:349–73, 4:33off., 381ff.; Briggs, *Dictionary of British Folk-Tales,* pt. A, vol. 1, 277, pt. A, vol. 2, 238; Bushnaq, *Arab Folktales,* 318, 354 (Syria); Calvino, *Italian Folktales,* no. 72; Chauvin, *Ouvrages arabes,* 5:286, no. 171, 6:173, no. 331, 8:160, no. 168; Clarkson and Cross, *World Folktales,* no. 13; Clouston, *Popular Tales,* 2:327–31; Cole, *Best-Loved Folktales,* nos. 99, 125; D'Aronco, *Fiabe Toscane,* 100; Dawkins, *Forty-five Stories,* nos. 20, 21, 26 (Greece); Dawkins, *Modern Greek Folktales,* nos. 45, 65, 67; EB, nos. 192, 235, 366; García Figueras, *Yehá,* no. 67; Grimm and Grimm, *Tales,* no. 94; T. Hansen, *Types* (875, 875**A, **924 Argentina, Dominican Republic, Puerto Rico); J. Jacobs, *European Folk and Fairy Tales,* no. 23; Laoust, *Contes berbères,* no. 74; Legey, *Maroc,* no. 38; Mathers, *Thousand Nights,* 4:210, 366; Megas, *Folktales of Greece,* nos. 33, 50; Pino-Saavedra, *Chile,* no. 36; Rael, *Colorado y Nuevo Méjico,* nos. 1, 2; Robe, *Mexican Folktales,* 140; Thompson, *One Hundred Favorite Folktales,* no. 78 (Italy); Thompson and Roberts, *Indic Oral Tales,* 104; Walker and Uysal, *Tales in Turkey,* 135.

the King and the Son of the Peasant, shows a merchant who buys forty boiled eggs and sails away without paying. On his return, he offers to pay, but demand is made for the value of all chickens and their offspring that would have come from the eggs.[7]

The archetypal counterargument survives in our tale, albeit in an altered form. Rather than the boiled egg/chicken reasoning and the planting of cooked seed, the tale shows the gullibility and greed of the king, who believes that sowing wheat of gold will produce a fresh harvest (J1930). To stress the unreasonableness of the royal edict of eviction, the Sephardic teller uses a rather coarse but natural bodily function for which she apologizes to her audience.[8]

While in universal parallels it is not unusual for a clever young woman to be the one to show the king or judge the absurdity of his behavior, in Sephardic versions it is oftentimes youthful Solomon who shows his resourcefulness in his father's court. King David was a judge, and by pointing out to him the error of his judgment in difficult cases, Solomon teaches many a lesson, even to his father, and demonstrates a good understanding of human nature. While the hero is not specifically identified with Solomon in this particular tale, his youth and wisdom subtly speak for a parallel. It is also his father, the king, whom he tactfully reproves (J816).[9]

The motif of the banishment of a guiltless, persecuted wife by her cruel husband (S62, P210, S410, S411) appears in AT 705–12 and is usually brought about by an angry husband or by a lecherous or spurned lover. Our tale follows the traditional pattern: it shows the expulsion of an innocent queen for a minor infraction when she is with child (S411.2, S414, Q431) and her eventual reinstatement. Missing here are the usual mutilation and the miraculous limb and eye restoration present in other universal narratives. Ours is a simple tale of injustice put right by human cleverness (J1100). The maternal qualities of the exiled queen are stressed. Her love for her son and her struggle to raise him properly, despite her state of poverty, are shown to be paramount (S442).

---

7. A non-Jewish parallel is included in Megas, *Folktales of Greece,* 53.

8. A similar Judeo-Spanish version in which passing wind is central to the tale and causes the banishment of the queen appears in another of Koén-Sarano's publications (*Konsejas,* 97). There, as well, the son brings about the reinstatement of his mother by showing the king the absurdity of his judgment. The narrators of these tales are different, but the idiosyncratic character of the cause for the banishment (farting) calls for attention: it may well be that one of the tellers heard the tale from the other at the collector's regular storytelling circle. Both tellers are women.

9. See Ps. 72:1–2.

Ultimately the tale leads us to understand the son's need to find his unknown father (H1381.2.2.1). When the young child is twitted with being a bastard, the slanderous label of *mamzér*, thrown in his face by his taunting classmates (K2128), calls for clarification. Unlike other systems of law, in Jewish law, the mere fact that a child is born or conceived out of lawful wedlock does not make him a *mamzér*. Only the offspring of a forbidden relationship is a *mamzér*, one whose status or rights are impaired due to the fact that the parents cannot marry each other because their sexual relationship (incest, adultery) is forbidden by the Torah.[10]

---

10. Lev. 18 and 20 list such forbidden marriages.

26

The Donkey Knows How to Read

Narrated by HAYIM TSUR (1992)

At the time of the Turks, there was a *pashá* who gave much grief, much *tsarót*, to the Jews of Jerusalem, of Yerushalayim. He drove them crazy every day with a new decree, a new *gezerá*. One day, you must pay, who knows how much, for each child born to you! Another day, you must pay for each bucket of water you draw from the well!

One day the *vazír*, the vizier, came. He said to the *pashá:*

"Look at these Jews! Aren't you going to pay any heed to them? You must come up with a very, very strong way to finish with them once and for all! Every time you say to them: 'Bring money! Bring *parás*.' I don't know where they get it from! One has to come up with something they will be unable to do!"

The *pashá* said to him:

"Well, mister *vazír*, do you have any ideas?"

The *vazír* said:

"Yes! Tell them that you wish to see a donkey that can read."

What did the *pashá* do? He sent for the rabbi of the Jews. He said to him:

"Look. I know that everything I'll ask of you, you'll do. *Agora*, now, I want to see if you are able to make a donkey read."

The rabbi said:

"Blessed be the *Dió* Almighty! Can a donkey read?"

The *pashá* said:

"Look, I'm giving you a three-day respite. If in three days you don't do it, I'll kill you all, and we'll put an end once and for all to this Jewish problem!"

201

The rabbi left the *pashá*'s residence, weeping and *chapaleando,* greatly agitated:

"What shall we do *agora*? Blessed be God, *Dió!* What shall we do? We can't. A donkey is a donkey: it has four legs, long ears.... *Ma,* how is it going to read?"

The *pashá* said:

"Look, today is *alhád,* Sunday. On Wednesday morning you'll bring the donkey here, and we want to see how it reads."

The rabbi went to the community council of the Jews, the *váad akeilá*. He sat down there, and he asked them:

"What shall we do?"

First of all, they said:

"*Taanít*! A fast! A day without food, drink, or anything!"

They brought all the wise men, the *hahamím*. They sent for the *hahamím* of Safed, and they sat, weeping and thinking about what to do.

Monday night arrived. The synagogue beadle, the *shamásh* of the *kal,* came. An *amares,* an unlearned simpleton! He knocked at the door of the rabbi and said:

"Why are you all crying? What's the matter?"

They said to him:

"Nothing! Go away from here!"

He said:

"Just tell me!"

They said to him:

"Go away from here *agora*! Must you be so tiresome? Leave it to us!"

He said:

"Tell me about it too. Even the tiresome think, sometimes. I can think as well!"

The rabbi said:

"Look, the *pashá* said that he wants to see the donkey read! Can you make a donkey read? How can you do that? Go away! Let me think about what to do!"

The *shamásh* said to him:

"Don't worry, rabbi, I'll do it for you. I'll bring the donkey that'll read. Give me four hours. I'll think about it and I'll bring it to you. Don't be afraid!"

The *shamásh* left, and after four or five hours, he returned once again. He said:

"Rabbi, I've found a way to do it."

"How will you do it?"

"Very easily," said the *shamásh*. "It's no problem at all. We'll bring the donkey. We'll bring a large book of Gemará,[1] and also a ladder. We'll put the book on the ladder, so it'll be higher up. And we'll put some barley on each sheet. The donkey will come and will begin to eat the barley on the first sheet. Then he'll turn the page with his nose and 'read.' Don't worry: they'll see the donkey doing that, and everything will turn out okay. It's on my shoulders."

"What? You'll do it? The donkey will be there?"

"Don't be frightened!"

On the morning of Tuesday, they tried it out. They brought the donkey. They placed the book. The *hahamím* began to say a prayer, a *tefilá*. They gave charity, *sedaká*. And the donkey began to eat. The donkey finished eating the barley; he turned the page with his nose and ate from the next sheet. And he ate from the next, and the next. . . . When he finished, the rabbi said:

"*Addió*, my God! This one is a clever one, the bastard! A *pikéah*, the *mamzér*!"[2]

Well, the rabbi went before the *pashá* on Tuesday night. He said to him:

"Look, my lord *pashá*, tomorrow at ten o'clock in the morning, we'll call upon the entire city to gather. We'll bring the little donkey, and we'll show everyone how he's going to read."

"Let's see," said the *pashá*.

On Wednesday morning, they came with the little donkey and the Book of Gemará. They placed it on top of the ladder. Everyone is standing around to see. They said to the *pashá*:

"Look, we don't want you to stand very close to the donkey, so he doesn't get nervous."

"Fine!" said the *pashá*.

They stood the donkey in front of the book. They also placed spectacles on his nose to show that he is reading. The little donkey, which hadn't eaten all of Tuesday, saw the barley on the first sheet and ate it. He finished one page, he turned the second one with his nose. And so on, from page to page, he was eating barley and "reading," *meldohoneando*.[3]

---

1. One of the two parts that make up the Talmud, the Gemará, in Aramaic, is a compilation of commentaries and interpretation on the Mishná, which it supplements. The Mishná is the text of the Oral Law, made up of sixty-three tractates in Hebrew.

2. Colloquially, *mamzér* describes a sly sort of individual. The term can also be used affectionately.

3. This is a form of *meldár* (to read), probably aimed at ridiculing what the *azno* is doing.

The *pashá* was convinced that the little donkey had really learned how to read, and he said:

"Blessed be God! *Dió!* Those Jews have a solution to everything! We'll never be able to overcome them!"

COMMENTARY

The theme of our tale—confrontation between Jew and Gentile—is one that frequently appears in Sephardic tales, as we see in this anthology. Set in a realistic background of Jews in a foreign land, subject to the sometimes irrational caprice and fancy of a ruler, it reflects a real-life situation familiar to the narrating society. The undertone of fear and frustration that surfaces is rooted in the common struggle for survival that existed among anti-Jewish societies of the Diaspora. Without humor, life would be unbearable. Thus, they transfer conflict from a threatening environment to the safe venue of humorous absurdity.

The Jewish oicotype IFA 1750*B, *Task: Teaching Camel to Speak*, describes the task, contrary to the laws of nature and of animals, imposed in this narrative.[4] A Jew is forced by his landlord, his king, or the like to attempt to change nature by teaching an animal (calf, camel, dog, or donkey) the art of speaking (reading, praying). He is given a long respite to complete the task and accepts it, hoping that the animal, the landlord, or he himself would die in the meantime. The absurd disregard of natural laws (J1900, J1930, H1020, H1024.7) appears to be intentional and to be used as evidence of the unreasonableness of many of the imposed decrees. It also allows for laughter as a

---

4. A Judeo-Spanish parallel of this version appear in Koén-Sarano, *Djohá ké dize?* 115, "Komo amaestrar gameos," in which Djohá volunteers for the task as a way to provide for his family for twenty years. His logic is that during that time, one of the participants (the king, the camel, or he, himself) would surely die. Another version in the same collection, "Djohá maestro de aznos" (p. 119), shows Djohá's wife as the one who comes up with the solution of teaching the donkey to turn the pages of a book by inserting wheat between the pages. For other Judeo-Spanish versions of this type, see Koén-Sarano, "El gatiko estudiozo," in *Lejendas,* 175, and "Maestro de gameos," 187; Koén-Sarano, "El gatiko ke se ambezó a meldar," in *Saragosa,* 177; and Moscona, "El sultan i el gameyo," in *Sipurei Sefarad,* 81. See also Jason, "Types," 220, for Jewish versions, as well as Schwarzbaum, *Studies,* 185, 468. IFA versions exist from Eastern Europe, Iraq, Turkey, and Yemen. For versions from other traditions, see Chauvin, *Ouvrages arabes,* 8:117, no. 101, n. 1; García Figueras, *Yehá,* no. 84 (AT 1675); and Rotunda, *Motif-Index of the Italian Novella* (K511.11).

means of release, to diffuse tension and the sense of doom that often accompanied such decrees.

Related types should also be mentioned, such as AT 1750A, *Sending a Dog to Be Educated,* and AT 922, *The Shepherd Substituting for the Priest Answers the King's Questions (The King and the Abbot.)*[5] In type IFA 922*C, *King Sets Tasks to Jew,* also, Jews are requested to answer questions or perform tasks.[6]

Our tale follows the prototype by showing the Jewish community being forced by an antagonistic rival to perform a ridiculous task that goes against the laws of nature: to teach a donkey to read. This is set against an atmosphere of threat to the entire Jewish community. At first it looks like the plotting vizier, just like Haman, is gaining the upper hand, but then the unpromising hero triumphs against all odds.[7]

One does not have to look far to find the Haman equivalent in this tale. Already in the religious story of Purim, in the Book of Esther, the king's minister, Haman, an evil, spiteful man, plotted the Jews' destruction.[8] Hence the appearance, in many Jewish folk stories, of a ruler incited by a jealous, scheming

---

5. Cf. Grimm and Grimm, *Tales,* no. 152. IFA holds a large number of Jewish versions of this type from Afghanistan, Bukhara, Eastern Europe, Greece, Hungary, Iran, Iraq, Israel (Ashkenazi), Morocco, Poland, Russia, and Yemen. It also has an Israeli Arab version. For published versions, see Bar Itzhak and Shenhar, *Jewish Moroccan,* 73, 170, 184; Cheichel, *TEM 1968–69,* no. 19; Nehmad, *Glima,* no. 1; Noy, *TEM 1976–77,* no. 1.

6. IFA versions of this type originate from Afghanistan, Czechoslovakia, Egypt, Iran, Iraq, Israel (Sefardi), Kurdistan, Latvia, Lebanon, Libya, Morocco, Poland, Romania, Russia, Syria, Tunisia, Turkey, and Yemen. Published versions appear in Avitsuk, *Ha-ilan,* no. 11; Baharav, *Mi-Dor le-Dor,* no. 65; Baharav, *Ashkelon,* no. 31; Bar Itzhak and Shenhar, *Jewish Moroccan,* 73, 170, 184; Cheichel, *TEM 1968–69,* no. 13; M. Cohen, *'Edot Yisrael,* 2:קבץ; Noy, *Folktales,* no. 38; Noy, *Ha-na'ara,* no. 33; Noy, *Morocco,* nos. 49, 57, 62, 64; Noy, *Libya,* no. 22; Schwili, no. 88; Seri, *Ha-kame'a,* no. 7; Stahl, *Emunah ve-musar,* no. 6; Yeshiva, *Shiv'a sipurei 'am,* no. 5.

7. In the Torah portion of Balak (Num. 22:21–31), there appears a remarkable incident of an ass speaking. It also sees what Balaam, the seer, is blind to seeing: an angel is blocking their path. The message of that passage is that Balaam comes to realize that no amount of altars and sacrifices can manipulate the sorcerer's god into cursing Israel. This is when he is shown to be no longer a sorcerer but a prophet.

8. The story related in the Book of Esther may be interpreted as an allegory of the Jews' struggle, from time to time, against the enemies that sought to destroy them. The themes on which it is based are universal, present in many other tales of Jews in the lands of the Diaspora.

minister. It is not unusual in such narratives for tasks to be imposed at the suggestion of such a wicked counselor or envious rival. Suspicious or envious of the Jews, he tries to destroy them, first through his influence with the ruler and then by assigning them a preposterous task they cannot possibly accomplish.

Imposing such unachievable undertakings reveals that the intent is indeed to get rid of the Jew who is asked to do something difficult or impossible in order to earn the right to live. He can only emerge as the winner through the use of cunning and deceit, or else through the ability to outwit. The trick he uses here to save the community makes us chuckle, and we appreciate the prank played on those who assigned the senseless task to begin with. Such motifs of subtlety and deception are characteristic of the realistic tale, and our version is a good example of a novella of ingenuity, which gives us yet another lesson in popular, practical wisdom. Because the Jews end up victorious, this reflects the wish of the narrating society to assert the Jews' superiority.

The story's purpose is to demonstrate the astuteness of even the most ignorant among the Jews (J1100) in contrast to the gullibility or stupidity of the "other." The lesson taught reminds us of the Perrault tale of the lion and the mouse: better not to denigrate the weakest, poorest, or most ignorant, as one never knows where salvation will come from.[9] To find a clever solution for every problem and trial in such Judeo-Spanish tales, the hero is shown off as an innocent simpleton, an unpromising protagonist of a much lesser stature than the sage as leader of the community. Here the simpleminded beadle, the *shamásh* (P426.4 [Noy]), successfully assumes the rabbi's place to diffuse the grave situation through humor and deceit. He is the wag who finds an unusually clever solution to the problem: a deceptive stratagem to diffuse the tension of the hostile situation. While the learned sages are lamenting their doomed fate and their powerlessness before a demand that goes against nature, the innocent sexton is able to save the entire community. He performs a trick "miracle" for the sake of his browbeaten people. Although it is not clearly stated here, the assumption is that his "heart," his *kavaná* or good intention, is what makes him "holy" enough to perform the miracle, as God is believed to reward the heart. This tale, however, is not to be seen as a religious story. It focuses mainly on the threat to the Jews and the cunning of the least intelligent member of the community who is able to fool the Gentiles and save the Jews. Various Judeo-Spanish proverbs likewise highlight Jewish ingenuity and artful cunning: *Haríf komo djudió* points to the sharp mind of the Jew; another saying is even more in line with the ending of this tale: *Ni el*

---

9. See Perrault, *Contes de ma mère Loye*.

guerko no kita kon el djudió, which means that not even the devil can have the upper hand with the Jew. To the delight of the audience, the king's final words confirm that he himself has reached the same conclusion: "Those Jews have a solution to everything! We'll never be able to overcome them!"

At the end of the Purim story, the ingenuity and cunning of Queen Esther and her uncle Mordechai are what save the Persian Jews from destruction. Similarly, our tale's plot is structured so as perhaps to indicate that the narrating community views that kind of resourcefulness as fundamental to survival in an antagonistic environment. In a variety of ways, similar narratives display the ingenious survival schemes of the weak. Stories that chronicle the indestructibility of the Jewish people have appealed to Jews across time. Perhaps this explains the survival and success of such tales as examples of the continued existence and achievement of Jews. Through the use of laughter, the tales allow for release from tension and anxiety.

The setting of our tale could not be more Jewish. There are rabbis, a Jewish community council, a synagogue, a sexton, a book of Gemará, as well as the customary religious acts such as fasting, penitence, prayer, and the giving of charity as a means of seeking salvation from a calamity. In the Purim happening as well, Queen Esther had asked the Jews of Shushan, in Persia, to fast and pray for her for three days before she dared appear before the king, her husband, to appeal for her people's lives. Fasting is basically an act of penance, a ritual expression of remorse, submission, and supplication, an almost instinctive reaction to exigencies, observed in an effort to try to avert the danger and invoke God's help.

The precept or custom of refraining from eating and drinking, the origins of which are obscure and the purposes multiple, has been widely used in Judaism. It serves as a means of supplicating God to alleviate the oppression of foreign rule.[10] Its most widely attested function, for the community as well as the individual, is to avert or terminate a calamity by eliciting God's compassion[11] and as a way of winning divine forgiveness.[12] When a calamity, human or natural, threatens or strikes a Jewish community and morale is low, a public fast is immediately proclaimed[13] to try to avert annihilation.[14] Such a sign of divine punishment could surely only be averted by penitence.

---

10. Neh. 9:1.
11. See 1 Kings 21:27–29.
12. See Ps. 35:13, 69:11; Ezra 10:6.
13. Judg. 20:26; 1 Sam. 7:6; 2 Chron. 20:3.
14. Jer. 36:3, 9; Esther 4:3, 16.

27

Mushón and the *Papás*

Narrated by MALKA LEVY (1988)

There was a king who was very fond of the Jews, and the priest, the *papás,* always incited him, *lo ensatanava,* by saying:

"Why do you like them so?"

"The Jews are brainy! That's not it!" the king would say to him. "Whenever I have a thing to ask, I must ask it of them. That's why I am so fond of them!"

"Ah, nonsense! *Shtuyót!*" the *papás* would say to him.

"Look," the king once said to him, "I'll show you that the Jew who fills up water,[1] who doesn't know where the letter *alef* lives,[2] is better that the most learned, the *áhsan melumád,* among the Christians."

"Fine!" said the *papás*.

The king said:

"Go, call Mushón, the one who fills up water."

They called Mushón. The king said to him:

"On your life, can you turn these five hundred liras into one thousand for me, within a month?"

"Why not?" said Mushón.

This narrative was previously published in Koén-Sarano, *Konsejas,* 321. Mushón is a nickname for Moshé (Hebrew for Moses). He is usually a recognizable humoristic character in Judeo-Spanish anecdotes.

1. This probably refers to a water carrier.
2. *Alef* is the first letter of the Hebrew alphabet. The allusion here is to an illiterate individual.

Upon leaving the king, Mushón sees that the *papás* is going up to the king. He stared squarely at his face. He looks at him and keeps looking....

"Why are you looking at me, Mushón?" the *papás* said to him. "What? Is this the first time you see me?"

Mushón said:

"No! I am looking at your beard, which is wonderful! I have not seen such a beard in my own world! *Djánum, djánum,* my dear! Can you sell it to me?"

The *papás* said:

"How am I going to sell it to you? *Addió*! My God! Am I to shave off my beard so I can sell it to you?"

"No, *has ve-shalóm*! God forbid!" said Mushón. "Let the beard remain with you! I'll pay you for it, and you'll write me ... you'll give me a piece of paper stating that this beard is mine! And I, each time I look at it, I'll know that the beard is mine."

"Fine, how much will you give me?" the *papás* said to him.

"I'll give you as much as you like!" said Mushón. "I'll give you five hundred liras!"

"*Addió*," said the *papás,* "Mushón has gone mad!"

He took the five hundred liras, and he signed that the beard belongs to Mushón.

At night, around midnight: Knock, knock! *Tak, tak!* at the door.

"Who is it?"

"Mushón!"

"What do you want?"

"I want to see the beard!"

"What? Now? *Agora*? At midnight you felt the urge? Is tomorrow not soon enough?"

"No, I want to see it now, *agora*!"

Well, the *papás* opened the door, and Mushón looked at the beard. No sooner did he look at it that he began to shout:

"May death keep away from here! What is this? Is that what you did to the beard? It's all dirty! *Pishín,* quickly, put some water to heat! I want to wash it for you! I want to soap it up for you!"

"*Agora*? At midnight? Tomorrow morning, early...."

"No! *Agora*!"

Pishín, quickly! They put their hands to the task! That daughter of a bastard, of a *mamzér,* that beard has to be washed! Once he washed it for him, Mushón went home.

The next night, he came back once again. As soon as he knocked on the door at three in the morning, the *papás* said:

"*Addió*! My God! *Agora* you have come? I am half naked!"

"I want to see the beard!" Mushón said to him.

He went in. He looked at it. And he started to shout:

"*Addió*! I don't know what to do! You have dirtied the beard! It was so beautiful! You are dirtying it! What shall I do?" he said. "*Yalla*! Let's go! *Agora* I'll leave."

The following night, Mushón came in with a *kutí,* a can, of red paint, of red *buyá*. At three in the morning, he went: Knock, knock! *Tak, tak!* at the door!

"Who is it?"

"Mushón!"

"What do you want *agora*?"

"*Na,* here, I want . . . I want to look at the beard!"

When he came in, he said:

"No! This is not a life! You have spoiled the beard! You have made it very ugly! *Agora* I want to paint it with red *buyá* so that it looks beautiful."[3]

"What? Did you go crazy, Mushón? How can you put *buyá* on my beard?"

"Eh, that's the way it is! The beard is mine! I can dye it any color I want! If I want to make it green, I make it green! If I want to make it red, I make it red!"

"*Djánum,* my dear! Take your *parás* back!"

"I don't want the *parás*! *Bukra*! *Mañana*! Such a beard for five hundred pounds?! *Ma pit'óm?* Who has heard of such a thing?"

"*Djánum.* Look! Listen!"

"*Beshúm ofen*! On no account will I sell this beard!"

"Take a thousand liras!"

"Well, okay! *Yalla*!" said Mushón. "I'll do you a *hatír,* a favor, this time!"

He took the thousand liras and he went before the king. He said to him:

"You gave me a month and, *na,* I did it in three days!"

"How did you make these *parás*?"

"From the beard of your *papás*!"

Commentary

Tales showing off the cunning and resourcefulness of Jews in contrast to the lack of relative smarts of easily duped Gentiles are common in Sephardic and

---

3. Coloring one's beard with henna was a Muslim custom for older men, so the joke here is on them.

the rest of Jewish folklore. Our example represents another realistic tale, a novella of cleverness (J1100) illustrating the type of practical wisdom much appreciated among the common people.

This version of IFA 1542*C, *Man Sells House But for a Nail*, differs slightly from the more traditional account of the man who sells his house but for a nail.[4] Usually included among the jokes and anecdotes of Djohá,[5] this prototype allows for hearty and easy laughter. Djohá sells his house on one condition: he maintains ownership of a nail in one of the walls and must be allowed to continue to use it. Thinking this to be the request of a fool, the new owner agrees to the unusual stipulation. Djohá then visits the house at the most inconvenient times of day or night in the company of donkeys or other smelly animals that he ties to the nail, turning the house into a stinky, uninhabitable stable. The new owner soon becomes fed up and relinquishes the house to Djohá long before Djohá himself desists. "Djohá's nail" has become a recognizable phrase that elicits instant recognition and hilarity among Sephardim and Muslims alike.[6] Less popular than Djohá but no less familiar among Sephardim, Mushón is another popular character of humorous folk stories, jokes, and anecdotes.

Just like *The Donkey Knows How to Read* (tale 26), this narrative of the unpromising but cunning hero is set realistically among Jews whose fate depends on the whim of a ruler. Here, it depicts a benign king seeking yet another confirmation of the versatility of his Jewish subjects so as to demonstrate to his meddling religious counselor why he favors them. As a Judeo-Spanish proverb proudly states, "Djudió bovo no ay" (There is no stupid Jew). The reputation of the Jews as crafty is upheld in our tale, and this is achieved with the king's blessing after he sets out to prove that the least literate of the Jews is superior to and more quick-witted than the most learned among the non-Jews. As expected, the Jew-hating vizier is put to ridicule (J1210). The Jew ends up in the winning seat, revitalizing the relationship between the king and his Jews.

---

4. See Koén-Sarano,"El klavo de Djohá," in *Djohá ké dize?* 107, for a Judeo-Spanish version. A Jewish version appears in Bar-Itzhak and Shenhar, *Jewish Moroccan*, 167–68, "Juha Sells His House." Se also Hanauer, *Holy Land,* 65.

5. See the Djohá section in this anthology.

6. See also Elbaz's *Canadian Sephardim* for a version of "Jha's Nail," tale 22. Several other Jewish versions of this narrative type are housed in IFA, all of which derive from the Islamic world (especially Morocco, Libya, Yemen, and Persia) as well as from Israeli Arabs.

In addition to pointing to the established religious differences, the tale also contrasts two social classes. By intentionally pairing off the least accomplished of the Jews with a man of influence and affluence, the narrator establishes a jocular tone. The incongruous demands of the water carrier thus appear even more entertaining because they impose ridiculous inconveniences on a powerful man who can neither evade them nor punish the Jew. A beard is hardly a possession that one can buy or sell, yet the greedy vizier agrees to the deal, thinking his opponent a dupe (J2300, K100). He ends up paying for his gullibility when he loses face before the king. Seeing him outwitted, the audience laughs and rejoices at the Jew's cleverness.

IFA 1528*D, *Contest in Cleverness between Jew and Gentile,* is an umbrella type for tales in which the Jew naturally wins,[7] while IFA 922*C, *King Sets Task to Jew,* is another oicotype for tales in which Jews are forced to answer difficult questions or perform impossible tasks.[8]

---

7. IFA versions of this type have been collected from tellers from Greece, Iran, Tunisia, and Turkey. The type is also known among Israeli Sephardim. Published versions are found in Alexander-Noy, no. 67 (Turkey); Aminoff, *Ha-emir,* no. 11 (Bukhara); Bar Itzhak and Shenhar, *Jewish Moroccan,* 152; Learsi, *Filled with Laughter,* 301; [Noy] (C201, C22.1+, C888, V75.1, V82); Noy, *Ha-na'ara,* nos. 36, 73 (Iraq); Noy, *TEM 1970,* no. 12 (Tunisia); Noy, *TEM 1971,* 171; Schwarzbaum, *Studies,* 530; Shenhar and Bar Itzhak, *Shelomi,* 78. For other Judeo-Spanish versions under this type, see Koen, "No savesh lo ke pedresh"; KS, 299; Moscona, *Sipurei Sefarad,* 15.

8. IFA versions of IFA 922*C are collected from narrators from Afghanistan, Czechoslovakia, Egypt, Iran, Iraq, Israel (Sefardi), Kurdistan, Latvia, Lebanon, Libya, Morocco, Poland, Romania, Russia, Syria, Tunisia, Turkey, and Yemen. Published parallel versions appear in Avitsuk, *Ha-ilan,* no. 11; Baharav, *Mi-Dor le-Dor,* no. 65; Baharav, *Ashkelon,* no. 31; Cheichel, *TEM 1968–69,* no. 13; Noy, *Libya,* no. 22; Noy, *Folktales,* no. 38; Noy, *Ha-na'ara,* no. 33; Noy, *Morocco,* nos. 49, 57, 62, 64; Schwili, no. 88; Seri, *Ha-kame'a,* no. 7; Stahl, *Emunah ve-musar,* no. 6; Yeshiva, *Shiv'a sipurei 'am,* no. 5. For Judeo-Spanish parallels in which the king sets tasks to Jews, see KS, 271, 275, 289; Ben Ezra, "Midrashim"; MR, no. 11; Perez, "La diskulpa mas negra ke la kulpa"; Romero, "Los tres konsejeros del rey," 44; Shahar, "El rey de Persia i rabi Yeuda."

28

The Tale of the Questions

Narrated by IMANUEL BEN EZRA (1992)

There was in Tsfat[1] a very learned Jew, very intelligent also, *ma* he was old. This Jew was very capable, very *kapache,* and very wealthy, *ma* he was always sad because he had been married for a very long time and he had no children. He always thought:

"All the respect, all the *kavód,* that I have earned, all the good things that I have, to whom shall I leave them? I have no one. It will go to waste, to *timión!*"

The rabbi, the *rav,* of the city of Tsfat had [away be it from here][2] died. The city council, the *váad,* was considering who to name in his place, and all unanimously said that the post belongs to this Jew, and they named him as *rav* of Tsfat.

When he became *rav,* he began leading the people of Tsfat, and they were all very pleased with the leadership, the *anagá,* of this man. *Ma* he himself

---

For a Judeo-Spanish and translated Hebrew version of this tale, see Koén-Sarano, "La ija savia," in *Lejendas,* 217.

1. Safed (H. *Tzfat*) was once considered one of the four holy cities in the land of Israel, along with Jerusalem, Hebron, and Tiberias. In the sixteenth century it was the home of some of the greatest luminaries in Jewish spiritual history, among them Joseph Karo, Moses Cordovero, and Isaac Luria, all three of whom are buried there. With its wide panoramic views and pure air, Safed stands three thousand feet above sea level.

2. Teller's aside, as a protective device against death for herself and her audience. She believes in the power of words to effect evil, so she articulates this formula before uttering the dreaded word.

became sadder, more *triakí*. Why? Because he would go to the synagogue, to the *keilá,* and he would see all the fathers coming in with their children, and he had no children. He would return home weeping.

One evening, he came back from *arvít*.[3] He came home weeping. He did not even say shalóm to his wife.[4] He went to his room, shut the door, took a book, and sat down. He opened it. He is reading and weeping. The tears are falling on the book.

His wife noticed that. She saw that her husband had come home not himself. She entered the room slowly, slowly. She approached her husband. She said to him:

"My lord, I understand the grief that you feel. You have all the right, of course. *Amá* what can we do? I can advise you to take another wife over me, without leaving me. It's possible that you may be able to have issue, you may bear children with this woman. And life will become sweeter and better."

When he heard this, he stood up:

"*Has ve-halila*! God forbid! God, the *Dió,* has joined the two of us. It's unto death. We have had no children; that's the way the *Dió* has wanted it."

"Is it your fault?" she said to him.

"No!" he said. "We'll always be together!"

They spent the night. In the morning they got up. The wife said to him:

"My lord, do you know what occurred to me last night, thinking about our problem?"

"What, *hanum*?[5] What occurred to you?"

She says:

"I am thinking that we can go to the orphanage and adopt a child and raise him. Often the adopted child turns out better than a child born from the mother's belly. Maybe we'll have some luck, some *mazál*."

The man thought about it and said:

"You're right. I usually go to the orphanage to give donations. They already know me. Let's go together. We'll look. We'll pick a child, and if we find him to our liking, we'll take him."

And they went to the orphanage. They were at that time having a lesson, a *lesón,* in the classrooms. The director, the *menaél,* who already knew him, received him with great pleasure. He thought that he had come to give some donation. He said to him.

---

3. This is the evening prayer.

4. *Shalóm* is a greeting that has several meanings: "hello," "goodbye," and "peace."

5. Term of endearment, such as "my dear."

"My lord *rav*, what brings you here?"
He says to him:
"I often come here to give a donation *ma,* this time, that's not why I've come. I've come," he says, "so that you yourselves may give me a donation."
"What is it you want?" says the *menaél*. "We're ready."
He says:
"We want to select one of the children that are here and take him as our son."
"*Addió!*" said the *menaél*. "It would be a great fortune, a great *mazál*, for the child who will fall into your hands! Come along," he says, "come into the classroom. *Agora* they are having a *lesón*. So look, choose!"

Husband and wife entered the classroom; they sat in a corner, in a *kantón*, and they are listening to the *lesón* that the teacher is teaching. The teacher finished teaching the *lesón*. The *rav* stood up:
"So children, do you know why I've come?"
One of the children stood up:
"Yes!"
"Why have I come?"
The little boy says:
"Since you have come with your wife, I understand that it is to pick a child from amongst us and to take him as your son."
"Bravo, young boy!" said the *rav*. "If you know how to answer correctly the questions that I'm about to ask," he says, "you'll become my son."
The boy says:
"Ask. If I can answer you, I'll answer you."
The *rav* says:
"Do you know who I am? I am the *rav* of this city. Can you tell me, my son: when the sky is cloudy and all of a sudden, *ensupitó,* we see a light and, after the light, we hear a terribly loud noise. . . ."
The young boy says:
"It's lightning falling from above."
The *rav* says to him:
"How long did it take for the lightning to fall from the sky to earth?"
The young child started to laugh. He says:
"*Aba,*[6] it didn't take even half a second! When we hear the loud noise, it

---

6. This is the Hebrew word for "father." Here, however, it may be used as a title of respect toward an elderly man.

means that two clouds have collided and there was contact. And it's a ray of electricity that fell. It didn't take any time at all, not even half a second."

"Right, *nahón,*" says the rabbi. "I'll ask you another question. Can you tell me how long it takes for a person to go from this world to the next?"

"*Addió!*"

The boy thought and thought. He said:

"*Aba,* about this I can't give you an accurate answer."

"Why not?"

The young boy says:

"Because it's been eight years since my father died, and we still haven't received a letter from him. How can I tell you how long it took him? I don't know."

"Bravo, young boy," said the *rav.*

They took this young boy, went through all the procedures that were needed, and adopted him. And they are raising him the right way. When the youth reached the age of twenty, educated, wealthy, and good, one day, while his father is reading in his room, someone knocks on the door. The son comes in.

"What do you have to say, *bey?*"

"*Aba,* I came to ask for your consent, for your *askamá.*"

"My *askamá?* What is it you want?" says the father. "I am ready to do anything you wish."

The son says:

"I want to marry Marika!" [a young non-Jewish servant girl they had at home].[7] "I love her!"

The father shuddered:

"*Addió!* You want Marika?"

"Yes, I love her," says the son.

The father didn't want to censure the youth. He said to him:

"Look, *bey,* I'll give you my *askamá,* but on one condition. I'll ask you one question. If you can give me the answer to that question, you'll marry Marika."

"Ask!"

The father says to him:

"Can you tell me: when you take a kettle, a *djizvé,* of water, you place it on the fire, and the water starts to boil, what does the boiling water say?"

"*Addió,* father! That's the loud noise that the water makes because of the power of the fire which is making it boil!"

---

7. The teller feels the need to identify Marika, since she had not appeared in the tale before.

"No! The water is saying something! When you tell me what the water is saying while it's boiling, I'll give you my *askamá* so you can marry Marika."

The son says:

"*Aba*, I don't know! There are people in the world more intelligent and wiser than I. Allow me," he says. "I'll go, I'll wander the world. If I find what is needed, I'll come back and tell you."

"Go!"

The next morning, the mother prepared for him a few things for the road, and he left. He reached the road to Yafo.[8] On the way, he saw an old man walking. Where is he going? To Yafo! They are traveling on foot. The youth approached the old man. He said to him:

"*Aba*, will you carry me to Yafo or shall I carry you?"

"This one's crazy!" said the old man. "You have legs, and I have legs. You'll travel on your legs, and I'll travel on mine."

The youth kept silent. They are continuing. *Ensupitó* they saw a small field sown with wheat:

"*Aba, aba,* may you live long. Pray tell me: has the wheat that is sown been eaten already or is it yet to be eaten?"

"*Addió*, it has just been sown! What kind of questions are you asking?"

Let's finish with this as well. They arrived in Yafo. When they arrived in Yafo, they saw [far away be it from here][9] a funeral, a *levayá*, a coffin being carried away.

"*Aba*," the youth says. "This man they are carrying away, is he dead or alive?"

"*Addió*," says the old man. "They are carrying him away, and he's asking me if he is dead or alive?!" he says. "There is no doubt that he doesn't have all his marbles!"

And in truth, the man became sad, *triakí*, because it gave him sorrow to see a young man so charming, so well dressed, so *atakanado,* speaking in such a manner.

When they were about to part company, the youth said to him:

"*Aba*, I'm not from here. I'm from Tsfat. I have taken a room in such and such a hotel. In case you need to see me, this is where you'll find me."

"Very well," said the old man, and they parted company.

The old man entered his home. He had a young daughter of about

---

8. Jaffa (H. Yaffo) is an ancient port city by the rolling Mediterranean in Israel, developed today as an art center, a mixture of old and new, east and west, Arab and Jewish.

9. Teller's aside. See note 2 above.

seventeen. Miriam was the name of the young girl. The young girl saw her father with the color of his face altered. She said to him:

"*Aba,* did anything happen in the family?"

"No," the father says. "They're all well."

"So why is your face this color?"

"Don't ask! Something happened to me on the way."

"What?"

"I met this youth on the way. He asked me the questions of a crazy person! *Amá,* if you could only see him," he says, "such a charming youth! In truth, it made me sad to see him."

"What questions did he ask you, *aba?*"

The father related to the young girl what the youth had asked.

"*Addió,*" the young girl said. "He is very intelligent, father! He is not crazy! He only appeared crazy to you, *ma* he is not crazy! I'll answer him myself!"

The old man remembered that the youth had taken a room in such and such a hotel. He said:

"I know where he lives."

"*Aba,* may you live long," the daughter said to him. "Go, take him what I'll give you, and tell him to come here, that I want to speak with him myself."

The old man did not want to go, because he was already tired from the trip he had made, without drinking a glass of water or anything. And his daughter is sending him out! *Ma,* all the same, he got up to go.

His daughter said to him:

"Wait, *aba.*"

She went. She took a plate with a cake on it, an *ugá;* she placed ten hardboiled eggs around the *ugá.* And she gave it to her father. She said to him:

"May you live long, *aba,* when you give it to him, you'll ask him if the moon is full, and what day of the month it is."

The father took this and he is on his way. He is thinking:

"I have come from far without eating, without drinking. I'm about to faint," he says. "Does the youth know how much my daughter has given me? I can take some of it for myself *agora.*"

He sat down on a bench over there, he cut a piece of cake, he took three eggs, and he ate. And the rest, the *kusúr,* when he arrived at his destination, he gave it to the youth. He said to him:

"My daughter begs you to come to our home. She'll answer the questions you asked me on the way."

"Sure," said the youth. "I am on my way!"

"*Ma* my daughter begs you, before you come, to tell her if the moon is full and what day of the month it is. I'll tell her myself."

"*Bashustoné.*"

The man got up to go back home. The youth said to him:

"*Aba*, you'll tell your daughter that the moon is three-quarters full and that today is the seventh day of the month."

The man arrived back home. His daughter came. She said to him:

"*Aba*, what happened? Did he answer the questions that I asked him?"

"Yes."

"What did he say to you?"

"That the moon is three-quarters full and that today is the seventh day of the month."

"*Addió, aba*! What a trick you played on me!" said the young girl. "Aren't you ashamed? Why did you eat three eggs and a piece of the cake?"

"How do you know that?"

"He's telling me so in his answer!"

In the meantime, the youth had already arrived. He sat down. The girl said to him:

"Young man, you asked my father three questions. Being an old man, my father was unable to think much and didn't answer you. I'll answer you myself," she says. "The first question you asked him was whether you should carry him to Yafo or he should carry you. Look, when two people travel together to a far-away place, if one tells an interesting story to the other, they don't pay attention to the road and reach their destination before they know it."

"*Nahón*, young girl," says the youth. "That's the truth!"

"The second question you asked him was whether the wheat which had been sown had already been eaten or not. It is perhaps that he who had sowed it had borrowed money, *parás*, to do so. When he grounds it into flour, he'll sell it and have nothing left. That means that it has already been eaten," says the young girl.

"Bravo, young girl!" he said.

"And the third question was," she says, "whether he who was being carried away was dead or alive. It is because, when a person performs good deeds in the world, he doesn't die. The good deeds he performed accompany him no matter how long he has been gone. And people *yené*, still speak well of him, because they say that a person has three friends: the first are his children, the second are the *parás* that he has, and the third are the good deeds he performs. And the most trustworthy of the three, the most *neemán*, are the good deeds that one performs."

"*Nahón*, girl, bravo!" says the youth. "Look, *hanum*, what's your name?"

"Miriam," she says.

"*Addió*, that is good!" He says. "The other one is called Mary and you

Miriam. Look," he says, "I'll ask you a question. If you give me the right answer, I'll take you as my wife."

"Ask!" she said.

The youth says:

"When we put water on the fire, after a little while the water begins to boil. What does this water say while it's boiling?"

"*Addió,*" says Miriam. "I'll tell you: what do we do to light a fire? We plant a little tree. To make it grow, we water it and take good care of it. Once it has grown and reached a certain size," she says, "they cut it down and turn it into wood. Wood is used to make fire, and they put water to boil on it. While boiling, the water begins to *kafuriarse,* to get angry and grumbles furiously. It's saying to the fire: 'I made you grow; I gave you all my strength! And *agora* you're burning me???'"

Agora the youth understood what his father had meant to say to him.

"He took me out of the orphanage, he raised me, he gave me all good things. And God forbid—*barminán*—I wanted to burn him by marrying a Christian? And his name would never have been named?"

He said to the young girl:

"Leave everything here and let's go!"

He took her with him to Tsfat, and they were married.

And so the father was satisfied to see them happy. *orozos.*

COMMENTARY

This is an excellent combination of AT 875D, *The Clever Girl at the End of the Journey* (part 2, *The Journey*)[10] and AT 875A, *Girl's Riddling Answer Betrays a Theft.*[11] In our tale, a traveling youth makes seemingly absurd statements to

---

10. Jewish versions of this type can be found in Nahmad, *Portion in Paradise,* 89; and Schram, *Jewish Stories,* 195. Non-Jewish versions appear in Al-Shahi, *Wisdom from the Nile,* no. 25; Basset, *Mille et un contes,* 2:157, no. 71; BP, 2:349; Dawkins, *Forty-five Stories,* nos. 20, 21; Grimm and Grimm, *Tales,* no. 94; Laoust, *Contes berbères,* no. 74.

11. See Baruch, "El judeo-español de Bosnia," 140, and KS, "La endivinansa de la reyna de Saba," 259 (reproduced in Koén-Sarano, *Lejendas,* 83) for Judeo-Spanish versions. The beginning of the Baruch tale follows AT 875A, but the rest is more complex, as it also includes AT 875, *The Clever Peasant Girl,* AT 875D, *The Clever Girl at the End of the Journey,* and the Jewish oicotype IFA 875D I*. The KS version describes the legendary queen of Sheba testing Solomon with a gift of food she sends with her father. When Solomon responds appropriately to her riddle, the queen rebukes her

an older man he encounters on the way, and his puzzling remarks are interpreted correctly by the man's daughter at the end of the journey (H586, H600). The enigmatic questions asked along the way fit well into the universal tale type of the clever peasant girl who unveils the symbolic meaning of the questions. They are well-known motifs of mysterious wisdom riddles (H501) propounded from chance experiences (H565), and they usually come in threes:

1. Which of the two travelers will carry the other? The telling of stories will shorten the way (H586.3).

2. Is the uncut field already harvested? It is so because its owner has already spent the money (H586.4).

3. Is the deceased whose corpse is borne by dead or alive? The corpse is not entirely dead because the man has left behind a good reputation (H586.5).[12] After this last answer, the teller inserts the motif of the test of friendship (H1558.3): Who will accompany one to death? The deceased man calls upon riches, family, etc. Only good deeds remain with him (J230+ [Noy]). This is found in **750E, *The Best Friend*.[13]

In the archetype, AT 875D, the resolution of the original riddle wins the love of the hero for the clever but unassuming maiden. Rather than the boiling

---

father for drinking the wine and eating the loaf, and recognizes Solomon's reputed wisdom. IFA parallels come from Afghanistan, Egypt, Iran, Iraq, Israel (Bedouin), Turkey, and Yemen. Other Jewish versions are in Ausubel, *Jewish Folklore*, 97; Bar Itzhak and Shenhar, *Jewish Moroccan*, 148; *BJ*, vol. 4, 108–14, 280; bin Gorion, *Mimekor Yisrael*, vol. 3, no. 15, 1292,; Jason, "Types," 172; Mizrahi, *Be-yeshishim khokhma*, no. 5 (Iran); Nahmad, *Portion in Paradise*, 89; [Noy] (H561+, H768, J192+); Noy, *Ha-na'ara*, no. 101 (Iraq); Noy, *TEM 1976–77*, no. 22; Schram, *Jewish Stories*, 195; Schwili, nos. 11, 78; Shahar, "Reyna de Shva," 48; Shenhar and Bar Itzhak, *Bet She'an*, no. כ. Non-Jewish versions appear in Al-Shahi, *Wisdom from the Nile*, no. 25; Ashliman, *Guide to Folktales*, 175–76; Basset, *1001 contes arabes*, 2:39, no. 17; Boulvin, *Contes populaires persans*, 1:47, 2:46; BP, 2:349, 361; Dawkins, *Forty-five Stories*, nos. 20, 21, 26; Dawkins, *Modern Greek Folktales*, no. 67; Grimm and Grimm, *Tales*, no. 94; J. Jacobs, *European Folk and Fairy Tales*, no. 23; Legey, *Maroc*, no. 38; Mathers, *Thousand Nights*, 4:366; Walker and Uysal, *Tales in Turkey*, 135.

12. The implication here is that during his lifetime, an individual should strive to accumulate a store of worthy actions, which preserves its value even after death (Prov. 6:22; Abot 6:9; Eccles. 7).

13. See Haboucha, 242. Judeo-Spanish versions of this type can be found in Bardavid, "El mijor amigo" (Mexico); "Deklarasion de bienes (Me'am Lo'ez)" in *AY* 15, p. 30. This is a moral tale found in the Me'am Lo'ez, Bereshit, and in Pirke de Rabbi

water riddle of explanation that appears in our version (H770, U162 [Noy]), the original question in other versions is often that of the fish in the royal palace that inexplicably laughs. This bizarre occurrence usually leads to the revelation that there is a man in the harem dressed in women's clothes (H561.1.1.1). In the Judeo-Spanish repertoire, the motif of the enigmatic behavior of the fish survives, but it customarily appears in a separate tale about King Solomon and one of his wives.[14]

As was the case between the famous queen of Sheba and Solomon, the propounding of metaphorical riddles (H530, H540, H540.2.1 [Noy], H720) typically takes place in tales of cleverness and competition between future marriage partners in which each partner seeks to find out character traits of his or her intended.[15] Such tales by and large end in marriage. Here, the young man leaves home, demonstrates his ability to pose enigmatic questions and to solve riddles, and marries (T100). His bride is clever as well. She answers and asks riddles and proves herself at least the equal of her suitor. In the end, however, she demonstrates her superiority when she elucidates the riddle of the boiling water, the answer to which the young man was unable to provide. After the heroine explains that metaphor, the youth finally understands the lesson his adoptive father was trying to teach him.

The heroine's father serves as a messenger between his daughter and his traveling companion, conveying messages from one to the other without fully understanding their significance. When the girl sends her father back to the youth bearing a gift of food, a formulistic conversation takes place (Z18), which is also a contest of repartees. The youth in turn sends back a symbolic answer that betrays the father's action (H582.1). He thus shows the girl that her father has eaten a quarter of the tart and three of the ten eggs she had sent as a gift (H582.1.1). This riddle and the questions posed on the way represent an intellectual challenge for the audience, which keeps the interest in the tale

---

Eliezer 34 as well as in Yalkut Shimoni 2, no. 354 and in Roman and Greek gesta. In Jewish sources, parallels appear in *BJ,* 4:32–35, 226–28, 257, 269–70, 275, 286, 288; bin Gorion, *Mimekor Yisrael,* vol. 3, nos. 34, 35, 1321, vol. 3, no. 36, 1322, vol. 3, no. 37, 1323, vol. 3, no. 38, 1324, vol. 3, no. 111, 1386; Cheichel, *TEM 1968–69,* no. 16 (Hungary); Frankel, *Classic Tales,* no. 187; [Noy] (V405); Pascual Recuero, *Cuentos sefardíes,* no. 3 (Hulli); Schwarzbaum, "Alphonsi," 284. In other traditions, versions appear in *Barlaam e Josafat,* 116, 388; Chauvin, *Ouvrages arabes,* 3:100, no. 7; Dawkins, *Modern Greek Folktales,* no. 75; *Gesta Romanorum,* 129; Keller, *Spanish Exempla* (H1558.1.1); Sánchez de Vercial, *Libro de los exenplos,* no. 16.

14. See *King Solomon and the Golden Fish* (tale 1 in this collection).

15. See Noy, "Riddles," regarding the riddle in tales of suitors.

alive. Because they may have heard the tale before, some listeners know the answers and thus are made to feel superior to the father, who finds himself unexpectedly caught in the act.

Beyond its architecture, this tale deals with two central issues of the life cycle: birth and marriage. As has been pointed out elsewhere in this anthology, children are considered a great blessing in Judaism,[16] "a heritage of the Lord."[17] The greatest misfortune that can befall a couple is childlessness,[18] which causes great disappointment and anguish[19] and was once considered a curse and a punishment.[20] Infertility in this tale is seen as caused by Providence, a hidden plan that is not revealed to mere humans. Deeply unhappy because his wish for progeny is denied, the rabbi grieves privately when his prayer for issue is not answered.[21] He laments that his name will perish at the time of his death. As the teller reveals in the end, in the words of the adopted son, an offspring—especially a male offspring—is still particularly prized because it means that *kaddísh,* the naming of the dead parent in a special prayer, will be recited in one's memory. The tale, however, also shows us how righteous people suffer their burden with patience and continue their service to God, demonstrating piety in spite of their troubles.

At the same time the teller shows an ambiguity about infertility, which is presented as a woman's problem. It is now, of course, generally accepted that the cause of sterility may lie as much with the husband as with the wife. The Bible so indicates as well,[22] as does the Talmud, for both Abraham and Isaac.[23] Yet, it was customary for a husband to have the option to divorce his wife after ten years of childless marriage,[24] for a man without progeny was regarded as dead.[25] There would be no one to assure the continuance of the family name[26] and no one to say *kaddísh.*

---

16. This is found in Gen. 22:17, 32:13.
17. Ps. 127:3–5.
18. Gen. 30:23; 1 Sam. 1.
19. Gen. 30:1; 1 Sam. 1:10.
20. Lev. 20:20–21; Jer. 22:30.
21. God is said to hold the key to fecundity (Ta'an. 2a).
22. See Gen. 15:2.
23. Refer to Yev. 64a.
24. Since the purpose of marriage is to raise a family, a wife's sterility would defeat that purpose (Yev. 6:6; Sh. Ar., Even Ha-ezer 154:6).
25. This appears in Gen. R. 45:2.
26. See Num. 27:4, 8.

In some tales, universal as well as Jewish versions, divorce or banishment of a wife, sometimes due to infertility, may bring about the motif of *The Dearest Possession,* derived from the Talmud (J1545.4 [Noy]).[27] In that type, AT 875, *The Clever Peasant Girl,* part 4, *The Dearest Possession,* upon being banished, the wife is allowed to take along only one thing: her dearest possession. She often takes her sleeping or drugged husband along and thus moves him to take her back. Here, the rabbi's wife demonstrates her love for her husband in a different way when she proposes to him that he marry another wife to try to father a child (T282 [Noy]). This is a tacit admission—and an opinion probably shared by the teller—that she has failed him by not being able to bear his children after so many years. The implication is that that gives him ample grounds for divorce (T297+ [Noy]). This is also reminiscent of the Sarah and Hagar episode in the Bible, in which Sarah suggests to Abraham to take her slave Hagar as a concubine to father a son.[28]

Divorce was rare within the Sephardic community, and there are no instances in the Bible where a man sends his wife away lightly. Thus it is clear why the matter of divorce rarely appears in the tales. What is reinforced is the ideal of marriage as a permanent union.[29] Keeping within the norm of that society, when the husband proclaims the sacredness of marriage, he reveals a marital relationship full of love and mutual respect.[30] Only then, after he has dismissed her first suggestion, does the wife bring up the possibility of adoption, the most modern of solutions to resolve their personal crisis (T670). Although legal adoption was recognized in the ancient Near East as far back as the Code of Hammurabi, around 1700 BCE, there is no clear evidence that this institution existed in ancient Israelite law. On the other hand, to raise a Jewish orphan and to provide for the child as if it were one's own is a com-

---

27. This is a midrashic story (Pesikta de-Rav Kahana, 2:147, no. 2; Midrash Shir Ha-shirim Rabba 1:31; Pesikta Rabati, 31; etc.). See also Pesikta Rabbati 30, 141a; Shir 1:4, 2; Yalk 16; BP, 2:372f. For Judeo-Spanish examples of that type, see Baruch, "El judeo-español de Bosnia," 140; and Shahar, "La mujer i el marido ke keria divorsar." KS, "El marido, la mujer i el Rav," 219, gives an identical version to Shahar's. Koén-Sarano, "La koza mas presioza," in *Saragosa,* 146, "La mujer entelijente," in *Lejendas,* 95, and "La koza mas presioza," in *Lejendas,* 171, provide additional versions. For another Jewish version, see M. Cohen, *'Edot Israel,* vol. 1, no. קיה.

28. In Gen. 16:1–2, Sarah's words indicate that she would then become a mother by proxy.

29. Cf. Gen. 2:24.

30. The rabbis stated that when a man divorces his first wife, even the altar sheds tears (Gittin 90b).

mandment, a *mitzvá*. In the Bible, the commandment to treat orphans well is repeated frequently, and they are cited over and over again as the object of charity and the subject of social legislation.[31] The Talmud holds the community responsible for the support of orphans and considers those who raise an orphan givers of constant charity.[32] Whoever brings up such a child in one's household is considered the child's true parent. The father in this tale expresses his love for his adopted son by calling him "bey" affectionately, even when angry with him.[33]

The more contemporary concern about intermarriage appears in the narrative as a prelude to and cause for the journey that will lead the protagonist to meet his future bride and thus resolve the conflict. Jews have always frowned on intermarriage, not only because the law forbids it but primarily because such unions pose a severe threat to Jewish survival. In Jewish law there is no validity to a marriage between a Jew and a non-Jew.

The teller introduces parallels and contrasts in the structure of her narrative. The two fathers, while both old, are opposites: one learned, pious, and wise; the other foolish and literal-minded. The analogies between the hero and heroine are obvious. They are both young and clever. They both speak in riddles and test each other before agreeing to marry. As an orphan, the hero is of unpromising origin. Yet he reveals his ingenuity when still in the orphanage, a foreshadowing of his future show of intelligence (H680, H682.1). The heroine recognizes his cleverness even before she meets him and enters into a deliberate contest with him. She attracts his attention by posing the riddle of the cake and the eggs. In the end, however, she wins the unstated contest when she elucidates the riddle of the boiling water and thus proves herself superior to him. The youth marries her, apparently neither for love nor because of her beauty, which is never touched upon, but because of her sharp mind and cleverness. There is a play on words regarding the name of the two girls: Marika (Mary) and its Jewish equivalent, Miriam. No other character is given a name.

The teller also gives central importance to interpersonal relationships in her narrative. She describes the rabbi's relationship with his wife as loving and mutually respectful, and it remains solid and affectionate despite the heartbreak of barrenness. The rabbi's reputation and status in Safed are also clearly

---

31. Deut. 16:11, 14, 24:19–21, 26:12–13; Maimonides, *Yad,* De'ot 6:10.

32. Babylonian Talmud (Talmud Babli), Sanhedrin 19b.

33. In Ottoman society, *bey* was a title below that of a pasha and above that of an ağa (a Muslim title meaning "chief"). Today it is used to describe an important person or one of good extraction, and it is also a term of endearment.

established in the first part of the tale. As a leader within the Jewish community, he is shown to be learned, successful, generous, and widely respected, a model Jew. His studiousness and commitment to prayer and Jewish life (V112.6+ (Noy)) contribute to the pious atmosphere at the beginning of the tale. The father displays his wisdom in his relationship with his son as well. Before selecting him at the orphanage, he propounds riddles to him to test his cleverness and ability (H500, H502). He also tests his learning when he propounds the riddle of distance to him. He does not oppose the proposed marriage to a non-Jew directly but instead delays his approval and gives his son the opportunity to seek a solution to the problem of intermarriage in his own time and in his own way. This wise strategy is rewarded in the end when the son returns home, not only with a clever Jewish bride but also cognizant of the grief he would have caused his father had he married his original choice, a situation the teller clearly emphasizes. In contrast, the relationship between the heroine and her father in Jaffa is barely sketched out. It is made clear that the daughter is smarter than her father and embarrassed by his behavior. However, when she covers up for his lack of understanding of the questions posed by the youth, she does so out of respect for his old age.

Finally, unlike most tales set in indefinite places, the teller locates this one solidly in Israel and, as we have seen, gives it a definite Jewish character. The first setting is Safed, a city in upper Galilee, and the hometown of the protagonist and his parents. The character, learning, and reputation of the father is probably meant as a parallel to some of the early Safed luminaries. The other locale in the tale is Jaffa, the destination of the travelers and the home of the clever bride. Travel and quests are frequently used in folktales in order for the characters to reach maturity, and this is indeed what happens here. It appears also that when the father grants his son permission to leave home, he gives him permission to marry, as is also often the case in folktales. The end of the tale takes us back to Safed, where the rabbi's wishes are fulfilled and he is able to see with his own eyes the happiness of the young couple.

29

When the Mouth Is Used

Narrated by RAFAEL VALANSI (1992)

It so happened that at the court of the sultan in Estanból there was a priest, a *papás,* and there was also a rabbi, a *hahám.* The two of them played backgammon, *tavle,* together. Whenever they played *tavle,* the *papás* would say to the *hahám:*

"*Bay, pezevéng! Bay, kieratá!* You, cuckold! You, pander!"

The *hahám* would say nothing to him; he let him go on this way. And so they continued to play for a long time.

One day, the sultan says to the *hahám:*

"What are you playing?"

"*Tavle.*"

"I'll play against the winner," the sultan said to him.

"Why not?" the *hahám* said to him.

The *hahám* then played with the *papás* and threw the game. The *papás* then played against the sultan. While they are playing, the *papás* throws out at the sultan:

"*Bay, pezeveng!* You, cuckold!"

The sultan said nothing. When the *papás* said for the second time:

"*Bay, kieratá!* You, pander!"

The sultan said to him:

"I, a *kieratá?*"

See Koén-Sarano, "La fuersa del uso," in *Lejendas,* 175, for Judeo-Spanish and Hebrew versions of this narrative.

And he seized him and sent him to have his head cut off.

The *hahám* said to the *papás*:

"You used to say to me: '*Bay, pezeveng! Bay, kieratá!*' Here you have the result: *agora* they'll kill you for it!"

COMMENTARY

Backgammon is a popular game in the Middle East. Usually played by pairs of men in cafés or at home, it is taken very seriously and can elicit a great deal of passion. One often hears the sound of the dice being thrown forcefully and of the pieces being slapped down loudly on the board. It is not unusual for one also to hear arguments, curses, and exclamations of appreciation or dismay during a game.

This humorous narrative could be viewed as a tale of cleverness confronting Jew and Gentile, in which the Jew who sits in the court of the king wins because he counts on the power of habit to avenge a repeated slight from his opponent. By not responding to the name-calling he is subjected to whenever he plays backgammon with the priest, the rabbi bides his time to teach his opponent a lesson in his own fashion. In time, his skillful manipulation of circumstances brings about the downfall of his opponent. The priest becomes so accustomed to insulting his opponent that when he plays against the sultan, he foolishly insults him as well, out of habit (U130). This turns the attention of the ruler to the verbal abuse (K1657) and causes the punishment of the abuser. The sovereign apparently can bear being called a cuckold but not a pander.

IFA 1538*D, *Revenge of Insulted Person,* is a Jewish oicotype that serves as an umbrella for various forms of revenge by insulted or cheated individuals.[1] Our tale easily fits under this umbrella as well as under IFA 929*B, *Minister Insults Rival,*[2] another parallel Jewish type. Additional related types are IFA

---

1. Other Judeo-Spanish versions of contests of cleverness and revenge can be found in *AY* 4, p. 20, "Una konsejika de Djoha"; Koén, "No savesh lo ke pedresh" (1528*D); Moscona, *Sipurei Sefarad,* 15 (IFA 1528*D). For Jewish equivalents, see Bar Itzhak and Shenhar, *Jewish Moroccan,* 152; Grunwald, *Tales,* no. 64; Jason, "Types," 209; Jason, *Types,* 78; Noy, *Ha-na'ara,* nos. 36, 73 (Iraq); Shenhar and Bar-Itzhak, *Shelomi,* 78. IFA versions originate from Afghanistan, Eastern Europe, Greece, Iran, Iraq, Iraqi Kurdistan, Israel (Ashkenazic, Samaritan, Sephardic), Morocco, Turkey, and Yemen. For universal versions, see Haboucha, 595.

2. A Judeo-Spanish parallel of that type is found in MR, no. 11, p. 105, "Las

1528*D, *Contest in Cleverness between Jew and Gentile*,³ and AT 837, *How the Wicked Lord Was Punished*.⁴

Unlike many tales of Jews versus Gentiles, this narrative does not feature a confrontation between two religions. It does not pitch an enemy against the Jews nor does it include a threat to Jewish survival. It displays no envy or resentment on the part of rivals, nor incitement to persecute, nor undeserved accusations to the sultan against the entire Jewish community. It illustrates only an insult to one Jew's pride and dignity and the punishment of the offender. The Jew is eventually vindicated for his patience when he succeeds in outsmarting his tormentor. In the end, the unbridled arrogance of the priest brings him to a disastrous end, and the teller thus establishes the rabbi as the only remaining power with the king. This is undoubtedly meant to instill pride in and bring satisfaction to the audience.

---

señales de la mužer," in which a minister slanders the wife of his rival as an adulteress. She, in turn, accuses him of stealing something from her while being with her. The man then denies knowing her at all. IFA versions are from Algeria, Egypt, Iran, Iranian Kurdistan, Iraq, Morocco, and Turkey. See *BJ*, 1:274 (AT 882); Crews, no. 10 (Skoplje AT 882); Cheichel, *TEM 1972*, no. 3 (Algeria); Grunwald, *Tales*, no. 49; Jason, "Types," 174 (AT 882), 187; Marcus, *Mabu'a*, no. 1 (Morocco), no. 14 (Iranian Kurdistan); Noy, *Morocco*, no. 24. For non-Jewish parallels, see Haboucha, 433.

3. Judeo-Spanish parallels can be found in Koén, "No savesh lo ke pedresh"; KS, "El haham i el papás," 299; Moscona, "Harebi Mercado i el cura," in *Sipurei Sefarad*, 15. IFA versions of this type appear from Afghanistan, Egypt, Greece, Iran, Iraq, Iraqi Kurdistan, Israel (Ashkenazic, Sephardic), Lebanon, Lithuania, Morocco, Poland, Russia, Tunisia, Turkey, Yemen, and Yugoslavia. For other Jewish versions, see Alexander-Noy, no. 67 (Turkey); Aminoff, *Ha-emir*, no. 11 (Bukhara); Bar Itzhak and Shenhar, *Jewish Moroccan*, 152; Learsi, *Filled with Laughter*, 301; Noy, *Ha-na'ara*, nos. 36, 73 (Iraq); Noy, *TEM 1970*, no. 12 (Tunisia); Noy, *TEM 1971*, 171; Schwarzbaum, *Studies*, 530; Shenhar and Bar Itzhak, *Shelomi*, 78.

4. IFA versions of this type exist from Africa, Egypt, Eastern Europe, Iraq, Iraqi Kurdistan, Israel (Ashkenazic, Sephardic), Libya, Lithuania, Morocco, Poland, Rumania, and Turkey. See the following for Jewish versions: Alexander-Noy, no. 27 (Israel [Sephardic]); Alexander-Romero, no. 57 (Iraq), also p. 256; Jason, "Types," 168; Jason, *Types*, 35; Noy, *Egypt*, no. 33; Noy, *Folktales*, no. 17; Noy, *Libya*, no. 62; Noy, *Morocco*, no. 46; Ps. 7:15–16; *Schwili*, no. 17; Schwarzbaum, *Studies*, 332–33; Stahl, *Emunah ve-musar*, no. 10 (Turkey). For international parallels, see Haboucha, 288.

PART SIX

Jokes and Anecdotes

Humor can be found in sources as early as the Bible. It appears also in the Talmud, in the Midrash, and in rabbinic tales and sayings. The Talmud, for example, tells us of a legend in which Elijah identifies two comedians as men assured of a place in paradise because of the relief they provide to those who are in pain.[1]

While laughter is primarily associated with fun and enjoyment, in folklore it is customary to laugh at anyone who does not fit into the familiar and expected. Thus the immediate amusement such tales evoke. This makes them readily remembered and enjoyed, and quick to be retold. Still, it is important to keep in mind that humor requires an audience. Since humor is cultural, it is often understood only by a select few. What is funny to one group may not amuse another, and trying to dissect a joke often takes away from its interest.

Jewish folk humor is well-known, including the self-deprecating way in which Jews tend to poke fun at themselves and at their own misfortunes to make their sometimes difficult existence more tolerable. Among the Sephardim, humorous tales often concentrate on the matter at hand and provide bits of received wisdom that may be both literal and metaphorical. They may contribute an extreme perspective or a total vision of human experience. The mocking laughter they evoke is sometimes filtered through a veil of self-reflection or wishful vindication. Without humor, they seem to say, life would be unbearable. It is like the spoonful of sugar that makes the medicine go down and gives the strength to bear persecution, hostility, and the difficulties of daily life. The "unutterable" things can be said as humor. It provides an indispensable ability to maintain an inner balance. In short, humor is liberating.

Humor, in fact, is at its best when it deals with important issues and contentious matters, for it allows for a transfer of the conflict from a threatening environment to a safe venue and helps diffuse social tensions and conflict. The coarse texture of life colors such narratives, which often highlight the crushing burden of poverty and survival. In Sephardic tales, this is undoubtedly rooted in the ceaseless struggle for economic and sometimes physical survival depicted in an often unpredictable, anti-Jewish environment. The impoverished society—Jewish and non-Jewish—was often living under the threat of starvation. These social situations are often treated symbolically in these tales, and such jokes and anecdotes thus become a symbolic genre.

More often than not, the anecdotal character of the narratives depicts the routine and difficulties of everyday life in a realistic setting and draws attention to human resilience. Since human happiness is so precarious, much of this lore revolves around the duality of sadness and humor by portraying the many hardships of life and the stress and exigencies of Jewish existence.[2] It is not unusual to find both laughter and tears appearing in tandem in such tales. Through some narratives tellers and audiences are reminded of their own powerlessness, but with the success of Jewish heroes in the tales, they try to prove to themselves that grasping a higher truth ensures ultimate victory.

Judeo-Spanish jokes and anecdotes are likely to cluster around a central character, such as Djohá the prankster, or a specific group, such as the foolish inhabitants of Makeda, social misfits who are typically fools, liars, beggars, or tricksters. Both categories are highlighted in this section.

Notes

1. Ta'anit 22a.
2. See Haboucha, 579, for a classification of other Judeo-Spanish jokes and anecdotes.

Djohá

It is said that the Sufis believe that the common people tend to miss the deceivingly simple answers while the wise ones uncover them simply by circumventing conventional logic.[1]

In traditional Middle Eastern folklore, Djohá (or as he is often known, Nasreddin Hodja) cuts an amusing figure, just like the one the Muslim mystics may have had in mind. Characteristically, this legendary personage is reported to have said: "I am upside down in this life." A well-liked local wag of pre-medieval origin, Djohá is a marvelous and celebrated folk character, renowned for his foolishness as well as his ironic wisdom and inventive antics. He has garnered currency and has come to be known as an archetypal trickster figure or stock character, much beloved for his delightful pranks and whims as well as for his unexpected astuteness.

Many countries claim Djohá as a native, but Turkey goes so far as to display his grave and hold a festival named after him. In Akshehir, the supposed hometown of this legendary figure, people believe that Nasreddin, the Hodja, the name for a wise Islamic teacher, looks out from a small opening in his grave to observe the world.[2] They also believe that when ordinary people look for a way to enter through the gates of truth, he will be there to greet those who attain that truth by walking around his grave.

Reminiscent of Foolish John, Juan Bobo, Hershele Ostropoler, Gimpel the Fool, and other such popular noodles, Djohá's appeal is almost universal. His fame has spread far beyond the border of his original location. Not only do many of his tales of jocular foolishness or wisdom permeate the local storytelling environment but they have spread far and wide to become known in various parts of the world. He is quite popular in Italy and Greece and throughout the Arab-speaking world, as well as in India and China.

The actions and adventures of this ordinary, quite naïve character, who manages to overcome obstacles and adversaries to achieve some level of success, have become the focus of many an anecdote. He is the folk hero of all kinds of adventures and misadventures in which he plays the role of a delightful simpleton. At once very stupid yet incredibly clever and with common sense, Djohá illustrates the complexities characteristic of the human mind. Silly and illogical, he can also lie, steal, and perform foolish tricks. Underlying Djohá's harebrained actions, however, is an implication and representation of wisdom. He can show sound judgement and display a certain logic all his own. Often he appears as an ingenious, creative culture hero who at times tries to control the events of his life inappropriately while at other times he unexpectedly finds clever and unorthodox solutions to his trials and tribulations.

A rich tradition of equivalent Djohá tales exists among the Sephardim as well.[3] His name has become an allusion to the traditional wise-fool. In Judeo-Spanish versions, the realistic background may be Jewish, but not always, as can the characters. Intercultural affinities may influence and change the tales. In tales from the East, for example, Djohá is portrayed as an innocent simpleton, less likely to influence his surroundings than his North African counterpart. The acculturation process, however, does not take away from the character of the tale in which, as the typical numskull of Judeo-Spanish noodle stories, Djohá is sometimes showcased as an example of how not to behave.

Typically he misunderstands instructions or takes them literally. His bizarre, blundering actions are often alluded to delightedly as *fechas de Djohá*. A good-hearted, careless fool, he is habitually shown to let events happen to him, as when he makes a foolish bet, asks foolish questions, and loses. At times he may be serious and at other times rather playful.

Not only is Djohá a nitwit and a careless simpleton, but now and again he can just as well be filled with good sense. Many lessons of insightfulness and familiar logic are attributed to him, yet now and then his behavior is the result of his own mysterious reasoning. In one tale featured here, for example, rather than mixing salad ingredients before eating, he invents an unusual way of doing so: after the food is ingested. In another tale, he follows eating instructions literally, with typical amusing results. In yet another tale, he displays a total lack of logic in response to unusual circumstances.

Some Djohá tales may feature deception or display an obscene character. With shrewdness and wit, the delightful figure of this marvelous folk character sometimes gets to outwit the witty. He can be a resourceful swindler who fools his enemies, avenges the tricks they play on him, and gets away with it. In a couple of instances in this anthology, while he appears to be the victim in the beginning, he finds a clever way to trick the tricksters in the end, be they a king or forty thieves. He comes up with a resourceful way to feed his family at his neighbors' expense, cleverly discomfits his accuser in court, and puts a judge out of countenance by showing him the absurdity of his judgment. In other cases, he gets himself out of trouble through his quick wit or succumbs to his bad luck despite his best efforts.

Djohá stories are usually short and uncomplicated, with a humorous conclusion. All the while, he elicits spontaneous laughter of recognition and appreciation as well as cheers from the listeners. As a wise-fool, then, Djohá is used to comment on life's occurrences in his own incomparable way. He becomes Everyman.

Notes

1. Sufism is the ascetic and mystical arm of Islam, which may have been influenced in part by Midrashic literature and, in turn, influenced Jewish mystical and ethical figures, including Maimonides and his son, and Ibn Pakudah.
2. See tale 44.
3. For a substantive collection of Djohá stories in Judeo-Spanish, side by side with a Hebrew translation, see Koén-Sarano, *Djohá ké dize?* A volume by the same author, *Folktales of Joha, Jewish Trickster* (Jewish Publication Society, 2003), offers 273 Djohá anecdotes in English, among which appear some of the narratives included in this anthology but offered by a different translator. These are tales nos. 30 (appears as *The Unmixed Salad,* on p. 236 of *Folktales of Joha*), 32 (*Dinner at the King's Table,* p. 247), 33 (*Knowing How to Ask,* p. 26), 35 (*Better to Be Struck by a Sane Person Than Saved by a Madman,* p. 264), 37 (*The Patient Teacher,* p. 40), 38 (*How to Bring Food Home,* p. 212), 39 (*Invitation to a Feast,* p. 239), 40 (*Miracle a la Joha,* p. 152), 41 (*What a Watermelon!* p. 220), 42 (*The Case of the Hard-Boiled Eggs,* p. 231), 43 (*Born Unlucky,* p. 221), and 44 (*Stamp of Servitude,* p. 215).

30

Djohá's *Salata*

Narrated by MARIA DE BENEDETTI (1987)

Djohá said to his mother:

"Mother, I want salad! I want *salata*! *Ma* I want it *agora*! Now! Right now! *Agora, agora, pishín*!"

His mother said to him:

"Take it, cut it up, and eat it!"

Alora, he took the *salata,* he cut it up, and he put it in his mouth.

"*Ma* that's not how it's eaten!" his mother said to him. "One cuts it up, then one puts oil, one puts salt, one puts vinegar, one puts. . . ."

"Everything will be put into it!" Djohá said to her. "You just keep doing your chores! Everything will be put into it!"

Djohá put some *salata* in his mouth, added with his hand a bit of oil, and vinegar, and salt. He added a bit more, and then still a bit more. Three, four times. Hum! He was full, full! He could no longer speak!

And in the end, *a la fín,* his mother said to him:

"What is this?! The *salata* needs to be tossed. *Agora,* to toss it, what will you do?"

"*Agora* I'll toss it!" said Djohá. And he tossed himself out of the window!

COMMENTARY

In AT 1263, *The Porridge Eaten in Different Rooms,* the porridge is eaten in one room, the milk in another (J2167). This prototype shows foolish ignorance of certain foods and shortsightedness in how to eat them. More than one version of this tale circulates in the Middle East. While the ingredients to be mixed may vary according to the country in which the narration occurs, what remains constant is the fact that Djohá misinterprets instructions and, due to the peculiarities of his own mind, continues to eat the ingredients, one at a time, when the recipe calls for mixing them all together before eating.

Another version that comes to mind is an Egyptian adaptation in which Djohá is served a meal of fava beans, the Egyptian staple protein dish. The bean is typically cooked in water until tender, and it is served plain. One then mixes the beans with oil and salt to taste, as well as with a variety of other ingredients as one pleases: a hard-boiled egg, fried eggplant, and finely cut salad, with onions, tomatoes, cucumber, parsley, and lemon juice, and perhaps even cumin. This dish is often eaten with flat pita bread or the coarse wholegrain peasant bread that is so popular in Egypt, making a delicious and nutritious meal. When Djohá is served fava beans, rather than mixing all the items together before eating his meal, he eats them one at a time. When he is reproved for his foolishness, he lives up to his reputation by rolling himself on the ground so as to do the mixing directly in his stomach.[1]

This anecdote, illustrating the illogical behavior of the noodle character, invariably elicits much laughter.

---

1. A version of this Egyptian parallel appears in Koén-Sarano, "Djohá en Ejipto," in *Djohá ke dize?* 291.

31

Djohá in the King's House

Narrated by DEBBIE HASSON (1992)

They invited Djohá to the king's house, and he went. They sat down to eat. There were hard-boiled eggs. Djohá ate his egg in one mouthful, and everyone was surprised:

"What ugly manners Djohá has!"

Djohá returned home, and his mother says to him:

"What did they serve you at the king's house?"

Djohá says:

"They served eggs, but everyone was amazed...."

"Why?" his mother says to him.

He says:

"Because I ate it this way: whole! In one mouthful!"

His mother says to him:

"Djohá, how could you eat the egg that way?! Eggs must be cut in quarters, and you must eat them piece by piece!"

Once again they invited Djohá to the king's house, and they sat down to eat. This time it was lentils, and Djohá remained for hours, cutting each single lentil into quarters.

COMMENTARY

Types AT 1691B, *The Suitor Who Does Not Know How to Behave at Table*,[1] and AT 1696, *"What Should I Have Said (Done)?"*[2] are typical Djohá jokes in which he obeys instructions to the letter, with incongruous results (J2460, J2461.1). When told that he should have cut the eggs, which he had eaten

---

1. Judeo-Spanish versions appear in KS, "Djohá i las kieftés," 129; Sephiha, "Djoha ande la novia," in "Dos kuentos de Djoha," 42; and Koén-Sarano, "Kozas redondas," in *Djohá ke dize?* 43. In KS, Djohá attends a wedding where he eats rice with his hands and gobbles down the meatballs in one mouthful. At home he divides each lentil according to his mother's instructions. In Sephiha, the same faux pas occurs, but this time Djohá behaves foolishly at the table when he visits his fiancée. For a universal parallel, see Andrejev, (type 1696*B). Another related type is AT 1685, *The Foolish Bridegroom*, a Judeo-Spanish version of which appears in KS, "El ojo de Djohá," 139. In it, the fool follows his grandmother's advice literally when she tells him to cast an eye on his bride. He throws cows' eyes at her during the wedding ceremony. There are several Jewish versions of this type: Alexander-Noy, no. 44 (Greece); Jason, "Types," 218; Jason, *Types*, 86; K, 133–35, no. 1; Pinhasi, *Bukhara*, no. 6; Schwili, no. 140; Schwarzbaum, *Studies*, 141; Stern, *Los Angeles*, 165, 361. There are also IFA versions from Afghanistan, Eastern Europe, Greece, Iran, Iraq, Israel (Ashkenazic, Sephardic), Lithuania, Poland, Tunisia, and Yemen. For non-Jewish parallels, see Andrejev, (type *1012); Ashliman, *Guide to Folktales*, 205 (type 1006), 285; Baughman, *England and North America*, 24; Bødker, *European Folk Tales*, 28 (Sweden), 78 (Denmark); Boggs, *Spanish Folktales*, 138; BP, 1:311; Briggs, *Dictionary of British Folk-Tales*, pt. A, vol. 1, 191, pt. A, vol. 2, 354; Clouston, *Noodles*, 41, 126; D'Aronco, *Fiabe Toscane*, 111; A. Espinosa, *Cuentos populares*, vol. 1, no. 187, vol. 3, 191–98; T. Hansen, *Types* (Puerto Rico) (*1686 A, B, C Dominican Republic, Argentina); Grimm and Grimm, *Tales*, no. 32; Robe, *Mexican Folktales*, 155, 200; Thompson, *One Hundred Favorite Folktales*, no. 85 (Denmark); Thompson and Roberts, *Indic Oral Tales*, 160.

2. In "Džuhá si kižu kazar" (Bitolj), K, no. 1, pp. 133–35, Kolonomos gives a Judeo-Spanish version of this type. Here Djohá once again obeys recommendations from his grandmother literally and at the most inappropriate moments. He throws sheep's eyes at his fiancée, laughs and jokes at a funeral, and expresses sorrow at the birth of a child and pleasure at his father-in-law's ill health. The engagement is broken. Jewish parallels can be found in Jason, "Types," 218; Learsi, *Filled with Laughter*, 94; Pinhasi, *Bukhara*, no. 6; Schwarzbaum, *Studies*, 91; Stern, *Los Angeles*, 165, 361. IFA versions come from Afghanistan, Bukhara, Iran, Iraq, Israel (Sephardic), Lebanon, Morocco, Tunisia, Turkey, and Yemen. For versions from other traditions, see Andrejev, (type 1696A); Ashliman, *Guide to Folktales*, 287; Baughman, *England and North America*, 44; Bødker, *European Folk Tales*, 28 (Sweden); Boggs, *Spanish*

whole, into four pieces, he takes the advice literally and applies it in an inappropriate way with amusing results. Such stories sometimes feature a mother-and-son relationship (P231), which makes them even funnier because the fool is often depicted as an adult who acts like a child.

This tale is set in two different spaces: the private space, where the numskull interacts with his mother and is taught a lesson in table etiquette, and the public space, where he showcases himself to others as a fool on two occasions. The mother's voice represents the collective voice of reason and propriety. Her help, however, is for naught, and the public space appears in a parallel manner to stress the hopelessness of Djohá's literal mind. In the first visit to the king's table, the teller sets the stage by making Djohá appear inept; during the second visit, by showing how he misapplies the helpful advice, the narrative highlights both his literal outlook and the absurdity of the resulting action.

In AT 1691B, the numskull skins the peas. In our version, Djohá cuts the tiny lentils into four parts (J2461.1.4). The choice of lentils in the Sephardic parallel is a logical cultural substitution, as lentils are eaten by the poor in the Middle East as an economical source of protein. In other versions the Djohá character performs all kinds of ridiculous acts at the dinner table, revealing his absurd ignorance of foods and table manners (J1730), which most audiences, including the Sephardic ones, find hilarious. The portrayal of Djohá as a literal fool is widely enjoyed (J1700, J2450).

Folktales, 139; Boulvin, *Contes populaires persans,* 1:77, 2:76; BP, 1:315, 524, 3:145–51; Briggs, *Dictionary of British Folk-Tales,* pt. A, vol. 1, 340, pt. A, vol. 2, 134, 150, 284; Calvino, *Italian Folktales,* no. 190.4; Carvalho-Neto, *Ecuador,* no. 31; Chauvin, *Ouvrages arabes,* 7:155, no. 437; Clarkson and Cross, *World Folktales,* no. 60 (England); Clouston, *Noodles,* 123, 137; Cole, *Best-Loved Folktales,* no. 51; Diaz and Chevalier, *Cuentos castellanos,* no. 41; EB, no. 328; A. Espinosa, *Cuentos populares,* vol. 1, nos. 181, 190, 191, vol. 3, 191–206; García Figueras, *Yehá,* no. 129; Grimm and Grimm, *Other Tales,* 95; Grimm and Grimm, *Tales,* nos. 32, 143; T. Hansen, *Types* (Argentina, Chile, Puerto Rico) (*1690 Puerto Rico, *1703 Puerto Rico, *1703 A–D Argentina); Megas, *Folktales of Greece,* no. 67; Paredes, *Mexico,* no. 64; Robe, *Mexican Folktales,* 202; Thompson, *One Hundred Favorite Folktales,* no. 98 (Russia); Thompson and Roberts, *Indic Oral Tales,* 163; Walker and Uysal, *Tales in Turkey,* 159; Wesselski, *Hodscha Nasreddin,* 1:251, no. 169.

32

Djohá Eats at the King's Table

Narrated by LEA BENABU (1993)

Djohá was very hungry. One day, walking down the street, he saw a large sign, a large *plaka*. On this *plaka* it was written: "Food and drink and a ducat in hand."

He knocked on the door. They opened it for him. He went inside. They said to him:

"*Buyrún!* Please!"

It was the king who had said that he would give food to all.

Djohá went inside. He sees a large room. In the middle of the room there is a large, large table, entirely empty. At one end the king took a seat, and at the other end Djohá himself took a seat.

The king clapped his hands for the waiter, saying:

"Bring in the first course!"

Djohá sees that the waiter came back with a make-believe tray, a *tavlá kiviahól,* in his hands, a *tavlá* filled with food, and he placed it on the table. He looked at the king. He started to taste, *kiviahól,* and he said:

"My lord king, in my life I have never eaten such an excellent fish. How tasty it is!"

The king said:

"Our cooks are famous. Our *tabahimes* are *mefursamím*. They cook food that can't be found in any other city."

Tov! Djohá pretended to cut the food with a fork, a *pirón,* a knife, and everything, and he is eating very nicely. He finished. He said:

"Ah, it was very tasty, my lord king!"

The king clapped his hands, and the waiter came in once again:

"Bring me the second course, the second *maná*!" the king said to him.

The waiter came back; he brought the second course. Djohá sees: there is nothing to eat. He held up the *pirón* and said:

"What is this?"

"This is wonderful lamb meat," the king said to him. "We roast it."

Djoha said:

"Very tasty meat," he said. "My lord king, in my life I have not eaten such tasty meat. It's the first time in my life!"

And he ate and ate, *kiviahól;* that is, he pretended to eat.

"*Tov,*" said the king, "now the waiter will bring something quite nice!"

The waiter brought in some *shorbét,* some sherbet, such as the Turks make. And he is eating, *kiviahól, shorbét* and compote. But there is neither *shorbét* nor compote!

"*Agora,*" the king said to the waiter, "from the *martéf* downstairs, from the cellar, you'll bring a *bokál,* a jug, of wine. Of the aged wine that I like so much."

"Ah, my lord king," said Djohá, "everything is wonderful, *avál,* wine, ... wine I don't drink!"

"You shall drink!" said the king. "We shall toast *lehayim*! To life! Together."

Tov, the waiter went downstairs, *kiviahól;* he brought him back a *bokál* of wine. There was neither wine nor *bokál*! Djohá held up his glass. He said:

"My lord king, don't force me. Afterward I'll do crazy things."

"No!" said the king, "you'll do no crazy things! Let's drink together."

Djohá filled the glass. He said:

"My lord king, and you, would you like some?"

"Yes," said the king, and Djohá filled up his glass, *kiviahól.*

"*Lehayim*!"

The two of them started to drink. Djohá drank one glass. He drank two. The *bokál* was now empty, *kiviahól.* He said:

"My lord king, the wine was very tasty. The *bokál* is already empty."

"Go, bring another *bokál* of wine," the king said to the waiter.

The waiter brought, *kiviahól,* another *bokál* of wine. Djohá kept drinking and drinking. He stood up, *sozdé,* as if he were drunk, and he punched the king, throwing him off his chair.

"What are you doing?" the king said to him.

"My lord king," said Djohá, "the fault is not mine. The fault is the wine's. I drank wine and lost my senses. Didn't I tell you that I don't drink wine? You forced me to."

He made as if to get up, and the king tried to help him. Djohá raised his hand and gave the king another punch, throwing him off the chair.

"What are you doing?" the king said to him.

Djohá said to him:

"I am drunk, my lord king. I don't know what I'm doing."

The king said to him:

"You are the first one to *lesadér* me, to put me in my place in my entire life. Until now," he said, "I have given food to everyone this way, as I have given you, and they all left weeping. You," he said, "you have given me a *haftoná,* a beating that I'll remember for the rest of my life. *Agora,*" he said to the waiters, "bring him all that you were going to bring him. Let him eat and drink. And you'll give him not only a ducat, *ma* a purse filled with gold coins, with *midjidiés.*"

They brought him food and drink. And he ate and drank, and he left with the gold liras. When he came out, someone said to him:

"I saw you when you entered there. What did you eat?"

"What did I eat?" Djohá said to him. "I ate fish. I ate meat. I ate compote...."

"Did you eat real food?" he said to him.

"Eh," said Djohá, "I must tell you the truth: the first time around it was not real, *avál* the second time it was indeed real."

And so it was that Djohá put the king in his place, and he left satisfied.

Commentary

This narrative is a clever hero tale that highlights the other side of Djohá's personality: his ingenuity and success in dealing craftily to avenge mistreatment by a trickster, no matter how powerful the trickster is.

The setting of the narrative provides a sharp contrast between wealth and poverty in two discrete spaces, separated by a door. Djohá uses that door to step between two distinct worlds. Even as people are starving on the outside, on the inside, the king's cooks serve delicious fish and lamb, sherbet and compote, and fine aged wine. When the king perpetuates hunger despite the lavish wealth he displays in mock fashion, however, the world of hunger outside is mirrored by an artificial situation created by the royal wealth on the inside.

As often is the case in such tales, the narrative tale opens bluntly with Djohá down on his luck. The teller describes him simply as being very hungry. In turn, she displays the king as showing little generosity toward the needy and going so far as to play an unkind trick on them, extending a deceptive invitation to a feast during which he serves pretend food (J1577). With a simple clapping of the hands, he calls for service. This is the characteristic way of catching the attention of a waiter in a restaurant. The tantalizing menu listed is mouth-watering and the pretense cruel, but as would be expected, the absurd make-believe backfires in the end. The objective of the tale appears to be both didactic and humorous, and Djohá's surprising rebuke of the ruler's lack of hospitality and his inappropriate form of entertainment (J1536, J1561, J1565) serves that dual purpose. At the conclusion of the tale, the king concedes that he has been beaten at his own game as never before, and he recognizes that Djohá has taught him a valuable lesson. For Djohá, the situation described is a multiple test: of resourcefulness (H506), patience (H1553), and character (H1550), and he passes it with flying colors.

By warning the king that his guest cannot be held responsible for his actions should he be forced to drink wine, Djohá and the narrator alert the listeners that a typical Djohá response is in the offing. After playing along with the king's charade throughout a four-course pretend meal, Djohá indeed cannot resist punching his cruel and stingy host and giving him a well-deserved beating (J1561.4, J1522) not once but twice. He shows skill in reproving him (J1110, J1675, J816, J1340), however, and in cleverly putting him out of countenance (J1210, J1214) he unexpectedly turns the tables on him with impunity (K1600).

Besides providing a delightful example of Djohá getting revenge, the teller takes pleasure in displaying for her audience how an unpromising character rises above his circumstances through resourcefulness and brings about an unexpected change of luck. She does so artfully by setting the stage for Djohá to play the same game as the king: pretend wine-drinking, pretend drunkenness. The punishment itself, however, and the reward could not be more real. While the royal table is set in imaginary mode at the beginning, the tale shows Djohá eating the described delicacies to his heart's content in the end. Once again, Djohá proves victorious against all odds.

33

It's All in the Asking

Narrated by ALEX KORFIATIS (1993)

Djohá was in class, and the schoolteacher wanted to teach the children about animals. He said to them:
"How does a dog bark?"
They all went:
"Woof! Woof!"
"And how does a cat mew?"
They all went:
"Meow! Meow!"
The teacher said to them:
"Good! Who knows how a wolf howls?"
Djohá raised his hand and said:
"My *nono*, my grandfather knows!"
The teacher says to him:
"Bring your *nono* here."
Djohá brings his *nono* to class, and the teacher asks him:
"How does the wolf howl?"
The *nono* goes:
"Eh?"
"How does the wolf howl?"
The *nono* goes:
"Eh?"
Djohá says:
"Not this way, my teacher! *Nono,* what was it like with all the beautiful young girls when you were a young man?"

The *nono* goes:
"AOOUUH!"

Commentary

Starting out as an uncomplicated child's tale, this short, unclassified narrative evolves from a semblance of teaching young children to recognize animal sounds into a slightly off-color joke, attributed to Djohá in childhood. Told by a man, this is clearly a masculine joke, one that looks back with nostalgia to times gone by of youthful vigor, the wolf's whistle, and sexual prowess.

34

Djohá and the Oil

Narrated by HAYIM TSUR (1992)

Djohá's mother once sent him out to buy oil. Djohá took a flask, went to the grocer, the *bakál,* and said to him:

"Look, my mother wants olive oil for the salad, for the *salata.*"

"Very well," the *bakál* said to him. "Give me the flask."

The man placed the funnel into the flask and is pouring the oil. And the oil reached the tip of the flask. *Agora,* there were still some drops of oil left; let's say, about a quarter of a cup. The *bakál* said to him:

"Look, you have this much left over. Come back tomorrow with the flask, and I'll fill it for you."

Djohá told him:

"No! Tomorrow I'll be busy. I'll forget. Look, this flask has a little space on the other side," he said. "I'll turn the flask over, and you'll pour the remainder there."

Well, he pushed the cork in and closed the flask. He turned it over, and the *bakál* poured the remaining oil there for him.

Djohá went home. He is walking with the flask upside down, saying to himself:

"Look what a *pikéah,* what a clever fellow I am!"

He is walking and walking, and the weight of the oil is pressing against the cork. While climbing up, his foot caught on the stairs. The flask opened up, and all the oil came pouring out. His mother came out and started to shout:

"Look at what you've done! Not only did the oil flask empty out, *ma* I now must clean up the stairs! Otherwise, your grandfather, your *papú*, will slip! Your grandmother, your *bavá*, will slip!"

And she gave him a good beating, a good *haftoná*!

Commentary

An umbrella type, AT 1349*, *Miscellaneous Numskull Tales,* serves as the appropriate classification for this narrative in which young Djohá is assigned a simple task by his mother (P231, H934).[1] The bungling fool makes a mess of it, of course (J1700, J2650), by thoughtlessly carrying the container of oil upside down and, true to form, tripping on the stairs (J2133). When the additional pressure on the cork forces the oil out, the predictable misstep by Djohá, who thinks himself clever, is what provides the humor in the tale.

The two clear-cut spaces, which appear at both ends of the tale—the grocery shop and the staircase of Djohá's home—are linked by a middle space in which we become unusually privy to the goings-on in Djohá's mind. On his way home after having made the oil purchase, he displays much self-satisfaction and compliments himself for having had the smarts to put the overflow of oil in the bottom groove of the container and thus avoid a second trip to the store. Yet, at the same time, he shows an absurd disregard for the law of gravity (J1930).

In the course of his narration, the teller gives us a glimpse of Djohá's home life. He depicts a harried housewife and mother, a walk-up dwelling, and an extended family arrangement where grandparents live together with their children and grandchildren. He shows the interaction with the grocer and between mother and son. He also describes a family environment in which it is acceptable for corporal punishment to be used by an irritated mother to chastise her numskull of a son.

---

1. A Judeo-Spanish parallel of this tale is found in Koén-Sarano, "Redoma sin fondo," in *Djohá ké dize?* 45.

35

Better a Wise Man Should Strike You Than a Fool Help You

Narrated by SHMUEL BARKI (1992)

One day, as he was leaving his house, Djohá saw a cluster of children, a *hamula*, shouting after a man:

"He has a *karahat*! He has a *karahat*! He is a baldhead! He is a baldhead!"

He, too, said it without knowing what it was all about:

"He has a *karahat*!"

The man, hearing that Djohá was saying to him that he had a *karahat*, took his hatchet, his *baltá*, and started running after him. Djohá runs and the man runs after him! Djohá runs, and the man runs! Soon, Djohá had no breath left, no *reflo*, from so much running. He saw a tree; he climbed on it. The one with the *baltá* said to him:

"Come down! Watch out, I'll chop down the tree with the *baltá,* and I'll make you fall as well!"

"No!" said Djohá. "Do whatever you want. I'm not coming down!"

A madman passed nearby and said:

"What's happening?"

"Djohá said to me that I have a *karahat*, and then he climbed on the tree. He doesn't want to come down," the man said. "Let him come down, I'll forgive him."

Djohá says:

"I'm not coming down!"

What did the madman do? He took out a Gillette.[1] He said:

"Look, Djohá! If you don't come down I'll chop down the tree, and you'll fall down!"

Djohá came down! The man stood there, staring at him:

"With the *baltá* that I have, he didn't want to come down; with the Gillette, how come he agreed to come down?!"

He said to Djohá:

"Look, next time don't talk to me like that. *Avál*, tell me. Why didn't you want to come down when I have a *baltá* in my hand, but you came down for that one who has a Gillette?"

"He said that he would cut down the tree!" Djohá said.

"Can the tree be cut down with a Gillette?"

"Yes!"

"How?"

"That one is a madman. He can do it. You are not mad, so you can't!" Djohá said to him.

Commentary

Once more, the absurd lack of logic of fools takes center stage in this short, unclassified narrative where pursuit (R260), tree refuge (R311), and stubbornness (W167) are featured together with incongruous behavior resulting from diminished common sense.

The introduction to this tale, with the children mocking the passerby for being bald, is reminiscent of biblical Elisha. On his way to Bethel from Jericho, the Bible tells us, Elisha was mocked by some young lads who called him a baldhead. Soon after, Elisha turned around and cursed the boys in the name of God. Two bears came out of the forest and tore forty-two of the youngsters apart.[2] The Talmud explains that Elisha punished the boys so harshly because he foresaw that no good would ever come of them.[3]

There is no moral judgment in our story, nor is there a supernatural curse or punishment. This is simply a numskull joke in which, true to his nature,

---

1. The Gillette Company, maker of blades and razors, is well-known all over the world, and its trademark products are so widely used that "Gillette" is often used to refer to any blade or razor.

2. 2 Kings 2:23. I am indebted to my mother, Emilia K. Haboucha, for calling my attention to this parallel. Her intimate knowledge of the Bible is inspiring.

3. Sotah 46b.

the fool behaves in a puzzling way (J1700). From the beginning, Djohá exhibits the same childish characteristics as the *hamula* of children who chase after the bald man. He then follows his own inner logic in showing implausible fear of a madman with a flimsy razor blade rather than of the hatchet man who threatens to fell the tree Djohá is sitting on. Beware of fools (J171+ [Noy])!

36

What a Sweet Death!

Narrated by SARA YOHAY (1992)

Djohá traveled on a hot summer day until he reached the neighboring town. There he ran into an acquaintance, who invited him to his home to drink iced *sherbét* to refresh himself.

They placed in front of them a *tendjeré,* a pan, filled with *sherbét* with *buz,* with ice. The friend gave Djohá a small teaspoon, and he himself took hold of a soup ladle. *Meskino* Djohá! Poor Djoha! How to satisfy his thirst with this tiny teaspoon? He sweated even more from the effort!

The other one *englutía*, swallowing up ladles and ladles, and he kept saying:

"Ah, *Dió Santo*! I'm dying! Oh, Holy God! I'm dying!"

And so he repeated every time the ladle would enter his mouth. Until Djohá, feeling worn out, could stand it no longer. He gave a sigh like a lion's roar and said:

"*Amán*! Have mercy, brother! Pass me the ladle so that I too can die, even if only once!"

COMMENTARY

With typical Middle Eastern humor, this tale's focus is on the oppressive, debilitating regional heat and on the attempt to overcome it by gulping down a refreshing iced drink. It uses a play on words: dying figuratively as a result of the stifling heat as opposed to dying from the pleasure derived from the relief provided by the cool drink. No equivalent type is known to exist.

37

Djohá's Questions

Narrated by ESTER VENTURA (1992)

When Djohá was a boy, he used to go to school, to the *skola*. He was always obstinate, showing *innát,* and wagering with his friends that he would win against them always. And he always won.

One day, they all came out of the *skola*. One of them said:
"What a good teacher, a good *moré,* we have! He never gets annoyed! He is always patient!"
Another one said:
"He'll never get annoyed!"
Djohá jumped in and said:
"I'll get him annoyed! Do you want to see? *Aval*," he said, "how much will you give me if I get him annoyed?"
His friends said to him:
"We'll give you a hundred liras, a hundred pounds each, if you get the teacher to become annoyed! *Avál,*" they said to him, "you always win! We'd like to win against you once! How much will you give us if you don't succeed?"
"I'll give you only a hundred, *avál* I want one hundred from each one of you!" said Djohá.
Djohá went home. He pondered and pondered, and he said:
"*Agora,* I know just what to do!"
He got up at midnight and went knocking on his teacher's door. The teacher got up, came downstairs, and looked. What did he see but that Djohá had come!
"What is it you want, *bey*?" he said to him. "What is it you want at midnight?" *Avál,* without becoming annoyed.

255

Djohá said to him:

"I wanted to ask you why it is that, in France, they all have large feet. Why is it that French people have large feet?"

The teacher said to him:

"Everyone is tall over there; that's why they have large feet. You did well in asking me," he said to him. "These are things you ought to know. Is there anything else you want to ask me?"

"No!" Djohá said to him.

"Oh, well, then," the teacher said to him, "*agora* go home, *bey*. Go in good health."

The man didn't get annoyed. He went back inside the house.

"What shall I do?" said Djohá. "I didn't get him annoyed."

He went back and knocked on the door once again. The *moré* put his clothes back on and once more came down the stairs. He opened the door and said to him:

"*Yené,* you've come back again? What do you want?"

Djohá said to him:

"I came to ask you why it is that, in Japan, they all have wide feet?"

The teacher said to him:

"That's the way they are over there. It's because there is a lot of sand, a lot of *holót*. They walk barefoot, and that's why their feet become wide. You did well to ask," he said. "*Ayde, bey*. Let's go now, my dear boy. *Agora* go home."

When he told him that, Djohá started to cry. The teacher said to him:

"Why are you crying? You came here to learn, to *ambezár,* no? So why are you crying?"

Djohá said to him:

"Because of you, I am about to lose a hundred liras!"

Commentary

Talmudic evidence indicates that some rabbis were remarkable in their humility. One of the most eminent and humblest is believed to be Hillel,[1] about whom the following anecdote is told. It seems that two of his disciples had wagered about whether they would succeed in making the rabbi lose his temper. One day, while Hillel was washing up in anticipation of the Sabbath,

---

1. Hillel was a Jewish teacher, scholar, and rabbi (30 BC–9 AD). He was the first to formulate definite hermeneutic principles. See n.13, p. 121.

one of the men brusquely interrupted him and asked: "Why are the Babylonians round-headed?" "You have asked an important question," Hillel responded evenly. "That is because there are no skilled midwives amongst them." The man left, only to return later and interrupt the rabbi's ablutions once again: "Why are the inhabitants of Palmyra[2] bleary-eyed?" "You have asked another important question," Hillel answered again. "The reason is that they reside in sandy districts." When the disciple returned for the third time, his question was: "Why are the Africans broad-footed?" This time, also, Hillel responded with equanimity: "You have asked an important question. That is because they live in marshy areas." The man finally gave up: "May there not be many like you in Israel! Because of you I have now lost 400 *zuzim.*"[3]

Our unclassified version is obviously a secular adaptation of the Hillel story.[4] Just like Hillel's disciple, Djohá behaves inappropriately and at inopportune times, testing the patience of his teacher and seeking to get him to display irritation and a rare lack of self-control. With the stress on the contrariness of the pupil rather than the serenity of his teacher, however, our narrative no longer belongs with other religious tales but with jokes about foolish behavior. This change results in part from the narrator's decision to identify the student with Djohá, thus evoking for the audience the quirkiness of the folk hero and setting the stage for his apparent silliness. At the same time, the identity of the teacher becomes blurred, and he remains nameless, thus expunging the connection with the renowned rabbi and distancing the story from the pious and humble character of the original.

This narrator also gives us a rare and realistic glimpse of school life among young pupils. The teacher's tolerance of his charges' rowdiness in the classroom, indirectly alluded to, and their recognition of his self-discipline illuminate an aspect of life seldom depicted in folk stories: that of the teacher/student relationship (P340) and the forbearance needed to control the youngsters. Just like Hillel, who remains calm and never shows anger, the teacher treats Djohá kindly and patiently even outside of class (W26). By calling him *bey,* a form of endearment such as "prince" or "my dear boy," he thwarts Djohá's intent of making him lose his self-control and temper despite

---

2. Palmyra was an ancient Syrian city, located northeast of Damascus on the northern edge of the Syrian Desert.
3. Shab. 30b ff.
4. For another Jewish version of this tale, see Serwer-Berstein, *Jewish and Arab Folktales,* no. 5, pp. 31–34.

the repeated intrusion on his private space and on his sleep. Just like Hillel, he respects inquiries and knows the answers sought, no matter how irrelevant and out of the ordinary.

As can be noted in this Djohá section, each individual Djohá anecdote contributes yet another facet of the personality of this folk hero/antihero. His obstinate and contrary streak is stressed here, first when the teller clearly identifies this character trait at the onset of the narrative and then again through the frequent betting that he apparently initiates among his friends, always setting himself up against the rest of them. His tears of frustration in the end upon realizing that he has lost the wager (No) are the final highlight of that depiction. Once removed from the devout context of the Hillel milieu, the seemingly foolish questions Djohá poses to his teacher at inconvenient times reinforce the image of the noodle who follows his own clock and his own logic.

38

Djohá's Retorts

Narrated by SARA YOHAY (1992)

Djohá was not born a hard worker, a *lavoradór*! Yet, *iné,* he still had to bring food home! One night he decided that very early the next morning, before the birds awake, he'll do something.

No sooner thought than done! *Beemét,* before the birds awoke he had entered a vegetable garden, a *bahché,* with a *torvá* that *boy,* a sack that size! And he filled it up with all the good things he found: with watermelons, *karpuzes,* tomatoes, vegetables, *zerzvá,* and fruit.

As he was getting ready to throw it over his shoulder, the watchman presented himself before him. And what a watchman he was! Two meters tall, with the face of a killer, a head entirely bald, and eyes as large as eggs, that protruded!

Djohá's *pachás,* his legs, wobbled under him, and his kidneys, his *renes,* dropped. The watchman stood before him and said to him:

"What are you doing here?"

And Djohá:

"Nothing! I'm not doing anything! Do you recall that a couple of days ago there was that strong wind? That wind lifted me up and dropped me here!"

"Well," said the watchman, "let's suppose, *supozamos,* that it is so. Tell me who cut these things?"

And he pointed to the *torvá* that was full. Djohá played dumb:

"Do you recall how strong that wind was? Well, as it lifted me up from here to there, I held on to one thing or the other. That's how they were cut."

"Well," the watchman said, "let's admit it was so. Who put them into the *torvá*?"

And Djohá [who wouldn't be the Djohá we know if he wouldn't answer him this way][1] said:

"You're right, *Musiú* Watchman! Here I am, looking and wondering...."

And his voice was filled with sweetness, his eyes as those of a young child! And walking slowly, slowly, without turning his head, he moved toward the gate.

"Hey," shouted the watchman, laughing. "Take away your *torvá!* You've earned it!"

COMMENTARY

The structure of this tale is identical to that of AT 1624, *Thief's Excuse: The Big Wind,* in which a vegetable thief is caught in a garden.[2] "Owner: How did you get into the garden? A wind blew me in. How were the vegetables uprooted? If the wind is strong enough to blow me in, it can uproot them. How did they get into your bag? That is what I was wondering."

Rather than depicting Djohá as the typical needy pauper seeking to feed his family, this teller sketches him out as a lazybones who is forced to come up with an easy scheme to assuage his hunger and that of his family. An inexperienced thief, though, he makes the same far-fetched excuse as in the universal type above (J1391, J1391.1). And, as is usually the case with Djohá, he gets away with his plan because he makes people laugh, within and without the tale.

Relevance and humor are what make these anecdotes entertaining and enduring.

---

1. Teller's aside, building up her listeners' expectations.

2. A close Judeo-Spanish parallel appears in Koén-Sarano, "Buena repuesta," in *Djohá ké dize?* 251. For universal parallels, see Basset, *Mille et un contes,* 1:286, no. 28; *Libro del Cavallero Cifar,* 40a; Clouston, *Noodles,* 11; García Figueras, *Yehá,* no. 256; Wesselski, *Hodscha Nasreddin,* 1:207, no. 7.

39

Djoha's Invitation to *Pranso*

Narrated by LEA BENABU (1993)

Djohá didn't have anything to eat. His wife is saying to him:

"Djohá *efendi*! Mr. Djohá! Are we always to remain without food? I'm hungry! The children are crying!"

"Don't worry!" Djohá said to her. "You just get the *odják,* the stove, ready. We'll eat a feast of good things, better than we've eaten until now, until *agora*!" he said.

Djohá went out to the street and called upon all those in the alley, in the *kaleja,* to come to dinner, saying:

"Come to my house for dinner! Come to my house for dinner!"

They said to him:

"Djohá, have you become rich?"

"No, I haven't become rich," Djohá said. "Only today is my day. I want you all to come to my house and eat!"

They all went in. The Turks have the custom of taking off their shoes at the door. When they all went in, Djohá collected all the shoes, put them in a sack, went to the *bazár,* and sold them for almost nothing. For thirty pairs of shoes, he earned, let's say, thirty liras! Thirty pounds! He went to the grocery, to the *bakál,* he bought lamb; he went to the fishmonger, the *baluhchí,* he bought fish; he bought green *salata;* he picked up some radishes *[ke mal te kere]*.[1] He got everything.

He went home; he gave food to everyone.

---

1. Teller's aside. See commentary.

They say to him:

"So, Djohá. Where did you get all of this? What day is today?"

"I can't tell you!" Djohá says. "Eat up! It's from your own goods!"

He fed his children. He fed his wife. They ate and drank.

"Eat up!" Djohá says.

"Djohá," they are saying to him, "there is no more room!"

"Eat up!" Djohá tells them. "It's all yours! It's from your own goods! Eat it up!"

Everyone had now eaten. Everyone had drunk. They went outside; they looked around: the shoes are not there!

They said:

"Where are the shoes?"

"Oh," said Djohá, "didn't I tell you that you were eating your own goods? You have eaten from your own goods!"

COMMENTARY

Poverty and the daily struggle to stay alive are pervasive in many of our tales and reflect the economic and social conditions that surrounded Sephardic Jews and their neighbors in the Ottoman Empire. Survival often depended on one's wit and ability to manipulate circumstances.

Here, Djohá conceives of yet another deceit of a humoristic nature, a plan to provide his family with plenty of food, even if only for one night (J710). To achieve his goal, he misappropriates goods he can sell (K254). This tale illustrates how he hoodwinks his neighbors into relinquishing control of some of their belongings (K330). With an unexpected and deceptive invitation to dinner (J1577), they are tricked into losing sight of their shoes and distracted while the shoes are stolen (K330.1, K341). This is a cultural adaptation of AT 1526A, *Supper Won by a Trick,* in which another person is made to pay.[2]

---

2. A Judeo-Spanish version exists in Koén-Sarano, "Kome, kome, ke de lo tuyo komes," in *Djohá ke dize?* 271. Another Judeo-Spanish parallel appears in Elnecavé, no. 14, p. 332, in which a traveling Jew succeeds in winning an invitation to spend the Sabbath at the home of a rich but inhospitable man by promising to save him a good amount of money. He should wait until after the end of Shabbat, however, to hear the details of the business proposition. At the close of the day of rest, the rich man finds out that the way to save money is to give his daughter in marriage to the guest at half the dowry intended for her. IFA versions are represented from Afghanistan, Eastern Europe, Egypt, Iran, Iraq, Israel (Ashkenazic, Sephardic), and Lebanon.

In this tale, unlike many other Djohá anecdotes, the teller does not give Djohá a Jewish identity. The neighbors leave their shoes outside the door, as is usually done at the entrance to a mosque, thus evoking a Moorish setting of close communal living. Marketing, hospitality, and the relation between host and guests (P320) are described in full. The close quarters provided by narrow alleys, where everyone knows the conditions under which the others live, are easily called to mind. The unexpected gallantry of Djohá's invitation to dinner and the surprising extravagance of the meal astonish his neighbors. There can be no other explanation but that Djohá has come into new money. The shrewdness of Djohá's trick, on the other hand, is that by making his guests benefit directly from the theft of their shoes and by telling them all along that they are profiting from their own goods, he produces a clever double entendre. Middle Eastern hospitality includes making one's guests feel at home by telling them figuratively that one's house and its belongings are their property. It is easy to see how the neighbors are fooled. Since they benefited from the sale of their shoes, however, they cannot really take Djohá to task for his trick at their expense. Once again, he shrewdly gets away with it.

Another cultural characteristic that surfaces in the tale is one related to the pervasive apprehension among the popular masses in the Middle East, including Sephardic Jews, that if you mention the word for something evil, that evil will surely materialize. To protect themselves, therefore, they conjure up help through the use of a special formula to exorcize the danger. The expression used here, "ke mal te kere," is really "a kyen mal te kyere!" the intended meaning being: "May the evil that we speak of not affect you but strike your enemies!" It is also used as an expression of sympathy for one who has suffered a personal loss. The formula follows the word *rávano* (radish), which, in Judeo-Spanish, may also refer to someone who is both unlettered and of little intelligence, that is, someone stupid, a condition to be pitied.

Other Jewish versions can be found in Jason, "Types," 207; Jason, *Types,* 76; [Noy], (C631.1); Richman, *Jewish Lore,* 111. For parallels from other sources, consult Ashliman, *Guide to Folktales,* 259, 267 (type 1544); Boggs, *Spanish Folktales,* 150 (type *1848); Briggs, *Dictionary of British Folk-Tales,* pt. A, vol. 2, 318; Bushnaq, *Arab Folktales,* 270 (Algeria AT 1544); Chauvin, *Ouvrages arabes,* 6:132, no. 285; A. Espinosa, *Cuentos populares,* vol. 1, no. 197, 3:233–39; Paredes, *Mexico,* no. 48; Robe, *Mexican Folktales,* 180.

40

Djohá's *Mirákolo*

Narrated by SARA KENT (1992)

Djohá made shoes, *kondurias*. Whatever he earned each day, he would eat and drink from at night with his wife and friends. Every night he had a big party!

One evening, one of the sultan's watchmen passed by, and he says to the sultan:

"Look at that Jew! He parties every night! Who knows how much money he earns?!"

The sultan issued a decree, a *firmán*, ordering all shoemakers' shops, all *kondureros*, closed. Djohá comes to his shop, to his *botika* in the morning. . . . It is shuttered! What can he do? He stood in front of the *botika* to give people a shave. At night, he parties once again with his friends.

Again the same watchman passed by and told the sultan about it. The sultan issued another *firmán:*

"Let all the barbers, all the *berberes,* be closed!"

Djohá saw that he has no work, no *lavor.* What is he going to do? Whoever doesn't have *lavor* becomes a soldier. So Djohá went and became a soldier. They put a sword, a *spada,* in his hand, and he doesn't know what to do to party that night. He made a wooden sword, a *spada de tavlá;* he put it in the place of the good one and sold the good one. At night he skips and dances with his friends.

That watchman passed by and said:

"How is this possible?"

He dispatched someone to ask Djohá. Djohá said:

"I sold the *spada* and put in its place one made of *tavlá*. And with the money I got, from the *parás,* we are now eating and drinking!"

"Oh," said the sultan, "*agora* we'll see!"
He brought in a man. He summoned Djohá and said to him:
"This is a bandit. Cut off his head on the spot!"
How will Djohá do that? He said to the sultan:
"Magnanimous sultan! This is not an evil man. It shows on his face! The *Dió* is going to make it so that I'm unable to kill him!"
And he unsheathed his *spada de tavlá*. . . .
The sultan said:
"This Jew is a very clever one! One cannot have one's way with him! *Ayde*! Go about your business!"

Commentary

This is a tale distinctly set in the Ottoman diaspora. While AT 1736A, *Sword Turns to Wood*, is used as the clever conclusion to this tale, Djohá's versatility and his ingenuity in handling every restriction that comes his way are really the focus of this narrative.[1] Here he represents the symbol of the legendary Jew, who somehow survives by overcoming every hurdle put in his path. No other Jewish elements appear in the tale.

The teller focuses on Djohá as a bon vivant shoemaker, a typical Sephardic occupation, and on how he continues to prosper even when constrained by restrictions that become increasingly more stringent (P715.1). As a Jew, he is depicted as a reed supple enough to resist the strong winds of adversity. He moves from being a shoemaker (P453), to being a barber (P446), and ultimately a soldier (P461), as the king's apparent capriciousness makes earning a living more and more difficult for him (M2). The sultan's guards, who resent the Jew's apparent success, encourage the ruler to deal harshly with Djohá. Throughout the royal testing of his resourcefulness (H506), however, Djohá personifies the Jewish hero who retains his morale, ingenuity, and adaptability, as well as his joy of life.

---

1. For Jewish versions, see Frankel, *Classic Tales*, no. 170; Noy, *Folktales*, no. 30; Patai, *Gates to the Old City*, 631; Richman, *Jewish Lore*, 212; Schwartz, *Elijah's Violin*, 89. Non-Jewish parallels appear in EB, no. 309; Laoust, *Contes berbères*, no. 57. See also Chauvin, *Ouvrages arabes*, 5:173, no. 96 n. 1; Grimm and Grimm, *Tales*, nos. 3, 6, 120; Keller, *Spanish Exempla*. The philosopher Hillel Zeitlin, who died in 1943 in the Warsaw Ghetto, published a version of this tale in which he highlights Simha, a simple, content, and resourceful man with a strong faith in God. Zeitlin's version was reproduced in *The Bar Mitzvah Treasury*, ed. Azriel Eisenberg, 98.

In AT 1736A, the man to be executed is said to be guilty unless his sword turns to wood. When this happens he is freed, but he had substituted a wooden sword, as in our version. No miracle occurs in the type or in our tale, despite the attempt to make it appear as if it had. This is in contrast with other types in which a magic manifestation takes place at an execution that proves the innocence of the person about to be decapitated. The person's life is spared when the execution sword miraculously turns to wood (D473.1, D2086.1.1). Our tale retains the gist of this extraordinary motif but changes its supernatural assumption by turning it into a motif of clever deception to fit the theme of the tale, just as it appears in AT 1736A. When ordered by the king to decapitate a prisoner, Djohá is caught at his own game and faces punishment. Realizing that his wooden sword will not be up to the task, he uses the precept that one must not draw a sword against the innocent (J21.2.3), predicting that his sword will magically make it impossible to kill the accused so as to prove that the prisoner is guiltless and should be spared (H215.1). In the process, Djohá thus saves both his own life and that of the prisoner. In the end, his stratagem and quick wit as a Jew also win over the sultan (K500).

The motif of the sultan going out in disguise at night to observe his subjects (K1812, P14.19) and to learn their secrets (N467) is widespread in folk stories. When the Turkish sultan (P10) is not roaming his city himself to take the pulse of his people, his spies serve as his substitutes to keep an eye on everyone, including the lowest of the low. The tale calls attention also, from the perspective of the victimized, to the capriciousness of kingly power and to the irrationality of some of the royal decrees that affected the livelihood of the poor (P19.4), especially the Jews.

41

Djohá and the *Karpúz*

Narrated by ALEX KORFIATIS (1993)

Djohá was very poor. He had nothing. Life was difficult. One day he said:

"I'll direct a channel of river water this way and, *ansí,* I'll be able to grow vegetables in my garden."

The government gave each person only a little bit of water, *ma* he had not heard about that. He took the pickaxe, the *makúsh,* and he is digging and digging, *kavakando, kavakando. Ensupitó,* he found a little box. He brought it home, placed it on the table, opened it, and saw gold!

Ensupitó, his neighbor came in and said:

"Oh, what's that? Gold? I want half of it!"

"*Ma* ... I haven't even counted it yet!" Djohá says to him.

"If that's so," says the neighbor, "I want two-thirds. If not, I'll go to the sultan. I'll denounce you, and you'll receive a punishment, a *punisión*!"

"Okay! Okay!" Djohá said to him. "You may be right, *amá* wait a bit. I'll bring out a watermelon, a *karpúz,* from the kitchen. We'll eat *karpúz,* and then we'll split up the treasure, *divizaremos.*"

Djohá went into the kitchen; he cut open a *karpúz,* carved out the inside, threw it away, and filled up the green shell of the *karpúz* with meatballs, with *kubbe.* He closed it up, turned it over, and went back into the room with the *karpúz.* He cut it open and, suddenly, the *karpúz* is filled with *kubbe*!

He said to the neighbor:

"Eat some *kubbe*!"

The neighbor said to him, in amazement:

"What? This is a *karpúz*!"

Djohá says to him:

"*Amá* it's filled with *kubbe*. Why do you care? Eat some *kubbe*!"

Both of them ate *kubbe*. Djohá held up a stick and said to the neighbor:

"Out! Neither a half nor a third! Not a thing! Go to the sultan if you want!"

The neighbor went to the sultan; he denounced him. The sultan went and sent for Djohá. He says to him:

"I've heard that you have found gold!"

Djohá says to him:

"From whom did you hear?"

"I've heard it from this man," the sultan says to him.

Djohá whispers in his ear:

"My lord sultan, he'll tell you that inside the *karpúz*, we found *kubbe*! Ask him and you'll see!"

"Tell me," the sultan said to the neighbor, "what did you find inside the *karpúz* when you cut it open?"

"*Kubbe*!" the neighbor said.

Djohá says:

"You see, my lord sultan? This man is a little crazy. As he found *kubbe* inside the *karpúz,* so I found gold!"

Commentary

This is another tale of poverty in which ingenuity, cleverness, and quick thinking save the day. Djohá shrewdly puts in doubt the testimony of his opponent, making him look like a fool by creating an absurd point of reference and thus foiling his plan (J1521).

AT 1642A, *The Borrowed Coat,* based on motif J1151.2 in which the witness claims the borrowed coat and is discredited, exemplifies this tale.[1] In both type and motif, the trickster is summoned to court in response to a Jew's complaint but refuses to go unless he has a new coat. The Jew lends him his. In court, the trickster says that the Jew is a liar: "He will even claim that I am

---

1. For Judeo-Spanish versions, see Camhy JS, 355; Kamhi, "El prove ke supo enganyar al riko," 40; KS, 161. For other Jewish versions, see Jason, "Types," 211, 215. IFA variants exist from Israel (Ashkenazic), Turkey, and Yemen. Universal parallels appear in Basset, *Si Djeha,* 31; Boggs, *Spanish Folktales,* 1848; A. Espinosa, *Cuentos populares,* vol. 1, no. 197, vol. 3, 233–39; García Figueras, *Yehá,* no. 121; Moulieras, *Si Djeh'a,* nos. 20, 53; Sánchez de Vercial, *Libro de los exenplos,* no. 68; Timoneda, *Patrañuelo,* no. 18.

wearing his coat." When the Jew does so, no one believes him. In these examples, the joke is on the Jew, which presumably adds to the humor and glee of a non-Jewish audience. For obvious reasons, this anti-Jewish element is eliminated altogether from our version. What is retained are the motifs of clever pleading and inducing the witness to talk foolishly so as to be discredited. AT 1525L, *Creditor Falsely Reported Insane When He Demands Money*,[2] and AT 1587**, *Accuser Is a Madman,* both are illustrations of this motif.

When he makes his accusation before the king (K242), Djohá's neighbor is set up to appear insane and thus not credible. By inducing him to talk foolishly (J1151.1), Djohá cleverly ensures that the king will not believe the neighbor (K1265) and that his testimony will be discounted (J1151). The stratagem used by Djohá in planning his defense is reminiscent of motif J1151.1.2 in which the husband is made to look foolish with the reporting of an absurd truth. His wife had put fish in the furrow, where he plows them up. When he tells about it, he is laughed at scornfully (AT 1381A, *Husband Discredited by Absurd Truth*). See also AT 1381B, *The Sausage Rain,* in which, in order to discredit her foolish son's testimony after he has killed a man, a mother makes him "believe" that it has rained sausages. When he says that he has killed the man on the night it rained sausages, his testimony is discredited (motif J1151.1.3)[3] Our tale retains the gist of the motif: the telling of the absurd truth. In this case, the foolish assertion is that there were *kubbe* inside the watermelon. Djohá's defense of falsely accusing the witness of being insane is well planned. It illustrates his resourcefulness, which often helps him overcome his adversaries.

The teller uses common and easily identifiable regional food products as a way for ingenious Djohá to put his opponent out of countenance (J1210).

---

2. For non-Jewish parallels, refer to Chevalier, *Siglo de Oro,* no. 166; A. Espinosa, *Cuentos populares,* 3:233–39 (AT 1587**, *Accuser Is a Madman*); Rael, *Colorado y Nuevo Méjico,* nos. 358–59; Robe, *Mexican Folktales,* 179; Timoneda, *Patrañuelo,* no. 18.

3. See Koén-Sarano, "La mujer bova," in *Djohá ké dize?* 149, for a Judeo-Spanish version that illustrates AT 1381B, *The Sausage Rain,* in which a husband discredits the testimony of his foolish wife by making her believe that it has rained figs and raisins. When she says that her husband slaughtered the king's camel when it rained figs, her evidence is dismissed. See Shenhar, *TEM 1973,* 108, no. 5, "The Termagant and Her Husband's Secret." For parallels from non-Jewish traditions, see Briggs, *Dictionary of British Folk-Tales,* pt. A, vol. 2, 225, 229, 265; Clouston, *Noodles,* 156; Cole, *Best Loved Folktales,* no. 137; A. Espinosa, *Castilla,* no. 20; García Figueras, *Yehá,* no. 7; Lorimer and Lorimer, *Persian,* no. 21; Moulieras, *Si Djeh'a,* no. 38; Rael, *Colorado y Nuevo Mejico,* no. 331; Robe, *Mexican Folktales,* 172; Thompson and Roberts, *Indic Oral Tales,* 141.

The two food items, the watermelon and *ḳubbe*, are popular in the area. The audience recognizes the refreshing watermelon and knows that it is green on the outside and red on the inside. Reporting that one has found anything else inside a watermelon but red juicy flesh and black seeds provokes mirth at the expense of the fool who asserts it. The thought of finding *ḳubbe* or dumplings inside a watermelon is so ridiculous that the reporter must be insane.

Kubbe, or *ḳibbeh*, is the national and much appreciated dish of many countries in the Middle East, particularly Syria and Lebanon. Each culture prepares *ḳubbe* in its own way, differing in the shell or in the filling. The word refers to the round or dome shape of *ḳubbe*. Some are round balls; others are flattened half-moons; still others are oval or elongated-shaped shells. All of them are hollow and stuffed with minced chicken or meat, often mixed together with nuts and spices. Their preparation is a ritual, including the pounding of the meat and wheat with a heavy metal pestle in a stone or metal mortar. Some women are known to have a special knack, a "hand" or "finger," for making *ḳubbe*, especially those with a torpedo shape.

There are countless variations of *ḳubbe*, some of which are widely known throughout the region. The most common is a mixture of finely grounded cracked wheat or *burghul*, grated onion, and minced lamb. *Kubbe* can be eaten raw, deep-fried, grilled, baked, or cooked in a special sauce. It can even be added to vegetable stews and soups. One kind of *ḳubbe*, popular in Egypt, is made with ground rice instead of cracked wheat and is stewed in stock. Sephardic Jews have developed a variation made with *matzá* meal (called *massá*), evolved for Passover but prepared throughout the year because of its particular lightness.

42

The Eggs and the Grain

Narrated by SARA YOHAY (1991)

Mr. So and So, a *fulaniko,* woke up one morning and decided to take to the road and travel from village to city to get to know the country. When dusk fell, he saw a light from afar. He drew closer and found himself before an inn, a *han.* The innkeeper, the *handjí,* greeted him with salaams, with *temenés,* and he seemed to be a good fellow. He set the table for him and served him a roasted chicken and two boiled eggs.

"*Buyrún*! Please! Eat, drink, and sleep here," he said to the client. "The jackals come out at night, and it is dangerous to be on the road."

No sooner said than done! In the morning, the *fulaniko* took some *parás,* some money, out of his pocket, out of his *djep,* to pay. *Amá* the *handjí* said to him in a voice filled with sweetness:

"*No te siklees!* Don't worry yourself about this, *agora.* Easy, *koláy,* may your travels be! When you return in good health, stop by and pay me the *pará.*"

Amazed to have come upon a man of such good heart, the *fulaniko* said his good-byes and left, very touched. Two months went by, and the *fulaniko* returned to the *han.* He went in and said:

"*Musiú handjí,* Mr. Innkeeper, let's settle our account *agora.* I'll pay up my debt."

"Look here, young man," said the *handjí.* "The debt is now a bit *kashkereada,* a bit mixed up. *Sha.* . . . Let's see. Give me two hundred *akchés,* two hundred silver coins, and let's clean up the slate!"

"*Amán!* My God!" shouted the *fulaniko, aharvándose,* striking his forehead. "Two hundred *akchés* for one chicken and two eggs??!!"

"The thing is like this," said the *handjí*. "A hen lays one egg every day; in one month, that's so many eggs. Each egg turns into a chick. What do you want? That I give you a hen that makes chicks every day? Are you crazy! Lay out the *pará* and have a safe trip!"

The *fulaniko* said that he wants to go before a *kadi*, a judge, and the *handjí* agreed. *Agora,* it was known that the *kadi* was a man who took bribes, *rusfetes.* What did the *handjí* do? He grabbed a sack, *aferró* a *torvá,* filled it with hens with their head sticking out, and went before the *kadi.* Seeing the hens, the *kadi* felt gladness in his soul, and he said to the *fulaniko:*

"The *handjí* is right! Pay up, and if you have *shaetes,* witnesses, bring them."

And he appointed an hour for him.

The unfortunate man left, pulling his hair out and, *na,* he found himself face to face with no other than Djohá.

"What's the matter?" Djohá asked.

And when he heard what had happened, he said:

"Here I am! Don't worry! I'll be your *shaét.* Just wait a while."

And he disappeared. The *fulaniko* waited and waited; *amá* Djohá was nowhere to be seen. It was now past the hour assigned by the *kadi.* More hours passed until Djohá could finally be seen from afar, running and soaking wet with sweat.

"*Ayte!*" he said. "Let's go before the *kadi.*"

And they went. The *kadi* asked why they were late, and Djohá started to speak:

"Don't ask, *musiú kadi*! I had to prepare grain for my partner, for my *havér,* and as I don't have *parás* to waste, I took boiled grain that I had at home! And it took me a few hours to count the grains, onc by one!"

The *kadi* thought that he had caught Djohá trying to be a wise guy, a *hahám,* and he said to him:

"Aren't you afraid of the *Dió,* you, Djohá?! How can cooked grain turn into seed to be sown?"

And Djohá:

"Wait a minute, *musiú kadi*! If, from your boiled eggs, hens can be hatched, why can't seedlings grow from my boiled grain?"

The *kadi* reconsidered; then he issued a fair judgment. And the *handjí patladeó*! He exploded!

COMMENTARY

This tale of cleverness is an adaptation of AT 821B, *Chickens from Boiled Eggs,* the type that describes how, many years after the guest has eaten them, a host demands an enormous sum for twelve boiled eggs, claiming that by this time they would have hatched out chickens who would have in turn laid eggs, and so on.[1] In the type, the devil comes in as an advocate and demands that the host cook his peas for planting. "Boiled peas may grow as soon as chickens can be hatched from boiled eggs." The type ends with the devil carrying off the judge.

Part 2 of a related type, AT 920A, *The Daughter of the King and the Son of the Peasant,* also describes *The Suit over Eggs* and tells of a merchant who buys forty boiled eggs and sails away without paying for them. On his return he offers to pay, but demand is made not only for the value of the meal but also for the potential chicks that would have come from the eaten eggs. The case is laid before the king, who takes four years to consider it. In part 3 of the

---

1. Shahar, "La valor del guero haminado," 51, gives another Judeo-Spanish version of this type, with the chicken-from-boiled-egg motif. This version focuses on the contrast between King David, who sides with the accuser, and his son, young Solomon, who demonstrates to him the absurdity of his judgment. Other parallels appear in Koén-Sarano, "El guevo haminado," in *Lejendas,* 23, and "La mujer entelijente," in *Lejendas,* 95. See also her *Djohá ké dize?* 87, which points to Djohá's gullibility in believing that seeds will produce camels. When a camel herder brings his flock to Djohá's field to graze, he believes that the seeds have borne the expected camels. A suit ensues (AT 1660, *The Poor Man in Court*). IFA archives also show versions from Libya, Iran, and Turkey. Additional parallels from Afghanistan, Greece, Iran, Iraqi Kurdistan, Israel (Sephardic), Morocco, Tunisia, Turkey, and Yemen follow the Jewish oicotype IFA 920*E, *Children's Judgment,* in which children (often young King Solomon) indirectly show the absurdity of the judgment passed by an adult. Jewish sources for AT 821B versions are *BJ,* 3:58, 61, 64, 83, 259, 301; bin Gorion, *Mimekor Yisrael,* vol. 1, no. 60, 120; Frankel, *Classic Tales,* no. 86; Gaster, *Exempla,* nos. 329, 342, 403, 441; Ginzberg, *Legends,* 6:285; Jason, "Types," 167, 181 (920*E); Jason, *Types,* 35, 49–50 (920*E); Nahmad, *Portion in Paradise,* 44; Noy, *Libya,* no. 23; Ps. 72:1–2; Noy, *TEM 1970,* 178 (AT 920A, Turkey IFA 8892); Schram, *Jewish Stories,* 69, 112 (AT 920A). Sources from other traditions include Andrejev; Ashliman, *Guide to Folktales,* 165; BP, 2:368 n. 1; Briggs, *Dictionary of British Folk-Tales,* pt. A, vol. 2, 100, pt. B, vol. 1, 145; Clouston, *Noodles,* 120; Delarue, *Conte populaire français,* 4:262; EB, nos. 294, 295; A. Espinosa, *Castilla,* no. 31; García Figueras, *Yehá,* no. 91; Megas, *Folktales of Greece,* no. 53 (AT 920A); Rael, *Colorado y Nuevo Méjico,* no. 34; Robe, *Mexican Folktales,* 131; Walker and Uysal, *Tales in Turkey,* 236.

type, *The Real Princess and the Real Peasant Son,* two children play at trying the case of the eggs (J1179+ [Noy]), and the princess shows that boiled eggs cannot bear chickens. The king overhears, understands the situation, and judges the case accordingly.

The motif of chickens from boiled eggs appears in Jewish Scriptures and folklore. Rather than focus on the absurd ignorance regarding the hatching of boiled eggs that is a central feature of the types above (J1902), our narrative retains that motif, as well as the reductio ad absurdum motif, but turns the tale into a trickster tale. Instead of the devil or the princess, it is Djohá, the unpromising protagonist, who cleverly discredits the argument (J1151) and wins the case.

The narrative depicts a corrupt society in which a devious innkeeper, carefully planning his scam from the beginning (K451), and a dishonest judge, known for taking bribes (J1192), are entangled in a suit over chickens hatched from boiled eggs. Djohá appears late in the tale as an unpromising bystander but eventually draws on one absurdity to rebuke another (J1530). The counterargument he uses in his unexpectedly clever pleading (J1160, J1130) is the sowing of cooked seeds (J1191.2, H1023.1.1). Through the use of this ridiculous claim and by pointing out that a rule must work both ways (J1511), he draws the attention of the judge to his equally ridiculous verdict and puts him out of countenance (P421, J1212). As a consequence, he reduces the judgment to absurdity (J1191) and brings the judge to recognize the foolishness and injustice of his sentence and to reverse it.

The enclosed spaces that appear in the tale—the inn and the courthouse—should represent shelter and justice, respectively, yet they are where the deceits and absurdities take place. The *fulaniko* and Djohá, on the other hand, depict naïve country bumpkins who are easily fooled. While his travels are meant to make him acquire the wisdom he apparently lacks to defend himself, the *fulaniko* clearly needs help, and it comes from the most unpromising source. The outdoor space where he meets Djohá can be interpreted as the place where wisdom is gleaned. Djohá's late arrival is used by the teller to raise the level of anticipation of the listeners as well as to remind them of Djohá's frequent absentmindedness. The late appearance of a breathless and sweaty Djohá elicits their appreciative and knowing laughter. This unpromising interlude, coupled with the words the teller puts in the mouth of the gloating judge, set the stage for the big surprise of Djohá's cleverness in court. While the judge is thus brought to his senses, it comes as no surprise to the audience that Djohá succeeds in pulling yet another good one.

The *temenés* performed by the crooked innkeeper when he first welcomes his unsuspecting guest are a distinctive Eastern ceremonial salute among

Muslims, which includes bowing very low without bending the knees, as a sign of deference. The hand touches the ground, then the chest, and finally the forehead. One can also bring the fingers of the right hand to the lips and then to the forehead. This was a common salute, especially toward one of a superior station, with less colorful gestures used for those of equal or inferior condition.

43

Djohá's Merás

Narrated by ESTER VENTURA (1993)

Djohá was not rich. He was poor. He worked during the day to eat at night. One day, he received a letter that in such and such a village, he had an uncle. This uncle had died, and an inheritance, a *merás,* was left to him.

Djohá said:

"My luck, my *mazál,* has lifted! Let me go find out!"

And he got up and left. They said to him:

"Yes! Here was left everything that was your uncle's. This is your share."

Djohá took the money, the *parás.* He returned home and bought a *binyán,* a large building. He had two friends; he got them married. He bought clothes for his family. He did everything. And for himself, he bought fine clothing, and every day he went out handsomely dressed.

One day, a neighbor met him. He said to him:

"Djohá, all you've done is fine. You have bought all that was necessary for yourself and for your family, *avál* you have bought no shoes for yourself!"

Djohá said to him:

"You're right. *Avál,* to me, these shoes feel very comfortable!"

"*Avál* it can't be!" his neighbor said to him. "It isn't nice! As well dressed as you are! Buy yourself some new shoes!"

What is Djohá to do? They told him to buy himself. . . . He got up and went to the store, to the *butika*. He bought himself a new pair of shoes. True, they were a little tight on him, *avál* it can't be helped. It's until he gets used to them. He put them on.

Now, *agora,* what he used to wear was a pair of sandals, of *sandalas*. He took the *sandalas* and carried them home.

"*Agora,*" he said, "what shall I do with these *sandalas?*" He thought and thought and thought:

"What shall I do *agora?*" he said. "*Agora,* I'll go to the bathhouse. I'll take my new shoes. I'll take the *sandalas* also. I'll leave the *sandalas* there, and I'll go home."

Djohá went to the bathhouse. He soaped himself, washed himself, put on his new shoes, and he returned home.

In the morning:

"*Tak, tak!*" at the door.

"What is it?"

"*Addió,* Djohá!" someone said to him, "You forgot your *sandalas* at the bathhouse. *Na!* Here! I've brought them back for you."

Agora Djohá thought, and thought, and thought, and thought about what to do. He took them and threw them in the river.

"*Agora,*" he said, "I'm finished with them!"

He returned home. In the morning:

"*Tak, tak!*" at the door. Who is it? The fishermen. They said:

"You threw away your *sandalas.* They messed up our *trata,* our nets! We haven't caught even a single fish!"

They gave him back his *sandalas. Agora,* he had thrown them into the river. They brought them back to him wet! Djohá put them out to dry on the balcony. The puppy came, and while playing and playing with them, he threw the *sandalas* down, breaking open a woman's head! She went upstairs shouting:

"Djohá, what have you done? Look at what has happened to my head!"

Djohá said to her:

"Take some *parás,* keep quiet, and go away!" [*Agora* he has a lot of *parás!*][1]

So she left.

In the end, Djohá said:

"These *sandalas* will not remain with me. I've thought about what to do. When it'll be nighttime," he said, "I'll dig up a hole in the field across the way, I'll bury them, and let that be the end of the matter!"

When it was nighttime, he looked to see that there was no one around, and he went and *kavakó,* he dug up a hole, put in the *sandalas,* and came back home.

In the morning, police!

"Djohá," they said to him, "last night you went out and dug up the field. Right there was buried the entire *otsár,* the entire treasury of the government! All the *parás,* all the money of the government! You are the one who took it!"

---

1. Teller's aside, in explanation.

"I took it?!" said Djohá, "I have no *habér* of it! I know nothing about it!"
"No, it isn't so!"
"Yes, it's so!"
A *mishpát*! A trial!
He went to the *mishpát*. They are saying:
"Look, this man has stolen all the *parás* of the government!"
"I stole them?!" said Djohá. "*Na*! I'll tell you what happened. I received," he said, "a large *merás*. And *ansí,* I wanted to get rid of those *sandalas;* I went and buried them!"
"You can tell false tales!" the *shofét,* the judge, said to him. "You are the one who stole it all!"

And they went to his house; they took away all the *parás* from the *merás,* and he was left with nothing!

Commentary

This tale of ill-starred fate is the equivalent of AT 946B*, *Shoes of Poverty,* which describes how poverty attaches itself to the poor man's sandals.[2]

Our version begins with wealth and poverty (U60) and an apparent change of fortune. The teller emphasizes Djohá's misery from the start, through a contrasted repetition: "Djohá was not rich. He was poor." When he suddenly acquires wealth (N170+ [Noy]) through an unexpected inheritance (J706), all seems to indicate a change of luck. Djohá himself believes that his doomed luck has lifted, and he acts as if it has. Although he demonstrates decisive conduct and a generous spirit when he first collects his money, he does not please everyone (J1040, J1041), and the well-meaning advice provided by a neighbor eventually leads to the adverse ending.

The prevalent message here is fatalistic, and the teller chooses a series of well-known motifs to develop her narrative. The capriciousness of lady luck (N170) is highlighted when Djohá's unpropitious fate pursues him in the form of his old sandals. No matter how he tries to rid himself of them, they always find their way back to him (N211). In fact, the sandals repeatedly serve as an identification token (H111), connecting Djohá to his former station in life despite his continuous efforts to distance himself from it. Burying his sandals in an isolated field is his last resort, yet it turns out to be a ruinous under-

---

2. A parallel version appears in Serwer-Bernstein, *Jewish and Arab Folktales,* no. 25.

taking. When he is falsely accused of having absconded with the state treasury (K401, K2127), justice and injustice merge (U10, P421). He loses his inheritance in undeserved punishment (Q595) and returns to his original destitute condition (J2100). Bad luck attaches itself to him and refuses to desert him (AT 947A*), leading him to ruin.

Why make Djohá the main character in this tale? The teller weaves in a series of amusing vignettes that fit well into the Djohá repertoire, singly and cumulatively: the new shoes that fit too snugly; the sandals that everyone easily identify as his; the frisky puppy that causes a minor accident; the embarrassment of Djohá and his expensive effort to silence the victim; and the unlucky coincidence that brings him to bury his shoes in the one spot that causes his ruin.

Djohá's society is described here realistically as a close-knit community in which generosity, honesty, and easy interaction are commonplace. People are familiar with one another to the point of interference, appearing at one's doorstep unexpectedly. Poverty is the norm, though, and all need to work hard just to earn enough to eat. Fishing is always a popular occupation with the poor, and regular visits to the public bath are common. At the same time, the government is said to bury its treasury in an open field.

44

Djohá and the Forty Thieves

Narrated by REBEKA COHEN-ARIEL (1989)

There were forty thieves who liked to annoy Djohá, to *kizdirialdo*, and make fun of him.

Djohá's mother had a little hen. One day, the thieves stole the hen from her. They fried it and ate it, one piece each.

"*Na*! Here is your chicken, Djohá! *Na*!"

Djohá said to them:

"*Agora* I'll buy a lamb. I want to see you eat it!"

He bought a little lamb. He brought it home and was raising it. Barely a week went by, and the thieves stole it.

"*Na*, Djohá!" they said to him, licking their fingers. "We're eating a piece each," they said. "Just die! And we'll defecate on your grave, on your *kever*!"

Djohá said:

"Good!"

He said to his mother:

"Look, I'll buy a seal. I'll pretend to be dead. You'll make me a little window in my grave, in my *kever*. When they come to defecate, I'll show them!"

"Good," said the mother.

Djohá pretended to be dead. The mother cried. The gravediggers came, and she gave them *parás*, so they would leave a little window open for him. Djohá took along the seal.

The thieves came. They saw that they buried him. They said:

"Let's go defecate on his *kever*!"

One would come; he would defecate. Djohá would brand him with the seal. The first one got it; he said:

"Let the next one get it too."

And the second one squatted down to defecate. Djohá branded him with the seal. He said:

"As I got it, so let the next one get it also!"

And so, all the thieves got the seal on their bottom. *Amá,* not even a single one of them told the others.

Djohá rose from the grave and said:

"I didn't die! *Agora,* I'll show all of you!"

He went before the judge, the *kadi,* and said to him:

"These forty thieves were my father's servants."

"Your father's servants?!"

"Yes," he said, "they were my father's servants."

"Where do you have proof of that?"

"Look," Djohá said. "Take off the pants of each and every one of them and let them stand up! Look at the bottom of every one of them! Of every single one of them!"

They all had the seal! The *kadi* came. He said:

"You are Djohá's servants!"

Djohá took them as his servants. He made them work in his vegetable garden. He would give them a beating, a *haftoná:*

"Work the vegetable garden! You're my servants! Didn't you eat the chicken? Didn't you eat the lamb?"

He had won.

Commentary

Through the depiction of petty rivalry and bullying in a rural setting, this tale illustrates the triumph of the weak (L300) through humorous deceit. Humor and laughter are often the only weapons of the underdog, who cannot otherwise prevail.

Initially Djohá is portrayed as a dupe (J1700, L121) whose goods are easily and repeatedly misappropriated (K254) and whose precious domestic animals are destroyed (K1440). The rights of the strong (U30) thus seem to prevail, and the band of thieves derives enjoyment from tormenting its pitiable victim. Effortlessly and repeatedly cheated, Djohá appears to make an easy target. Eventually, however, he succeeds in avenging the harassment by putting his tormenters into a humiliating position (K1200, Q470).

By feigning death (K1860) and hiding in a grave (K1892), Djohá conceives a plan that first deceives and then subordinates the forty thieves

(K2130): he degrades them one by one by branding them (Q472) in castigation for the trouble they have caused him (K911.1). In one episode of AT 1539, *Cleverness and Gullibility,* a youth has himself buried alive and stabs his enemy from out of the grave. In an acceptable adaptation, which substitutes the stabbing for a less lethal compromise, Djohá lets himself be buried alive to brand his enemies from the grave when they come to defile his body, as they had threatened they would. The branding event is not an isolated motif in Judeo-Spanish tales. It appears also in a tale from Skoplje collected by Cynthia Crews, in which a clever woman, falsely accused of being unchaste, forces her accuser to establish her innocence after branding him and claiming him to be her father's old slave.[1]

Ultimately Djohá displays his cleverness in the courtroom (J1130) by using the branding as a means of identifying and winning the robbers legally as his slaves (H55, P475). In the end, the victim triumphs over the bullies (L121.1), and the damages he has suffered are recuperated manifold (Q212). Such tales of deception sometimes display obscene elements. Characteristically, when graphic language is used and off-color imagery evoked, as is the case here, such tales tend to be told by men. It is surprising that this version is narrated by a woman.

---

1. See Crews 10, p. 162 (Skoplje). This tale is classified in Haboucha, under AT 882, *The Wager on the Wife's Chastity.* For another Judeo-Spanish parallel of Djohá's feigning death and hiding in a grave, see Koén-Sarano, "Djohá merka a fyado," in *Djohá ké dize?* 273. This, however, is a version of AT 1654, *The Robbers in the Death Chamber.*

Numskulls

Tales from Makeda

The ten fools' anecdotes in this section are set in a fictitious but recognizable place, which inevitably elicits the anticipatory attention and complicit laughter of the audience. The town of Makeda is an imaginary village, which has its own unique niche in Sephardic humor because of the apparent naïveté of its inhabitants, a community of simpletons. The Makeda tales are set in the equivalent of Chelm, the fabled Eastern European village of Jewish fools that Isaac Bashevis Singer helped popularize in America. In universal oral tradition, other variants of tales about noodles in towns of "wise men" are about the inhabitants of Gotham, England, or those of Emassa in Persian tales.

Historically, there are two references to a place by the same name, one biblical and the other medieval. In the Bible, five Amorite kings (Jerusalem, Hebron, Jarmuth, Lachish, Eglon), united to punish Gibeon in the second or third century before the modern era. They were defeated at Ajalon. The sun had stood still for Joshua, and to escape the Israelite pursuit the kings fled to a cave at Makkedá, the Canaanite city, in the Shephelá, where they were captured and executed and the town destroyed.[1] Maqueda is also the name of a small town in Castile, in central Spain, northeast of Toledo. It was founded around 1177 CE on the territory of the Order of Calatrava. In 1492, King Ferdinand the Catholic ordered an investigation to look into whether the Jews of Maqueda were really ready to convert to Christianity. The town is mentioned in the second chapter (Tratado Segundo) of the anonymous Spanish picaresque novel, *Lazarillo de Tormes*.

Because of the resemblance to the biblical Makkedá, some Jewish commentators have maintained that the Spanish town was founded by Jews from Makkedá, after their exile by Nebuchadnezzar.[2] Then again, Moses Arragel, a fifteenth-century scholar who had been commissioned by the Order of Calatrava to undertake a biblical translation into Spanish, tried to make the opposite case before the head of the order: that the Israelite Makkedá had been established by the king of Maqueda, in Spain. Arragel himself had settled in Maqueda.

A third theory, which Matilda Koén-Sarano proposes, is that Makeda may well refer to Macedonia. This, she submits, is because the Greeks apparently consider the Macedonians to be less than quick-witted.

The Makeda of Sephardic folklore has become the familiar home of noodles. Numerous stories are told about their simple-minded and inept doings and the needless dilemmas they create for themselves. Some of the tales in this section contain Jewish elements, either religious or cultural. They depict individuals bewildered by their daily lives and unable to cope with the complexity of putting intricate theory into everyday practice. They include jokes on peculiar character traits, such as a surprising ignorance of routine matters and a total lack of common sense. The fools prove ignorant of the laws of nature and treat animals as though they are human. They cannot keep instructions straight and turn ordinary matters into major obstacles. Their characteristically inappropriate or dim-witted behavior and their inability to handle routine situations in their surroundings make them fall outside the social norm, causing the listeners to feel subliminal superiority and to savor their own cleverness and abilities in comparison. The predicaments that arise and their resolutions are often both comical and far-fetched.

These numskull tales tend to be uncomplicated. Short, simple, and entertaining, they streamline the plots to emphasize the action. Sometimes limited to a single motif, they have no use for the supernatural. They feature the inhabitants of Makeda as fools to be amused by and laughed at.

Notes

1. Josh. 10:10–28. In Ethiopian tradition, an important place is reserved for the marriage of Solomon and Makeda, the queen of Sheba. The long version of the story is found in the Kebra Nagest. The royal house of Ethiopia claimed its ancestry back to this union. Tradition has it also that the Falashas descend from the Jews who accompanied Menelik I, the son of Solomon and the queen of Sheba when he returned from Jerusalem to Ethiopia.

2. Among these commentators is Isaac Abrabanel in his commentary to Kings.

45

The Tales of Makeda

Narrated by SHOSHANA LEVY (1988)

One day, a man went to the city of the inhabitants of Makeda. Before he went to bed, they put a hammer in his hand and said to him:
"Here it doesn't dawn. We'll call you as well. You'll get up and hit the mountain with this hammer (this ax). Dawn doesn't break here!"
"Dawn doesn't break?!"
"No," they said to him. "Not unless we strike the mountains with these axes, with these hammers!"
"Well," he said.
And he went along after them. They struck the mountains and the sun started to rise.
He said to them:
"If you give me a lot of money, I'll arrange it so that no one will have to get out of bed. The sun will rise on its own!"
They said:
"Let's give him whatever it takes!"
What did the man do? He went to another city and brought back ten roosters. He said to them:
"When you hear the roosters crow, it means that a new day has dawned."

COMMENTARY

This anecdote focuses on a town of fools (J1703) whose inhabitants display absurd ignorance of universally familiar physical phenomena and natural laws

(J1700, J1730, J1810, J1930), as well as a complete lack of common sense and a disregard for established facts (J1960). The tale shows that they seem to take no notice of well-known, natural, basic facts in the course of their daily lives. They have a curious theory concerning the sun and how to make it rise (J2272), believing that dawn will not break without their aid. On such a mistaken assumption (J2210) they behave in a bizarre manner (J1820) until a man with common sense introduces a few roosters in town to greet the sunrise (B755).

The teller has selected an observable and predicable occurrence—the dawning of a new day—to show the utter hopelessness of the Makeda inhabitants, who often turn a simple matter into a hurdle over which they must find a way to leap. Their solution, as always, turns out to be at once foolish and entertaining. Feeling superior, the Sephardic audience predictably responds with mirth.

This tale falls under a generic type, AT 1346*, *Easy Problem Made Hard*.

46

The Seven Repudiated Wives of Makeda

Narrated by REBEKA COHEN-ARIEL (1989)

There were in Makeda seven *kitas,* seven repudiated wives who, one day, all went to the bathhouse and are bathing. Each one is telling a story about all the *tsarót,* all the problems, she has.

"Did your husband throw you out?"

"Yes!"

"*Na,* my husband threw me out!"

"Me too! My husband threw me out!"

"Why?" one of them said.

The other said:

"My husband had hens and he had *lules,* chicken coops. I went there and saw filth! Excrements! I opened up the *lules,* I put a string on the hens and a coin, a *grosh,* and I said to them, 'Kisht! Shoo!' so they would go to the bathhouse. At night, my husband came home; he looked for the hens: they are not there. He said to me:

'Where are the hens?'

I said to him:

'I tied each one with a string and I put a *grosh* for each one so they would go to the bathhouse. They were filthy!'

My husband said to me:

'*Arrematasión!*[1] Women such as you will be the death of me! Go back to where you came from!'

---

1. This exclamation suggests total despair: "This is the end! May you cease to exist!" See glossary.

Did you ever see such a thing? That's why he threw me out! I was doing him a favor!" [A blind favor: she sent his hens flying across the mountains!]²

The other woman came. She says:

"Let me tell you: my husband asked me for flour broth.

'How is it made?' I said to him.

He said:

'One pours flour into the water, one stirs it, and one has flour broth.'

What did I do? We had a flour bin, I poured flour into the well, and I stirred it with the bucket. I poured flour in, and until evening I kept stirring. There was no more flour left, *ama,* still no flour broth was coming out of the well! When my husband finally came, I said to him:

'I am dead tired!'

'What did you do?'

'You asked me for something that I was unable to make!'

'What was that?'

'No matter how much flour I poured into the well, it just didn't turn into flour broth!'

'*Shemá* Israél!³ Did you pour all the flour into the well? Can one make flour soup there?'

He gave me a *haftoná,* a beating. He said to me:

'Go away! I don't want you!'

Na, here I was, making flour broth for him, and he beat me up and sent me away!"

Another one came. She said:

"Look, my husband had oil drums: a storeroom full of drums. I leaned over to look into one drum and I saw a black woman inside. I leaned over another one and I saw another black woman inside. 'Oh,' I said, 'my husband has lovers in here and I know nothing about it?' I overturned all the drums and emptied them out for him. In the evening, my husband came home. I was dead tired.

'What from?'

'*Vadáy*! Of course! You had lovers inside the drums! In the oil! I emptied them all!'

---

2. Teller's aside, pointing out the foolishness of the woman.

3. "Hear Oh Israel!" These are the first two words of the central creed of Judaism, the Jewish declaration of faith, solemnly affirming divine unity: "Hear Oh Israel, the Lord our God, the Lord is One" (Deut. 6:4–9, 11:13–21; Num. 15:37–41). Here it is an expression of consternation and dismay.

'*Addió!* My God! You spilt out all the oil? I had lovers in there?!'

He gave me a good *haftoná* and he sent me away. Did you see why he threw me out? He had lovers, so I spilt his oil!"

The next one came. She said:

"My husband had fabrics of many, many colors: red, green, yellow.... One day, I said:

'They're stained. I'll soak them in the river. I'll wash them. I'll remove these stains.'

She took all the fabrics and carried them to the river, and she keeps washing and washing and washing and washing so that the color would run out. And she spread them out in the sun. At night she is dead tired.

Her husband said to her:

'What did you do?'

'All your fabrics were stained. I went to the river and washed them.'

'*Ija d'un mamzér*! Daughter of a bastard! Idiot! The fabrics have stains? These were roses!'

The husband gave her a *haftoná,* and he threw her out of the house.

Another one came. She said:

"Let me tell you: my husband said that in his soul he felt a craving for chicken legs."

'Fine. Bring them and I'll make them for you,' she said.

He brought her four chicken legs. She said:

'How shall I cook them?'

He said:

'Look, you dip them in boiling water, you pluck the hair out, then you sear them over a flame, you scrape them, and when they're clean, you put them in water to boil.'

In the morning she asked him again:

'How do you make the legs?'

'You put them in boiling water, you pluck the hair out, you clean them, you sear them, you scrape them, and you boil them.'

He had already told her once, and he told her again. In the end, as he was ready to leave for work, she said to him:

'I have forgotten how to make them.'

He was so fed up that he said to her:

'*Enkáshatelas al kulo!* Stuff them up your arse!'

And he went to work. Here she is, stuffing and stuffing, when her mother came to visit:

'What's this, my daughter? What are you doing?'

'My husband told me to stuff them up my arse.'

The mother said to her:

'You take two and I'll take two.'

When the husband came home in the evening, he found them both dead tired. He said:

'What's going on? Why are you like this?'

'Didn't you tell me to stuff them up my arse?'

'I told you yesterday and last night and again at midnight how to make them, but it didn't stick in your mind! When I was fed up, I said to you: "Put them up your arse!" Only this stuck in your mind? *Ijas d'un mamzér*! Daughters of a bastard! You and your mother, take to the street!'

The other one said:

"We have no children. One evening, we were eating dinner. My husband came. He said:

'What we need is a toothless mouth and a little crawling bottom.' [That is, a child!]⁴

'What? What did you say?'

'We need a little naked bottom, a bottom *desbragado,* and a little toothless mouth.'

The dunce! In the morning, she went to the dentist and had all her teeth pulled. She took off her panties. In the evening, her husband came home: she is dragging her naked bottom on the floor, *desbragada,* and doesn't speak because she had her teeth pulled out.

'*Mamzertá*! Bastard! What is this?'

'You.... Didn't... you... say... that... you... wanted... a... toothless... mouth... and... a... little... crawling... bottom?'

He gave her a *haftoná,* a beating, and threw her out of the house.

The last woman said:

"My husband said: 'How beautiful the woman becomes with a little henna on her hands, feet, and face!'"⁵

She didn't do anything. She went and bought a good quantity of henna. Her husband likes henna. Now she'll show him! She took her clothes off and

---

4. Teller's aside.

5. Henna is a reddish-brown or reddish-black dye obtained from the powdered leaves of the henna plant (mignonette tree). It has long been in use, as evidenced by Egyptian mummies. In more recent days, the dye has been used to color hair. Additionally, in many Middle Eastern countries a henna ceremony takes place a few days before a wedding, at which time the fingers and toes of the bride are freshly colored with a touch of red henna for luck and beauty.

smeared henna all over her body. The husband had a *bakal,* a grocery store downstairs, and she lived upstairs. She stood on the balcony so he can see her naked. He isn't looking.

'Psst! Psst!'

She calls out to her husband so he can come outside and look at her. Everybody is looking at her on the balcony when the husband finally comes out.

'*Ija d'un mamzér*! Daughter of a bastard! The entire world is seeing you naked!'

He went upstairs, gave her a good *haftoná* and said to her:

'Go away!'

The seven *kitas* of Makeda said:

"Only for this did our husbands throw us out!"

COMMENTARY

This tale is a conglomerate of types describing foolish wives (J1701) and their absurd behavior (J1730). Similar to AT 1384, *The Husband Hunts Three Persons as Stupid as His Wife,*[6] here there are seven women who compete with each other in terms of dim-witted domestic behavior (J1700, J2463). The women waste their husbands' valuable property and show absurd ignorance of the nature of objects, animals, food, and cooking. Their ignorance is accompanied by a bizarre lack of logic (J2200). As a consequence of their foolish behavior, all seven wives receive a sound beating from their husbands before being sent away. A similar Sephardic version was collected in Monastir,[7] in which a

---

6. For Jewish parallels, see Marcus, *Mabu'a,* no. 15; Mizrahi, *Be-yeshishim khokhma,* no. 4 (Iran). Universal parallels appear in Baughman, *England and North America,* 34; Briggs, *Dictionary of British Folk-Tales,* pt. A, vol. 2, 301, 304, 305; Thompson, *One Hundred Favorite Folktales,* no. 88 (Italy).

7. It appeared in L, no. 22, p. 70 (Monastir) and is classified in Haboucha, under *1328, *Woman Does Not Know Her Housework.* Jewish parallels can be found in Gaster, *Ma'aseh Book,* vol. 1, no. 123; Jason, "Types," 200; Jason, *Types,* 70–71; Marcus, *Mabu'a,* no. 15 (Iranian Kurdistan); Mizrahi, *Be-yeshishim khokhma,* no. 4 (Iran); Schwili, no. 121. IFA versions were collected from Eastern Europe, Iran, Iraq, Israel (Sephardic), and Yemen. Non-Jewish parallels appear in Andrejev, (type 1386); Baughman, *England and North America,* 33 (J1813.9), 34 (AT 1384), 35 (AT 1386); Boratav, *Contes turcs,* 171; Boulvin, *Contes populaires persans,* 1:72, 2:73; BP, 1:335 (AT 1384), 520 (AT 1386), 2:440 (AT 1384); Briggs, *Dictionary of British Folk-Tales,* pt. A, vol. 2, 301, 304, 305 (AT 1384); D'Aronco, *Fiabe Toscane,* 174 (type 1225); EB, nos. 331

man marries seven times but ends up killing all his wives because of their absurd lack of common sense. In the end he remains single. The number seven for the seven wives is a common formulistic number.

Wife no. 1 in our tale sends her hens to the bathhouse on their own, giving them a coin to pay for the entrance fee. This is similar to *The Woman from Makeda and the Ducks* (tale 47), classified under AT 1291**, *Fools Let Horse Loose to Find Road Home*. Here, also, the stupid wife treats animals as if they were human (J1880), disregarding their animal nature (J1900). By expecting them to go by themselves to the bathhouse (J1881.2), she also displays absurd shortsightedness (J2050).[8]

As in IFA *1328, *Woman Does Not Know Her Housework*,[9] in which the wife does not admit to her ignorance but cooks and carries on with disastrous results, wives nos. 2 and 5 show little culinary inclination. They are ignorant of certain foods (J1732) and misunderstand the cooking process (J1813). Wife no. 2 uses the well as a cooking pot and wastes an entire reserve of flour in her vain attempt to prepare a single meal (J1813.9.1, J2465). This action is described in AT 1260A*, *Flour in River*, in which a woman who is to mix flour for bread puts it in a river and loses it all. AT 1339E, *All Cooked for One Meal*, illustrates similar waste, when the foolish wife cooks all the beans for one meal. Wife no. 5 is forgetful (J2671). She asks her husband to repeat cooking instructions several times, but she always forgets them (J2671.2), as in AT 1204, *Fool Keeps Repeating His Instructions*.[10] Exasperated, he gives her sarcastic instructions, which she remembers and follows literally and inappropriately, with unappetizing results (J2465.7, J2489) and to the sorrow of the husband (J2516). Interestingly, this section describes the old way of plucking feathers and the searing procedure needed to clean a chicken before cooking it.

Wife no. 3 does not recognize her own reflection in several oil drums (J2012) and spills out the stored oil in a jealous rage (J1791.7, J1791.7.1). A similar ignorance appears in AT 1284, *Person Does Not Know Himself*,[11] and

---

(AT 1384), 333; Grimm and Grimm, *Tales*, nos. 34 (AT 1384), 59 (AT 1386), 104 (AT 1384); T. Hansen, *Types* (AT 1384, Puerto Rico); Lorimer and Lorimer, *Persian*, no. 21; Thompson, *One Hundred Favorite Folktales*, no. 88 (Italy, AT 1384); Thompson and Roberts, *Indic Oral Tales*, 138 (AT 1328*).

8. See Koén-Sarano, "Aprontijos para la boda," in *Djohá ke dize?* 139, in which Djohá sends the hens he had bought in preparation for his wedding home alone.

9. See note 7 above.

10. See Rael, *Colorado y Nuevo Méjico*, no. 29; Robe, *Mexican Folktales*, 162.

11. See Confino, "Djuha, pasha de la madre!" 642. This is classified in Haboucha,

AT 1336A, *Man Does Not Recognize His Own Reflection in the Water (Mirror).*[12]

Wife no. 4 ruins her husband's merchandise stock when she washes the cloth and exposes it to the sun, thus causing it to fade. Wives nos. 6 and 7 misinterpret the husband's wishes with disastrous and somewhat obscene results (J1820). Literal obedience leads to unexpected consequences (J2460) and foolish extremes (J2500), with a disregard of personal danger and shameful exposure (J2130, J2134) in the bargain.

This is a woman's tale, told by a woman, probably to other women who would easily understand the references, absurdity, and inappropriateness of the domestic behavior described. It gives the listeners a sense of superiority and allows them to laugh condescendingly at the foolishness of it all.

---

under **1288B and has Jewish parallels in Frankel, *Classic Tales,* no. 275; Noy, *Folktales,* nos. 69, 70 (Afghanistan). See also Briggs, *Dictionary of British Folk-Tales,* pt. A, vol. 2, 362; García Figueras, *Yehá,* no. 13*; Megas, *Folktales of Greece,* no. 58; Thompson and Roberts, *Indic Oral Tales,* 135; Wesselski, *Hodscha Nasreddin,* 1:274, no. 298, 1:214, no. 43.

12. See Briggs, *Dictionary of British Folk-Tales,* pt. A, vol. 2, 84; Chevalier, *Siglo de Oro,* no. 103; EB, no. 329; Thompson and Roberts, *Indic Oral Tales,* 139; Wesselski, *Hodscha Nasreddin,* 1:276, no. 311.

47

The Woman from Makeda and the *Papías*

Narrated by STREA KOHEN (1990)

A woman from Makeda had all sorts of good things in her home. She even had a large gander. Her husband bought her a *papia,* a female goose, and she kept them in the garden.

The big goose would come to the door and go squawking and squawking:

"Da . . . dada . . . dada . . . dada . . . dada. . . ."

"*Addió*! *Hanum*! *Bula*! Oh my goodness! My dear!" she said to her. "Do you want to go to your daddy's? I'll send you!"

The woman took off all her jewels and placed them on the *papias*. She put on them chain necklaces, *sharsherotes,* bracelets, and everything! And she sent them.

After she sent them, which way did the good *papias* go? One went this way and the other one that way. She is waiting for them to come back. It was already evening, and soon her husband came and went to feed them. He looks for the *papias*; they aren't there.

"Wife," the husband says to her, "where are the *papias*?"

She says to him:

"What shall I tell you? They killed me all day: 'Dada . . . dada! . . . ' In the end," she said, "I adorned them with my jewels, I fixed them up, and I sent them to you."

"Daughter of a so and so!" he said. "Look at what you have done to me! You've sent all the gold with the *papias*?!" he said. "You go as well, together with them!!"

COMMENTARY

This tale is a parallel of AT 1291**, *Fools Let Horse Loose to Find Road Home*.[1] It is also one of several tales in the category of AT 1380 to AT 1404 that focus on the stupid wife (J1700, J1701) and her absurd behavior (J1730). It is worth noting that in this collection such tales tend to be narrated by women.

The foolish wife here treats animals as if they were human beings (J1870, J1880), as if they were her children. First she misinterprets their squawking (J1818, A2426.2), then she gives them her expensive jewelry as gifts (J1851.2), and lastly, disregarding their animal nature and habits (J1900), she shows absurd shortsightedness (J2050) by expecting them to go by themselves to the destination she intends for them to go to (J1881.2). Her ignorance reveals an odd lack of common sense (J2200).

The mention of the gold jewelry the brainless woman literally gives away, apparently oblivious to the fact that they will disappear with the birds, is deliberate. In the Middle East, gold jewels for the wife are a reflection of the wealth and stature of the husband. The more gold a woman displays the more successful the husband looks in the eyes of his neighbors. It is often also the only asset many families have. Thus the husband's reaction to the loss of his wife's gold possessions in this tale, despite the fact that he is comparatively well-to-do since his wife had "all sorts of good things in her home."

---

1. See also AT 1291D, *Other Objects Sent to Go by Themselves*. A similar Judeo-Spanish version appears in Sevilla-Sharon, "Las bovedades de Yusiko," 19, in which, in preparation for his wedding feast, Yusiko goes to the market to buy hens. When he finally returns home late at night, he is quite surprised that the hens have not arrived yet; he had sent them home on their own much earlier in the day. A related saying appears in Benazéraf's collection of *refranes*: "Kix! Kix! Para casa, gainas para la boda" ("Psst! Psst! Hen, find your way home for the wedding"). Koén-Sarano shows another Judeo-Spanish parallel in "Solusion para haraganes," in *Djohá ké dize?* 59, in which Djohá throws flour up in the air with the expectation that the air will take it home, and in "Aprontijos para la boda," in *Djohá ké dize?* 139. Alexander-Noy, no. 45, lists an additional Sephardic version. Other Jewish parallels appear in Jason, "Numskull Tales," 31 (Yemen, IFA 848); *Schwili*, no. 118. For non-Jewish parallels, see García Figueras, *Yehá*, no. 176; Wesselski, *Hodscha Nasreddin*, 1:272, no. 281.

48

Djenitores in Makeda

Narrated by ETY EYLAM (1992)

There were in Makeda a man and his wife who had no children. After many years, a son was born to them. In those days, it was known that for the first forty days, the newborn did not go out of the house. And they waited for forty years.

When he turned forty, they dressed up the "little boy" in beautiful clothes. They put a small hat on him and gave him a pacifier. They put him in the *arabá,* the baby carriage, and the father went for a stroll in the country with the "child."

The first thing they saw was a duck. How did the father tell the "child" how to say duck? He said to him:

"This is called a quack-quack-quack!"

And the "child" repeated after him:

"Quack! Quack! Quack!"

Next they saw a little lamb, and the father taught him to say:

"Baa! Baa! Baa!"

And then they saw a cow; the father taught him to say:

"Moo! Moo! Moo!"

The father said:

"Three words in one day, that's enough and more than enough!"

He took him home and immediately told his wife that the "child" is very tired because he has learnt a lot in one day. And he said to the "child":

"Tell *ima,* tell mother, what you've learnt today!"

The "child" climbed on a chair and said:

"Quack-quack-quack! Baa-baa-baa! Moo-moo-moo!"

His father and mother clapped their hands for him and pinned on him a little eye of *ayin ará,* to protect him against the evil eye, because the forty-year-old "child" had learned to say three words in a single day!

Commentary

This is an exaggerated cartoon of the old-fashioned custom of confining a new mother and her infant in the home for forty days to protect them both from disease and the evil eye. Newborns and their mothers were believed to be easy targets for demons such as Lilith and her followers, and they were seldom left alone.[1] Later in the tale, the teller refers to the use of a protective amulet to safeguard the child from the evil eye. A child was believed to be particularly vulnerable to evil influences and needed to be protected.

In some patriarchal societies, parents would disguise their children so as to avoid the evil eye and make them less an object of envy. Probably influenced by the customs of their Arab and Turkish neighbors in the Ottoman Empire, Sephardic Jews have used both amulets and the color blue to counter the evil eye (D2071 [Noy], D2071.1 [Noy]). According to Maimonides' Code, an amulet is permitted because of the psychological relief it offers to the disturbed mind and as a protection from harm. Protective charms were usually placed on the baby or on the cradle. Such amulets, mostly in the form of an eye or a hand, were used superstitiously to shield the newborn not only from envy but also from malevolent spirits (G302.16+ [Noy]). Blue was often associated with these preventive measures, as compared with coral or even black, for example, in other parts of the world.[2]

The intent of the teller here may be to give a caricature of this old-world custom while poking fun at the simplemindedness of the inhabitant of Makeda (J1700) and the overprotective parents (J1713). The image of a forty-year-old man being fussed over and treated as an infant is ludicrous, and thus it elicits peals of laughter. At the same time, as part of its larger-than-life comical intent, the tale turns a blind eye to the process of intellectual and physical development.

This tale belongs under AT 1349*, *Miscellaneous Numskull Tales*. It can also easily fall under the category of *Foolish Couples*, AT 1430–39.

---

1. See more on Lilith in note 6 of tale 6, *The King's Lost Son Transformed to a Dog*.

2. When I inquired about the significance of the use of the color blue among Arabs in Israel, the response was that it possibly had to do with the Crusades, as many fearsome Crusaders had blue eyes. Whether true or not, this makes for a colorful folk theory.

49

The Mice of Makeda

Narrated by SHOSHANA LEVY (1992)

In the city of Makeda, they invited a good group of people, a good *hevrá*. They set a table filled with many good things and to each, rather than a *pirón,* a fork, and a knife, they gave a stick to hold in their hand.

If one said it, the other said it, too:

"These sticks, what are they for?"

Suddenly an *aláy,* a procession, of mice appeared: one comes out from here, a second comes out from there, and yet another from over there!

And everybody already knew: *Tak! Tak! Tak! Tak!* Instead of eating, they are smacking the mice on the head!

Among the *hevrá,* there was a clever man from Istanbul, an *estanbullí*. He said:

"What's going on?"

"Hey," they told him, "here, when we set the table to eat, the mice appear...."

The *estanbullí* said:

"How much will you give me if I rid you of all these mice?"

"We'll give you as much as you want!" they said to him. "We're a large city, a *kodjamá sivdá!*"

The man went to Stanbol,[1] where there is no shortage of cats, and filled a sack full of cats. Customs, the *mehes,* did not ask what it is, because they could well hear the meowing! And he brought them there.

---

1. Istanbul, Turkey.

When they came in for the meal with the stick in their hands, he came in with the sack of cats. When the mice started to come out, he let out all the cats in the middle. They did not let a single mouse escape!

The next day he brought another sack, and soon there was not a mouse to be found in the city!

The *estanbullí* said to them:

"Fools! Is there a city without cats?"

COMMENTARY

A version of AT 1651, *Whittington's Cat*,[2] this tale shows that in a mouse-infested land where cats are unknown (F708.1), they are sold for a fortune (N411.1). In a follow-up type, AT 1281, *Getting Rid of the Unknown Animal*, after the cat is bought and eats many mice, it is thought to be a monster. To get rid of it, the fools set the house on fire (J2101). This second part is not displayed in our tale. For obvious reasons, this narrative also falls within the parameters of AT 1346*, *Easy Problem Made Hard*.

Unlike the Whittington type (part 1), this tale does not focus on the lucky accident of ownership of the unknown animal. In this assembly of Makeda simpletons (J1703), the stress is rather on the fools (J1700) who do not know how best to deal with an invasion of mice, although it interferes with the simple activity of eating. While they take matters into their own hands in their inimitable way and seem to adjust to the situation, as often is the case in Makeda, they turn a relatively simple problem into one that is hard to resolve (J2700) in a land in which there are no cats.[3]

---

2. Our tale incorporates only part 2 of the type. See KS, "Los kolas enkolgando," 195, for a Judeo-Spanish version of AT 1651A, *Fortune in Salt*, a close parallel. Jewish versions of AT 1651 and 1651A appear in *BJ*, 2:133, 346; Fus, *Khavilot zahav*, no. 2 (Lithuania); Gaster, *Exempla*, no. 368; Jason, "Types," 216; Learsi, *Filled with Laughter*, 25; Richman, *Jewish Lore*, 195; Schwarzbaum, *Studies*, 12. Non-Jewish parallels can be found in Ashliman, *Guide to Folktales*, 281; Baughman, *England and North America*, 42; Bødker, *European Folk Tales*, 26 (Finland-Sweden), 98 (Luxembourg); Briggs, *Dictionary of British Folk-Tales*, pt. B, vol. 2, 139; Calvino, *Italian Folktales*, no. 173; Clouston, *Popular Tales*, 2:65–78; Cole, *Best-Loved Folktales*, nos. 55, 196; Keller, *Spanish Exempla* (N411.5); Thompson, *One Hundred Favorite Folktales*, no. 96 (Russia); Thompson and Roberts, *Indic Oral Tales*, 158.

3. See Jason, "Numskull Tales," 27, in which she describes a tale recorded from a Sephardic teller from Turkey. In that tale, monks in a monastery give the newcomer

The quandary is tackled effortlessly by a visiting *estanbullí* who turns it into a profit-making business transaction. *Djudió estanbullí* generally refers to a particularly quick-witted and sharp individual. Introducing the feline animal and enriching himself in the process by exploiting the situation, the obliging guest represents the sophisticated urban dweller as opposed to the ignorant country bumpkins of Makeda.

---

a club to defend himself from the innumerable mice that would otherwise snatch his food. The youth releases the cat he had inherited from his father. When the cat kills the mice, the monks pay the youth a large sum of money to purchase the cat, an animal the likes of which they had never seen.

50

The *Makedanos* and the Cat

Narrated by MATILDA KOÉN-SARANO (1984)

In the city of the *Makedanos,* a wedding was to take place. On the day they displayed the bride's trousseau, her *anshugár,* for all her friends and relatives to see, and the house was filled with people, suddenly a cat came in and sat down on top of the bride's quilt!

The Makeda women, who had never seen a cat in all their lives, were very frightened, and they began to screech. But the cat remained sitting on top of the quilt and wasn't budging!

The men came in and began to argue among themselves, asking themselves how they would remove this strange beast from atop the bride's *anshugár.* But they hadn't a clue as to how to go about doing it!

At that moment a Jew, who was passing through by chance, entered the house. Seeing all that *galú,* all that commotion, the Jew asked what the fuss was all about, and they showed him the cat, sitting on the quilt. The man said nothing. He approached the side of the cat very, very slowly and then went:

"Psst! Shoo! Son of so and so!"

In no time at all the cat scrambled down and disappeared. And so the *Makedanos* rushed to the side of the Jew, kissed his hand, and hailed him as a national hero.

COMMENTARY

Once again we find ourselves in a town of noodles (J1700, J1703) in a city where cats are unknown (F708.1). The fear that the sudden appearance of that mysterious species provokes in the inhabitants of Makeda and their inability to think of a way to get rid of the cat are meant to be funny. Men and women alike think that the cat is a monster (J1736, J2600), and as in AT 1346*, *Easy Problem Made Hard,* the straightforward situation is turned into a hard-to-solve problem. In AT 1231, *The Attack on the Hare (Crayfish)*, a similar incident takes place,[1] and seven men make elaborate plans to attack the fierce animal. When one man screams with fright, the animal runs away (J2612). In our version, it is a stranger who intentionally shouts to scare the animal away. The fools are very thankful (J2550).

This narrative provides the opportunity for the teller, a woman, to give some information about the pre-wedding ritual of publicly showing off the bride's trousseau. The immediate crowd is made up of female friends and relatives who have come to admire the displayed goods. The strange animal sitting on top of the bride's matrimonial bed linen could well be interpreted superstitiously as a bad omen. The elderly Sephardic audience would intuit this immediately.

---

1. This tale was published previously in Judeo-Spanish in KS, 269, and in Koén-Sarano, *Saragosa,* 179. See Attias, *Nozat ha-zahav,* 23–25; Alexander-Noy, no. 21 (Greece); Kurt, *Zar prakhim,* 203–4, nos. 73, 74 (Afghanistan) for Jewish parallels. For non-Jewish versions, see Ashliman, *Guide to Folktales,* 223; BP, 2:556, 3:286; Boulvin, *Contes populaires persans,* 1:74, 150; Briggs, *Dictionary of British Folk-Tales,* pt. A, vol. 2, 354; Grimm and Grimm, *Tales,* no. 119.

51

The Eve of Yom Kippúr in Makeda

Narrated by MATILDA KOÉN-SARANO (1992)

On the eve of one Yom Kippúr, a father and his son came out of their home in Makeda to go to the synagogue, to the *kal,* to say Kol Nidré. And both of them were dressed in white.

While walking, the father sees a puddle of water in the middle of the alley. Knowing full well that his son always does the opposite of what he tells him to do, the father says to him:

"Step into the puddle, my son!"

The child does just as his father told him: he steps into the middle of the puddle, getting himself all muddied!

Filled with fury, the father says to his son:

"Why did you step into the puddle?"

"I did what you told me to do!" the child replies.

"*Ma,* I said that to you because you always do the opposite of what I tell you to do!" the father said to him.

"Ah," said the son, "*ma agora* is the eve of Kippúr. If I don't listen *agora* to what my father tells me, when am I going to do so?"

Commentary

Our narrative is a judaized variant of AT 1365J*, *Asking by Opposites,* an archetype about married couples, which tells of a man who always asks his obstinate wife for the opposite of what he wants.[1]

Our teller adapts her tale from a domestic anecdote about a husband and his wife to a religious tale about a father and his son (P233). The tale takes place on the eve of the holiest of days in the Jewish calendar, the Day of Atonement (*Yom Hakipurím*) (V79.2 [Noy], V79.2 + [Noy]). The narrative is thus set in Jewish time, directing the listeners' or readers' attention to the familiar solemnity and customs of the Yom Kippúr ritual.

On the eve of the Day of Atonement, the most solemn holiday of the year, the community assembles in the synagogue, where young and old join in worship to ask God for forgiveness through fasting, prayer, and charity. A few minutes before sundown, the service begins with a very old prayer, chanted three times, which has a sad but most beautiful melody: the Kol Nidré.[2] The community thus comes together to ask for God's forgiveness. On Yom Kippúr it is also traditional to dress in white and not to wear leather

---

1. An almost identical tale told by a male informant appears in Koén-Sarano, *Konsejas,* 241. Two other Judeo-Spanish versions exist: Elnecavé, no. 9, p. 330 and KS, "El ijo de Djohá," 163. Elnecavé's version is identical to ours, while KS identifies Djohá as the father and substitutes a business trip for the Jewish holiday of Yom Kippúr, thus eliminating the religious character of the tale. The ending shows Djohá losing his goods in the stream when his son obeys his instructions and throws them in. The boy later explains that he did so because he was annoyed by his father's foolish orders. An identical tale appears in Koén-Sarano, "Buen ijo," in *Djohá ké dize?* 177. Other Jewish versions can be found in Avitsuk, *Ha-ilan,* no. 8 (Rumania); Gaster, *Exempla,* no. 411; [Noy], (V79.2); Richman, *Jewish Lore,* 27; Schwarzbaum, *Studies,* 48. Among non-Jewish parallels are Ashliman, *Guide to Folktales,* 239; Manuel, *Conde Lucanor,* no. 27; García Figueras, *Yehá,* no. 2; Hikmet, *Hodja,* 63.

2. The Kol Nidré is a legal formula that releases individuals from vows made to God. Its theme is the seeking of forgiveness for unfulfilled promises made to God. It was in use as early as the eighth century, during the Gaonic period. It is recited in its archaic form a few minutes before sundown to usher in Yom Kippur. Many believe that the beautiful melody to which the Kol Nidré is chanted has come down from Spanish Jews who were forced to convert to Catholicism and risked their lives to observe their Jewish faith clandestinely. On Yom Kippúr they would assemble in secret to celebrate the holiest of days. The Kol Nidré does not absolve sins and oaths between individuals. These are not forgiven until amends are made.

shoes. White garments on that day are believed to signify a state of spiritual preparedness.

The belief in atonement permeates the tale (V315), as the usual disobedience (W126) and stubbornness (W167) of the obstinate son are put aside for the day (P236) when the boy, longing for a clear conscience, obeys his father literally (J2460). This is because the ten days between the Jewish New Year, Rosh Hashaná, and Yom Kippúr are a solemn period during which Jews are supposed to reflect on their actions of the past year and try to atone for their mistakes. It is said that during those ten days the Book of Life is open and human actions judged (F889+ [Noy]). Yom Kippúr prayers are considered the most important of the year and are the longest.

The holy day is a day of fasting. Adults don't eat or drink from sundown on the eve of Yom Kippúr—*erev* Kippúr—until sundown the next day. They are supposed to devote the entire day and all their thoughts to prayer and to moving closer to God rather than on more mundane activities such as eating. God is said to record the yearly fate of each person before closing the Book of Life at the end of the day on Kippúr as the *shofár* (the ram's horn) is blown. Hence the reasoning behind the boy's change of behavior.

52

Yom Kippúr in Makeda

Narrated by SHIMON ASAYAS (1990)

A man went to a town in Makeda and passed himself off as a *hahám,* a rabbi, in order to *ramayár,* to swindle, the people. He gathered them all at the synagogue, at the *kal,* and announced that the next day is Yom Kippúr. He said to them:

"Tomorrow evening at six thirty we'll say the Kal Nidré."

And so, on the eve of Kippúr, they all gathered at the *kal* and started the prayer. Among them was one who suspected that something was amiss. But he didn't say anything. The next day the entire town went to the *kal.* They recited the prayer, the *tefillá.* They finished the *perashá* of Balak,[1] the Balak portion of the Torah, and they are in the Musáf service,[2] the prayer of the priests, of the

---

1. Num. 22:2–25:9. The Pentateuch is traditionally divided into an appropriate number of weekly readings, and the *parashá* of the week is the portion of the Torah read on the Saturday of that week. The one referred to here, the Torah portion of Balak, shows how the recent victory of the Israelites over the Amorites filled both the king and people of Moab with dread, as the Israelites were now settled on the border of Moab. Balak, son of Zippor, was king of Moab. By insidious and pernicious ways, he sought the destruction of Israel and followed the instructions at Balaam: he prepared seven altars and seven sacrifices and used magic formulas to defeat his enemies, the Israelites. His intent was to curse them through magic. The *haftará,* recited after the *parashá* of Balak includes Mic. 5:6–6:8.

2. The Mussáf service mentioned is an additional part of the holiday prayers in which *Shemoné Atzeret,* the twelve benedictions of the Yom Kippúr service, are repeated in the afternoon.

koaním. The man who understood what was going on could no longer bear to keep silent, and he began chanting along with the melody of the prayer:

"Hahám, hahám, lo raíti 17 be-Tamúz be-Yom Kippúr!..."³

The *hahám* realized that a man born on a Friday wants to expose him.⁴ He answered him with the same melody:

"Hamishá zeuvím lakahti. Hatsí shelí ve-hatsí shelhá."⁵

"Hahám, hahám, shetiká."⁶

COMMENTARY

This is a universal tale usually set in a church and pointing to the unethical behavior of a priest and the shrewdness of a member of the congregation who catches him in the act and threatens to expose him. In the end, when the imposter proposes to share the profits he makes with the astute congregant and the man agrees not to reveal the deceit, the power of greed is highlighted in a humorous fashion.

The tale parallels AT 1824, *Parody Sermon*⁷ (K1961, K1961.1.2.1), and AT 1831, *The Parson and Sexton at Mass*.⁸ In the latter type, the sexton has been sent to steal the lamb. At mass, he discusses the theft with the parson in antiphony. In Catholic stories, the antiphonies are made to sound like Latin. Here, in our judaized version, the antiphony takes place in Hebrew, the language of prayer, which few men in the noodle town of Makeda probably understand.

De-Christianized, our tale fits the Jewish oicotype IFA 1831*C, *Ignorance of Holidays*.⁹ It describes country Jews who are ignorant of religious matters

---

3. "Rabbi, Rabbi, I have never seen the seventeen of Tamúz on Yom Kippúr." This is a pointed remark since both the *parashá* and the *haftará* of Balak are read on the Sabbath before the fast of Tamúz, several months before Yom Kippúr.

4. This expression probably refers to someone clever, who catches on quickly and takes advantage of the situation.

5. "I have taken five *zeuvím*. Half are mine and half are yours."

6. "Rabbi, Rabbi, mum's the word!"

7. Versions of this type appear in Briggs, *Dictionary of British Folk-Tales*, pt. A, vol. 2, 315, pt. B, vol. 2, 125; Robe, *Mexican Folktales*, 211.

8. For parallels, see Boggs, *Spanish Folktales*, 147; D'Aronco, *Fiabe Toscane*, 121; Paredes, *Mexico*, no. 73; Rael, *Colorado y Nuevo Méjico*, no. 422; Robe, *Mexican Folktales*, 213.

9. See KS, "La askará," 69, for a comparable Judeo-Spanish version classified under the same type in Haboucha. While retaining the religious character of the type,

(J1738) and who do not know the exact dates of holidays (J1743). Taking advantage of this ignorance, a villain posing as a rabbi proclaims the holiday of Yom Kippúr in our storyline. This is a solemn and serious day (K1900 [Noy]), and most Jews, whether traditional or secular, tend to respond to the call of their religion and attend synagogue services on that occasion (V112.3, V112.6+ [Noy]).

The teller sets his narrative in Jewish time and focuses on the Jewish calendar, with its religious feasts and fasts. The Jewish year is divided into twelve months: Tishré,[10] Heshván, Kislév, Tevet, Shevát, Adár, Nisán, Iyár, Siván, Tamúz, Av, and Elúl. Rosh Hashaná, the Jewish New Year, falls on the first day of Tishré, and Yom Kippúr, the Day of Awe or Day of Atonement, falls on the tenth. Another fast, the fast of Tamúz, falls on the seventeenth of that month, almost three months before Yom Kippúr, thus the pointed reference to that holiday in Tamúz during the secret dialogue in our tale. Considered by some to represent a lesser obligation than the Day of Atonement, the fast of Tamúz, known in the Bible as the fast of the fourth month (Tamúz is the fourth month of the Hebrew calendar after Nisán[11]) commemorates the beginning of the siege of Jerusalem by the Romans.[12] It is one of the four fasts

---

KS gives it an additional twist. When the rabbi reminds a man to recite the memorial prayer for his parents, he receives a donation. A few weeks later, he calls upon the man once again to recite the prayer of the dead for his father. The man does so and pays. When the rabbi calls him within a short time to honor his mother's memory once again, the man balks. He may conceive of having more than one father, he says, but he is sure of having only one mother. See also Crews, no. 6, p. 97 (Bitolj) and L, no. 99, p. 34 (Monastir), both classified under **1825D, *The Thief as Sham Priest*, in Haboucha. For Jewish variants, see Grunwald, "Motifs," no. 42; Grunwald, *Tales*, no. 23; Jason, "Types," 221; Jason, *Types*, 87; [Noy], (V60+); Noy, *Ha-na'ara*, nos. 68, 88 (Iraq); Noy, *TEM 1965*, no. 10 (Rumania); M. Noy, *Manguinah*, no. 3 (Rumania), 39–42; Pipe, *Sanok*, nos. 5, 20 (Poland); Richman, *Jewish Lore*, 274; Schwarzbaum, *Studies*, 30, 445. IFA versions exist from Afghanistan, Eastern Europe, India, Iraq, Israel (Sephardic), Rumania, and Yemen. Universal parallels are found in Ashliman, *Guide to Folktales*, 297 (type 1848A); Bødker, *European Folk Tales*, 213; Briggs, *Dictionary of British Folk-Tales*, pt. A, vol. 2, 240, 249; Megas, *Folktales of Greece*, no. 13.

10. Tishré begins at the first new moon after the autumnal equinox.

11. Nisán is an important month in Jewish life, commemorating Passover and the miracle of the Exodus from Egypt, when the Egyptians proved powerless to harm the Jews. According to the Torah, it is the "head of the months," the first month, although Jews count the New Year from the first day of Tishré.

12. The seventeenth of Tamúz is observed as a fast day because on that day the enemy breached the wall surrounding Jerusalem and was able to enter the city, which then led to the destruction of the Temple. (According to tradition, the breaking of

ordained by the prophets of Israel in memory of the destruction of the Holy Temple.

The Jewish calendar follows the cycle of the moon, with twenty-nine-and-a-half days between one moon and the next. Thus it is that some months have twenty-nine days and others thirty. Since it takes twelve-and-a-half cycles of the moon for the earth to travel once around the sun, an extra month, called Adár Shení (the Second Adár) appears every two or three years, right after the month of Adár, on lunar leap years. In addition, every nineteen years the months of Heshván, Kislév, and Adár have thirty days instead of twenty-nine; this is what makes the Jewish holidays so irregular with regard to the solar calendar. In the old days the common people relied on their rabbis or on the more learned members in their communities to alert them to the dates of the holidays.

The religious content and details of this anecdote make it an appropriate one to be told by a male narrator.

---

the Tablets of the Law by Moses, when he came down from Mount Sinai to find the people worshiping the golden calf, also took place on that day.) There were two destructions of the Temple in ancient Jewish history, the first by the Babylonians and the second by the Romans. Both are observed with the fast of the ninth of Av, *Tish'á be-Av*. Tradition has it that the Jews were expelled from Spain on that day as well. The three-week period between the two fasts, Tamúz and Av, is observed in commemoration of both destructions and shows a progression of intensified mourning during which many Jews abstain from doing joyful things and eating delicacies, including red meat.

53

The *Makedanos* at the Bathhouse

Narrated by DJOYA ALBUKREK (1990)

In Makeda they were going to have a wedding. The brocade coverings, the *bogos sirmalís,* the high-heeled sabots, the *galechas,* the *tas,* the *borundjúk,* they were all ready. And by now they were going to the bathhouse. [Years ago, there were no bathrooms at home. They went to the public bath.]¹

The bride was very tall; the entrance to the bathhouse was very low; the people of Makeda were very stupid! They tried it this way, and then they tried it that way. The bride just doesn't fit through the door! They began to wail in the street. As one is wailing, the other one wails as well.

"Tomorrow we have a wedding! We are unable to get the bride into the bathhouse! She must go in so she can bathe, because tomorrow we must dress her in a white dress, a white *fostán*!"

Wailing and crying! A clever man passed by. He inquired:

"Why are you all crying?"

"*Na,* we want to get the bride into the bathhouse and bathe her, because we have a wedding. She is very tall. We can't fit her through!"

The clever man came; he gave the bride a poke on the back, a *yumúk.* As he did so, the bride bent down and entered the bathhouse. All her relatives entered as well; they all sat together and are overcrowding each other. There were so many people that soon their legs became entangled. One woman said:

"This is my leg!"

Another said:

"This leg isn't yours! It's mine!"

---

1. Teller's aside.

They are killing each other! From the outside they overheard shouts. People paid attention:

"What's going on?"

"*Na,*" they said. "The legs! The legs! We can't pull them apart!"

One said:

"The fat leg is mine!"

Another said:

"The slender leg is mine!"

The clever man came from the outside and said:

"What are you fighting about?"

They said to him:

"Our legs are all mixed together!"

The clever man got hold of a stick; he started to hit the legs. They all scooted away!

COMMENTARY

A judaized version of AT 1295A*, *Tall Bridegroom Cannot Get into Church,*[2] in which the groom is hit on the back and falls down and thus can enter, our tale transforms the inappropriate church into a suitable Jewish substitute. First, the groom is turned into the bride, and then the church becomes a *mikvá,* or ritual bath, to which each bride must go to immerse herself before her wedding (V96).[3] Such tales illustrate local marriage customs (T130) and accompaniments at a wedding (T136).

The *bogo de baño,* which is apparently what is happening in this narrative, is a special party given by the mother of the groom in honor of her future daughter-in-law, right before she goes to the *mikvá* (V99+ [Noy], V96). It is a festive occasion, at which the bride receives lavish gifts from her bridegroom

---

2. See Cohen-Sarano, "Los Makedanos," and KS, "Los Makedanos i la novia," 269, for identical versions. Also see Koén-Sarano, "La novia alta," in *Djohá ké dize?* 289. For additional Jewish versions, see Alexander-Noy, no. 22; Attias, *Nozat hazahav,* 25 n. 2; Hanauer, *Holy Land,* 83, 95; Jason, "Types," 199; Jason, *Types,* 70; Jason, "Numskull Tales," 34 (Iraq, IFA 1588), 37 (Egypt, IFA 5464); Noy, *TEM 1970,* 174 (Tunisia, IFA 8881); Schwili, no. 117 (AT 1294). For other universal parallels, see Briggs, *Dictionary of British Folk-Tales,* pt. A, vol. 2, 11; Chevalier, *Siglo de Oro,* no. 97; Clouston, *Noodles,* 202; Lorimer and Lorimer, *Persian,* no. 25.

3. See Tale 21, *The Arranged Marriage,* for more on the ritual of immersion.

and his family, such as jewelry, lingerie, perfume, and soaps. The mother-in-law is traditionally the bearer of these gifts.

In this town of fools (J1703), however, a series of seemingly insurmountable hurdles arise. Even easy matters become difficult (J2700). First, the tall bride cannot enter the low gate of the bathhouse until a stranger's blow causes her to lower her head (J2171.6). Then her family and guests, women and numskulls all (J1700), cannot find their own legs after they get them mixed up at the bathhouse where they have joined the bridal party to bathe themselves. The same stranger helps solve their problem with a stick (J2021). AT 1288, *Numskulls Cannot Find Their Own Legs*,[4] adds this new twist to the prenuptial *mikvá* ritual, highlighting the absurd ignorance of the people of Makeda (J1730) and their bizarre inability to identify their own limbs (J2020).

---

4. Versions exist from other traditions: Robe, *Mexican Folktales,* 165; D'Aronco, *Fiabe Toscane,* 114; Paredes, *Mexico,* no. 47; García Figueras, *Yehá,* no. 276.

54

Snow in Makeda

Narrated by ESTER LEVY (1988)

One morning, those living in Makeda woke up and saw that the entire city was white with snow.

"*Addió!* My God!" they said. "What a gift God has given us! Everything is white, pure, beautiful! *Amá,* what are we going to do? How shall we go and summon the people so they can come to the synagogue, to the *k̠al?*"

They pondered . . . and pondered . . . and pondered. . . . How will the *shamásh* go from door to door?

In the end, one man came and said:

"What's the problem? Let four men come. They will lift the *shamásh* and they will carry him from door to door to wake up the people so they can come and say their *tefillá!*"

COMMENTARY

Still in Makeda, the Sephardic imaginary town of noodles (J1703), the inhabitants provide us with yet more evidence of their absurd lack of common sense (J1700, J2200) by displaying their illogical use of numbers (J2213) as well as their ignorance of and disregard for natural laws (J1930).

In the old days, it was customary in small towns for the *shamásh* or synagogue beadle to make the rounds of homes before sunrise to rouse the men for early-morning prayer. Their presence at the synagogue was necessary for a full *minyán* or the required quorum of ten men for prayer. Our tale is a Jewish variant of AT 1201, *The Plowing,*[1] in which four men carry the horse so as not to tramp up the field. Likewise, here, rather than one set of footprints in the untouched snow, the solution the people of Makeda come up with shortsightedly quadruples the imprints on the purity of the white snow they wish so much to preserve (J2163). Clearly, the remedy is worse than the disease (J2100).[2]

---

1. For other versions, see Andrejev; Baughman, *England and North America,* 28.
2. See Jason, "Numskull Tales," 36 for a version in IFA (Israel [Sephardic]) in which the numskulls conduct themselves in exactly the same way.

El rey Shelomó i el pishkado de oro

Narrated by Moshé Ibn Ezra (1987)

En los tiempos del rey Shelomó bivía en el Galíl, al lado del Kineret, un viejo peshkador, ke tinía siete ijas, una mas ermoza de la otra. Ma la chika, Shulamít, era la mas ermoza de todas.

Un día se prezentó la bohora al padre, disho:

"Oy, en echando la trata, diga: 'Esta trata es el mazál de mi ija bohora, la primera.' Veremos a ver kualo va salir. Pue' ser le sali el mazál por mí."

Ansí izo el peshkador, en viniendo la ora, ayá en el Kineret. S'entró en el barko i echó la peshka en medio de mar.

"Esto es el mazál de mi ija bohora, la primera."

I asperó a la tadre.

A la tadre, travando la trata, está pezgada. Muy pezgada! Kon munchos esforsos travó la trata a l'arena, vido una grande piedra. Retornando a kaza, disho a la ija:

"Esto fue tu mazál! Una piedra."

Al sigundo día se prezentó la sigunda ija. Enfín, lo aremos en kurto. Todas las ijas provaron. Una vez salió un maso de kalsados viejos, ke echaron a l'agua.... Otra vez salieron yervas.... Kada una i una tuvo otro mazál. A la fin se prezentó Shulamít, la chika:

"Papá, esta vez es por mí!"

"Ma ya estás viendo lo ke está saliendo! No ay nada!"

"Esta vez echa por mí!"

Era día de viernes, el peshkador kijo eskapar demprano para vinir a kaza i resivir el shabbát. De madrugada s'echó al lado del Kineret, echó la trata:

"Echo la trata a nombre de Shulamít, mi ija chika."

I asperó. Después de medio día tiró la trata. Vido, está un poko pezgadika! Avagar, avagar la tiró. En lo ke la retiró, ke vee? Un peshe enorme, senteando de oro i de diamantes! Kedó enkantado! En lo ke stava enkantado, avrió el peshe la boka, le disho:

"De vista kítame de akí, tráeme a tu kaza i ázeme una djépea de agua, para ke pueda bivír!"

De vista el peshkador se fue en kaza kon muncha pena. Todos salieron en su enkuentro.

"Kayados!" disho él. "Mos metermos al lavoro!"

I kavakaron una djépea en el kurtijo de sus kazas, la incheron de agua i ponieron el peshe adientro.

De akel día el gusto de la famiya era éste: kada demanyana se alevantavan i bevían el kafé al derredor de la djépea, i el peshe dava solanses i les kontava kuentizikos de mil i una noche del tiempo viejo. Ansina pasavan la ora.

Un día, mientres ke stavan asentados delantre del peshe, stava pensando el peshkador ké va ser la suerte de sus siete ijas, komo las va kazar, i él no tiene una agorá! Avrió la boka el peshe, disho:

"Ké ay de pensar? Estira la mano, toma un punyadiko de diamantes, va a Yerusháláyim i véndelos!"

"Buena idea!"

El peshkador stiró la mano, tomó de la kavesa del peshe un punyado de diamantes i perlas, tomó un pedaso de pan, se lo metió en l'aldukera i partió para Yerusháláyim. Después de tres días arivó en la sivdá i s'enkantó de ver su splendor i su ermozura. Todas las kayes yevavan al sentro, ke era el Bet-Amikdásh, ke senteava de oro. Enfín demandó ande es la kaye de los bijutiés. Se la amostraron. En Yerusháláyim avían kayes kayes: la kaye de los djoyeros, la kaye de los karneseros, la kaye de los tisheros. ... En kada kaye avía una sorte de profesión.

Enfín arivó a la kaye de los djoyeros. El primer djoyero al kual se prezentó, le disho:

"Regreto. Me es emposible de pagarte! Lo ke mos stas prezentando es muy de muy karo! Aval akí ay un djoyero ke se yama Aminadáv. Este es el ke traye bijús a la korte de Shelomó. Este te puede merkar esto."

El peshkador se adresó a Aminadáv, ma, examinando las perlas, éste vido ke no tinía todo el montante menesterozo.

"Siente," le disho, "toma la metá del dinero. Oy vo arrekojér mas. Vienes amanyana demanyana!"

Desharemos esto i veremos la korte del rey Shelomó. El rey Shelomó amava munchas mujeres de todas las sortes i los grados, i por medio de eyas kosuegró kon Paró, el rey del Ejipto, i tomó a la ija, Tantanhís, ke era una de las mas ermozas ijas de Paró. La trusho a Yerusháláyim, le fraguó un palasio, i Tantanhís vino kon una korte de munchos sirvidores, i entre eyos un sirvidor djigante, negro.

Enfín, akontesió ke akel día salió Tantanhís al charshí de los djoyeros, entró ande Aminadáv i vido las perlas. De vista se fue ande el rey Shelomó i demandó absolutamente ke le merke estas perlas. El rey Shelomó vino a ver la merkansía i observó entre las perlas una eskama de peshe. Le entró un sospecho:

"Alguna koza ay akí!"

Enkomendó a sus soldados ke lo asperen al ke vendió las perlas: apenas va vinir demanyana a tomar el resto del dinero, ke lo apanyen i lo traygan delantre d'él. Ansí fue. La demanyana, en viniendo el peshkador a tomar el resto del dinero, se le echaron ensima los soldados i lo trusheron delantre del rey Shelomó.

El rey Shelomó le disho:

"La mi espada en la tu kavesa! Me vas a kontar komo vinieron en tu poder estas perlas!"

I el peshkador disho:

"Al rey no se enkuvre nada! Vo avlar la pura verdá!"

I le kontó todo.

El rey no pudo estar. De vista tomó a todos los ministros i se fue para ver el peshe en el Galíl, en el Kineret. Se yevaron i a las mujeres, i vino i Tantanhís kon su korte.

Enfín, vieron el peshe. Todos se kedaron maraviyados de ver su ermozura. Stava entero senteando! S'asentaron al derredor de la djépea, la patrona de kaza les trusho kafé, i el peshe empesó a dar solanses.

En arivando delantre la reyna Tantanhís, el peshe skupió un fishék de menopresio, ke la mojó entera. Al rey Shelomó le vino muy afuerte de esto, i de vista le demandó al peshkador de matar al peshe, ke tuvo la ozadía de azer esto.

El peshe avrió la boka i le disho:

"A ti es ke te yaman el re Shelomó, ke es el mas grande savio de todo el mundo? Ma tú no saves lo ke sta akontesiendo adientro de tu kaza! La reyna Tantanhís sta namorada kon el negro ke tiene en su kaza. Este sta eskundido detrás de la státua de Amún-Ra...."

I ke vayan i ke lo topen.

Ansina fue. Fueron de vista a Yerusháláyim i toparon a este negro, ke tinía la morada detrás de la státua de Amún-Ra. De vista los tomaron a los dos i los exekutieron sigún la Ley de Moshé.

Pasando tiempo, el rey estava bien triste, siendo ke amava muy muncho a la reyna Tantanhís, i lo ke le akontesió le kemó el korasón. Para afalagar un poko su tristeza desidió de irse al Galíl i estar en la kompanía del peshe tan ermozo. Tomó unos kuantos sirvidores, se fue al Galíl, i kada demanyana, sigún lo ke uzavan los miembros de la famiya del peshkador, s'asentava al derredor de la djépea, i el peshe empesava a kontar.

En viendo al rey Shelomó tanto triste, le disho el peshe:

"Ké estás pensando tanto? Mankan ermozas ijas en Israel, ke te stas atristando tanto?! Abolta tu kara i vee la ermozura ke tienes al lado!"

Aboltó la kara Shelomó i vido a la ija chika del peshkador, a Shulamít, i de entonses se le avrieron los ojos i desidió de tomarla por mujer i de meterla sovre todas las mujeres de su armón.

Pasando un poko de tiempo, izieron delantre del Kineret un talamó ermozo, i ayí s'izo la boda del rey Shelomó kon Shulamít. Entonses eskrivió el rey Shelomó en su poema, el "Shir Ashirím": "Setenta son las reynas, i las namoradas i las ijas son sin fin, ma una es Shulamít."

El rey Shelomó se okupó de kazar a las otras sesh ijas kon ministros del estado, i de entonses todos bivieron orozos.

Eyos tengan bien i mozós también.

Note: The Judeo-Spanish accentuation used in this tale conforms to that applied throughout this volume, keeping in mind the English-speaking reader. Thus, it differs somewhat from the system used by Koén-Sarano in the Judeo-Spanish version of this tale she published in *Lejendas,* 29.

Informants

DJOYA ALBUKREK (KOHEN) Born in Ankara, she completed her education there and today lives in Istanbul. After Matilda Koén-Sarano's husband was sent to Turkey to manage a Talmud Torah, Matilda interviewed Djoya in Istanbul in 1990 at the home of mutual friends. Djoya refused to give her date of birth, saying simply: "I was born sixty-five years ago." The repertoire she displayed included only humorous jokes and anecdotes. She is fluent in Turkish, Judeo-Spanish, and French. (tale 53)

SHIMON ASAYAS was born in the neighborhood of Balat, Istanbul, in 1948, where he still lives. Matilda Koén-Sarano recorded his tales there in 1990 during boat trips she and her husband took on the Bosphorus with Shimon and his wife and also at a café on the island of Hebely. He studied at the Rabbinical Seminary and is the *hazan* at the synagogue Kal de Shalom in Istanbul. He speaks Turkish, Judeo-Spanish, Hebrew, and French. (tale 52)

JULIDE AVZARADEL (ISRAEL) was born in Milas, Turkey, in 1931 and studied at the Lycée Kuz in Izmir. She went on *aliyá,* that is, she immigrated to Israel in 1950, then lived in the Belgian Congo from 1952 to 1960. Presently she resides in Ashdod, in southern Israel. Not only is she a storyteller but she is also a singer in Judeo-Spanish. She served as a tale informant for Matilda Koén-Sarano between 1987 and 1992. Julide speaks Judeo-Spanish, French, Hebrew, Turkish, and Swahili. (tale 25)

SHMUEL BARKI was born in Izmir, Turkey, in 1924, where he attended a Turkish school as well as the B'nai B'rith School. He made *aliyá* to Israel in 1949 and lived in Jerusalem until his death in 1993. Matilda Koén-Sarano interviewed him with his wife at their home in 1992 through the intercession of their daughter, who had heard Matilda give a lecture about Sephardic oral narratives on the occasion of the five hundredth anniversary of the Expulsion of the Jews from Spain. Shmuel contributed many stories to Matilda's collection. He knew Hebrew, Turkish, and Judeo-Spanish. (tale 35)

LEA BENABU (COHEN) was born in Istanbul in 1932 and attended the B'nai B'rith School there, going on *aliyá* to Israel in 1948. She lives in Jerusalem, where her stories were recorded by Matilda Koén-Sarano in 1993 during Lea's participation in Matilda's Storytellers' Circle, which she attended for almost a year. She speaks French, Judeo-Spanish, Turkish, Hebrew, Rumanian, and Yiddish. (tales 32, 39)

ALICIA BENDAYAN (BENASSAYAG) was born in Tetuán (Spanish Morocco) in 1922 and was educated there, moving to Israel in 1962. She lives in Ashkelon. This particular tale was recorded in 1992 by Gladys Pimienta, a scholar of Sephardic narratives from Spanish Morocco. Alicia speaks Spanish, Hakitía (the Judeo-Spanish dialect spoken in northern Morocco), Hebrew, and French. (tale 18)

IMANUEL BEN EZRA was born in Izmir, Turkey, in 1917 and studied at the Talmud Torah as well as at the school of the Alliance Israélite Universelle. He made *aliyá* to Israel in 1948 and lived in Bat-Yam, a suburb of Tel Aviv, where he recently passed away. He was the brother of Moshé Ibn Ezra and the uncle of Maty Shalem, another informant, who gave his name to Matilda Koén-Sarano. The latter interviewed him in 1992 at his home in Bat-Yam, in the presence of his wife and daughter. He told her many tales. Imanuel spoke French, Judeo-Spanish, Turkish, and Hebrew. (tales 21, 28)

SARA BENREY (FRANCO) was born in Izmir, Turkey, in 1920 and was educated there at the school of the Alliance Israélite Universelle. She made *aliyá* to Israel in 1960 and lived in Bat-Yam, a Tel Aviv suburb, where she recently passed away. She was a poet and a writer of comedies. She published her book, *Espertando el djudeo-espanyol,* in 1996. Matilda Koén-Sarano interviewed her in 1989, after she told a tale during one of Matilda's presentations in Bat-Yam. Sara spoke French, Judeo-Spanish, Turkish, English, and Hebrew. (tale 22)

SIMHA COHEN (HASSON) was born in the Old City of Jerusalem in 1911. Her mother was born in Yugoslavia. She studied at the Lebanot B School in the Old City and presently lives in Jerusalem. When Simha's daughter heard Matilda Koén-Sarano's folklore program on the radio, she called her and invited her to interview her mother who lives in Mea Shearím, an ultra-Orthodox neighborhood of Jerusalem. Simha received Matilda alone at home while she was recovering from a fall. She spoke mostly about her life and confided that she had always wanted to acquire an education but had been married off at a relatively young age and given birth to twelve children. As

Matilda was getting ready to leave, assuming that that was all Simha was going to tell her, Simha surprised her by saying: "Agora te vo a kontar una konseja!" ("And now I'll tell you a tale.") She speaks Judeo-Spanish, Yiddish, Hebrew, Arabic, and English. (tale 20)

REBEKA COHEN-ARIEL (COHEN) was born in Shama, at the foot of Mount Zion, in Jerusalem in 1910. She studied at the Old City School and at the Evelyna de Rothschild School. She lives in Jerusalem. Rebeka was introduced to Matilda Koén-Sarano by Dr. Tamar Alexander, who had interviewed her and published some of her tales. Rebeka told many hard-to-find tales that she had heard from her father who, she said, had been a gifted storyteller around whom the entire neighborhood gathered every evening to hear him tell tales. Matilda interviewed Rebeka several times in 1989, once as a result of Rebeka's initiative when she remembered a few tales to tell. In 1992, Matilda visited her to present her with a copy of a book of tales she had published for the Midrashiat Amalia School in Jerusalem, in which one of Rebeka's tales appeared. Rebeka asked Matilda to read her the tale because she was having trouble with her eyes, and while Matilda was reading the tale, Rebeka would complete each sentence from memory, using exactly the same words that were recorded in the book. After about a half-page of reading, Rebeka began to cry, leading Matilda herself to shed some tears and to conclude that the older woman had been greatly moved by finding herself immortalized in the book. Rebeka speaks Hebrew, Judeo-Spanish, Arabic, English, and French. (tales 10, 44, 46)

MARIA DE BENEDETTI (CAPOANO) was born in Istanbul in 1904. She studied at a French school run by nuns in Pyraeus, at a public school in Naples, and at a lycée in Marseilles. She lived in Turin, where she died in 1987. Matilda Koén-Sarano interviewed her in 1987 at the Jewish Rest Home in Turin, where Matilda used to have lunch every day and tell tales to entertain the residents during a period of two summers when her husband served as the rabbi of the Jewish community of Turin. Maria was fluent in Italian, Judeo-Spanish, French, English, and Greek. (tale 30)

YAAKOV ELAZAR was born in the Jewish Quarter of the Old City of Jerusalem in 1913. He studied at the Sephardic Talmud Torah there and completed the Seminary Mizrahi Lemorim to become a schoolteacher. He continued his studies at Sephardic yeshivas and learned ritual slaughtering. He is a writer and lives in Jerusalem. He told Matilda Koén-Sarano his first tale in 1983, when she visited him with her husband on a Shabbát afternoon. Afterward she went back to interview him and his wife, Ester. In 1991 she interviewed him once more, at his initiative. Yaakov speaks Hebrew, Judeo-Spanish, French, English, and Arabic. (tale 13)

Ety Eylam (Bejarano) was born in Tel Aviv in 1947, where she still lives. She studied at the Tel-Barukh School. When Matilda Koén-Sarano was presenting at the Museum Bet Hatfutzot in 1992, she met Ety, who was working there and who told her this tale. Ety speaks Hebrew, Judeo-Spanish, and English. (tale 48)

Debbie Hasson was born in Miami in 1964 to a Sephardic family. She still lives there and teaches linguistics. She is the daughter of Matilda Koén-Sarano's cousin Vitorina Hadjes Hasson. Debbie took Matilda for rides around Miami during her visit there to participate in a congress commemorating the five hundredth anniversary of the Expulsion of the Jews from Spain, and she told her this single tale while having lunch at a restaurant. As Matilda did not have a tape recorder along, she took the narrative down on a piece of paper. The languages Debbie speaks are Spanish, English, French, Judeo-Spanish, Italian, and Hebrew. She now holds a doctorate in linguistics. (tale 31)

Moshé Ibn Ezra was born in Izmir, Turkey, in 1909. He studied there with his father and made *aliyá* to Israel in 1945. He studied in Kfar Malal, lived in Netania, and died in Kfar Saba in 1988. Matilda Koén-Sarano met Moshé in Netania through his daughter, Maty Shalem, who introduced him when Matilda was there with her husband. She was able to interview him only for an hour at his home, but that short time left her with a profound impression. He told her tales he had learned from his mother, some of which he had represented as plays at his children's school. Shortly afterward Matilda organized a radio program and invited Moshé to participate as one of the storytellers. She called him, asking him to record the tales he recalled, but he responded through the mail: "I am trying to record but only incomprehensible sounds come out." She called him back to let him know that she would visit him in Netania to record him, but he died unexpectedly before she was able to do so. Moshé spoke Hebrew, Judeo-Spanish, Greek, Turkish, Italian, Spanish, French, and German. (tale 1)

Ester Kamar (Navon) was born in the Old City of Jerusalem in 1906 and died there in 1998. She studied at the Lemel School. In 1990 Yaakov Bonano, former director of the Division of Archives at the Interior Ministry in Jerusalem, where Matilda Koén-Sarano worked for many years, took her to the old age home where Ester lived. Ester was the sister of Itzhak Navon, the fifth president of the state of Israel. Matilda used to visit the home periodically to tell tales to the elderly residents. On these occasions she interviewed Ester and recorded several tales. Ester gave Matilda the idea of publishing a volume of Judeo-Spanish ballads and songs, *Vini kantaremos,* suggesting that such a book was needed to bring together a collection of songs that everyone loved to sing. Ester knew Hebrew, Judeo-Spanish, Moroccan Arabic, and French. (tale 4)

SARA KENT (BARUH) was born in 1925 in Istanbul, where she completed her studies, making *aliyá* to Israel in 1972. She lives in Tel Aviv. Matilda Koén-Sarano met Sara at a WIZO Sephardic women's group where she was asked by those present to tell humorous tales (Djohá, Makeda, etc.). At the end of the session, Sara told Matilda a Djohá tale, which Matilda took down in writing since she did not have her tape recorder. Sara's languages are Judeo-Spanish, French, Hebrew, English, Greek, Turkish, and Italian. (tale 40)

MATILDA KOÉN-SARANO was born in Milan in 1939 to parents from Turkey. She attended the Jewish Community School there and later the University of Bocconi. She made *aliyá* to Israel in 1960, where she completed her studies in Italian literature, folklore, and Judeo-Spanish at the Hebrew University of Jerusalem. For twenty-three years she worked at the Ministry of Foreign Affairs in Jerusalem, a position from which she is now retired. She taught Judeo-Spanish at Ben-Gurion University in the Negev for five years, and is about to begin teaching Judeo-Spanish culture at the Centre for Classical Oriental Music and Dance in Jerusalem. She also teaches Judeo-Spanish at the National Authority for Ladino and Its Culture in Jerusalem. Matilda contributes twice a week to the radio news in Judeo-Spanish, broadcast by Kol Israel, the national Israeli radio station, and has published a number of Judeo-Spanish collections of tales. She lives in Jerusalem and had heard the tale "La ija del rey i los tres fostanes" in her youth in Italy and retold it in 1988 in Judeo-Spanish. She speaks Italian, Judeo-Spanish, Hebrew, French, Spanish, and English. (tales 19, 50, 51)

STREA KOHEN (LEVY) was born in Izmir, Turkey, in 1926. She studied at the neighborhood school in the Budurali neighborhood. She made *aliyá* to Israel in 1949 and now lives in Jerusalem. She belongs to the Storytellers' Circle run by Matilda Koén-Sarano since 1987 and told many tales during the monthly meetings at the home of one of the members. Anyone could attend these sessions and participate, telling tales, singing and dancing, as long as they did so in Judeo-Spanish. Strea speaks Turkish, Hebrew, and Judeo-Spanish. (tale 47)

ALEX KORFIATIS was born in Jerusalem in 1947. His grandparents had come from Corfu. He was educated at Geula High School and later studied art in Germany and Greece. He told this tale in Hebrew in 1993. Matilda Koén-Sarano met Alex through the singer Betty Klein, with whom she collaborates on Judeo-Spanish programs of songs and tales. Each time Matilda meets Alex, he tells her new tales. He is a jeweler, and while making bracelets for Matilda he told her a few tales. Alex speaks Hebrew, Greek, English, Arabic, and German. (tales 33, 41)

ESTER LEVY (IFRAH) was born in Jerusalem in the old neighborhood of Yemín Moshé in 1920. She studied at the school of the Alliance Israélite Universelle and still lives in Jerusalem. Matilda Koén-Sarano met Ester in 1987 through one of her colleagues from the Ministry of Foreign Affairs, Ester's daughter Rahel, who had bought Matilda's book, *Kuentos del folklor de la famiya djudeo-espanyola,* for her mother in 1986. Ester then invited Matilda to interview her friend Sol Maymaran, but when she visited her, she discovered that Ester was no less of a storyteller herself. The two of them founded the Storytellers' Circle. She is a vital informant for Matilda, who often sends her students to her to complete their assignments if there are no Judeo-Spanish speakers in their own families. Matilda also invited Ester to her radio program several times and to conferences as a storyteller who also knows many songs. She is fluent in Hebrew, Judeo-Spanish, Arabic, French, and English. (tales 14, 54)

MALKA LEVY (DASA) was born in Jerusalem in the old neighborhood of Yemín Moshé in 1918. She attended the school of the Alliance Israélite Universelle and lived in Jerusalem until her death in 1994. Matilda Koén-Sarano met Malka in 1988, after a pain in her arm brought her to a health clinic for an examination. The doctor who examined her mentioned a woman who knew many tales. That same evening Matilda went to visit Malka. Matilda recorded her tales on several occasions at her home as well as part of the Storytellers' Circle, which Malka joined. She was a limitless source of tales of every genre. Matilda invited her to the radio station to tell tales and also to join her and Ester Levy at a *nochada* (an evening of performance) in celebration of the end of a course on performance at the Bet-Ariela Center in Tel Aviv. At that time they were all introduced as "genuine" storytellers, that is, as tellers who had not studied the art of performance. Malka knew Hebrew, Judeo-Spanish, French, English, and Arabic. (tales 16, 27)

SHOSHANA LEVY (GERSHON) was born in Istanbul in 1927. She studied at the school of the Alliance Israélite Universelle and made *aliyá* to Israel in 1948. She lived in Jerusalem until her death in 1998. Matilda Koén-Sarano came in contact with Shoshana at the meetings of the group Sefarad in the 1980s. In 1988, when she asked her if she knew any tales and Shoshana responded in the affirmative, Matilda invited her to her home where she narrated many tales. Matilda immediately invited her to join the Storytellers' Circle. In addition to telling tales, Shoshana also enjoyed singing and dancing. She spoke Judeo-Spanish, Hebrew, English, French, Turkish, and Greek. (tales 9, 45, 49)

KOHAVA PIVIS (CHIKUREL) was born in Izmir, Turkey, in 1943 and came to Israel in 1949. She attended the Givat Washington School and then took a course on performance at Bet-Ariela. She lives in Petah-Tikva, and Matilda Koén-Sarano met her in 1992 at a Storytellers' Day organized by the Ministry of Education and Culture as part of the events commemorating the five hundredth anniversary of the Expulsion of the Jews from Spain. She now has joined Matilda's Storytellers' Circle. She performs as a storyteller and has published a children's book of Judeo-Spanish tales in Hebrew, *Sir Haplayím* (The magic pot), (Yaron Golan, Tel Aviv, 1996). Kohava speaks Judeo-Spanish, Hebrew, Turkish, French, English, Yiddish, and Arabic. (tales 5, 12)

LEVANA SASSON (SABA) was born in Jerusalem in 1942 to a mother from Turkey and a father from Greece. She attended the Seligsberg School and lives in Jerusalem. Matilda Koén-Sarano met her in the 1970s during her activities in the women's movement, Emunah. When she founded her Storytellers' Circle, she invited Levana to join it. Levana tells many tales originating from the Me'am Lo'ez, which she had heard from her family. She speaks Hebrew and Judeo-Spanish. (tale 8)

MATY (MATILDA) SHALEM (IBN EZRA) was born in Tsur Moshé, Israel, in 1945. She studied at the Teachers' School in Netania, where she lives. Matilda Koén-Sarano met her in Netania in 1988, when she participated in a study weekend organized by the Association for the Preservation and Development of the Yemenite Jewish Heritage where Maty was secretary. Maty took Matilda to interview her father. Maty told her tale in this volume in 1992, during a radio program in memory of her father. She speaks Hebrew, Judeo-Spanish, Greek, and English. (tale 6)

HAYIM TSUR was born in Jerusalem in 1938. He attended high school there and pursued his education at the Academy of Music at the Hebrew University of Jerusalem. He also studied in the United States and now lives in Jerusalem. A violinist, he serves as director of the Division of Folklore at Kol Israel, the national Israeli radio station. Matilda Koén-Sarano has known him since 1979 but never thought of interviewing him until he asked her to participate in his program *El narrador de kuentos* (The teller of tales) and she discovered that he was a good performer. In 1992, when she asked him to narrate tales in Judeo-Spanish, he told her not only tales but also proverbs, blessings, curses, etc. He encouraged her to write poetry and songs, and together they have issued two CDs and produced four musicals. He is fluent in Portuguese, Hebrew, English, Arabic, French, Spanish, and Judeo-Spanish. (tales 26, 34)

RAFAEL VALANSI was born in Entreríos, in the Argentine province of Córdoba, in 1925, to a mother from Izmir. He studied in Buenos Aires and still lives there. Matilda Koén-Sarano met him in 1992 in Buenos Aires when she attended an international conference of Spanish and Latin-American writers. He sought her out at Clara Salem's house, at the latter's invitation, and he told tales in Judeo-Spanish, which was clearly no longer his language but that of his parents. The effort he had to make to use the language was evident, but it was as apparent that he was willing to do so with much pleasure and affection. He speaks Spanish and some Judeo-Spanish. (tale 29)

ESTER VENTURA (ROMANO) was born in Izmir, Turkey, in 1930. She made *aliyá* to Israel in 1949 and studied at the Ulpan Katznelson in Jerusalem, where she still lives. Matilda Koén-Sarano met her through the late Valentina Tsoref, who was one of the best tellers of the Storytellers' Circle. The tales in this collection are some of the many Ester told at the circle. She would never agree to being recorded separately. Her languages are Turkish, Judeo-Spanish, Hebrew, and Greek. (tales 11, 15, 24, 37, 43)

SARA YOHAY was born in Barcelona in 1937. Her grandparents were from Turkey but lived in Kavala, Greece. She moved to Athens in 1939 and attended Greek schools as well as Saint Joseph, a French high school. She studied ballet at the Royal Academy of London and lived in Milan from 1959 to 1967, when she made *aliyá* to Israel. She was a dancer with Imbal, an Israeli dance company, and ran a children's dance school in Netania, where she lived until her death in 1997. In the 1960s she worked for the Jewish Community of Milan where Matilda Koén-Sarano's father also worked as secretary of the community. After Matilda's first book appeared, Sara contacted her through a common friend, Hanna Adorian, and informed her that she knew a large repertoire of tales and was willing to be interviewed. In 1988 she went to Matilda's office in Jerusalem, and Matilda recorded her there. They stayed in touch after that. Sara would often send Matilda her Judeo-Spanish prose or poetry writings and Matilda would look for a publication venue for her work. Sara also attended the Storytellers' Circle and would often participate as a teller in the *nochadas* of "Vini kantaremos," Matilda's monthly evenings of songs and tales. She spoke Greek, Spanish, Judeo-Spanish, French, English, Italian, Hebrew, Turkish, Portuguese, and Catalan. (tales 2, 3, 7, 17, 23, 36, 38, 42)

A Note on Judeo-Spanish

Spanish Jews whose ancestors were forcibly banished from the land of their birth for religious—and some say economic, social, and even racial—reasons and were subsequently scattered all over the welcoming Ottoman Empire still display an extraordinary attachment to the language of the Inquisition. This much beloved tongue, the language of everyday life, severed long ago from its original homeland and from the still evolving peninsular vernacular and left to undertake its own isolated linguistic journey, still preserves archaic terms and expressions from the medieval Spanish of the exiled ancestors of modern-day Sephardim. Today the use of Judeo-Spanish conveys nostalgia for the way of life of the Sephardic communities in the Mediterranean that thrived until the devastation of World War II.

Only after the forced exile from Spain did the language of Spanish-speaking Jews actually become a specifically Jewish language. Within the communities of the Ottoman Empire where Sephardic Jews found refuge and settled, there was no urge to extirpate the old ways. This was a polyglot world. Over time and under the external pressures of the local languages and, later, of French—due to the powerful influence of the Alliance Israélite Universelle[1]—the language slowly evolved. Judeo-Spanish speakers adopted terms from local languages. As a result of geographical diversity, these languages have had a significant influence on the development of what is today the surviving language of the Sephardim.

Like Yiddish, Judeo-Spanish used to be phonetically represented with Hebrew letters, identified as Rashi characters.[2] Today, there is still no agreement on how to transliterate this predominantly romance dialect into Latin characters. Likewise, this spoken tongue is referred to by many names—Judeo-Spanish, Judezmo, Spanyol, Spanyolit, and Ladino.[3] Scholars cannot seem to agree on any one term.

Over the centuries the language has become an expressive and beautiful means of communication that conveys both common sense and mental images in succinct and expressive ways and easily delivers a lesson or message. As they traveled in different countries and absorbed different cultures into their own, Sephardic Jews amassed a new set of words and expressions they hold dear.

In the speech of Sephardim who now make their home in Israel, Judeo-Spanish is at a crossroad in time and space. It still reflects some of the basic phonetics and syntax of medieval Castilian Spanish, and its morphology follows descriptive characteristics of gender and number. Some adverbs that have disappeared from modern Spanish are preserved (*agora:* now; *aínda:* still; *muncho:* much). Preserved also are archaic (*ambezár:* to learn; *chapeo:* hat; *hazino:* grieved, afflicted, ill) or specialized Spanish words (*meldár:* to read), and some that have undergone a change of meaning (*escapár:* to finish). The use of diminutive forms of nouns and adjectives is widespread and varied. All of these forms coexist in this period of perpetual change.

Many of our tellers engage in the common Sephardic practice of word corruption, drawing missing words from other languages and adapting them to their speech. They give a representative sample of the communicative forms borrowed from various linguistic media interwoven in the tales, highlighting natural dynamism and a process of ongoing linguistic change. The tales are performed in a Judeo-Spanish infused with everyday words in Greek, Turkish, French, and Italian, as well as heavy borrowing from the Hebrew acquired in Israel, especially but not only terms of religious significance. They are peppered with names of holidays in Hebrew, with Sephardic names, and with names of Jewish or Turkish cities and biblical characters.

Substitutions and contaminations are commonplace. Hebrew words such as Yom Kippúr, Kol Nidré, Brit Milá, *hahám,* arvít, musáf, *ketubá, alef-bet, amares (am ha-aretz), berahá,* and *sedaká* appear side by side with common everyday Hebrew words and expressions such as *az, tov, avál, yalla, aba,* and *ben.* In addition to the implanted Hebrew lexicon, one finds Hispanicized French, Hebrew, or Turkish words. Some of these borrowings are given Spanish form simply by adding prefixes and suffixes (*seheludo:* intelligent; *atakanado:* well-groomed). One also finds Spanish words with Hebrew prefixes or suffixes (*ladroním:* thieves).

In short, Judeo-Spanish provided the glue that bonded the Sephardic community for centuries, part of the larger society yet separate from its neighbors. By keeping alive language, customs, and cookery, generations of women and men were actually the upholders of the Sephardic tradition, the bearers, transmitters, and sustainers of its rich culture.

Notes

1. Founded in 1860, this is the first modern international Jewish organization intended for Jews to help fellow Jews wherever they were in distress due to their religion. Its aims were to work everywhere for the emancipation and progress of Jews, to offer effective assistance to Jews suffering from anti-Semitism, and to encourage all publications that promoted this aim. It was administered from Paris, with a resulting French centralism. It conducted diplomatic activities, provided assistance to emigrants, and concentrated on education, especially in the Ottoman Empire—the Balkans and the Middle East—where most of the Sephardim lived. This eventually created some controversy since the propagation of the French language and culture in the schools, while very successful in educating the Jewish population, was often viewed as a danger to the local culture of the communities and to traditional Jewish life. As a consequence of the creation of the state of Israel and after the exodus of Jews from the Arab world, the Alliance schools were either closed or they steadily lost their character.

2. Rashi, Rabbi Solomon bar Isaac, was an eleventh-century French Jewish exegete, grammarian, and legal authority. He wrote commentaries on the Bible and the Talmud that still rank among the most authoritative. He used a cursive writing referred to as the Rashi script.

3. *Hakitía* is the Judeo-Spanish spoken by the Sephardim of northern Morocco.

Glossary

Key

Alb.	Albanian	Moz.	Mozarabic
Ar.	Arabic	O. Sp.	Old Spanish
Aram.	Aramaic	Ot. T.	Ottoman Turkish
Bulg.	Bulgarian	Pers.	Persian
Fr.	French	Port.	Portuguese
Gr.	Greek	S.-Cr.	Serbo-Croation
H.	Hebrew	Sp.	Spanish
It.	Italian	T.	Turkish

Guide to Pronunciation: Since there is no established, uniform mode of transliteration for Judeo-Spanish, the method used here is for the convenience of the English-speaking reader who may not be familiar with the language. The placement of an accent on a vowel indicates that the oral stress is on that syllable. When no accent appears, the stress is on the penultimate syllable of the word.

a	as in	"ah"
e	as	"eh"
i	as in	"feel"
o	as in	"old"
u	as in	"boot"
ch	as in	"check"
g	as in	"goal"
j	as in	"abajour"
k	as in	"car"
sh	as in	"show"
z	as in	"zebra"
h	as in	"Chanukah" (Judeo-Spanish)
h	as in	"heaven" (Hebrew)
kh	as in	"Chanukah" (Hebrew)

aba. (H.) Father.
achetó. (achetaron [plural]) (It. *accettare*) Accepted; agreed.
addió. Oh God! An invocation of God due to surprise, grief, etc.
adjilé. (T. *âcil*) Haste; hurry; urgency.
adovár. To repair; to fix.
afalagár. (Sp. *halagar*; maybe through Catalan from the Arabic *halaq*) To smooth out; to polish; to treat kindly. Also to flatter; to give comfort to; to console.
afartásh. (O. Sp. *hartar*) You surfeit; satisfy; satiate.
aferró. (Sp. *aferrar*) Grabbed; caught; seized.
afilu. (H.) Even; even though; even if; also.
afsikó. (H. *lehafsik*) Stopped.
agora. (O. Sp.) Now.
agorá. (H.) Penny.
agrafe(s). (Fr.) Hooks; clasps; buckles. Here, probably pins; brooches.
a-hafetsá. (H. *ha-khafetsá*) The one who wishes.
aharvár. (H., Ar., T.) Beat up; hit; strike. *Aharvándose* is the reflexive form.
áhsan. (T. *ahsen*; Ar. *ahsan*) Good; better; best; prettiest; more/most beautiful.
ahvát. (H. *ahavá*) Love; peace.
aikár. (H. *ha-ikar*) The most essential point; the main thing.
aínda. (O. Sp.) Still; yet; in addition.
aite. *See* ayde.
akchés. (T. *akçe*) Money; small coin; farthing; half or one-third of a *pará*.
a la fín. (Fr.) In the end. *See enfín*
alat(es). (T. *alât*) Set of tools, instrument(s), implement(s).
aláy. (T.) Procession; pageant; group; cohort; a band of people; a good number; countless; a cohort of rowdy people.
alé. (H.) Rise up.
alef. (H.) First letter of Hebrew alphabet.
alef-bet. (H.) The Hebrew alphabet. Figuratively, the most elementary knowledge.
alhád. (Ar.) Sunday, the first day. (It had already come into the Sp. spoken by Jews before the Expulsion.)
almaná. (H.) Widow.
almenara(s). (O. Sp., Ar. *minha*r) Multiarm chandelier, candelabra, light. Here it means the house, filled with chandeliers, nothing but bright lights shining.
almisklár. (Sp. *almizcle*; T. *misk*) Perfume oneself, usually with musk or sweet-smelling soap.
alora. (It. *allora*) So; then; in that case; at that time.

amá. (T. *ama*) Still; but; yet; however.

amahó. (Ar. *maha:* to wipe out, eradicate; H. *maha:* to erase, rub off) Was cured. *Amahar* was already used in pre-Expulsion Judeo-Spanish and in the language of moriscos.

amán. (T. *amân*) Pardon! Mercy! Help! Alas! For goodness sake! Also an interjection of unhappiness: Oh! Ah! Oh my God!

amares. (H. *am ha-aretz*) Ignoramus; illiterate.

ambezár. (O. Sp.) Teach; learn; become accustomed to (*ambezen:* they learn).

ameleh. (H. *ha-melekh*) The king.

anagá. (H. *hanagá*) Leadership; guidance.

aní. (H.) I.

aní. (H. *'aní*) Poor. The expression *prove aní* emphasizes the poverty and need of the character. The repetition of the concept of poverty in *prove* (Sp. pobre: poor) and *aní* creates a particular narrative style.

anshugár. Trousseau; dowry.

ansi. (O. Sp. *así*) So; thus

arabá. (T. *araba*) Turkish carriage; coach; cart, small wagon; usually horse-driven.

arabadjí. (T. *arabaci*) Coachman.

argish(ates). (H. *leharguish*) You felt.

arivó. (It. *arrivare*) Arrived; reached.

armón. (H.) Palace.

arrematasión. An exclamation of despair, such as "Go to the devil!" Wishing the total destruction of the one causing trouble.

arremendár. Mend; patch up; repair.

arvít. (H. *arvit*) Evening prayer.

Ashmedáy. (H.) Asmodeus, king of demons.

askamá. (H. *haskamá*) Decision; consent; agreement. Here, religious guidance.

askér (es). (T.) Soldier.

aspera. (It.) Wait

atakanado. (H. *letaken*) Fixed up; ordered; well groomed. (T. *takinmak*) To wear (ornaments).

avál. (H.) But.

Avramachí. Nickname or affectionate name for Abraham. (*Achi* is a Turkish suffix added to names of titles.)

ayde. Pan-Balkanic exclamation or interjection like *yallah* (let's go!). (Sp. *ala*; vámonos!) (T. *haydi*: hurry up; go on; now then; let's go) (S.-Cr. *hajde*; [it takes verb endings]) (Alb. *hajde*) (Bulg. *haide*: come on; jump to it; run or go along.)

ayin ará. (H. *ayin ha-ra*) Evil eye.
az. (H.) So; then; at that time.
aziéndose hadras. Coquettish gestures; playing the coquette; putting on airs; to give oneself an air of importance. The expression *hadras y baraná* is used to describe someone trying to be noticed or a woman who takes great pains to attract a man's amorous attention.
azno. Donkey; ass. Also ignorant; stupid; idiot; incompetent.

baayót. (H.) Problems.
bafo. (O. Sp., Port.) Breath.
bahché. (T. *bahçe*) Garden; vegetable garden.
bakál. (T. *bakkal*) Grocer; storekeeper. Also grocery.
baklabá (T. *baklava*) Sweet pastry-cake filled with nuts (walnuts or pistachios) and honey, cut in lozenges (diamond-shaped pieces).
baklabadjí. (T. *baklavaci*) Baklava maker/vendor.
balo. (It. *ballo*; T. *balo*) Ball; dance party.
baltá. (T. *balta*) Axe; hatchet.
baluhchí. (T. *balikçi*) Fisherman; fishmonger.
baraná. (T. *bapirma*) A great deal of noise and commotion. See *aziéndose hadras* and *hadras*.
barminán. (H. or Aram.) Alas; God forbid; away be it from us.
barúh abá. (H.) Welcome! Blessed be the newcomer.
bashustoné. (T. *baş üstüne*) Very well, sir! Alright, sir! At your service; with great pleasure. Literally, "on top of one's head," meaning that your wish or request will be taken care of.
bavá. Grandmother.
bay. (T. bey/bay) See *bey*.
bazár. (Pers.) Bazaar; an oriental market consisting of rows of shops or stalls with miscellaneous goods for sale.
be. (H.) In.
beemét. (H. *be emet*) Truthfully; in truth; really. Sometimes appears as *bemét*.
beit(í). (H. *bayit*) My house (possessive case).
bekleando. (T. *beklemek*) Guarding; watching over.
bel. (T.) Waist; loins.
belá. (T. *belâ*) Troubles; misfortune; calamity; grief; nuisance.
bemét. See *beemét*.
ben. (H.) Son.
benadám. (H. *ben adam*) Son of Adam; man; person; human being.
berahá. (H.) Blessing.
berbér (es). (T.) Barber(s).

beseder. (H. *be seder*) Okay; alright; fine.
beshúm ofen. (H.) On no account; by no means.
bet. (H.) Second letter of Hebrew alphabet.
Bet Amikdásh. (H.) The Holy Temple.
betamús. Of the Jewish month of Tamuz.
bey. (T.) Bey; gentleman; lord; prince; chief; mister. Here, also a term of endearment: my dear.
bezrát Ashém. (H. *be ezrat ha-shem*) With the help of God.
bienfezensias. (Fr. *bienfaisance*) Good deeds; philanthropy.
bijú. (Fr. *bijou*) Jewel.
bijutié. (Fr. *bijoutier*) Jeweler.
biko. (Port. *bico*) Beak. It was used by Spanish-Portuguese Jews of Amsterdam in the seventeenth century.
binyán. (H.) Building.
birít. (H.) Covenant; the covenant of circumcision.
blú. Blue, in Monastir dialect.
bogo. (T. *bohça*) Cloth; wrapper; bundle of clothes. It may also be *bürgü*: cover; scarf; cloak; kerchief; veil; woman's cloak; wrapper.
bohora. (H. *bekhorá*). Firstborn; often the name of the firstborn.
bokál(iko). Small jug, pitcher, or bottle. First appeared in 1517. Found in the Arabic of the Iberian Peninsula in the thirteenth century. Probably of Italian influence.
borundjúk. (T. *bürümcük*) Wrap.
bosko. (It.) Woods; small forest.
botika. (T; Sp. *botica*) Retail shop; drugstore. Also *butika*.
boy. (T.) Size; length; height; measurement.
bre. (Sp. *hombre?*) Hey you! Now then! Used to catch someone's attention; to express fear surprise, indignation, admiration, disapproval.
brit. (H. *berit*) Covenant; the covenant of circumcision. Also *birít*.
bruto. (It. *brutto*) Ugly; bad.
bufár. (Fr. *bouffer*) Eat to excess; to become inflated.
bukra. (Ar.) Tomorrow; euphemism for never.
bula. (H. *beulah, balabayit*; T. *bulisa*) Lady; spouse. Used to address a woman of a certain age.
bundjúk (es). (T. *boncuk*) Bead.
butika. (T. *botika*; O. Sp.; Fr. *boutique*) Shop; store; commercial business.
buyá. (T. *boya*) Dye; paint; color; rouge.
buyrún. (T. *buyurun*) Welcome! Will you please come in, sit down, help yourself? You are welcome! Sometimes appears as *buyrúm*.
buz. (T.) Ice.

chafteár. (H. *khavat*; T. *çarpmak, çatişmak*, or *çiftlemek*) Strike; knock on something. (*Chafteó/chafteamos:* he struck/we strike.)

chambís. Bunches.

chapaleando. (T. *çabalamak/çabalanmak*) Strive; endeavor; work hard at; make convulsive movements or efforts; an indication of agitation and distress.

chapeo. (O. Sp.) Hat.

charé. (T. *çaşe*) Care; remedy; solution; help.

charshí. (T. *çarli*) Marketplace; bazaar; street with shops; shopping district (usually for non-food items).

chay(iziko). (T. *çai*) Tea (with the Spanish diminutive suffix *"iko"*).

chelték. (T. *koltuk*) Armchair; fauteuil (or T. *çilte:* mattress).

chiní. (T. *çini*) Fine china; porcelain; dish; plate.

chizmé. (T. *çizme*) Top-boot; high-boot; Wellington.

churap. (T. *çorap*) Sock; hose; stocking.

dag. (H.) Fish.

dalet. (H.) Fourth letter of Hebrew alphabet.

dallál. (T. *tellâl, dellál*; Ar. *dallál*) Public crier; broker. *See delales.*

dantela(s). (T. *dantelâ*) Lace; lacework.

dechizó. (It. *decidere*) Decided; made up one's mind; resolved.

delales. (T. *tellâl, dellál;* Ar. *dallál*) Town criers. *See dallál.*

depasates. (Fr. *dépasser la mesure*) You exaggerate, exceed the limits.

desbragado. Very poor person (figuratively); literally, having no breeches on.

deynda. (Port.) Just; still; more.

dezmazalado. (H. *mazal*) Unlucky; unfortunate; without luck; deprived of luck.

diezén. (Fr. *dixième*) Tenth.

Dió. God, the Almighty. Note the singular use in contrast to the Spanish *Dios*. One interpretation indicates that Sephardic Jews use the singular as opposed to what they interpret to be the plural *Dios* of the Trinity.

divizaremos. (Fr. *diviser*) We'll divide up.

djánum. (T. *hanim*) Lady; Mrs.; Miss. Also an expression of affection: darling, dear (T. *canim:* my soul). *See hanum.*

djenitores. (It. *genitori*) Parents.

djep. (T. *ceb*) Pocket; purse.

djépea. (T. *kepya*) Pool or basin in a garden or a patio.

djevaerdjí. (T. *cevherci*) Jeweler.

djirando. (It. *girare*) Running around; whirling; revolving; rotating.

djizvé. (T. *cezvé*) Oriental coffeepot with long handle.

dubara. (T., Pers.) Tumult; disturbance; a great deal of confused, clattering noise; loud voices; racket. It derives from the backgammon game when the dice are thrown and come up with all twos. The player shouts out: *Dubara!*

edá. (H.) Community.
efendi. (T.) Master; sir; gentleman. Formerly used after a name, as Mister.
elevos. (Fr. *élèves*) Pupils.
Eliau Anaví. (H. Eliyahu *Ha-naví*) Elijah the Prophet.
emuná. (H.) Faith.
enfasár. (Fr. *effacer*) To erase, change, alter, or wipe out.
enfín. (Sp. *en fin;* Fr. *enfin*) Finally, at last. See *a la fín*
englutír. (Fr. *engloutir;* O. Sp.) Gulp; swallow up; absorb in large quantity.
enkashar. To stuff. Here it appears in the imperative of the reflexive: *enkáshate (la)*.
ensatanár. (H. *satán?*) To incite; tempt with devilish ideas. In the reflexive form, to become violently agitated or engage in frenetic activity as if possessed by the devil.
ensupitó. (It. *subito*) Suddenly; at once; right away.
erev. (H.) Eve; evening.
Estanból. (T.) Istanbul.
estanbullí. (T.) Inhabitant of Istanbul. Also, a very clever person.
Esterina. Woman's name, diminutive of Esther.

facha. (It. *faccia*) Face.
facha kon facha. (Fr. *face à face*) Face-to-face.
fiksár. (Fr. *fixer*) To fix; to arrange; to set (*fiksí, fiksó, fiksaron* are all past tense: arranged).
firmán. (T. *ferman*) Imperial or royal decree, edict, or command.
fishék. (T. *fişek/fiskiye*) Forceful jet of water; spurt; firecracker; firework.
fistán. (T. *fistan*) Skirt; petticoat; dress. Found in peninsular Arabic and Spanish since 1289. See *fostán*
fluka. (T. *floka*) Felucca; ship.
fostán(ikos). (T. *fistan*) Skirt; petticoat; dress ("*ikos*" is a Spanish diminutive suffix). See also *fistán*
fulán. (H., Ar.) An undetermined individual; a person whose name is unknown; a so and so. *Fulano* and *fulana* are the masculine and feminine terms.

gadér. (H.) Fence.
galecha. (Gr. *galéntza;* Fr. *galoche*) A wooden shoe; a sabot.

Galíl. Galilee; the Sea of Galilee.
galú. (H. *galut*) Literally, exile; captivity. Here a scandal; a disorderly situation.
garón. (H.) Throat.
gató. (Fr. *gâteau*) Cake.
gefen. (H.) Vine.
gevír. (T. *kebir*) Notable; great; important; eminent; rich person; a gentleman.
gevúl. (H. *gvul*) Border; frontier; limit.
gezerá. (H.) Divine decree (usually as a chastisement); sentence; condemnation. Also calamity; edict; predestination. Often it is an anti-Semitic law, hence, by extension, a disaster, a public misfortune.
gimel. (H.) Third letter of Hebrew alphabet.
gizandón. (O. Sp.) A cook.
grosh. (T. *kuruş*, Ot. T. *guruş*, H. *grush*) One one-hundredth of a Turkish pound; a silver coin; a piastre.
guáy(as). (O. Sp., from Ar. *wai;* It. *guaiare:* to lament) Lament; lamentation; cry; exclamation of anguish; pain; grief. The Spanish expression *echar guayas* is an interjection of lament that existed in the early Middle Ages.
guezmava. (O. Sp.) Smelled; filled up with the smell of (usually a good smell).

habér. (T.) News; knowledge; information. *No tener habér:* not to know anything about it. See *havér*
hadras. Exaggerated effort to give oneself an air of importance; affectation. *Hazerse hadras:* to be coquettish, to endeavor to attract attention in an exaggerated fashion. See *aziéndose hadras*. See also *baraná*.
haftoná. (H. *khavatá*) Strike; blow; slap; spanking; a good beating.
hahám. (H.) Clever; intelligent; knowledgeable; educated; wise. (*hahamá* is the feminine; *hahamím* is the plural). Also a Sephardic rabbi.
hal(es). (T. *hal*) Condition; situation; state; circumstance.
hamám. (T.) Public bath, esp. a Turkish bath (different from *mikvá*).
hamishá. (H.) Five.
hamula. (T. *hamule*) A family clan; load; charge. Here, a large group of children.
han. (T.) Inn; caravansarai.
handjí. (T. *hanci*) Innkeeper.
hanum(es). (T. *hanim*) Turkish lady; madam; my lady. Also an affectionate name: my dear.
has ve-halila. (H.) God forbid! Sometimes *halila ve- hal.*
has ve-shalóm. (H.) God forbid.

hatír. (T. *hatir*) Favor; courtesy; consideration; a special kindness one person expects from another; a favor afforded a friend.
hatsí. (H.) Half.
havér. (H.) Partner; associate. See *habér*.
havúz. (T. *havuz*) Lake; pond; pool; artificial basin with jet of water.
hayál(es). (H.) Soldiers.
hazán. (H.) Cantor.
hazinientos. (T. *hüzün*) Tending to be sick; sickly; diseased; sad; melancholy.
hazino. (Ar., T. *hazin*) Sad; mournful; sorrowful; grieved; afflicted; ill; sick; indisposed. T. borrowed *hazin* from Ar., but *hazino* existed in O. Sp so Judeo-Spanish word is of Iberian Peninsular origin; Ibn Quzman uses *hazin* in a bilingual verse, as if it were a Moz. romance word.
hazinura. (T. *hüzün, hazin*) Sadness; sorrow; melancholy; grief; illness; sickness; the state of being *hazino*.
hazné. (T. *hazine*) Public treasury; exchequer. Figuratively, treasure; riches.
hevrá. (H.) Company; group; club; fraternity.
hol(ót). (H.) Sand (plural).
hursh. (T. *hurç*) Saddlebag; packsaddle; large leather bag or sack; hold-all.

i. (H. *hi*) She (is).
ija d'un mamzér. (H.) Daughter of a bastard.
ima. (H.) Mother.
improvizo. (It. *improvviso*) Suddenly; unexpectedly; impromptu.
iné. (T. *yine*) Again; once more; still; yet; despite everything; in spite of; nonetheless.
innát. (T. *inat*) Obstinacy; contrariness; stubbornness; obduracy; defiance; persistence beyond reason; capriciousness.
ishtí. (H.) My wife.

jaketiko. (T. *ceket, caket;* from Fr. *jacquette*) Jacket; vest; coat (with the Spanish diminutive *"iko"*).
jurnál. (Fr. *journal*) Newspaper.

kadayíf(es). (T.) Any of various kinds of sweet oriental pastry made of fine shredded wheat with honey and nuts (particularly pistachio nuts) or with custard.
kadi. (T.) Moslem judge.
kafuriarse. (T. *küfür,* H. *kafrar*) To swear, curse, blaspheme; to deny God's existence; to get angry, growl, become furious. Reflexive verb.

kal. (H. *kahal*) Community; multitude; public assembly; congregation; synagogue.
kaleja. Alley; lane.
kambúr. (T.) Hunchback(ed); round-backed; crooked; warped.
kampanya. (Fr. *campagne*) Countryside.
kantón. Corner
kapache. (It. *capace*) Clever; able; capable (Monastir dialect).
karahat. (H.) Baldness.
karár. (T. *kadar* + *karar*) Right quantity; reasonable degree; so much; so many; about; approximately; amount; degree.
kare ke/kale ke. (O. Sp.) It's necessary to; one must.
karpúz. (T.) Watermelon.
kartié. (Fr. *quartier*) Quarter; district; neighborhood.
kasáp. (T. *kasap*) Butcher.
kaskereado. (T. *karişmak/kariştirmak*) Confused, mixed up, jumbled, muddled, complicated. (It should be *karishtereado* or *kashtereado*.)
katifé. (T. *kadife*) Velour; velvet.
kavakár. To dig. Also *kavakando*: digging.
kavalier. (Fr. *cavalier*) Horseman; rider.
kavané. (T. *kahvehane*) Coffeehouse; café.
kavé. (T. *kahve*) Turkish coffee.
kavód. (H.) Honor; respect.
kazál. (Port. *casal*) Hamlet; village (outside of a big city).
keilá. (H. *kehilá*) Congregation; synagogue; community. See *killá*.
kelár. Cellar.
kestión. (Fr. *question*) Question; matter.
ketubá. (H.) Marriage contract.
kever. (H.) Grave.
kieratá. (T. *kerata*) Pander, knave; scoundrel; rascal (referring to a very clever, very skilled person).
killá. (H. *kehilá*) congregation; synagogue; community. See *keilá*
Kineret. (H.) Sea of Galilee, in Israel.
kish. Cry to frighten or to chase animals such as cats, dogs, hens, etc.
kita. (O. Sp.) A divorcee; repudiated wife (usually due to barrenness).
kiviahól. (H.) Pretend.
kizdirialdo. (T. *kizdirmak*) To anger, annoy, irritate him.
koan(ím). (H. *kohen*) High priest(s).
kodjamá. (T. *kocaman*) Huge; large; great; enormous. Note syntactic difference: *kodjamá sivdá*.
koláy. (T.) Easy; simple; without hassle.

koliés. (Fr. *colliers*) Necklaces.

Kol Nidré. (H.) Solemn opening prayer on the eve of the Day of Atonement liturgy to ask God's forgiveness for any vows or promises made to Him that may have been broken (also appears as *Kal Nidré*).

kolonia. (T. *kolonya*) Eau de cologne.

kómo. (Sp.) How?

konchentos. Morning sickness.

kondurero. (T. *kundura*) Shoemaker.

konduria. (T. *kundura*) Shoe, footwear.

konseja. Tale, folktale, anecdote, story.

koraje. (Fr. *courage*) Courage; determination; daring.

korridór. (Fr. *corridor*) Narrow hallway.

kos.huegra. (Sp. *Consuegra*) Co-mother-in-law. Relationship between women whose son and daughter are married to each other.

kubbe. (T.) Dome; cupola (here, typical delicacies filled with meat in the form of balls or torpedoes).

kushák. (T. *kuşak*) Belt; girdle; sash used as a belt.

kusúr. (T.) Remainder of a sum of money; change (here, the remainder of a cake).

kutí(ko). (T. *kutu*) Small chest, box, or case with a cover.

kuyumjulár. (T. *kuyumculuk*) Jeweler; goldsmith; silversmith.

lakah(ti). (H. *lakahat*) I have taken.

lampo. (It.) Lightning flash; a flash; an instant (Sp. *como un relámpago*).

landra. (O. Sp.) Pest; budding ulcer; pustule; tumor; illness. Also devil; devilish (the sixth plague of Egypt in the biblical story of Moses).

lavór. (It. *lavoro*) Work.

lavoro. (It. *lavoro*) Work.

laylek. (T. *leylek*) Stork.

lehayim. (H.) To life! To your health! Cheers! Skoal!

lesadér. (H.) To fix.

lesón. (Fr. *leçon*) Lesson.

letra. (Fr. *lettre*) Letter. The diminutive is *letrezika* (little letter).

levayá. (H.) Funeral.

líbero. (It. *libero*) Free.

lira. (T.) Turkish currency equal to the pound; one hundred piastres.

lo. (H.) No, not.

lo raíti. (H.) I have not seen.

lules. (H.) Chicken coops.

ma. (Pan-Balkanic conjunction, supported by It.) But; yet; still.
madám. (Fr. *madame*) Madam; lady (in Turkey, used only for non-Turkish women).
magazén. (Fr., Ar., T.) Storeroom; bin; large store; shop.
mahshefá. (H.) Witch.
mahsús. (T.) Specially; expressly; on purpose.
makúsh. (T. *makus*) Pickaxe.
malgrado. (It.) Despite; in spite of.
Malkuna. A woman's name, deriving from *malká* (queen).
malón. (H.) Inn; hotel.
mamzér. (H.) Bastard (*mamzertá* is the feminine; *mamzerím* is the plural).
maná. (H.) Course (on menu).
mantél. (Sp. *mantel,* from Latin *mantel,* T. *mendil*) Tablecloth. Also handkerchief; napkin; towel. Note also modern Gr. *manētli:* handkerchief.
ma pit'óm. (H.) How come? Why suddenly?
martéf. (H.) Cellar.
mashiah. (H.) Messiah.
maskeniko. Poor one. *See meskino; miskén*
maskín. Poor one. See *maskeniko; meskino; miskén*
matrá. (H. *matridá*) Disturbs.
mazál. (H.) Fate; luck; destiny; lot; stars.
meará. (H.) Cave.
medayón. (Fr. *médaillon*) Medallion.
mefursam(ím). (H.) Well-known; famous ("*im*" is the masculine plural ending in Hebrew).
mehes. (H.) Custom; custom tax.
mehubád. (H.) Honorable.
mekubál. (H.) Cabalist; mystic; popular, well-respected scholar.
meldár. (O. Sp.; ultimately, Gr. *meletán?*) To study the Bible and, by extension, simply to read (specialized terminology, always used in a Jewish context; *melden* [they read]).
meldohoneando. (Gr. *meletán?* alteration of *meldar*) To read with wisdom and good understanding. Here the term is aimed at ridiculing what the *azno* is doing, that is, pretending to read with thoughtfulness. *Meldahón* is someone who reads too much and becomes a nerd, an idiot; *meldohonear* may then mean *lire à l'excés, lecturonner.*
meleh. (H.) King.
melumád. (H.) Learned.
menaél. (H. *menahél*) Director; manager.
merás. (T. *miras*) Inheritance; legacy.

Merkada(ucha). Woman's name used as a substitute for a young girl who survives a grave, mortal illness (*ucha* is an affectionate diminutive).
meskino. (O. Sp. *smezquino;* T. *miskin;* It. *meschino*) Poor; wretched; miserable; needy. See *maskeniko; miskén*
mezé. (T. *meze*) Appetizer; snack; tidbits; hors-d'oeuvres.
midbár. (H.) Desert.
midjidiés. (T. *mecidiye*) Formerly, silver coin of about twenty piastres or one-fifth of a gold Turkish pound.
mikvá. (H.) Ritual bath.
milizina. (O. Sp. *melezino*) Medicine; remedy (Rhodes or Bosnian pronunciation; Salonika: *melezina*).
mirákolo. (It. *miracolo*) Miracle.
mirikiyes. (T. *merak*) Become anxious, worried, melancholy, depressed, afflicted, sorrowful, or upset (second-person singular, present tense).
mishpahá. (H.) Family.
mishpát. (H.) Trial.
miskén. (T. *miskin*) Poor, wretched creature; indigent. *Miskeniko* is the diminutive; appears also as *miskin*. See *maskeniko; meskino*.
mitzvá. (H. *mitzvah*) Commandment; good deed.
moré. (H.) Teacher.
mosas. (O. Sp. *mozas*) Girls.
musáf. (H.) Appendage; additional. Refers to a prayer
musafires. (T. *misafir*) Guests; visitors; travelers; company.
musiú. (Fr. *monsieur*) Sir; mister; gentleman.
mutáv. (H.) To reform; to restore to the right way.
mutbáh. (T. *mutbak*) Kitchen.

na. (T., Pan-Balkan) So; so it is; there; here; there it is; behold; take it.
nahón. (H.) True; right; correct.
neemán. (H.) Trustworthy; faithful; conscientious; honest.
nehmadá. (H.) Nice; pleasant.
niddá. (H.) Ritual uncleanliness of a woman caused by her menses.
nishán. (T. *nişan*) Mark; birthmark.
niur. Manners.
nono. (It. *nonno*) Grandfather. Also appears as *nonno*.

odják. (T. *ocak*) Kitchen furnace; oven; fireplace; range (Fr. *fourneau;* Sp. *hogar*).
oka. (T. okka) Oke; an old unit of weight, corresponding to 1282 grams, 400 drams, or 2.83 lbs.

orozo(s). (Fr. *heureux*) Happy.
otsár. (H. *otzar*) Treasury.

pachá. (T. *paça* or *bacak*) Bottom part of the leg(s), from the knee to the ankle. Also cooked drumstick; shank (usually a lamb dish).
palto. (T. *palto;* Fr. *paletot*) Jacket; overcoat.
papás. (Gr. *pappās;* T. *papaz*) Priest; generally a Greek orthodox priest.
papia. Female goose.
papú. (Gr.) Grandfather.
pará. (T. *para*) Money; small coin; currency. A *pará* is one-fortieth of a piastre.
parientes. (Sp.) Relatives.
parnasá. (H.) Livelihood; sustenance; earnings; means of support; financial means by which to subsist; to earn one's bread (to sustain, support oneself).
Paró. (H. *paró*) Pharaoh.
parvino. (Fr. *parvenir*) Reached; achieved; arrived at; accomplished; succeeded in (past tense, third-person singular).
pashá. (T. *paşa*) Honorific title, formerly the highest title of Turkish civil and military officials, now reserved for generals. Among Sephardim, an affectionate nickname for a son or a young man.
patladeár. (T. *patlamak,* with Spanish infinitive ending) To burst; to explode; to burst open; to be furious; to burst with jealousy. *Patlatmak* is the causative form of *patlamak; patladeó* uses the ending for the past tense in Spanish.
patrón(a). Owner; boss.
perashá. (H. *parashá*) Section; division; chapter; book.
permisión. (Fr. *permission*) Permission.
peskésh. (T. *peşkeş*) Gift, present.
pezevéng. (T. *pezevenk*) Cuckold; pander; pimp. A term of general abuse.
pikéah. (H.) Astute; clever; shrewd; intelligent.
pirón. (Gr. *pēroūni*) Fork.
pishín. (T. *peşin*) First; in the first place; suddenly; quickly; on the spot; immediately; as soon as; at once.
plaka. (T. *plâka;* It. *placca;* Fr. *plaque*) Plate; sign.
polís. (T.) Police; policeman.
posta. (T.) Mail; post office. By extension the postal service.
povereta. (It. *poveretta*) The poor one; the needy one. *Povereto* is the masculine adjective.
pranso. (It. *pranzo*) Dinner; banquet.
presto. (It.) Fast; quickly.

preta. (Port.) Black; a black female.
primus. Brand name for an alcohol stove.
puliz(is). (T. *polis*) Police; policemen.
punisión. (Fr. *punition*) Punishment.

ramayár. (H.) To deceive; to swindle.
randevú. (Fr. *rendez-vous*) Date; appointment; meeting.
rango. (Fr. *rang*) Line.
rashá. (H. *rasha*) Wicked; sinful; bad individual.
rav. (H.) Rabbi.
rávano. (Sp.) Radish (person deprived of culture and intelligence; a stupid, worthless individual).
reflo. (It. dialect *reflare?*) Breath.
refuzó. (Fr. *refuser;* O. Sp.) Refused.
regalada. Dearest daughter.
regreto. (Fr. *regretter*) I regret.
remark(en). (Fr. *remarquer*) They notice.
ren(es). (Fr. *rein;* O. Sp. *ren*) Kidney(s).
rengraziár. (It. *ringraziare*) To thank (for).
reshet. (H.) Net.
reushír. (It. *riuscire*) To be successful; to succeed at. Appears also as *riushir.*
rima. (H. *aremá;* T., Ar. *rizma*) A heap, a pile.
rizá. (T. *rida*) Handkerchief.
rodancha. May come from *roda ancha* (a slice). Used as in *rodancha de pertukal* (a slice of orange) or *rodancha de limon* (a slice of lemon). Here, it depicts large circles.
rusfet. (T. *rüşvetçi*) Bribe.

salata. (T.) Salad; lettuce.
sandák. (H.) Godfather who holds the newborn during circumcision ceremony. Appears also as *sandek.*
sandal(as). (T. *sandal*) Sandal(s).
sandelár. (H.) Shoemaker.
sar. (H. *tzaar*) Anguish; fear.
saráy. (T., Ar.) Palace; mansion; royal court.
savá. (H. *tsavaá*) Last will, testament, order. Recommendation given by a dying person that must be obeyed.
sedaká. (H. *tzedaka*) Charity; alms.
sehorá. (H. *shkhorá*) Sadness; sorrow; gloom; depression.
sehoriento. (H. *sekhorá*) Grieving.

semít. (T. *simit*) Ring-shaped sesame-covered bread-roll or bun.
senteando. Sparkling; glistening. Also *senteas:* sparkles.
sha. (O. Sp. *dexa;* Sp. *deja*) Let's see. Apocope; this can be a shortened, contracted imperative of *dexa,* as in *sha que venga,* etc.
shabát. (H.) Jewish Sabbath.
shabonár. (O. Sp. *xabón;* T. *sabun*) To soap up; to wash with soap. Appears also as *shavonár. Shavonó* is the past tense: he soaped himself up.
shaét. (T. *şahit*) Witness.
shalóm. (H.) Hello; peace be upon you.
shamásh. (H.) Synagogue beadle.
sharsherotes. (H. *sharsheraot*) Chains; necklaces.
shed(á). (H.) Demon. *Shedá* is the female demon; *shedím* is the masculine plural.
she'elót. (H. *she'elá*) Queries asked of a religious scholar to resolve a problem of rite, custom, cult, or conscience as for rabbinical *Responsa*. Plural *she'elot.*
shehuná. (H. *shkhuná*) Neighborhood.
shelhá. (H.) Yours.
shelí. (H.) Mine.
Shelomó. (H.) Solomon. Also appears as Shlomó.
Shemá Israel. (H.) Hear O Israel. This is the Jewish creed
shematá. (T. *şamata*) Commotion; great noise; tumult; uproar; hubbub; din.
sherbét. (T. *şerbet*) Sweet drink; sherbet; refreshing drink. Also *shorbét.*
shetiká. (H. *shtiká*) Silence.
shilín(is). (T. *şilin*) Shilling, coin.
Shir Ashirím. (H.) Biblical Song of Songs.
shofét. (H.) Judge.
shorbét. (T. *şerbet*) Sweet drink; sherbet. Also *sherbét.*
shotr(ím). (H. *shoter*) Policemen.
shtuyót. (H. *shtut;* pl. *shtuyót*) Nonsense (plural).
shuk. (H.) Oriental market. See *soko*
sikleó. (T. *sikilmak,* passive of *sikmak*) Cause annoyance, embarrassment, or discomfort; *sikilmak* means to be bored, annoyed, uneasy, ashamed. Here it appears in the reflexive form, both in the present *siklees* (don't be annoyed, don't worry) and in the past *sikleó* (he was annoyed, he worried).
Simha. (H.) Joy. Also the name of a woman.
sirmalís. (T. *sirma;* O. Sp. *sirma*) Embroidered; worked with gold or silver thread; brocade; filigree (may adorn a wedding trousseau).
skapó. (Sp. *escapar*) It's finished. It's over.
skola. (It. *scuola*) School.

sofrita (o). (Sp. *freír,* participle *frita*) Sauté; lightly fried. *Sofreír* is found in the sixteenth century.

soko. (Sp. Arabism *zoko*) Marketplace; market; public square. (T. also has *suk,* but the "o" seems to indicate this is the O. Sp. form. *Soko* is also used in Sp. toponyms, such as Zocodover in Toledo.)

solanses. Whirls; a whirling or circling course.

sorte. (Fr. *sorte*) Manner; type; class.

sozdé. (T. *sözde*) Make-believe; pretend; fictitious; as though; as if; in words only; so-called; supposing that.

spada. (It. *spada;* Sp. *espada*) Sword.

spondjár. To mop the floor; to clean with a sponge. Also appears in the gerund as *spondjando.*

stampa. (It.) Print; photograph.

suivió. (Fr. *suivre*) He followed.

sultán. (T.) Ruler; sovereign; sultan (ruler of the Ottoman Empire).

Sultana. Wife of the sultan. A common woman's name, deriving from *sultán.*

supitó. (It.) Suddenly; at once; right away.

supoz(amos). (Fr. *supposer*) Let's suppose.

sutlách. (T. *sütlâç*) Rice pudding.

taanít. (H.) A ritual fast. See also *taní*

tabahím (es). (H.) Cook(s). Note the double plural: *im* from H. and *es* from Sp.

taf. (H.) Last letter of Hebrew alphabet.

tak tak. Onomatopeic sound of a knock on the door.

taksa(s). (Fr.) Taxes.

tálamo. (O. Sp.; Gr. *thálamos*) Wedding dais; *huppah* or nuptial canopy under which the bridal couple stands. Also room, house for newlyweds; bedroom; nuptial bed.

talega. (T. *talika;* O. Sp. *talega:* a bag, sack) Container, four-wheeled cart suspended on straps; carriage for travel. The Sp. word is also of Ar. origin (Ar. *taçliqa*) and is related etymologically to T. *talika.*

talmíd hahám. (H.) A learned man; a scholar; a student of the Torah.

taní. (H. *taanít*) A ritual fast. See also *taanít.*

tapét(es). (O. Sp.) Rugs; carpets. In Mod. Sp., *tapete* is a tablecloth or a small carpet.

tas. (T.) Metal cup; bowl; basin (used for washing oneself in a Turkish bath, usually with rounded bottom).

taván. (T.) Ceiling.

tavlá. (T.) Wood; board; plank.

tavlá. (T. *tabla*) Large, circular metal tray (for serving sweets).
tavle. (T. *tavla*) Backgammon; tric-trac; *shesh besh;* dice game.
tefilá. (H. *tfilá*) Prayer.
temená. (T. *temenna*) Low bow; oriental salute bringing fingers of right hand to lips and then to forehead. *Temenés* is the plural.
tendjeré. (T. *tencere*) Saucepan; stew pan; cooking pot. *Tendjereniko* is the Spanish diminutive.
tevá. (H.) Chest; cover. Among Sephardim, the synagogal platform (*bimá*) or raised place on which the reading book is situated; the reader's desk; the highest point at the synagogue.
tifsín. (T. *tepsi*) Large metal tray with a lip around the edges.
timión. (H.) Waste; go to waste.
tipésh. (H.) Stupid; fool.
tisheros. (Sp. *tijeras*) Scissors.
tnáy. (H.) Condition.
todá rabá. (H.) Thank you very much.
top. (T.) Round; ball; collected together; in a mass.
Torá. (H.) Torah.
torvá. (T. *torba*) Bag. Also appears as *torbá*.
tov. (H.) Good; well; okay; so.
tová. (H.) A favor; a good turn.
trata. (T. *trata:* a fishing boat; Gr. *tráta:* a net) Fishing net.
triakí. (Gr. *teryaka*) Sad; melancholy.
tsarót. (H.) Sorrow; grief; suffering; pain; problems.
tsavá. (H.) Army.
tsavaá. (H. *tsavaa*) Testament; will; order; last wishes.
Tsfat. (H.) Safed.
tsrif. (H.) Hut.

udá. (T. *oda*) Room; chamber.
udún. (T. *odun*) Log; blockhead; stupid; coarse fellow.
ugá. (H.) Cake.
uzinyól. (Fr. *rossignol*) Nightingale.

váad. (H.) Committee; council.
váad akeilá. (H. *vaad ha kehila*) Community council.
vadáy. (H.) Of course.
vazír. (T. *vezir*) Vizier; minister. *See also* vizír.
ve. (H.) And.
ve-halóf. (H. *lakhlóf*) And go away; pass.

verso. (It.) Toward.
vistozo. One who sees; euphemism for blind.
vizír or vijír. (T. *vezir*) Vizier; minister. A vizier sits in the *diwan* or council.
vulkán. (It. *vulcano;* T. *volkan*) Volcano.

yalla. (Ar. *yallah*) Come; let's go; let's get it over with. Abbreviation of *"Ya Allah!"*
yatagán. (T. *yatağan*) Heavy, curved knife; yataghan.
yaudí. (T. *Yahudi*) Jew.
yené. (T. *yine*) Here; still; again; once more; yet; besides; all the same; nonetheless.
yerushá. (H.) Inheritance.
Yerushalayim. (H.) Jerusalem.
yetser ará. (H. *yetzér ha-rá*) Evil inclination.
yoffi. (H) Beautiful; good. Also an interjection meaning "Bravo!"
Yom Kippúr. (H.) Day of Atonement.
yumúk. (T. *yummak*) A closed fist; a punch.

zatén. (T.) As a matter of fact; of course.
zerzavát. (T. *zerzevat*) Vegetables. Also appears as *zerzvá*.
zeuvím. (H.) Gold coins; guilders.
zikarón. (H.) Memory.
zug. (H.) Couple; pair.
zuz(im) (H.) Old silver coin. One fourth of a shekel.
zveltés. (Fr. *sveltesse*) Slenderness; suppleness; agility.

TYPE INDEX

Type	Tale	#	Page
AT 841	One Beggar Trusts God, the Other the King	11	92
AT 842	The Man Who Kicked Aside Riches	11	92
AT 875	The Clever Peasant Girl	25	198
		28	224
AT 875A	Girl's Riddling Answer Betrays a Theft	28	220
AT 875C	The Queen as Gusli-player	20	167, 168
AT 875D	The Clever Girl at the End of the Journey	1	10
		28	220
**881B	The Suspected Maiden Proves Innocent	18	144
AT 882	The Wager on the Wife's Chastity	44	282
AT 888	The Faithful Wife	20	167
AT 888A	The Wife Who Would Not Be Beaten	20	167
AT 891B*	The King's Glove	18	144
IFA *895	The Miraculous Child	1	10
IFA 899*H	The Friendly Tree (Tree of Sorrow)	16	124
AT 900	King Thrushbeard	7	50
		10	84
AT 910	Precepts Bought or Given Prove Correct	10	83
AT 910B	The Servant's Good Counsels	10	86
AT 910G	Man Buys a Pennyworth of Wit	10	85
AT 911*	The Dying Father's Counsel	8	61
AT 920A	The Daughter of the King and the Son of the Peasant	25	198
		42	273
IFA 920*E	Children's Judgment	42	273
AT 921A	The Four Coins (Focus)	22	186
AT 922	The Shepherd Substituting for the Priest Answers the King's Questions (The King and The Abbot)	26	205
IFA 922*C	King Sets Tasks to Jew	26	205
		27	212
AT 923B	The Princess Who Was Responsible for Her Own Fortune	10	83, 84
IFA *923	Love Like Salt	10	83, 84
IFA 929*B	Minister Insults Rival	29	228
AT 930	The Prophecy	9	72
		12	98
IFA 934*F	Charity Saves from Death	13	108
AT 946B*	Shoes of Poverty	43	278
AT 947A	Bad Luck Cannot Be Arrested	11	92

Type Index

AT refers to tale types included in Aarne and Thompson, *The Types of the Folktale*. IFA classification is based on Heda Jason's indices (see list of abbreviations) of the Israel Folktale Archives. Types that begin with ** are found in Haboucha.

Type	Tale	#	Page
AT 303	The Twins or Blood Brothers	3	24
AT 425C	Beauty and the Beast	7	49
AT 425D	Vanished Husband Learned of by Keeping Inn (Bath-House)	6	43
AT 510	Cinderella and Cap o' Rushes	19	153
		20	167
AT 510B	The Dress of Gold, of Silver, and of Stars	19	152
IFA 510*C	The Maiden in the Chest	19	152
AT 554	The Grateful Animals	17	138
AT 555	The Fisher and His Wife	4	31
AT 559	Dungbeetle	23	189
AT 571	"All Stick Together"	23	189
AT 591	The Thieving Pot	5	38
AT 737A*	Why Have I Nothing?	10	84
AT 737B*	The Lucky Wife	10	84
AT 745A	The Predestined Treasure	11	92
AT 750A	The Wishes	14	113
**750E	The Best Friend	28	221
AT 750F*	The Old Man's Blessing	2	17
		16	127
AT 780	The Singing Bone	3	25
AT 821B	Chickens from Boiled Eggs	25	197
		42	273
AT 837	How the Wicked Lord Was Punished	29	229

TYPE INDEX · 355

Type	Tale	#	Page
AT 947A*	Bad Luck Refuses to Desert a Man	11	92
		43	279
AT 960	The Sun Brings All to Light	3	24
AT 981	Wisdom of Hidden Old Man Saves Kingdom	2	20
		23	189
IFA *981			
I (Andrejev)	Tales of the Talking Birds	20	165
AT 983	The Dishes of the Same Flavor	18	146
AT 1201	The Plowing	54	314
AT 1204	Fool Keeps Repeating His Instructions	46	292
AT 1231	The Attack on the Hare (Crayfish)	50	302
AT 1260A*	Flour in River	46	292
AT 1263	The Porridge Eaten in Different Rooms	30	238
AT 1281	Getting Rid of the Unknown Animal	49	299
AT 1284	Person Does Not Know Himself	46	292
AT 1288	Numskulls Cannot Find Their Own Legs	53	312
AT 1291D	Other Objects Sent to Go by Themselves	47	295
AT 1291**	Fools Let Horse Loose to Find Road Home	46	292
		47	295
AT 1295A*	Tall Bridegroom Cannot Get into Church	53	311
IFA *1328	Woman Does Not Know Her Housework	46	292
AT 1336A	Man Does Not Recognize His Own Reflection in the Water (Mirror)	46	293
AT 1339E	All Cooked for One Meal	46	292
AT 1346*	Easy Problem Made Hard	45	286
		49	299
		50	302
AT 1349*	Miscellaneous Numskull Tales	34	250
		48	297
AT 1365J*	Asking by Opposites	51	304
AT 1381A	Husband Discredited by Absurd Truth	41	269
AT 1381B	The Sausage Rain	41	269
AT 1384	The Husband Hunts Three Persons as Stupid as His Wife	46	291
AT 1431	The Contagious Yawns	25	196
AT 1510	The Matron of Ephesus (Vidua)	20	166
AT 1525L	Creditor Falsely Reported Insane When He Demands Money	41	269
AT 1526A	Supper Won by a Trick	39	262

Type	Tale	#	Page
IFA 1528*D	Contest in Cleverness between Jew and Gentile	27 29	212 228 229
IFA 1538*D	Revenge of Insulted Person	29	228
AT 1539	Cleverness and Gullibility	44	282
IFA 1542*C	Man Sells House But for a Nail	27	211
AT 1572F*	Turning the Shovel Backwards	11	43
AT 1587**	Accuser Is a Madman	41	269
AT 1624	Thief's Excuse: The Big Wind	38	260
AT 1642	The Good Bargain, Part V: The Borrowed Coat	41	268
AT 1642A	The Borrowed Coat	41	268
AT 1651	Whittington's Cat	49	269
AT 1651A	Fortune in Salt	49	299
AT 1685	The Foolish Bridegroom	31	241
AT 1691B	The Suitor Who Does Not Know How to Behave at Table	31	241
AT 1696	"What Should I Have Said (Done)?"	31	241
AT 1736A	Sword Turns to Wood	40	265
AT 1750A	Sending a Dog to Be Educated	26	205
IFA 1750*B	Task: Teaching Camel to Speak	26	204
AT 1824	Parody Sermon	52	307
AT 1831	The Parson and Sexton at Mass	52	307
IFA 1831*C	Ignorance of Holidays	52	307

Motif Index

The majority of motifs in this index are found in Thompson's monumental *Motif-Index of Folk Literature*. When a motif number is followed by the notation "[Noy]," however, it comes from the classification of motifs from Jewish texts produced by Dov Neuman [Noy], included in this volume's bibliography.

Motif	Tale	#	Page
A102.16	Justice of God	2, 3	18, 25
A182.11.3 [Noy]	Moral law received by man from God	2	18
A1012.1	Flood from tears	23	189
A1344.1	The "three first cries that made their way to God": the cry of the blood of Abel, etc.	3	26
A1614.1 [Noy]	Negroes as curse on Ham for laughing at Noah's nakedness	12	99
A1614.1+[Noy]	Negroes as curse on Ham for breaking sex taboos in the ark	12	99
A2426.2	Cries of birds	47	295
A2426.1.1	Nightingale's song	17	140
B11.2.11	Fire-breathing dragon	17	139
B11.2.12	Dragon of enormous size	17	139
B11.3.2	Dragon's home at top of mountain. His breath forms clouds to hide the mountain	17	139
B175	Magic fish	1, 4	10, 33
B178 [Noy]	Magic frog	10	87
B211	Animal uses human speech	1	10
B211.3	Speaking bird	17	140
		20	166
B211.9 [Noy]	Speaking bird	17	140
		20	166

Motif	Tale	#	Page
B211.11 [Noy]	Speaking fish	1, 4	10, 33
B211.12 [Noy]	Speaking frog	10	87
B242+ [Noy]	Ziz king of birds	17	140
B242.1.1	Eagle king of birds	17	139
B242.1.10	Ziz as king of birds	17	140
B292	Animal as servant to man	1, 17	11, 140
B292 [Noy]	Animal in service of man	1, 17	11, 140
B350	Grateful animals	17	140
B360	Animals grateful for rescue from peril or death	17	138
B375.1	Fish returned to water: grateful	4	31
B450	Helpful birds	17	138
		20	166
B455.3	Helpful eagle	17	139
B470	Helpful fish	1, 4	11, 31
B552	Man carried by bird	8	61
B560	Animals advise men	17	140
B571	Animals perform tasks for men	17	140
		20	166
B582.2	Animals help hero win princess	17	139
		20	166
B755	Animal calls the dawn. The sun rises as a result of the animal's call	45	286
C600	Unique prohibition. A person is forbidden to do one particular thing; everything else he is free to do	8	62
		20	167
C610	The one forbidden place	8	62
C611	Forbidden chamber. Person allowed to enter all chambers of house except one	8	62
C631.2+ [Noy]	Taboo: fishing on Sabbath	1	11
C773.1	Taboo: making unreasonable requests. Given power of fulfilling all wishes, person oversteps moderation and is punished	4	32
D5	Enchanted person	7	51
D30	Transformation to person of different race	12	100
D141	Transformation: man to dog	6	46
D473.1	Transformation: sword to wood	40	266

Motif	Tale	#	Page
D562.1	Transformation by application of water	6, 12	46, 100
D683	Transformation by magician	7	51
D700	Person disenchanted	6	46
		7	52
		10	87
D732	Loathly Lady. Man disenchants loathsome woman by embracing her	7	50
D735	Disenchantment by kiss	7	52
D766	Disenchantment by liquid	6	46
D921	Magic lake (pond)	12	99
D1171.1	Magic pot	5	38
D1273	Magic formula (charm)	4	33
D1311+ [Noy]	Divination by the stars	9, 12	74, 98
D1318.2	Dead fish reveals guilt	1	10
D1470	Magic object as provider	5	38
D1470.1.19	Magic wishing-pot	5	38
D1470.2	Provisions received from magic object	5	38
D1472.1	Food or drink received directly from magic object	5	38
D1472.1.9	Magic pot supplies food and drink	5	38
D1473	Magic object furnishes clothes	5	39
D1520	Magic object affords miraculous transportation	5	40
D1532	Magic object bears person aloft	5	40
D1602	Self-returning magic object	5	38
D1605.1	Magic thieving pot. Boy sells pot to neighbors and when they have put things into it the pot returns to the boy	5	38
D1651.3	Magic cooking-pot obeys only master	5	38
D1712 [Noy]	Soothsayer	2	18
		9	73
		12	98
D1713+ [Noy]	Magic power of Elijah	14	114
		15	121
D1720.1	Man given power of wishing	4, 14	31, 114
D1722+ [Noy]	Magic power from Elijah the Prophet	15	121
D1761	Magic results produced by wishing	4, 14	32, 116
D1761.0.2	Limited number of wishes granted	4, 14	31, 114

Motif	Tale	#	Page
D1761.0.2.2	One wish granted	14	114
D1810	Magic knowledge	1, 13	10, 109
D1812	Magic power of prophecy	13	109
D1870	Magic hideousness	7	51
D1871	Girl magically made hideous	7	51
D1872	Man made hideous	7	51
D2071 [Noy]	Evil Eye	48	297
D2071.1 [Noy]	Averting Evil Eye	48	297
D2086.1.1	Execution sword turned to wood	40	266
D2121.5	Magic journey: man carried by spirit or devil	8	65
D2122	Journey with magic speed	8	65
D2135	Magic air journey	8	65
D2198+[Noy]	Solomon's dominion over animals (ruler of birds)	20	166
E631	Reincarnation in plant (tree) growing from grave	3	26
E631.0.3	Plant from blood of slain person	3	26
F162.2.12	River in underworld from tears of living	23	189
F402.2.1 [Noy]	Asmodeus—Ashmedai—as king of demons	8	63
F411.0.1	Spirit travels with extraordinary speed	8	65
F575.1	Remarkably beautiful woman	7	51
F576	Extraordinary ugliness	7	51
F591	Person who never laughs	23	189
F695.3	Learning to read in extraordinarily short time	15	121
F708.1	Country without cats	49	299
		50	301
F713	Extraordinary pond (lake)	12	100
F715.2.5	River of tears	23	189
F811	Extraordinary tree	3	26
F815.4 [Noy]	Extraordinary vine	3	26
F821	Extraordinary dress (clothes, robe, etc.)	19	154
F821.1.5	Dress of gold, silver, color of sun, moon, and stars	19	154

Motif	Tale	#	Page
F821.2	Dress so fine that it goes in nutshell	19	154
F889+ [Noy]	Book of Life	51	305
F979.12	Trees spring up from blood spilled on ground	3	26
F991	Object bleeds	3	26
F1041.9.1	Going to bed for sorrow	17	138
F1082	Person changes color	12	99
G200	Witch	7	51
G263	Witch injures, enchants or transforms	7	51
G269.4	Curse by disappointed witch	7	51
G302.2+[Noy]	Kingdom of the demons	8	61
G302.2+[Noy]	Asmodeus—Ashmedai as king of demons	8	63
G302.9+[Noy]	Lilit injures baby boy during first night of his life, baby girl during first twenty days	6	44
G302.9+[Noy]	Demons observe the Torah	8	64
G302.12+[Noy]	Sexual relations between man and demons	8	63
G302.16+[Noy]	Amulets ward off demons	6, 48	44, 297
G302.16+[Noy]	Amulet with names of the three angels sent by Satan to capture Lilit, keeps her away from children	6	44
G302.22 [Noy]	Demons as helpers	8	65
G303.12+[Noy]	Lilit deserted her husband, Satan. Three angels sent to capture her	4	32
G500	Ogre defeated	17	140
G530.2	Help from ogre's daughter (or son)	8	63
G610.3	Stealing from ogre as task	17	139
H11.1.1	Recognition at inn (hospital, etc) where all must tell their life histories	6	43
H36.1	Slipper test. Identification by fitting of slipper	20	167
H55	Recognition through branding	44	282
H94	Identification by ring	19	155
H94.1	Identification by ring baked in cake	19	155
H111	Identification by garment	43	278

Motif	Tale	#	Page
H151	Attention drawn and recognition follows	19	155
H151.6	Heroine in menial disguise discovered in her beautiful clothes. Recognition follows	19	155
H175	Recognition for force of nature. Unknown member of family immediately and magically recognized	6	46
H192	Recognition by supernatural manifestation	6	46
H215.1	Sword magically changed to wood when executioner is to decapitate innocent person	40	266
H300	Tests connected with marriage	7	49
		17	139
		20	166, 167
H301	Excessive demands to prevent marriage	17	139
		19	155
H310	Suitor tests. A suitor is put to severe tests by his prospective bride or father-in-law	17	139
H326	Suitor test: skill	17	140
H328	Suitor test: power of endurance	17	139
H331	Suitor contests: bride offered as prize	7, 17	50, 139
H335	Tasks assigned suitors. Bride as prize for accomplishments	7	50
		17	139
		20	165
H335.0.2	Girl assigns tasks to her suitors	17	139
		20	165
H360	Bride test	20	167
H363	Deceased wife marriage test. Man will marry woman meeting certain specifications prescribed by his deceased wife	19	154
H363.2	Bride test: wearing deceased wife's ring	19	154
H465	Test of wife's endurance. Haughty princess married to beggar and must endure poverty and menial work	10	84
H500	Test of cleverness or ability	28	226
H501	Test of wisdom	28	221
H502	Test of learning	28	226
H506	Test of resourcefulness	17	140
		32	246
		40	265

Motif	Tale	#	Page
H530	Riddles	28	222
H540	Propounding of riddles	28	222
H540.2.1 [Noy]	Queen of Sheba propounds riddles to Solomon	28	222
H561.1.1.1	Clever daughter construes enigmatic sayings	1, 28	10, 222
H565	Riddle propounded from chance experience. On way to riddle trial youth sees things that give him a clue for his riddles	28	221
H582.1	Riddling answer betrays theft	28	222
H582.1.1	The full moon and the thirtieth of the month. Prince sends servant to clever girl with a round tart, thirty cakes, and a capon and asks her if it is full moon and the thirtieth of the month and if the cock has crowed in the evening. She replies that it is not full moon, that it is the fifteenth of the month, and that the capon has gone to the mill; but the prince should spare the pheasant for the partridge's sake. She thus shows him that the servant has stolen half the tart, half the cakes, and the capon	28	222
H585	Enigmatic conversation of king and peasant	22	186
H585.1	The four coins. (Focus.) King: What do you do with the four coins you earn? Peasant: First I eat (feed myself); second I put out at interest (give my children); third I give back (pay debts); fourth I throw away (give my wife)	22	186
H586	Riddling remarks of traveling companion interpreted by girl (man) at end of journey	28	221
H586.3	One traveler to another: Let us carry each other and shorten the way. (Let us tell tales and amuse ourselves on the way.)	28	221
H586.4	One traveler to another: that field (uncut) is already harvested. (Belongs to spendthrift who has already spent the money.)	28	221

Motif	Tale	#	Page
H586.5	One traveler to another (as they see corpse borne by: he is not entirely dead (Has left good property.)	28	221
H600	Symbolic interpretations	28	221
H680	Riddles of distance	28	225
H682.1	Riddle: how far is it from earth to heaven?	28	225
H720	Metaphorical riddles	28	222
H770	Riddle of explanation	28	222
H931	Tasks assigned in order to get rid of hero	9	74
H934	Relative assigns tasks	34	250
H970	Help in performing tasks	17	140
		20	166
H982	Animals help man perform task	17	140
H1010	Impossible tasks	17	139
H1020	Tasks contrary to laws of nature	26	204
H1023.1.1	Task: hatching boiled eggs; countertask: sowing cooked seeds and harvesting the crop	42	274
H1024.7	Task: teaching animal to speak	26	204
H1130	Superhuman tasks	17	139
H1381.2.2.1	Son seeks unknown father	25	200
H1381.3.1	Quest for bride	20	167
H1400	Fear test. A person is put to various tests in the attempt to make him show fear	17	139
H1550	Tests of character	7, 14	51, 114
		18	147
		32	246
H1553	Tests of patience	32	246
H1556	Test of fidelity	20	166
H1558.3	Test of friendship: to go with one to death. Everyman. He calls in Riches, Family, etc. Only Good Deeds remains with him	28	221
J21	Counsels proved wise by experience	10	85
J21.2	"Do not act when angry": counsel proved wise by experience. Man returns home and sees someone sleeping with his wife. Though he thinks it is a paramour, he restrains himself and finds that it is a newborn son	10	86

MOTIF INDEX · 365

Motif	Tale	#	Page
J21.2.3	"Do not draw your sword against the innocent": counsel proved wise by experience	40	266
J21.2.6	"Control your anger at the beginning": counsel proved wise by experience	10	85
J21.22	"Do not tell a secret to a woman": counsel proved wise by experience	12	100
J81	The dishes of the same flavor. Man thus shown that one woman is like another and dissuaded from his amorous purpose	18	146
J151	Wisdom from old person	2, 23	18, 189
J151 [Noy]	Wisdom of old man	2, 23	21, 189
J154	Wise words of dying father. Counsel proved wise by experience	8, 20	61, 167
J163	Wisdom purchased	10	85
J163.1	Man buys pennyworth of wit	10	85
J163.4	Good counsels bought	10	85
J166	Wisdom from books	2, 18	18, 146
J171+[Noy]	If you have learned much, do not take credit for yourself	16	125
J171+ [Noy]	Let not anger master you	10	86
J171+ [Noy]	Repent one day before your death (today, you may die tomorrow).	13	109
J171+ [Noy]	Beware of fools	35	253
J171.1	Counsel: if you take it you will be sorry; if you don't you will also be sorry. This advice given hero by helpful horse	10	87
J192+ [Noy]	King Solomon as "father of wisdom"	1	14
J230+ [Noy]	Good name is preferable to abundant riches	28	221
J320+ [Noy]	Man with bread in his basket not to ask: "what will I eat tomorrow?"	13	110
J347.4	Rich merchant is poorer in happiness than poor man	13	110
J513	One should let well enough alone	4	34
J514	One should not be too greedy	4	34
J530	Prudence in demands	4	34
J570	Wisdom of deliberation	10	85

Motif	Tale	#	Page
J571	Avoid hasty judgment	10	86
J571.4	Avoid hasty punishment	10	86
J706	Acquisition of wealth	43	278
J710	Forethought in provision for food	39	262
J815	Unpleasant truths must be withheld from the great	12	98
J816	Tact in reproving the great	25	199
		32	246
J816.4	Woman tactfully restrains amorous king	18	146
J900	Humility	16	125
J910	Humility of the great	16	125
J914 [Noy]	R. Hillel teaches Gentile who wants to make him angry the whole Torah "on one leg" by quoting one sentence: "Love thy neighbor like yourself"	15	121
J1040	Decisiveness of conduct	43	278
J1041	Impossibility of pleasing everyone. One must act therefore without awaiting everyone's approval	43	278
J1100	Cleverness	14	115
		25	199
		26	206
		27	211
J1110	Clever persons	32	246
J1112	Clever wife	14	115
		20	167
		21	178
J1130	Cleverness in law court	42	274
		44	282
J1151	Testimony of witness cleverly discredited	41	269
		42	274
J1151.1	Testimony discredited by inducing witness to talk foolishly	41	269
J1151.1.2	Husband discredited by absurd truth. Wife puts fish in furrow where husband plows them up (or like absurdity). At mealtime the husband says, "Where are the fish?"—"What fish?"—"Those I plowed up." He is laughed to scorn	41	269

Motif	Tale	#	Page
J1151.1.3	The sausage rain. (Or rain of figs, fishes, or milk.) A mother, in order to discredit testimony of her foolish son who has killed a man, makes him believe that it has rained sausages. When he says that he killed the man on the night it rained sausages, his testimony is discredited	41	269
J1151.2	Witness claims the borrowed coat: discredited. Trickster summoned to court on Jew's complaint refuses to go unless he has a new coat: Jew lends him his. In court the trickster says that the Jew is a liar: "He will even claim that I am wearing his coat." The Jew does so and no one believes him	41	268
J1160	Clever pleading	42	279
J1179+ [Noy]	Man who borrowed an egg with promise to return all that might come of it. Condemned to pay enormous sum of money by a judge. A clever child helps judge to find out that egg was boiled and could not produce anything	42	274
J1190	Cleverness in the law court	25	196
J1191	Reductio ad absurdum of judgment	42	274
J1191.1	Reductio ad absurdum: the decision about the colt. A man ties his mare to a second man's wagon. The mare bears a colt which the wagon-owner claims, saying that the wagon has borne a colt. Real owner of the colt shows the absurdity (1) by fishing in the street or (2) by telling that his wife is shooting fish in the garden. Neither of these things is as absurd as the decision	25	196
J1191.2	Suit for chicken produced from boiled eggs. Countertask: harvesting crop produced from cooked seeds	25 42	197 274
J1192	The bribed judge	42	274
J1210	Clever man puts another out of countenance	27 32 41	211 246 269

Motif	Tale	#	Page
J1212	Judge put out of countenance	25	197
		42	274
J1214	Absurd pretense, when allowed, puts pretender out of countenance	32	246
J1280	Repartee with ruler (judge, etc.)	25	197
J1340	Retorts from hungry persons	32	246
J1391	Thief makes a lame excuse	38	260
J1391.1	Thief's excuse: the big wind. Vegetable thief is caught in a garden. Owner: How did you get into the garden? A wind blew me in. How were the vegetables uprooted? If the wind is strong enough to blow me in, it can uproot them. How did they get into your bag? That is what I was just wondering	38	260
J1511	A rule must work both ways	42	274
J1521	Swindler's plans foiled	41	268
J1522	Rebuke to the stingy	32	246
J1530	One absurdity rebukes another	25	197
		42	274
J1536	Ruler's absurdity rebuked	25	197
		32	246
J1545.4 [Noy]	The exiled wife's dearest possession. A wife driven from home is allowed by her husband to take her one dearest possession. She takes her sleeping husband and effects reconciliation	28	224
J1561	Inhospitality repaid	32	246
J1561.4	Servant repays stingy master (mistress)	32	246
J1565	Inappropriate entertainment repaid	32	246
J1577	Deceptive invitation to feast	32	245
		39	262
J1675	Clever dealings with a king	20	167
		25	197
		32	246
J1700	Fools	31	242
		34	250
		35	253
		44	281

Motif	Tale	#	Page
		45	286
		46	291
		47	295
		48	297
		49	299
		50	301
		53	312
		54	313
J1701	Stupid wife	46	291
		47	295
J1703	Town (country) of fools	45	285
		49	299
		50	301
		53	312
		54	313
J1713	Foolish married couple	48	297
J1730	Absurd ignorance	31	242
		45	286
		46	291
		47	295
		53	312
J1732	Ignorance of certain foods	46	292
J1736	Fools and the unknown animal	50	301
J1738	Ignorance of religious matters	52	308
J1743	Ignorance of dates	52	308
J1791.7	Man does not recognize his own reflection in the water	46	292
J1791.7.1	Simpleton thinks his reflection in jar of melted butter is thief; strikes at the jar and breaks it	46	292
J1810	Physical phenomena misunderstood	45	286
J1813	Cooking processes misunderstood	46	292
J1813.9.1	Stupid servant cooks all the rice for one meal	46	292
J1818	Animal's action misunderstood	47	295
J1820	Inappropriate action from misunderstanding	45	286
		46	293
J1851.2	Gifts to birds. Numskulls hear birds calling and give them gifts	47	295

Motif	Tale	#	Page
J1870	Absurd sympathy for animals or objects	47	295
J1880	Animals or objects treated as if human	46	292
		47	295
J1881.2	Animal sent to go by itself	46	292
		47	295
J1900	Absurd disregard or ignorance of animal's nature or habits	26	204
		46	292
		47	295
J1902	Absurd ignorance concerning the hatching of eggs	42	274
J1930	Absurd disregard of natural laws	25	199
		26	204
		34	250
		45	286
		54	313
J1960	Other absurd disregard of facts	45	286
J2012	Person does not know himself	46	292
J2020	Inability to find own members, etc.	53	312
J2021	Numskulls cannot find their own legs	53	312
J2050	Absurd shortsightedness	46	292
		47	295
J2100	Remedies worse than the disease	43	279
		54	319
J2101	Getting rid of the cat. In a land in which cats are not known, one is bought at a great price. It eats many mice. By misunderstanding, they think the cat is a monster. In order to get rid of it, they set the house on fire	49	299
J2130	Foolish disregard of personal danger	46	293
J2133	Numskull falls	34	250
J2134	Numskull makes himself sick (uncomfortable)	46	293
J2163	Carrying the plow horse so as not to tramp up the field	54	314
J2167	Porridge eaten in different rooms. The porridge in one, the milk in another	30	238
J2171.6	Man on camel has doorway broken down so he can ride in. It does not occur to him to dismount	53	312

Motif	Tale	#	Page
J2200	Absurd lack of logic	46	291
		47	295
		54	313
J2210	Logical absurdity based on certain false assumptions	45	286
J2213	Illogical use of numbers	54	313
J2272	Absurd theories concerning the sun	45	286
J2300	Gullible fools	27	212
J2412.1	Hot onion to the eye. A friend has cured his foot with this remedy	23	189
J2450	Literal fool	31	242
J2460	Literal obedience	31	241
		46	293
		51	305
J2461.1	Literal following of instructions about actions	31	241
J2461.1.4	Literal numskull cuts peas into four parts. Told that he should have cut up the pancakes which he has eaten whole	31	242
J2463	The foolish bride	46	291
J2465	Disastrous following of instructions	46	292
J2465.7	Oh bother! Put it on my head! Numskulls asking old woman where to put grain obey and smother her	46	292
J2489	Metaphors literally interpreted	46	292
J2500	Foolish extreme	46	293
J2516	Directions followed literally to the sorrow of the giver	46	292
J2550	Thankful fools	50	302
J2600	Cowardly fool	50	302
J2612	The attack on the hare (crayfish). Seven men make strenuous plans for the attack on the fierce animal. One screams with fright and the animal runs away	50	302
J2650	Bungling fool	34	250
J2671	The forgetful fool	46	292
J2671.2	Fool keeps repeating his instructions so as to remember them. (He usually forgets them.)	46	292

372 · MOTIF INDEX

Motif	Tale	#	Page
J2700	The easy problem made hard	49	299
		53	312
K100	Deceptive bargains	27	212
K242	Creditor falsely reported insane when he demands money	41	269
K254	Goods misappropriated	39	262
		44	281
K330	Means of hoodwinking the guardian or owner	39	262
K330.1	Man gulled into giving up his clothes	39	262
K341	Owner's interest distracted while goods are stolen	39	262
K401	Blame for theft fastened on dupe	43	279
K451	Unjust umpire as trickster's confederate	42	274
K500	Escape from death or danger by deception	40	266
K511	Uriah letter changed. Falsified letter of execution. A messenger is sent with a letter ordering the recipient to kill the bearer. On the way, the letter is changed so that the bearer is honored	9	75
K512.1	Compassionate executioner: bloody coat. A servant charged with killing the hero smears the latter's coat with the blood of an animal as proof of the execution and lets the hero escape	12	99
K551.4.7	Escape by pretending to go for bath	18	146
K675	Sleeping potion given to a man who is to pass the night with a girl. (Sometimes magic pillow or magic sleeping card.)	17	140
K911.1	Sham death to wound enemies. Trickster lets himself be buried alive and stabs his enemies from the grave when they come to defile his body	44	282
K951.0.1 [Noy]	Deserted wife chokes departing husband. Asks for one last kiss	8	66
K978	Uriah letter. Man carries written order for his own execution	9	74

MOTIF INDEX · 373

Motif	Tale	#	Page
K1200	Deception into humiliating position	44	281
K1227	Lover put off by deceptive respite	19	155
K1265	Man falsely reported insane. No one will believe him	41	269
K1355	Altered letter of execution gives princess to hero. On his way robbers steal the letter and change it so that instead of being killed he is married to the princess	9	75
K1440	Dupe's animals destroyed or maimed	44	281
K1600	Deceiver falls into own trap	32	246
K1657	Unjust official outwitted by peasant who quarrels with him and thus turns the attention of the ruler to the abuses	29	228
K1811	Gods (saints) in disguise visit mortals	14	114
		15	120
		16	127
K1811.3+[Noy]	Prophet Elijah in disguise	13	109
		14	114
		15	120
		16	127
K1812	King in disguise	22	187
		40	266
K1816	Disguise as menial	19	155
K1816.0.2	Girl in menial disguise at lover's court	19	155
K1817.1	Disguise as beggar (pauper)	16	126
K1821.7	Beautiful woman in hideous disguise	19	155
K1837	Disguise of woman in man's clothes	20	168
K1843.2	Wife takes mistress's place in husband's bed. Brings about reconciliation	21	178
K1860	Deception by feigning death (sleep)	44	281
K1892	Deception by hiding	44	281
K1900 [Noy]	Impostures	52	308
K1961	Sham churchman	52	307
K1961.1.2.1	Parody sermon	52	307
K2112.5.1	Handkerchief left in woman's room to cause accusation (Othello)	18	144
K2127	False accusation of theft	43	279
K2128	Slander: prince is bastard	25	200

Motif	Tale	#	Page
K2130	Trouble-makers	44	282
K2150	Innocent made to appear guilty	18	145
K2213.1	Matron of Ephesus. (Vidua.) A woman mourns night and day by her husband's grave. A knight guarding a hanged man is about to lose his life because of the corpse he has stolen from the gallows. The matron offers him her love and substitutes her husband's corpse on the gallows so that the knight can escape	20	166
K2371.3	Ingeniously worded boon asked of God combines riches, issue, and restoration of eyesight: "Oh God! I want to see from above the seventh story of my mansion my great-grandsons playing in the streets and eating their cakes from golden vessels"	14	115
L100	Unpromising hero (heroine)	21	175
L102	Unpromising heroine. Usually, but not always, the youngest daughter	20	168
L111	Hero (heroine) of unpromising origin	10	85
L111.4.2	Orphan heroine	19	154
L113.1.0.1	Heroine endures hardships with husband. Rewarded by his success	10	85
L121	Stupid hero	44	281
L121.1	Half-wit successful	44	282
L123	Pauper hero	10	85
L123.1	Penniless hero. Loved by a courtesan, he proves later to be a great man	10	85
L160	Success of the unpromising hero (heroine)	10	85
L161	Lowly hero marries princess	9	75
		17	140
L162	Lowly heroine marries prince (king)	21	175
L300	Triumph of the weak	44	281
L420	Overweening ambition punished	4	34
M2	Inhuman decisions of kings	40	265
M205	Breaking of bargains or promises	8	61

Motif	Tale	#	Page
M250	Promises connected with death	8	61
		18	144
		19	154
		20	167
M255	Deathbed promise concerning second wife. Promises his dying wife that he will not marry unless the bride meets the specifications the dying wife imposes	19	154
M256	Promise to dying man broken	8, 20	61, 167
M258	Promise to dying man sacred	8	61
M302.4 [Noy]	Prophesying by means of stars	9, 12	74, 98
M340	Unfavorable prophecies	9, 12	74, 98
M369.2	Prophecies concerning love and marriage	9	74
M369.2+ [Noy]	Future husband (wife) foretold	9, 12	74, 98
M369.2.1	Future husband (wife) foretold	9	74
M370	Vain attempts to escape fulfillment of prophecy	9, 12	74, 99
M391	Fulfillment of prophecy	9, 12	75, 98
M411.12	Curse by witch	7	51
M420	Enduring and overcoming curses	7	52
N0	Wagers and gambling	37	258
N101	Inexorable fate	11	93
N120.0.1 [Noy]	Fate decided by God	9, 12	75, 98
N121	Fate decided before birth	11	93
N121+ [Noy]	Marriages decided by God	9, 12	75, 98
N130	Changing of luck or fate	14	114
N131	Acts performed for changing luck	11	93
N131.5	Luck changing after change of place	10, 15	85, 119
N134	Persons effect change of luck	10	85
N141	Luck or intelligence? Dispute as to which is the more powerful. Man with intelligence remains poor (is brought into court). Saved by mere luck	11	93
N145	Cast-out princess prospers because of Good Luck	10	85
N170	The capriciousness of luck	43	278
N170+ [Noy]	Rich man becomes poor (and vice versa)	43	278

Motif	Tale	#	Page
N201	Wish for exalted husband realized. Girls make wish that they may marry king (prince, etc.). It so happens	5	39
N201 [Noy]	Wishes realized	14	116
N211	Lost object returns to its owner	43	278
N250	Persistent bad luck	11	93
N270	Crime inevitably comes to light	3	25
N271.7	Murder discovered on digging foundation of house. House burns. Digger discovers body	3	26
N351	Money (treasure) unwittingly given away. Unlucky man given a loaf filled with gold exchanges it for another loaf	11	93
N411.1	Whittington's cat. A cat in a mouse-infested land without cats is sold for a fortune	49	299
N455	Overheard (human) conversation	12	100
N467	King in disguise to learn secrets of his subjects	22	187
		40	266
N630	Accidental acquisition of treasure or money	12	100
N810	Supernatural helpers	4	33
		8	65
		9	74
		15	121
N813	Helpful genie (spirit)	8	65
N831	Girl as helper	6	44
		10	85
		20	168
N835	Wealthy (powerful) man as helper	24	192
N836	King as helper	11	93
N847	Prophet as helper	9	74
		13	109
		14	114
		15	121
		16	127
N848	Saint (pious man) as helper	15	120
		24	192

Motif	Tale	#	Page
N848 [Noy]	Saint (prophet, pious man) as helper	15	120
P10	Kings	20	165
		40	266
P14.19	King goes in disguise at night to observe his subjects	11	93
		22	187
		40	266
P19.4	Kingly powers (rights)	40	266
P30	Princes	19	155
P161	Beggars' many children	2	18
P193 [Noy]	Am Haarets—unlearned in Torah	15	119
P210	Husband and wife	8	61
		12	100
		14	115
		18	145
		20	167
		21	177
		25	199
P231	Mother and son	21	178
		31	242
		34	250
P233	Father and son	8	61
		18	144
		20	167
		51	304
P234	Father and daughter	8	61
		10	88
		12	100
		19	155
P234+ [Noy]	Father expels daughter from home for not marrying a suitable man	10	84
P236	Undutiful children	51	305
P253	Sister and brother	18	145
P320	Hospitality. Relation of host and guest	39	263
P340	Teacher and pupil	37	257
P420+ [Noy]	Astronomer	9, 12	73, 98
P421	Judge	42	274
		43	279

Motif	Tale	#	Page
P426.4 [Noy]	Beadle *(Shamash)*	16	126
		26	206
P431 [Noy]	Merchant	1	12
		5	39
		8	61
		12	99
P446	Barber	40	265
P453	Shoemaker	22	187
		40	265
P461	Soldier	40	265
P475	Robber	44	282
P715.1	Jews	40	265
Q40	Kindness rewarded	24	193
Q42	Generosity rewarded	24	193
Q45	Hospitality rewarded	16	127
Q45.1	Angels entertained unawares. Hospitality to disguised saint (angel, god) rewarded	16	127
Q46	Reward for protecting fugitive	24	194
Q64	Patience rewarded	10	85
Q91	Reward for cleverness	14	116
		22	186
Q113.0.1	High honors as reward	24	193
Q151	Life spared as reward	13	111
Q211	Murder punished	3	25
Q212	Theft punished	44	282
Q241	Adultery punished	1	10
Q243.2.1	Attempted seduction punished	20	167
Q255+ [Noy]	Husband's refusal to resume conjugal relations punished	18	145
Q288	Punishment for mockery	7	51
Q338	Immoderate request punished	4	34
Q431	Punishment: banishment (exile)	25	199
Q470	Humiliating punishments	44	281
Q471	Spitting in face as punishment	1	10
Q472	Branding as punishment	44	282
Q559.2 [Noy]	Blindness as punishment	7	51

MOTIF INDEX · 379

Motif	Tale	#	Page
Q595	Loss or destruction of property as punishment	43	279
R10.3	Children abducted	6	43
R11.2.2	Abduction by demon	6	43
R17	Abduction by whirlwind	6	43
R110	Rescue of captive	20	168
R152	Wife rescues husband	20	168
R152.1	Disguised wife helps husband escape from prison	20	168
R153.4	Mother rescues son	6	46
R175	Rescue at the stake	24	194
R210	Escapes	19	155
R213	Escape from home	19	155
R260	Pursuits	35	252
R311	Tree refuge	35	252
S50	Cruel relatives-in-law	16	126
S62	Cruel husband	25	199
S410	Persecuted wife	25	199
S411	Wife banished	25	199
S411.2	Wife banished for some small fault	25	199
S414	Woman abandoned when with child	25	199
S442	Outcast wife and her son live in poverty	25	199
S451	Outcast wife at last reunited with husband and children	25	197
T10	Falling in love	17	138
		19	155
		20	165
T11.2	Love through sight of picture	20	167
T22 [Noy]	Future husband and wife born on the same day	9	72
T24.1	Lovesickness	12	98
		17	138
		19	155
T24.6	Lover refuses food and drink	17	138
T53.0.1	Matchmakers arrange weddings	21	175

Motif	Tale	#	Page
T53.4	God occupied with matchmaking	12	98
T68	Princess offered as prize	7, 17	50, 139
T85	Woman mourns dead lover	20	66
T91.6.1	Lowly person falls in love with king (queen)	17	138
T100	Marriage	8	61
		17	140
		18	145
		19	154
		21	174
		28	222
T107 [Noy]	Marriages made in heaven	9, 12	75, 98
T111	Marriage of mortal and supernatural being	8	63
T111.3 [Noy]	Marriage of mortal and demon	8	63
T121	Unequal marriage	10, 20	85, 168
T121.3.1	Princess marries lowly man	9	75
		10	84
		12	100
T130	Marriage customs	53	311
T132	Preparation for wedding	21	174
T134.1	Bridal couple must never see each other before wedding	21	176
T135.8 [Noy]	Marriage contract (ketuba)	8	66
T136	Accompaniments of wedding	53	311
T151.0.1	Respite ruse. Captive maiden assigns quest, agreeing to marry when it is accomplished	19	155
T211.9	Excessive grief at husband's or wife's death	20	166
T231	The faithless widow	20	166
T231.1	Faithless widow betrothed anew at husband's funeral	20	166
T232.2	Adulteress chooses loathly paramour	1	10
T271	The neglected wife	21	177
T282 [Noy]	First (barren) wife insists her husband should take second wife	28	224

Motif	Tale	#	Page
T297+ [Noy]	Ten years of married life without children grounds for divorce	28	224
T298	Reconciliation of separated couple	21	178
T311.1	Flight of maiden (bridegroom) to escape marriage	19	155
T315	Continence in marriage	18	145
		21	178
T315.2	The continent husband	18	145
		21	178
T320	Escape from undesired lover	18	146
T320.4	Wife escapes lust of king by shaming him	18	146
T411.1	Lecherous father. Unnatural father wants to marry his daughter (Manekine)	19	155
T411.1 (Huerta)	Lecherous father. Unnatural father wants to marry his daughter. The daughter exacts a price and then escapes	19	155
T463 [Noy]	Sexual intercourse between men and demons	8	63
T481	Adultery	1	10
T481.2.1	Queen commits adultery with lowborn man	1	10
T481.5	King takes subject's wife while her husband is sent away	18	147
T548	Birth obtained through magic or prayer	6	43
T600	Care of children	2	18
T670	Adoption of children	28	224
U10	Justice and injustice	43	279
U30	Rights of the strong	44	281
U60	Wealth and poverty	2	18
		10	84
		13	108
		16	128
		21	175
		24	192
		43	278
U110	Appearances deceive	21	177
U130	The power of habit	29	228

Motif	Tale	#	Page
U162 [Noy]	Tree cut down with axe for which it has furnished a handle. When tree weeps at creation, God says: "If you do not give of your wood there will be no axe"	28	222
V50	Prayer	14	44
		15	119
V51	Learning to pray	15	121
V51.1	Man who does not know how to pray so holy that he walks on water	15	120
V79.2 [Noy]	Day of Atonement (Yom Hakipurim)	51	304
V79.2+ [Noy]	Day of Atonement day of repentance	51	304
V82	Circumcision	16	127
V96	Ritual bathing	21	176
		53	311
V97	Study of Tora as religious service	2	18
V99+ [Noy]	Ritual bathing	21	176
		53	311
V112.3	Synagogues	14	114
		15	121
		16	128
		52	308
V112.6+ [Noy]	Prayer in synagogues	14	114
		16	128
		28	226
		52	308
V112.6+ [Noy]	Circumcision performed in synagogue	16	128
V136	Bible	2	18
V221	Miraculous healing by saint	14	114
V221.12	Saint cures blindness	14	114
V223	Saints have miraculous knowledge	13	109
		15	121
V223.4	Saint helps with learning	15	121
V235	Mortal visited by angel	14	114
		15	120
		16	127
V238	Guardian Angel	15	120
V238+ [Noy]	Guardian Angel accompanies man on journey to protect him from harm	15	120

Motif	Tale	#	Page
V246	Angel counsels mortal	15	121
V246+ [Noy]	Wisdom received from angel	15	121
V246+ [Noy]	Angel-teacher (instructor) of man	13	109
		15	121
V246+ [Noy]	Angel reveals decree of God to man	13	109
V295 [Noy]	Prophet Elijah—the most miraculous figure among Jewish "saints"	9	74
		13	109
		14	114
		15	120
		16	127
V315	Belief in the Atonement	51	305
V315+ [Noy]	Atoning power of good deeds	13	109
V400 [Noy]	Charity	13	110
		24	192
V404 [Noy]	*Tsedaka* = righteousness (almsgiving—monetary help to poor	13	110
		24	192
V405 [Noy]	*Gemilut Hasadim*—"bestowal of loving acts"	13	110
		24	193
V405+ [Noy]	Helping poor bride with dowry (*Hakhnosat kala*)	21	175
V407 [Noy]	Charity to be practiced in secret	21	176
		24	193
V410+ [Noy]	Charity saves from death	13	110
V440+ [Noy]	God created poor to enable others to earn reward for almsgiving	2	19
		24	193
W26	Patience	10	84
		37	257
W27	Gratitude	17	140
W45 [Noy]	Humility and modesty	16	125
W45+ [Noy]	The greater the man the deeper his humility	16	125
W126	Disobedience	51	305
W137	Curiosity	8	62
W151	Greed	8	62
W167	Stubbornness	35	252
		51	305
X370+ [Noy]	Teaching the whole Tora on one leg	15	121

Motif	Tale	#	Page
Z0	Formulas	4	32
Z18	Formulistic conversations	28	222
Z71.1 [Noy]	Formulistic number: three	4	33
		10	87
Z71.5 [Noy]	Formulistic number: seven	1	11
Z140 [Noy]	Letter symbolism. Each has its numerical value *(Gimatria)* and Meaning; each acts as symbol	15	120
Z183	Symbolic names	21	179
Z320	Object will fit only one thing (or person)	19	152
		20	167

Bibliography

Aki Yerushalayim, Revista kulturala djudeo-espanyol. Jerusalem.
Alcalay, Reuben. *The Complete Hebrew-English Dictionary*. Bridgeport, CT, 1965.
Alexander, Tamar, and Elena Romero, eds. *Érase una vez . . . Maimónides. Cuentos tradicionales hebreos*. Córdoba, 1988.
Alexander, Tamar, and M. Govrin. "Story-Telling as a Performing Art." *Assaph: Studies in the Theatre* 5 (1990): 1–34.
Alexander, Tamar, and Dov Noy, eds. *Ozaroh shel Abba: Me'ah Sipurim ve-Sipur mi-Pei Yehudei Sefarad (The Treasure of Our Fathers. Judeo-Spanish Tales)*. Jerusalem, 1989.
Alexander-Frizer, Tamar. *Ma'aseh ahuv va-hetsi: ha-sipur ha-'amami shel yehude Sefarad (Beloved Friend-and-a-Half: Studies in Sepharadic Folk-Literature)*. Yerushalayim, c. 1999.
Alfonso, Pedro. *Disciplina Clericalis. Introducción y notas de María Jesús Lacarra. Traducción de Esperanza Ducay*. Zaragoza, c. 1980.
Al-Shahi, Ahmed, and F.C.T. Moore, trans. and eds. *Wisdom from the Nile: A Collection of Folk-Stories from Northern and Central Sudan*. Oxford, 1978.
Aminoff, Irit. *Ha-emir ve ha-almanah ha-yehudiah (The Emir and the Jewish Widow)*. Haifa, 1974.
Andrejev, Nikolai Petrovich. *Ukazatel' Skazocnich Síuzhetov po-Sisteme Aarne*. Leningrad, 1929. Reprint, Berkeley, 1993.
Andriotes, Nikolaos P. *Etymologikò lexikò tēs koinēs neoellēnikēs*. Salonica, 1983.
Antti Aarne and Stith Thompson. *The Types of the Folktale*. 2d rev. Folklore Fellows Company (FFC) 184. Helsinki, 1973.
Apuleius. *Cupid and Psyche*. Ed. E. J. Kenney. Cambridge, 1990.
———. *The Golden Ass*. Trans. with intro. and explanatory notes by P. G. Walsh. Oxford, 1994.
Armistead, Samuel G., and Israel J. Katz. "Tres cuentos tradicionales de la provincia de Soria." *Celtiberia* 24, no. 47 (1974): 7–19.
Ashliman, D. L. *A Guide to Folktales in the English Language. Based on the Aarne-Thompson Classification System*. New York, 1987.
Attias, Moshe. *Nozat ha-zahav Shel Tsipor ha-pele. Esrim sipurei-'am mi pi yehude yavan (The Golden Feather: Twenty Folktales Narrated by Greek Jews)*. Haifa, 1976.
Ausubel, Nathan, ed. *A Treasury of Jewish Folklore*. New York, 1948.
Avitsuk, J. *Ha-ilan she-safag dma'ot (The Tree That Absorbed Tears)*. Haifa, 1965.

Ayoun, Richard, and Haïm Vidal Séphiha. *Los sefardíes de ayer y de hoy: 71 retratos.* Madrid, Mexico, 2002. Trans. Tomás Onaindía. (*Séfarades d'hier et d'aujourd'hui: 70 portraits.* Paris, 1992.

Babay, Refael. *Tovah be-'ad tovah; 'asarah sipure-'am mi-pi yehude Paras.* (*A Favor for a Favor: Ten Jewish-Persian Folktales*). Jerusalem, 1980.

Babylonian Talmud. English translation ed. I. Epstein. 18 vols. London, 1935–52.

Baharav, Zalman. *Mi-Dor le-Dor: Sipure-'am mi-pi 'edot Yisrael.* (*From Generation to Generation*). Tel Aviv, 1968.

———. *Shishim Sipurei 'Am mi-pi Mesaprim me-Ashḳelon* (*Sixty Folktales Collected for Narrators in Ashḳelon*). Haifa, 1964.

Balys, Jonas. *Motif-Index of Lithuanian Narrative Folklore.* Kaunas, 1936.

Bardavid, Beki. "El mijor amigo." *Aki Yerushalayim, Revista kulturala djudeo-espanyol.* 36–37 (Enero–Djunio, 1988): 88.

Bar-Itzhak, Haya, and Aliza Shenhar. *Jewish Moroccan Folk Narratives from Israel.* Detroit, 1993.

Barlaam e Josafat. Ed. John E. Keller and Robert W. Linker. Madrid, 1979.

Baruch, Kalmi. "El judeo-español de Bosnia." *Revista de Filología Española* 17, no. 2 (1930): 113–54.

Basgöz, Ilhan. *Turkish Folklore and Oral Literature.* Ed. Kemal Silay. Bloomington, 1998.

———. "Turkish Hikaye-telling Tradition in Azerbijan, Iran." *Journal of American Folklore* 83/330 (1970): 391–405.

Basile, Giambattista. *The Pentamerone, Translated from the Italian of Benedetto Croce.* Ed. with notes by N. M. Penzer. 2 vols. London, 1932. Reprint, Westport, CT, 1979.

Basset, René. *Études sur Si Djeha et les anecdotes qui lui sont attribuées.* Paris, 1892.

———. *Mille et un contes, récits et légendes arabes.* 3 vols. Paris, 1924–26.

Baughman, Ernest W. *Type and Motif-Index of the Folktales of England and North America.* The Hague, 1966.

Ben Ami, Issachar. "Customs of Pregnancy and Childbirth among Sephardic and Oriental Jews." In *New Horizons in Sephardic Studies,* ed. Yedida K. Stillman and George K. Zucker, 253–67. Albany, 1993.

———. "The Presence of Demons in the Moroccan Jewish Home." In *The Jews of Morocco—Studies in Their Culture.* 165–70. Jerusalem, 1976.

Ben-Amos D., and K. Goldstein, eds. *Folklore: Performance and Communication.* The Hague, 1975.

Benazéraf, R. *Refranero. Recueil de proverbes judéo-espagnols du Maroc.* Neuilly-sur-Seine, 1978.

Bendelac, Alegria. *Diccionario del judeoespañol de los sefardíes del norte de Marruecos.* Caracas, 1995.

Ben Ezra, Nissim. "Midrashim." *Le Judaïsme Séphardi* 17 (October 1958): 773.

Bin Gorion, Micha J. *Der Born Judas: Legenden, Märchen und Erzählungen.* 6 vols. Leipzig, 1919–24.

———. *Mimekor Yisrael: Classical Jewish Folktales.* 3 vols. Bloomington, 1976.

Birch, Carol, and Melissa Heckler, eds. *Who Says? Essays on Pivotal Issues in Contemporary Storytelling*. Little Rock, 1996.

Boccaccio, Giovanni. *Decameron*. The John Payne Translation. Rev. and annotated by Charles S. Singleton. Berkeley, c. 1982.

Bødker, Laurits, Christina Hole, and G. D'Aronco, eds. *European Folk Tales*. Copenhagen, 1963.

Boggs, Ralph S. *Index of Spanish Folktales: Classified According to Antti Aarne's "Types of the Folktale."* Trans. and enlarged by Stith Thompson in FFC, no. 74, FFC 90. Helsinki, 1930.

Bolte, Johannes, and George Polívka. *Anmerkungen zu den Kinder-und Hausmärchen der Brüder Grimm*. 5 vols. Leipzig, 1913–32. Reprint, Hildesheim, 1963.

Boratav, Pertev. *Contes turcs*. Paris, 1955.

Bornes-Varol, M. C. "Le judéo-espagnol vernaculaire d'Istanbul (Étude linguistique)." 3 vols. Ph.D. diss., Université de Paris, 1992.

Boulvin, Adrienne. *Contes populaires persans du Khorassan*. 2 vols. Paris, 1975.

Briggs, Katherine M., ed. *A Dictionary of British Folk-Tales in the English Language*. 4 vols. London, 1970–71. Reprint, London, 1991. 2 vols.

Bunis, David Marc. *Elementary Judezmo Language and Literature: A Manual for Judezmo*. New York, 1977.

———. *A Guide to Reading and Writing Judezmo*. Brooklyn, 1975, 1976.

———. *A Lexicon of the Hebrew and Aramaic Elements in Modern Judezmo*. Jerusalem, 1993.

———. *Sephardic Studies: A Research Bibliography Incorporating Judezmo Language, Literature and Folklore, and Historical Background*. New York, 1981.

Bushnaq, Inea, ed. and trans. *Arab Folktales*. New York, 1986.

Calvino, Italo. *Italian Folktales*. Trans. George Martin. New York, 1980.

Camhi, Gina. "Mi Nonna," *Le Judaïsme Séphardi* 8 (Septembre 1955), 353–55.

———. "La vida en el invierno en Sarajevo," *Le Judaïsme Séphardi* 9 (Décembre 1955), 389–91.

Carvalho-Neto, Paulo De. *Cuentos folklóricos del Ecuador: 52 registros de la tradición oral*. 4 vols. Quito, 1966.

Chauvin, Victor. *Bibliographie des ouvrages arabes ou relatif aux arabes publiés dans l'Europe Chrétienne de 1810 à 1885*. 12 vols. Liège, 1892–1922.

Cheichel, Edna. *A Tale for Each Month, 1967*. Haifa, 1968.

———. *A Tale for Each Month, 1968–1969*. Haifa, 1970.

———. *A Tale for Each Month, 1972*. Haifa, 1973.

Cherezli, Salomon Israel. *Nouveau petit dictionnaire judéo-espagnol français*. 2 vols. Jerusalem, 1898–99.

Chevalier, Maxime. *Cuentos folklóricos en la España del Siglo de Oro*. Barcelona, 1983.

Chouraqui, André. *L'Alliance Israélite universelle et la renaissance juive contemporaine, 1860–1960: Cent ans d'histoire*. Paris, 1965.

Clarkson, Atelia, and Gilbert B. Cross, eds. *World Folktales: A Scribners Resource Collection*. New York, 1980.

Clouston, William A. *The Book of Noodles: Stories of Simpletons; or, Fools and Their Follies.* London, 1888. Reprint, Detroit, 1969.

———. *Popular Tales and Fictions.* 2 vols. Edinburgh, 1887. Reprint, Detroit, 1968.

———, ed. *The Book of Sindibad; or The Story of the King, His Son, the Damsel, and Seven Vazirs.* From the Persian and Arabic. Glasgow, 1884.

Code of Jewish Law (Kitzur Shulkhan Arukh). Comp. Rabbi S. Ganzfried. Trans. H. Goldin. Rev. ed. New York, 1927.

Cohen, A. *Everyman's Talmud.* New York, 1975.

Cohen, Malka. *Mi pei ha-'am: sipurei-'am, mi pei 'edot Israel.* 3 vols. Tel Aviv, 1974–79.

Cohen-Sarano, Matilda. "Los Makedanos." *Aki Yerushalayim* 18 (Djulio 1983): 44–45.

Cole, Joanna, ed. *Best-Loved Folktales of the World.* Garden City, NY, 1982.

Confino, Jacques. "Djuha, pasha de la madre!" *Le Judaïsme Séphardi* 14 (May 1957): 642–43.

Cordovero, Moses. *Shi'ur Komah.* Yerushalayim, 1965/66.

Corominas, Joan, with José A. Pascual. *Diccionario crítico etimológico castellano e hispánico.* 6 vols. Madrid, 1980–91.

Crews, Cynthia M. *Recherches sur le judéo-espagnol dans les pays balkaniques.* Paris, 1935.

———. "Judeo-Spanish Folk-Tales in Macedonia," *Folk-Lore* 43 (1932): 193–225.

———. "A Salonica Conseja," *Le Judaïsme Séphardi* 6 (Mars 1955): 278–79.

———. "Some Arabic and Hebrew Words in Oriental Judeo-Spanish," *Vox Romanica* 14 (1955): 296–309.

———. "Two Salonica Consejicas," *Le Judaïsme Séphardi* 7 (Juin 1955): 294–95.

D'Aronco, Gianfranco. *Le Fiabe di Magia in Italia.* Udine, 1957.

———. *Indice delle Fiabe Toscane.* Firenze, 1953.

Dawkins, Richard M., ed. and trans. *Forty-five Stories from the Dodekanese.* Cambridge, 1950.

———, ed. and trans. *Modern Greek Folktales.* Oxford, 1953. Reprint, Westport, CT, 1974.

———, ed. and trans. *More Greek Folktales.* Oxford, 1955. Reprint, Westport, CT, 1974.

Delarue, Paul. *Le conte populaire français: Catalogue raisonné des versions de France et des pays de language française d'outre-mer.* 4 vols. Paris, 1957. Vols. 2 and 4, co-ed. Marie-Louise Tenèze. Vol. 3, ed. M. L. Tenèze. Reprint, Paris, 1964, 1976, 1985.

Devellioğlu, Ferit. *Osmanlica-türkçe ansiklopedik lûgat.* 14th ed. Ankara, 1997.

Diaz, Joaquín, and Maxime Chevalier. *Cuentos castellanos de tradición oral.* Valladolid, 1983.

Dobrinsky, Herbert C. *A Treasury of Sephardic Laws and Customs.* New York, 1986.

Dorson, Richard M., ed. *Folktales Told around the World.* Chicago, 1975.

Doyle, Richard. *Beauty and the Beast.* New York, 1973.

Eberhard, Wolfram, and P. N. Boratav. *Typen türkischer Volksmärchen.* Weisbaden, 1953.

Eisenberg, Azriel, ed. *The Bar Mitzvah Treasury.* New York, 1952.

Elbaz, André E. *Folktales of the Canadian Sephardim.* Toronto, 1982.
Elnecavé, David. "Folklore de los sefardíes de Turquía." *Sefarad* 23 (1963): 328–32.
Elisséeff, Nikita. *Thèmes et motifs des Mille et une nuits. Essai de Classification.* Beyrouth, 1949.
El-Shamy, Hassan M., ed. and trans. *Folktales of Egypt.* Chicago, 1980.
Encyclopedia Judaica. Jerusalem, 1971.
Epstein, Morris, ed. and trans. *Mishle Sendabar (Tales of Sendebar).* Philadelphia, 1967.
Espinosa, Aurelio M. *Cuentos populares españoles, recogidos de la tradición oral de España.* 3 vols. Stanford, 1923–26. 2d ed., 3 vols., Madrid, 1946–47. Reprint, New York, 1967.
Espinosa, Aurelio M., Jr. *Cuentos populares de Castilla, recogidos de la tradición oral.* Buenos Aires, 1946.
Espinosa, Manuel J., ed. *The Folklore of Spain in the American South-West: Traditional Spanish Folk Literature in Northern New Mexico and Southern Colorado.* By Aurelio M. Espinosa. Norman, OK, 1985.
Farhi, Yosef. *Sefer Osé Pelé (The Miracle Worker).* Livorno, 1930.
Frankel, Ellen. *The Classic Tales: 4000 Years of Jewish Lore.* Northvale, NJ, 1989.
Froger, Jean-François. *La voie du désir: Selon le mythe d'Eros et Psyché du conte d'Apulée dans les Métamorphoses ou l'Âne d'or; nouvelle traduction de Bernard Verten.* Méolans-Revel, c. 1997.
Fus, Dvora. *Shiv'a khavilot zahav (Seven Bags of Gold).* Haifa, 1969.
Gabai, Yehezkel, and Eliyahu Sha'uli. *Mi-Paris li-Yerushalayim: toldot Hevrat kol Yisra'el haverim (1860–1985).* Yerushalayim, 1986.
García Figueras, T. Ed. *Cuentos de Yehá.* Tetuán, 1950.
Gaster, Moses. *The Exempla of the Rabbis.* New York, 1968.
———. *Ma'aseh Book. Book of Jewish Tales and Legends Translated from the Judeo-German.* 2 vols. Philadephia, 1934.
Georges, Robert A. "Towards an Understanding of Storytelling Events." *Journal of American Folklore* 82 (October–December, 1969): 313–28.
———. "Using Storytelling in University Instruction." *Southern Folklore* 50, no. 1 (1992): 3–17.
Gesta Romanorum. Ed. Hermann Osterley. Berlin, 1872.
Ginzberg, L. *The Legends of the Jews.* Trans. H. Szold. 7 vols. Philadelphia, 1909–38. Reprint, Philadelphia, 1968.
Grimm, Jacob, and Wilhelm Grimm. *Grimm's Other Tales: A New Selection by Wilhelm Hansen.* Trans. Ruth Michaelis-Jena and Arthur Ratcliff. London, 1956.
———. *Grimm's Tales for Young and Old.* Trans. Ralph Manheim. Garden City, NY, 1977.
Grunwald, M. *Sipurei 'Am, Romansot, ve-Orakhot Khayim shel Yehudei Sefarad (Tales, Songs and Folkways of Sephardic Jews. Texts and Studies).* Ed. Dov Noy. Jerusalem, 1982.
———. "Sipurim spanyoliim ve-ha-motivim she-bahem" ("Spaniolic-Jewish Folktales and Their Motifs"). *Edot* 2 (1947): 225–45.

Haboucha, Reginetta. "Misogyny or Philogyny: The Case of a Judeo-Spanish Folktale." In *New Horizons in Sephardic Studies,* ed. Yedida K. Stillman and George K. Zucker, 239–51. Albany, 1993.

———. *Types and Motifs of the Judeo-Spanish Folktales.* New York, 1992.

Hadas, Moses, trans. *Berechiah ha-nakdan. Fables of a Jewish Aesop.* New York, 1967.

Haimovits, Zvi M. *Shomrim ne'emanim (Faithful Guardians).* Haifa, 1976.

Hanauer, J. E. *Folk-Lore of the Holy Land: Moslem, Christian, and Jewish.* Ed. Marmaduke Pickthall. London, 1907. Reprint, Folcroft, PA, 1977; Mineola, NY, 2000.

Handford, S. A., trans. *Fables of Aesop.* Harmondsworth, Middlesex, 1987.

Hansen, Terrence L. *The Types of the Folktales in Cuba, Puerto Rico, the Dominican Repulic and Spanish South America.* Berkeley, 1957.

Hertz, J. H. *The Soncino Edition of the Pentateuch and Haftorahs, with Hebrew Text, English Translation, and Commentary.* 2d ed. London, 1967.

Hikmet, Murat. *One Day the Hodja.* Ankara, 1959.

Howard, Richard, trans. *Beauty and the Beast: A Fairy Tale by Marie LePrince de Beaumont.* New York, 1990.

Huerta, Elias D. "A Motif-Index of Juan B. Rael's *Cuentos españoles de Colorado y Nuevo Méjico.*" Master's thesis, Arizona State University, 1963.

Israel, Gerard. *L'Alliance israélite universelle, 1860–1960. Cent ans d'efforts pour la liberation et la promotion de l'homme par l'homme.* Paris, 1960.

Jacobs, Joseph, ed. *European Folk and Fairy Tales.* New York, 1916.

———, ed. *The Fables of Aesop.* 1894. Reprint, New York, 1966.

Jacobs, Louis. *The Jewish Religion: A Concise Companion.* Oxford, 1999.

Jason, Heda. *IFA Tales in Print.* Israel Ethnographic Society, Memoir Series 4. Jerusalem, 1975.

———. "Jewish Near-Eastern Numskull Tales: An Attempt at Interpretation." *Asian Folklore Studies* 31, no. 1 (1972): 1–39.

———. "Types of Jewish-Oriental Oral Tales." *Fabula* 7 (1965): 115–224.

———. *Types of Oral Tales in Israel, Part II.* IES Studies no. 2. Jerusalem, 1975.

Kafka, Franz. *The Metamorphosis.* Ed. and intro. Harold Bloom. New York, 1988.

Kagan, Zipora. *TEM 1963.* Haifa, 1964.

———. *TEM 1964.* Haifa, 1965.

Kamhi, Djina. "El prove ke supo enganyar al riko." *Aki Yerushalayim* 8 (Enero 1981): 40–42.

Keller, John Esten. *Motif-Index of Mediaeval Spanish Exempla.* Knoxville, 1949.

Keller John E., and James H. Johnson. "Motif-Index Classification of the Fables and Tales of Ysopete Ystoriado." *Southern Folklore Quarterly* 18, no. 2 (1954): 85–117.

Kent, Margery, trans. *Fairy Tales from Turkey.* London, 1946.

Kitabevi, Tarhan. *Türkçe-Ingilizce Büyük Lûgat. Comprehensive Turkish-English Dictionary.* Ankara, 1959.

Koén, Matilda. "No savesh lo ke pedresh." *Aki Yerushalayim* 12 (Enero 1982): 55.

Koén-Sarano, Matilda. *Djohá ké dize? Kuentos populares djudeo-espanyoles.* Jerusalem, 1991.

———. *Folktales of Joha, Jewish Trickster.* Philadelphia, 2003.

———. *Konsejas i konsejicas del mundo djudeo-espanyol.* Yerushalayim, 1994.
———. *Kuentos del folklor de la famiya djudeo-espanyola.* Yerushalayim, 1986.
———. *Lejendas i kuentos morales de la tradisión djudeo-espanyola.* Yerushalayim, 1999.
———. "La pasensia es madre de la sensia," *Aki Yerushalayim* 36–37 (Enero–Djunio 1988): 86–87.
———. *De Saragosa a Yerushalayim: kuentos sefardís.* Zaragoza, 1995.
Kohen, Elli, and Dahlia Kohen-Gordon. *Ladino-English/English-Ladino Concise Encyclopedic Dictionary (Judeo-Spanish).* New York, 2000.
Kolonomos, Žamila, ed. *Proverbs, Sayings and Tales of the Sephardic Jews of Macedonia.* Belgrade, 1978.
Kurt, Z. *Bat ha-melekh she-hafekhah le zar prakhim.* Tel Aviv, 1974.
Laoust, E. *Contes berbères du Maroc.* 2 vols. Paris, 1949.
Larrea Palacín, Arcadio de. *Cuentos populares de los judíos del Norte de Marruecos.* 2 vols. Tetuán, Morocco, 1952–53.
Laskier, Michael Menachem. *The Alliance Israélite Universelle and the Jewish Communities of Morocco, 1862–1962.* Albany, c. 1983.
Lauterbach, Jacob. Z. "The Naming of Children in Jewish Folklore, Ritual and Practice." *Yearbook of the Central Conference of American Rabbis* 42 (1932): 316–60.
Lazarillo de Tormes. Ed. with intro. and notes by Francisco Rico. Barcelona, c. 1980.
Learsi, Rufus. *Filled with Laughter.* New York, 1961.
Legey, Françoise, trans. *Contes et légendes populaires du Maroc recueillis à Marrakech.* Paris, 1926.
Lehrman, S. M. *The World of the Midrash.* New York, 1962.
Le Prince de Beaumont, Madame (Jeanne-Marie). *Contes moraux.* Leipsick, 1774.
Levi, Israel. "Recueil de contes juifs inédits." *Revue des Études Juives* 33 (1896): 47–63.
Libro del Cavallero Cifar. Ed. Marilyn A. Olsen. Madison, 1984.
Livro de los engaños e los asayamientos de las mugeres. Ed. Emilio Vuolo. Messina, 1971.
Lomba, Joaquín, ed. *Ibn Gabirol, Ibn Paqûda, Pedro Alfonso. Dichos y narraciones de tres sabios judíos.* Zaragoza, 1997.
Lorimer, D. L. R., and E. O. Lorimer. *Persian Tales Written Down for the First Time in the Original Kermani and Bakhtiari.* London, 1919.
Luria, M. A. *A Study of the Monastir Dialect of Judeo-Spanish Based on Oral Material Collected in Monastir, Yugo-Slavia.* New York, 1930.
MacDonald, Margaret Read. *The Story-Teller's Start Up Book: Finding, Learning, Performing and Using Folktales.* Little Rock, AR, 1993.
———, ed. *Traditional Storytelling Today: An International Sourcebook.* Chicago, 1999.
Manuel, Juan. *Libro del Conde Lucanor.* Ed. Reinaldo Ayerbe-Chaux. Madrid, 1986.
Marcus, Eliezer. *Min ha-Mabu'a (From the Fountainhead).* Haifa, 1966.
Martínez Ruiz, Juan. "Textos judeo-españoles de Alcazarquivir (Marruecos), 1948–1951." *Revista de Dialectología y Tradiciones Populares* 19 (1963): 78–115.
Mathers, Powys, trans. *The Book of the Thousand Nights and One Night, Rendered into English from the Literal and Complete French Translation of Dr. J. C. Mardrus.* 4 vols. London, 1964. Reprint, London, 1986.

McCarthy, William Bernard, ed. *Jack in Two Worlds: Contemporary North American Tales and Their Tellers.* Chapel Hill, 1994.
Megas, Georgios A., ed. *Folktales of Greece.* Trans. Helen Colaclides. Chicago, 1970.
Meir, Ofra. "Ha-nuskhaot ha-yehudiyot shel ha-tipus ha-sipuri AT 875." *Yeda 'Am* 19, no.45–46 (1979): 55–61.
Meyukhas, Y. *Ma'asiyot 'am livne kedem.* Tel Aviv, 1938.
Mintz, Jerome. *Legends of the Hassidim.* Chicago, 1968.
Mishle Sendabar (Tales of Sendebar). Ed. and trans. Morris Epstein. Translation of the Hebrew version of the *Seven Sages,* based on unpublished manuscripts. Philadelphia, 1967.
Mizrahi, Hanina. *Be-yeshishim khokhma (With Elders Is Wisdom).* Haifa, 1967.
Moscona, Isaac. *Sipurei Sefarad (Tales of Sepharad).* Tel Aviv, 1985.
Moulieras, Auguste Jean, trans. *Les Fourberies de Si Djeh'a. Contes Kabyles.* Paris, 1892.
Moyle, Natalie Kononenko. *The Turkish Minstrel Tale Tradition.* New York, 1990.
Na'ana, R. Y. *Ozar ha-ma'asiyot (A Treasury of Fairytales).* Jerusalem, 1958.
Naddaff, Sandra. *Arabesque: Narrative Structure and the Aesthetics of Repetition in the 1001 Nights.* Evanston, IL, 1991.
Nahmad, H. M., trans. *A Portion in Paradise and Other Jewish Folktales.* New York, 1970.
Nehama, Joseph, with Jesús Cantera. *Dictionnaire du Judéo-espagnol.* Madrid, 1977.
Nehmad, Moshe. *Ha-glima ha-khadashah shel mullah Avraham (The New Garment of Mullah Avraham).* Haifa, 1966.
Neuman (Noy), Dov. "Motif index of Talmudic-Midrashic Literature." Ph.D. dissertation. Bloomington, Indiana, 1954.
Noy, Dov. "Animal Tales in Ancient Egypt." *Makhanayim* 105 (1966): 116–21.
———. "The First Thousand Folktales in IFA." *Fabula* 4 (1961): 99–110.
———. *Ha-mashal be sifrut ha-aggada: tipusim u-motivim (Tale Types and Motifs of Animal Tales: Aarne-Thompson).* Jerusalem 1960.
———. "Riddles in Wedding Ceremonies." *Makhanayim* 83 (1973): 64–71.
———. *TEM 1961.* Haifa, 1962.
———. *TEM 1962.* Haifa, 1963.
———. *TEM 1965.* Haifa, 1966.
———. *TEM 1966.* Haifa, 1967.
———. *TEM 1970.* Haifa, 1971.
———. *TEM 1971.* Haifa, 1972.
———. *TEM 1976–77.* Haifa, 1979.
———, ed. *Folktales of Israel.* Trans. Gene Baharav. Chicago, 1963.
———, ed. *Ha-na'ara ha-yefefiya u-sheloshet beney ha-melekh (The Beautiful Maiden and the Three Princes).* Tel Aviv, 1965.
———, ed. *Jefet Schwili Erzält.* Berlin, 1963.
———, ed. *Moroccan Jewish Folktales.* New York, 1966.
———, ed. *Shiv'im Sipurim ve-Sipur mi-Pi Yehudei Luv (Seventy-one Folktales from Libyan Jews).* Jerusalem, 1967.

———, ed. *Shiv'im Sipurim ve-Sipur mi-Pi Yehudei Tunisia (Seventy-one Folktales from Tunisian Jews)*. Jerusalem, 1966.
Noy, Meir. *Sipur ve Manguinah bo (Jewish Cante-Fables)*. Haifa, 1968.
Paredes, Américo, ed. and trans. *Folktales of Mexico*. Chicago, 1970.
Pascual Recuero, Pascual. *Antología de cuentos sefardíes*. Barcelona, 1979.
———. *Diccionario básico ladino-español*. Barcelona, 1977.
Passy, A. M. *Sephardic Folk Dictionary (English-Ladino/Ladino English)*. Ed. Beno Eskenazi. Los Angeles, 1999.
Patai, Raphael. *Gates to the Old City*. Detroit, 1981.
———. *The Hebrew Goddess*. Detroit, 1990.
Perez, Rebeka. "La diskulpa mas negra ke la kulpa." *Aki Yerushalayim* 13–14 (Avril–Djulio 1982): 76.
Perez, Yoel. *Hanasich me-Aragon (The Prince of Aragon: Jewish-Sefaradic Folktales)*. Tel Aviv, 1991.
Perrault, Charles. *Contes/Charles Perrault; textes établis et présentés* par Marc Soriano. Paris, c. 1989.
———. *Contes de fées tirés de Claude [!] Perrault, de Mmes d'Aulnoi et Leprince de Beaumont et illustrés de 65 vignettes dessinées sur bois par Bertall, Beaucé, etc*. Paris, 1878.
———. *Contes de ma mère Loye*. Trans. Charles Walsh. Boston, 1902.
Petronius Arbiter. *The Satyricon*. Trans. with intro. and explanatory notes by P. G. Walsh. Oxford, 1996.
Pinhasi, Jacob. *'Asarah sipurei 'am mi Bukhara (Ten Folktales from Bukhara)*. Jerusalem, 1978.
Pino Saavedra, Yolando, ed. *Folktales of Chile*. Trans. R. Gray. Chicago, 1967.
Pipe, Samuel Z. *Sipurei 'am mi Sanok (Twelve Folktales from Sanok)*. Haifa, 1967.
Propp, Vladimir. *Morphology of the Folktale*. Trans. Laurence Scott. Austin, 2000.
Quiller-Couch, Arthur Thomas, Sir. *The Sleeping Beauty and Other Fairy Tales from the Old French*. London, 1910.
Rael, Juan B. *Cuentos españoles de Colorado y Nuevo Méjico*. 2 vols. New York, 1977.
Rappaport, A. S. *The Folklore of the Jews*. London, 1937.
Redhouse çagdas Türkçe-Ingilizce sözlügü (Redhouse Contemporary Turkish-English Dictionary). Istanbul, c. 1983.
Redhouse Türkçe/Osmanl, ca- Ingilizce sözlük (Redhouse Turkish/Ottoman-English Dictionary). Istanbul, 1999.
Richman, Jacob. *Laughs from Jewish Lore*. New York, 1926.
Riquet à la houppe. (Deux versions d'un conte de ma Mère Loye). London, 1907.
Robe, Stanley L. *Index of Mexican Folktales, Including Narrative Texts from Mexico, Central America and the Hispanic United States*. Berkeley, 1973.
Rodrigue, Aron. *French Jews, Turkish Jews: The Alliance Israélite Universelle and the Politics of Jewish Schooling in Turkey, 1860–1925*. Bloomington, 1990.
Rojas, Fernando de. *La Celestina*. Buenos Aires, 1965.
Roland, Joan Gardner. "The Alliance Israélite Universelle and French Policy in North Africa, 1860–1918." Ph.D. diss., Columbia University, 1969.

Romano, Samuel. *Dictionary of Spoken Judeo-Spanish/French/German: with an Introduction on Phonetics and Word Formation.* Jerusalem, 1995.

Romero, Alberto. "Los tres konsejeros del rey." *Aki Yerushalayim* 6 (Djulio 1980): 44–45, 48.

Rotunda, Dominic Peter. *Motif-Index of the Italian Novella in Prose.* Bloomington, 1942. Reprint, New York, 1973.

Rozenzweig, Rivka. "El ijo del rey i la ija del karreador de agua." *Aki Yerushalayim* 6 (Julio 1980): 39–43.

Sabar, Yona, ed. and trans. *The Folk Literature of the Kurdistani Jews: An Anthology.* New Haven, 1982.

Salinas, Djeni. "Un diálogo entre el rey i el guertelano." *Aki Yerushalayim* 38–39 (Julio–Dis 1988): 84–86.

———. "Konsejo de un padre a su ijo." *Aki Yerushalayim* 43 (1991): 89.

Sánchez de Vercial, Clemente. *Libro de los exenplos por A.B.C.* Ed. John E. Keller. Madrid, 1961.

Schram, Peninnah. *Jewish Stories One Generation Tells Another.* Northvale, NJ, 1987.

Schwartz, Howard. *Elijah's Violin and Other Jewish Fairy Tales.* New York, 1983.

Schwarzbaum, Haim. "International Folklore Motifs in Petrus Alphonsi's *Disciplina Clericalis*." *Sefarad* 21 (1961): 267–99; 22 (1962): 17–59, 321–44; 23 (1963): 54–73.

———. *Studies in Jewish and World Folklore.* Berlin, 1968.

Séphiha, Haïm Vidal. *Contes judéo-espagnols. Du miel au fiel.* Paris, 1992.

———. "Dos kuentos de Djoha." *Aki Yerushalayim* 9 (Avril 1981): 42–43.

Seri, Rachel. *Ha-kame'a ha-kadosh* (*The Holy Amulet*). Haifa, 1968.

Serwer-Bernstein, Blanche L. *In the Tradition of Moses and Mohammed: Jewish and Arab Folktales.* Northvale, NJ, 1994.

Sevilla-Sharon, Moshe. "Las bovedades de Yusiko." *Aki Yerushalayim* 17 (Avril 1983): 1919.

Shahar, Kamelia. "Ayudar al menesterozo sin averguensarlo ni ofensarlo." *Aki Yerushalayim* 22–23 (Djulio–Oktobre 1984): 49–50.

———. "La konfiensa en el Dio." *Aki Yerushalayim* 19–20 (Oktobre 1983–Enero 1984): 41.

———. "Las letras de la alfabeta." *Aki Yerushalayim* 4 (Enero 1980): 21.

———. "La mujer i el marido ke keria divorsar." *Aki Yerushalayim* 12 (Enero 1982): 51.

———. "El prove i Eliyau Hanavi." *Aki Yerushalayim* 2 (Djulio 1979): 22.

———. "El rey de Persia i rabi Yeuda." *Aki Yerushalayim* 18 (Djulio 1983): 27.

———. "La reyna de Shva i sus enigmas al rey Shlomo," *Aki Yerushalayim* 38–39 (Julio–Dis. 1988): 48–49.

———. "La valor del guevo haminado," *Aki Yerushalayim* 22–23 (Djulio–Oktobre 1984): 51–52.

Shakespeare, William. *William Shakespeare's Othello.* Ed., with intro. by Harold Bloom. New York, c. 1996.

Shenhar, Aliza. *TEM 1973.* Haifa, 1974.

Shenhar, Aliza, and Haya Bar Itzhak. *Sipurei-'am mi-Bet She'an (Folktales from Bet-She'an)*. Haifa, 1981.

———. *Sipurei-'Am mi-Shelomi (Folktales from Shelomi)*. Haifa, 1982.

Shurman, Dvora, and Yoel Perez. "Storytelling in Israel." *Storytelling Magazine* 14, no. 2 (2002): 25–26.

Sider, F. *Shiv'a sipurei 'am mi Boryslaw (Seven Folktales from Boryslaw)*. Haifa, 1968.

Sobol, Joseph. *The Storytellers' Journey: An American Revival*. Chicago, 1999.

Stahl, A. *Sipurei emunah ve-musar (Stories of Faith and Morals)*. Haifa, 1976.

Stern, Steven. *The Sephardic Jewish Community of Los Angeles: A Study in Folklore and Ethnic Identity*. New York, 1980.

Stillman, Norman. *The Jews of Arab Lands*. Philadelphia, 1979.

Stone, Kay. *Burning Brightly: New Light on Old Tales Told Today*. Peterborough, Ont., 1998.

Straparola, Giovanni F. *The Facetious Nights of Straparola*. Trans. W. G. Waters. 4 vols. London, c. 1901.

Thompson, Stith. *The Folktale*. Berkeley, 1977.

———. *Motif-Index of Folk Literature: A Classification of Narrative Elements in Folktales, Ballads, Myths, Fables, Mediaeval Romances, Exempla, Fabliaux, Jest-Books and Local Legends*. FFC 106–9, 116–17. 6 vols. Helsinki, 1932–36. Rev. and enl. ed., 6 vols., Bloomington, 1955–58.

———, ed. *One Hundred Favorite Folktales*. Bloomington, 1974.

Thompson, Stith, and Warren E. Roberts. *Types of Indic Oral Tales: India, Pakistan and Ceylon*. FFC 180. Helsinki, 1960.

Timoneda, Juan. *El patrañuelo*. Ed. Alva V. Ebersole. Valencia, 1987.

Tolstoy, Leo, *Fables and Fairy Tales*. Trans. Ann Dunnigan. New York, 1962.

Trachtenberg, Joshua. *Jewish Magic and Superstition: A Study in Folk Religion*. New York, 1939.

Tubach, Frederic C. *Index Exemplorum: A Handbook of Medieval Religious Tales*. FFC 204. Helsinki, 1969.

Villa, Susie H. *100 Armenian Tales and Their Folkloristic Relevance*. Detroit, 1966.

Villeneuve, Gabrielle-Suzanne Barbot Gallon, Dame de. *La belle et la bête: suivi d'une lettre de la belle à la bête et d'une réponse de la bête à la belle; édition établie par Jacques Cotin et Elizabeth Lemirre*. Paris, c. 1996.

Voltaire. *Zadig ou, La destinée, histoire orientale*. Critical ed. with intro. and commentary by George Ascoli. Paris, 1929.

Wagner, Max L. *Beiträge zur Kenntnis des Judenspanischen von Konstantinopel*. Vienna, 1914.

Walker, Warren S., and Ahmet E. Uysal, eds. and trans. *Tales Alive in Turkey*. Cambridge, 1966.

———. *More Tales Alive in Turkey*. Lubbock, TX, 1992.

Wesselski, A. *Der Hodscha Nasreddin*. 2 vols. Weimar, 1911; abridged ed.: *Schwänke des Hodscha Nasreddin*. Frankfurt, 1964.

———. *Märchen des Mittelalters*. Berlin, 1925.
Yassif, Eli. *Jewish Folklore: An Annotated Bibliography*. New York, 1986.
———. *Sipur ha-'am ha-ivrí* (*The Hebrew Folktale*). Jerusalem, 1994; English version, Bloomington, 1999.
Yehoshua, Ben Zion. *Tsava'at av* (*The Father's Will*). Haifa, 1969.
Yeshiva, Miriam. *Shiv'a sipurei 'am* (*Seven Folktales*). Haifa, 1963.